A Spectrum
of Rhetoric

A Spectrum of Rhetoric

Dorothy Margaret Guinn
Florida Atlantic University

Daniel Marder
University of Tulsa

 Little, Brown and Company
Boston   Toronto

Library of Congress Cataloging-in-Publication Data

Guinn, Dorothy.
  A spectrum of rhetoric.

  Includes index.
  1. English language—Rhetoric.   2. College readers.
I. Marder, Daniel.   II. Title.
PE1408.G927   1987   808'.0427   86–7220
ISBN 0–316–33132–5

Library of Congress Catalog Card No. 86–7220

ISBN 0-316-33132-5

9 8 7 6 5 4 3 2 1

RRD

Published simultaneously in Canada
by Little, Brown & Company (Canada) Limited

Printed in the United States of America

CREDITS

  p. 2: "The Window" by Edwin Muir from *Collected Poems.* Reprinted by permission of Oxford University Press and Faber and Faber Publishers.
  p. 3 (definition of window): By permission. From *Webster's Ninth New Collegiate Dictionary* © 1986 by Merriam-Webster Inc., publisher of the Merriam-Webster Dictionaries.
  pp. 18–19: From "The Barrio" by Robert Ramirez and reprinted with permission.
  pp. 26, 36, 108, 119: From *The Lives of a Cell,* by Lewis Thomas. Copyright © 1971, 1972, 1973 by the Massachusetts Medical Society. Originally published in *The New England Journal of Medicine.* Reprinted by permission of Viking Penguin, Inc.
  pp. 29–30, 38: "From Song to Sound: Bing and Elvis" by Russell Baker. Copyright © 1977 by The New York Times Company. Reprinted by permission.

Continued on page 462

For our parents

Preface

Too often teaching composition involves students only in the forms and mechanics of written expression: how to construct a grammatical sentence, how to organize a report, how to describe, analyze, or summarize. These are important but only as supplementary to students' gaining an overall understanding of language and communication. In many instances students learn the "how to" but not the "why." This book attempts to remedy that situation by focusing not only on structure and mechanics, but also on the purposes and strategies of writing.

A *Spectrum of Rhetoric* emphasizes the types of discourse that people use in college, business, industry, and the professions. Poetry and fiction are not included, but essays, articles, reports, letters, and reviews are all examined at length. Underlying the text is a basic concept: that writing and speaking derive from a desire to bring others into agreement with one's own observations, thoughts, and feelings. From a consideration of motive students are led to think about the strategies and methods that various kinds of writing entail. What purpose and strategy are evident in a discussion of Grandma Moses's paintings? How do these differ in an ad for Estée Lauder lipstick? Or a study of New York traffic patterns? By thinking and practicing along these lines, students can strengthen their understanding of the choices they themselves must make when they write.

The spectrum of the book's title is the continuum formed by three fundamental ingredients of writing: fact, reason, and feeling. Students will learn that any piece of written discourse contains a combination of these ingredients. A technical report may be dominated by facts, though reason and feeling will also work on the audience. At the other end of the spectrum, a letter to a friend may be charged with feeling, but reason and fact will appear as well. Knowing how these three elements combine will help students to elaborate, shape, and refine their own expression so that it communicates its meaning to the chosen audience.

Though *A Spectrum of Rhetoric* can be used in a first-semester course, it should be most valuable to students who have already been introduced to the basics of composition. It lends itself especially well to writing-across-the-curriculum approaches and writing in the professions. The text contains a large number of examples, chosen for their range and diversity, as well as exercises that are meant to be both challenging and thought-provoking.

The book is organized into four sections. Section One, Rhetorical Operations, concentrates on the intrinsics of writing and thinking, such as description, comparison, classification, and analysis. Because these operations represent patterns of thought that all people use every day, the text attempts to draw on the student's existing skills and raise them to a conscious level. Even students who have already been taught about rhetorical operations may have a "Eureka" experience—a sudden insight into the nature of the writing process.

Section Two, Rhetorical Structures, covers the various means of beginning, ending, and developing a discourse. The building blocks of style—words, sentences, and paragraphs—are treated as means to achieve a coherent structure. In Section Three, Rhetorical Forms, students apply their understanding of operations and structures to the types of discourse found in the academic and workaday worlds: letters, essays, reports, and other standard forms. Finally, Section Four, Rhetorical Conventions, discusses grammar, punctuation, and mechanics from a rhetorical point of view. This last section, arranged for easy reference, can be approached in order or can be turned to whenever it is needed.

In its methodology and its treatment of cognitive process, *A Spectrum of Rhetoric* accords with the research of Linda Flower, William Perry, and George Hillocks, Jr. It also gives credence to the expressive/emotive views of rhetoricians like Donald Murray and William Coles, as well as the philosophies of Edward P. J. Corbett and Richard Hughes. As authors, we are indebted to all of these theorists, as well as the many other rhetoricians we have studied throughout our years in the profession.

Particular recognition is due to those who commented on *A Spectrum of Rhetoric* in manuscript, Jim Corder and Christiana Murphy of Texas Christian University and Judith Hert of San Bernardino Valley College. We are also grateful to Paul O'Connell, who first encouraged publication of the book, and to Carolyn Potts, who brought the publication to fruition with the help of Virginia Pye, Adrienne Weiss, and Amy L. Johnson. Special thanks go to Billie Ingram, our production editor, for her patience and careful work on the manuscript, to Nancy Butman for her tireless tracking of sources, and to Peggy Gordon, whose sharp eye and pen kept us from error.

Finally, we would like to thank our families, without whose patience and understanding we could not have finished this book.

Contents

A Spectrum
of Rhetoric

Introduction

Rhetoric: The Aim and the Means

Rhetoric is our verbal means of seeking agreement with others. Although seeking agreement may be human nature, achieving it, unfortunately, is not. To achieve agreement, writers must establish a common ground with their readers. Usually they appeal to existing agreements, which lead to further agreements. This appeal does not mean that writers pander to the audience. If the writer agrees totally with the audience, or knows nothing more, there is no need for rhetoric. In such situations we simply celebrate our shared knowledge, feelings, or actions.

An effort to identify as much as possible with the audience at the outset is a major strategy a writer uses to bring an audience into agreement. Writers build bridges between their beliefs and attitudes and those of their audiences. Some of these bridges are appeals to common knowledge, common experiences, common needs, common sense. Writers use words that readers will understand, and they emphasize shared goals and values. Writer and reader may hold different opinions on how to solve a certain problem, but they may agree that it exists and must be solved. However, even when the writer succeeds in establishing such common ground, the discourse may not persuade the reader that the view or belief presented is true or that the action advocated is best. Choices and differences abound. If authors fail to convince audiences, it is either because differences in culture, personalities, or beliefs and desires are too great to overcome, or because their rhetorical strategies are ineffective. The purpose of all rhetoric, on any occasion for discourse, is to overcome such differences through effective strategies.

A Spectrum of Rhetoric

We can view the entire range of rhetoric as a spectrum of persuasiveness. The spectrum ranges from representations of observations at one end to representations of feelings at the other end. In gross terms, it would look like the following diagram:

1

Report	Argument	Poem
(Fact)	(Reason)	(Feeling)

At one end fact dominates, in the middle reason dominates, and at the other end emotion dominates, although all are present to some degree in writing at every point in the spectrum. Reports with their facts appeal primarily to our rational powers, poetry with its metaphors to our emotional powers.

The word *report* is derived from a Latin term meaning "to carry back." Carrying back, the report confines meaning. *Metaphor,* on the other hand, derived from a Greek term meaning "to carry across," expands meaning. Reporting is usually identified as a primary medium of expository writing, metaphor the primary medium of literary writing. However, both occur in all types of writing.

Let us look briefly at some examples for illustration, first at a poem, "The Window" by Edwin Muir:

> There was a tower set in the wall
> And a great window in the tower
> And if one looked, beyond recall
> The twisting glass kept him in thrall
> With changing marvels hour by hour.

The poem does, of course, report a tower with a glass window, but its primary purpose is to create meanings beyond those of a report. The word *window* is ambiguous. It stands for an opening in the wall but also for an opening into the imagination, its "twisting glass" full of marvels, changeable as the imagination "hour by hour." Such ambiguity is a key virtue of a poem's metaphor, offering a multiplicity of meanings. Poets striving to "get it right" are guided not so much by the possibility of an audience recognizing meanings as by their own artistic sensibility. Poets work primarily to please themselves.

Authors of reports, on the other hand, including many student writers and most professional writers, have already reached their conclusions. Their effort to "get it right" means they strive to report, with as much accuracy as possible, not only their conclusions but also the reasoning that led to them, the data or evidence upon which their reasoning is based, and the procedures for obtaining the data. Just as we cannot conceive of poetry without metaphor, we cannot conceive of nonpoetic prose without reporting. The dictionary reports that a window is

an opening esp. in the wall of a building for admission of light and air that is usu. closed by casements or sashes containing transparent material (as glass) and capable of being opened and shut.
> *Webster's Ninth New Collegiate*
> *Dictionary*

Reports appeal mainly to the reader's intelligence rather than sensing powers, yet nonpoetic prose uses metaphor, just as poetic prose and poetry report. Nevertheless, metaphors do not occur as often in nonpoetic prose, and when they do, they are used to clarify thought, events, and objects. Helen Gardner uses metaphor this way in *Art Through the Ages:*

> For practical purposes, a building must have doors and windows; and as light envelops a building and penetrates its interior, the light and shadow created by these openings play an important role in breaking up surfaces into effective designs . . . statistically regular or dynamically varied with arresting accents.

With the metaphors "envelops," "breaking up," and "arresting," Gardner ventures along the poet's path — but only a short distance. The dictionary and Gardner more easily bring an audience into agreement with their notions of a window than Muir does with his. It is more difficult to bring an audience into agreement with our thought as we approach the emotive or poetic end of the spectrum. More of the total reader has to be moved, the emotions and sensibilities as well as reason. At the reporting end of the spectrum, writer and reader share the experience to a much greater extent. A writer, therefore, need only select words and arrange them to represent best the shared experience of reality, the "facts." But even writing "facts" requires selectivity, generalization, some judgment. In describing a bridge, for example, do you choose to speak of the nuts and bolts that hold it together? Is its color rust? Or brown? Shall the description begin with the location? Materials? Shape? Or principle of construction?

As we move away from the more simple reporting of observations along our spectrum, we apply more and more reason. At midpoint the main effort is reasoning from observations; we render hypotheses, theories, judgments, conclusions. We support these generalizations with facts or data, but it is the logic we emphasize. We reason about advantages and disadvantages. We predict what is likely or not likely to happen.

Beyond midpoint, reason is joined by emotive or psychological modes of expression; as the imaginative end of the spectrum is reached, the role of reason lightens, and factuality tends to disappear.

A more detailed and useful view of the waxing and waning of rhetorical intent across the spectrum of rhetoric would look something like the following diagram:

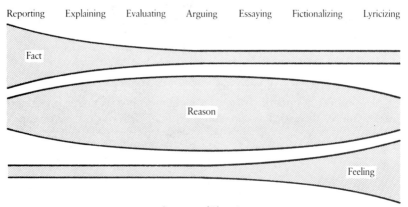

Reporting   Explaining   Evaluating   Arguing   Essaying   Fictionalizing   Lyricizing

Fact

Reason

Feeling

Spectrum of Rhetoric

The spectrum of rhetoric enables us to see that any form of discourse can be employed to fulfill any motive, whether weighed heavily or lightly with emotion or reason. The motive itself helps determine what material to seek, what form to use, and what language to employ. If the motive is, say, to explain how a machine operates, the materials selected will be mostly referential, objects and processes of the external world, in this case the parts of the machine. The form will likely be a report. Language will tend to be concrete and neutral, names of things and actions — in the case of a machine, levers and movements of cogs. Voice will tend to be passive unless the subject is active, as an operating machine would be. Tone will be impersonal.

If the motive moves to the middle of the spectrum — for example, if it is to convince someone to buy a particular machine — more reason will enter the material. Concepts will tend to dominate over reference. Language will become more abstract and connotative, tone less impersonal.

If the motive moves toward the other end of the spectrum — say to stir the imagination of readers with a fictionalized account of a personal experience — reason becomes colored more and more with feeling, tone becomes personal, the tendency toward abstract language is replaced by the tendency toward connotative symbol and metaphor, and images dominate.

The choices we make as we write, of language, tone, form of discourse, and the like, stem from an interaction of what we want to say, to whom we are saying it, and for what purpose. The overall aim in all writing efforts is to bring the audience into agreement with the writer's views and attitudes, even if a discourse offers what seems to be only information. All aspects of rhetoric are essentially means for achieving agreement.

As writers proceed to fulfill their purposes for writing, they begin to view their efforts in terms of genre, the form of discourse. When facts are the major component, a report comes to mind. When the proportion of reasoning begins to outweigh that of reporting facts, writers say they are producing an article or essay. As essays become more and more personal, emotive, fictive, even lyrical, they are recognized as story, play, and poem.

The traditional genre of a discourse, however, does not always signal its intention. A personal essay or a poem may be presented in the form of a report, and a report or essay may be versified. A famous poem that is more in the way of an essay, as its title suggests, is Alexander Pope's "Essay on Man":

> Two principles in human nature reign:
> Self-love, to urge, and reason, to restrain;
> Nor this a good, nor this a bad we call,
> Each works its end, to move or govern all:
> And to their proper operation still,
> Ascribe all good; to their improper, ill.

Personal letters to friends may possess the qualities of lyric poetry. Love letters are of this nature. On the other hand, business letters are often reports, but rarely present facts only; rather, they explain or argue from the facts.

Organization of the Book

The chapters of this book explore strategies for realizing in your writing the fundamental principle of agreement that underlies all discourse. Your motives—whether to present, explain, argue, or represent—lead to appeals. These appeals are efforts to establish common ground, the author's credibility, and the goodwill of the audience. The writer's appeal is also a promise to the reader: that something worthwhile is written here. The writer states or implies the promise of what is to be explored or rendered, along with its significance. The promise is developed and maintained throughout the discourse, from the beginning through the middle and into the ending.

The mental processes used to invent and develop the material for discourse are presented in Section One, Rhetorical Operations. Section Two, Rhetorical Structure, is devoted to effective ways of stating the promise of a discourse, concluding it, and developing the material coherently and with some style and grace. Section Three, Rhetorical Forms, presents various discourse forms along the spectrum of rhetoric, with emphasis on the vital middle of the spectrum where most of the world's writing is concentrated. Each chapter shows how the fundamental motive of gaining agreement is modified by specific motives or

purposes and how these guide the discovery of rhetorical means—
operations, forms, stylistic choices—to suit a particular writing situation and its audience.

The final section, Section Four, Rhetorical Conventions, addresses
the smaller but significant matters of effectiveness in sentence structure, punctuation, and other mechanics. Even these details are examined in terms of the principal rhetorical motive underlying all discourse—agreement.

SECTION ONE

Rhetorical Operations

We develop discourse by exploring our observations, ideas, and perceptions and rendering them for the reader's understanding. As readers encounter our discourse, they test it for validity against their own experience, logic, and opinions. We fulfill the expectations that our promises have aroused when readers are satisfied that we have rendered the subject without violating their sense of truth. Whatever agreement is possible accrues through the reading process.

Writers also verify for themselves their perceptions, ideas, and opinions through the writing process. The question is always, "Does it work out in the writing?" It is in the discourse itself that we order our jumbles of feelings and ideas into coherent and consistent wholes. During this process we rethink, reorganize, and rephrase in order to clarify our convictions and validate our ideas. Often this process of shaping and validating is called discovery.

The process of shaping or discovering the contents of our minds occurs in our internal as well as our external world, when we attempt to record feelings and thoughts for ourselves, as in a journal, or for others, as in personal narrative or fiction. Agreements reached at this end of the spectrum are more empathetic than logical or factual. Whatever our motives or effects along the spectrum of rhetoric may be—factual, rational, emotive—we employ the same rhetorical operations for exploring our promises, developing them, and rendering them.

Rhetorical operations are patterns of thought that direct and order our perceptions, ideas, and feelings. They comprise a system of principles we have been using everyday since we were infants, when we began to know things by comparing one with another and by generalizing the results. Rhetorical operations are means of understanding our world and the worlds of others. We mostly perform these operations unconsciously when we speak and write. We become more effective writers by learning to use them with conscious control. The operations presented in the following chapters are:

Description
Narration
Comparison
Classification
Analysis
Induction and Deduction
Definition

Seldom do these rhetorical operations work alone in discourse. One or another tends to dominate, and the other operations are used as suitable aids in rendering the whole composition. Description often helps to define. Classification often plays an important role in developing comparisons. Analysis usually provides the framework for descriptions and narrations. Induction and deduction occur in nearly all pieces of writing along the spectrum of rhetoric, even the most factual. The means of definition include all the other rhetorical operations.

Chapter 1

Description

To show the appearance of things, the features and qualities of things, writers describe. They paint verbal pictures of objects, scenes, persons, even ideas. Description arranges objects in space, in contrast to narration, which arranges events and processes in time. Most often description and narration work together, but usually one is the dominant operation and the other accessory. In reporting a horse race, the dominant rhetorical operation would be narration, but all the supporting material would be description: the color, noise, costumes, peculiarities of the crowd, the heraldry, the turf, the sun, wind, the horses and riders, and, of course, the winner's circle. If we were to focus the composition not on the race itself but on a horse within it, then our main intention would be descriptive. We would delineate the horse's contours, color, and other physical characteristics, that is, the way the animal occupies space. But these details would give us only a bare description. To describe the horse more fully, we would include not only features we have observed, but also other features as background, such as lineage, racing record, habitual racing behavior, and personality traits.

When description is aimed at giving qualities and characteristics to enlarge only the understanding, we have objective or technical description. Impressionistic or affective description, on the other hand, portrays color and tone and a way of understanding. Impressionistic descriptions tend to interpret as they describe. They give impressions of an external or internal world as it impinges upon the senses. Descriptions become more objective and technical as they eliminate personal impressions. They are said to be "factual," while impressionistic descriptions are said to be "subjective" or even "emotive," because they express the writer's personal interpretation. One emphasizes the observed, and the other emphasizes the observer.

The Language of Description

Whether description is technical or impressionistic, general and abstract words are of limited value because they do not convey an image, a verbal picture. Only concrete and specific language can visualize. "Dessert" is vague compared to "a pastry sat on a plate," and even this image can be sharpened considerably: "A steaming wedge of apple pie sat squarely on a plate, its golden brown crispness dominating the delicate bone white china."

The words in a technical description are chosen for neutral tone. The "magenta" of an impressionistic description becomes "red" or at most "bright red" in a technical description. Measurements and numbers abound in technical description:

> The glass tube is twenty inches long. One end is a cylinder with a diameter of three inches, which begins to enlarge in the middle until it reaches a diameter of thirty inches at the other end.

But through the use of metaphor and analogy the necessary numbers can be woven into the image:

> The glass tube is twenty inches long. One end is a three-inch cylinder which flares out about halfway down its length into the shape of a trumpet, ending in a round, flat surface thirty inches in diameter.

Although such figures of speech may allow the writer's feeling or attitude to edge into the description, it is still objective because the writer's aim is a clear picture, not the rendition of feelings about the picture. The most detached of scientific observers is still human and cannot totally repress individuality.

The metaphors of impressionistic description, on the other hand, carry the author's feelings and attitude. The description cannot be separated from the describer. In *Moby Dick*, Melville's awe of the whale's magnificence is inseparable from the physical description. This combination of awe and physicality cannot be rendered by direct statement. The author uses comparisons with images familiar to the reader:

> Most of the scientific drawings have been taken from the stranded fish; and these are about as correct as a drawing of a wrecked ship, with broken back, would correctly represent the noble animal itself in all its undashed pride of hull and spars.

The humor in Mark Twain's descriptions come largely from his outrageous comparisons. Tom Sawyer's unwashed neck is described as a "dark expanse of irrigated soil." The beggars in *Innocents Abroad* are "animated rags." In *Roughing It* a "coyote is a living, breathing allegory of want," and in *Huckleberry Finn* we hear a "a little piano that has tin pans in it."

Impressionistic description, we see, uses figurative language suggestively, or *connotatively,* adding associated meanings and attitudes to literal meanings. Technical description also uses these devices of language, but does so *denotatively.* The figurative language in technical description is used only to explain. It restricts itself as much as possible to singular meaning, but the language of impressionistic description reaches for possibilities beyond the main meaning.

As we move from the factual end of the spectrum of rhetoric to the emotive end, our descriptions become more impressionistic, and language tends to become more metaphorical. However, just as we are aware of the need for figurative language in denotative writing at the factual end, we should also be aware of using too much at the other end:

> The little man, agile as a monkey, balanced himself like a tight-rope walker on the thin edge of the curb above the running mud in the pigsty of a gutter.

Excessive use of metaphor and simile here produces the ring of artificiality. Figures of speech also ring artificially when they are repeated until they become buzz words — "interface," "paradigm" — or other cliches — "capitalistic pigs," "light as a feather," "ruby lips," "pursuant to."

Modifiers added to the base clause of a sentence enrich its descriptive power while controlling its accuracy. *Free modifiers* can be moved around in a sentence to create different effects, in contrast to *bound modifiers,* which occupy fixed positions (see pp. 167–170). The free modifiers are in italics in this example:

> The two regiments ran full-tilt up the hill toward the bridge, *men shouting madly in the midst of smoke and flames, falling at every step as muskets and cannon, in great unbroken roar, slashed the column.*

Free modifiers are usually derivatives of verbs (adverbs or participial phrases) and therefore carry the dynamic quality of verbs. They also create a sense of simultaneous action. Note the sequential one-thing-at-a-time effect of this group of sentences:

> He sat close, and leaned forward intensely. One of his hands toyed with a chopstick. The other hand absently touched his beard. His light blue eyes fixed her gaze.

When we combine these separate sentences and clauses into a single sentence through the use of free modifiers, we achieve simultaneity of action; all is happening at once:

> He sat close, leaning forward intensely, one hand toying with a chopstick, the other absently touching his beard, his light blue eyes fixing her gaze.

More emphasis can be shifted to the eyes by moving the last phrase:

> He sat close, leaning forward intensely, his light blue eyes fixing her gaze, one hand toying with a chopstick, the other absently touching his beard.

Free modifiers can enrich and enliven static descriptions at the factual end of the spectrum as well:

> The electrons of the hydrogen atoms merge with the four-prong patterns in twin-electron bonds, creating a tetrahedron in which the carbon nucleus is in the center and four hydrogen nuclei are at the corners.

Organization of Description

Although descriptions are ordered spatially, not every arrangement of detail in space will produce an effective composition. The details must be associated and combined into a composition for some purpose. The writer may describe a person from head to toe, an object from left to right or roundabout, a scene from near to far or from panorama to narrow focus. These are all lines of development. They are spatial rather than sequential as in narrative. Each spatial line of development assumes a different stance for describing and takes a particular point of view. The view focuses on a major trait, quality, or feature in the person, object, or scene described. A fourth element of organization — in addition to line of development, point of view, and focus — is level of generality, that is, how broadly or narrowly the subject is being described: in general terms, specific terms, or particular terms. Because level of generality establishes the scope of the whole composition, it is the first to be considered.

Level of Generality

If we had to describe an airplane to someone who did not know it, our description would state what an airplane does in general and what its basic flying principles are. Then we would name the parts — wings, fuselage, tail assembly, engines, landing gear. This general level of description would apply to any airplane. On a specific level, we would describe the type of wings, fuselage, and so on, and on the particular level — say, the DC-10 that Captain Flynn just landed without landing gear — we would describe particularly the damaged landing gear, belly, and wing tip. Often, the general description can serve as a covering statement for the specific description. The following example introduces a report that describes various types of gyros:

> For practical purposes, a gyroscope may be described as a spinning rotor supported in a framework which provides several degrees of freedom. In general the parts of a gyro are the rotor, the structure that supports it, and the sensing or control components that transfer the information obtained to usable form. All gyro instruments have additional components, numbers, and types, depending on the complexity of purpose.

Similarly, John Steinbeck begins *The Grapes of Wrath* with this general view of a part of Oklahoma:

> In the last part of May the sky grew pale and the clouds that had hung in high puffs for so long in the spring were dissipated. The sun flared down on the growing corn day after day until a line of brown spread along the edge of each green bayonet. The clouds appeared, and went away, and in a while they did not try any more. The surface of the earth crusted, a thin hard crust, and as the sky became pale, so the earth became pale, pink in the red country and white in the gray country.

The parts of the general description are sun, clouds, corn, weeds, earth. In the succeeding paragraphs, Steinbeck narrows the description to specifics:

> In the water-cut gullies the earth dusted down in dry little streams. Gophers and ant lions started small avalanches. And as the sharp sun struck day after day, the leaves of the young corn became less stiff and erect; they bent on a curve at first, and then, as the central ribs of strength grew weak, each leaf tilted downward. . . . The weeds frayed and edged towards their roots. The air was thin and the sky more pale; and every day the earth paled.

We notice that the parts are still the same: sun, air (for clouds), corn, weeds, earth. In the next chapter, Steinbeck arrives at the particular level of description where most of the action occurs: "A huge red transport truck stood in front of the little roadside restaurant."

The general view of a description can be given in a single sentence, the topic sentence of a paragraph, or the theme sentence of a whole essay. The first sentence in the following example introduces the specifics, which are given in the second and third sentences:

> A typical telephone consists of a handset, containing a transmitter and a receiver. An extendable cord connects the receiver to the base which houses a transformer system which separates outgoing and incoming speech signals. The base also houses a switch for connecting and disconnecting the telephone, a device that signals the required numbers to the central office, and a bell to signal an incoming call.

Topic or theme sentences at the impressionistic end of the spectrum also serve as general views of the whole, but they tend to name dominant qualities or mood rather than parts or overall characteristics of an object, for example, "breadth and suppleness" in addition to size in this description of a portrait figure:

> Nearly seven feet high, the picture was not only unusually large for women's work, it had a breadth and suppleness which bespoke complete mastery. The subject seemed to have been painted slightly larger than life size, for his body, self-conscious in its brand-new armor, was small in

proportion to his large, good-natured head and to his hands, which floated irresolutely, one over his sword pommel and one over the plush-covered table on which rested his plumed helmet, half as tall as he was. . . . It was woman's work, wise, witty, and compassionate. At last I had before me proof positive that a painter may be both female and great.

Germaine Greer, *The Obstacle Race: The Story of Women in Painting*

In this paragraph the general view given in the topic sentence serves to introduce a particular description. The description is neither definitive (paintings in general as distinguished from other arts such as sculpture) nor specific (a type of painting like watercolor, or a style like baroque), but particular or individual.

Point of View

The writer observes the subject from some location or other, a conceptual or physical point of view, or both. The point of view is either explicit or implied. Always it must be consistent. Selecting a point of view in writing is much like selecting a camera angle. The right location or attitude for viewing enables the writer to focus on the fundamentals of the object, person, scene, or concept; at the same time the writer can see the relative importance of details — that is, which are to be emphasized, which subordinated, which omitted.

The point of view should shift only with good reason, because frequent shifts back and forth destroy the coherence of a description:

He saw the flames spurt from the window. On the floor below, a woman flailed her arms and shouted. Trash had been accumulating in the cellar for years.

The last sentence above obviously departs from the established point of view. Violations of point of view occur in fiction when first one character speaks and thinks, then another, then back to the first, and so on. Another common violation is the shift in scale. A ship described from shore cannot show barnacles on its hull. After exhausting the view from the shore, the writer can shift to a close-up, and after exhausting that view, to another point within the ship where the interior arrangements can be described. These are successive points of view, all fixed.

If there is too little description for each fixed position, shifts become too rapid. The remedy is a continuously moving point of view rather than a series of fixed points of view. In the moving point of view, the writer observes continuously as if he or she is a camera moving over a scene from side to side, from near to far, from panorama to a single detail, or vice versa.

A moderate seabreeze had set in; yet over the city, and the water adjacent, was a thin haze, concealing nothing, only adding to the beauty. From my point of view, as I write amid the soft breeze, with a sea temperature, surely nothing on earth of its kind can go beyond this show. To the left the North river with its far vista — nearer, three or four warships, anchor'd peacefully — the Jersey side, the banks or Weehawken, the Palisades, and the gradually receding blue, lost in the distance — to the right of the East river — the mast-hemm's shores — the grand obelisk-like towers of the bridge, one on either side, in haze, yet plainly defin'd, giant brothers twain, throwing free graceful inter-linking loops high across the tumbled tumultuous current below — the broad waterspread everywhere crowded . . . all sorts and sizes of sail and steam vessels, plying ferryboats, arriving and departing coasters, great ocean Dons, iron-black, modern, magnificent in size and power . . . above all, those daring, careening things of grace and wonder, those white and shaded swift-darting fishbirds.

Walt Whitman, *Specimen Days in America*

Line of Development

The moving point of view in Whitman's description uses a spatial line of development; the observer, who is aboard a boat moving from the open bay into the Manhattan harbor, leads the reader through the parts of the scene. The effect of the moving point of view might seem to be chronological, but the whole describes stationary things, not events accruing sequentially as in narration. In Germaine Greer's description of a painting, on the other hand, there is no question that the line of development is spatial, even though she metaphorically inserts movement here and there, "hands, which floated irresolutely, one over his sword pommel and one over the plush-covered table."

Most spatial lines of development are logical progressions beginning at some point and following a path, up and down, in and out, around, and so on. The resulting descriptions would wear out the reader's attention if the writer did not provide some central point of interest, some emphasis of one thing at the expense of another, some focus.

Focus

Descriptions express the writer's purpose and become coherent by focusing on the heart of the matter and relating to that center the surrounding details, placing some in the foreground and others in the background. In the example that follows, notice how the focus on the "time base" describes the function of the PPI tube in relation to the entire radar system.

Many types of radar whose antennas "scan" various directions employ the PPI tube. Here the *time base* starts from the center of the tube and moves radially outward in a direction corresponding to that in which the antenna is pointing. This *time base* rotates in synchronism with the antenna. The returning signal, instead of causing a break in the *time base,* simply appears as a bright spot of light at a position corresponding to the range and bearing of the target. A maplike picture of all reflecting objects appears in the tube face.

This description has a sequential, rather than a spatial, line of development, and it is full of action. The time base starts, moves outward, rotates, and so on. Coherence and liveliness are more difficult to achieve in descriptions of static scenes and objects because movement cannot be traced in them. They require spatial lines of development. In static scenes, the writer must represent details one by one yet still produce the effect of a simultaneous whole, as in a photograph. To achieve this effect, the writer, using a spatial line of development, focuses on some central item, characteristic, or quality, and then introduces the elements of the scene or object one by one as they contribute to the center. That is how dominant impression is achieved, as we can see in the paragraph by Germaine Greer or this passage by Edgar Allan Poe from "The Fall of the House of Usher":

I know not how it was — but, with the first glimpse of the building, a sense of insufferable gloom pervaded my spirit. . . . I looked upon the scene before me — upon the mere house, and the simple landscape features of the domain — upon the bleak walls — upon the vacant eye-like windows — upon a few rank sedges — and upon a few white trunks of decayed trees — with an utter depression of soul. . . .

Most of Poe's story is told from another point of view, within the house, where the focus shifts from the effects of the house upon the narrator to the effects of Roderick Usher upon the narrator. The same technique can be applied to a static description at the factual end of our spectrum, such as that of the PPI tube. Using a spatial order, the writer shifts point of view from the outside of the tube to the inside:

The tube is essentially a glass cone with a round, flat surface for a base. The inner surface of this flat base is coated with a special paint, and it is on this surface that electricity is transformed into light. At the small end or apex of the tube an "electron gun," an incandescent element, shoots a thin stream of electrons at the coated surface. The source of the electrons is called the cathode, hence the name cathode-ray tube. The coated surface is called the screen.

Before focusing on the inside of the tube, the description arrives at an object — the surface of the conic base — that will serve as the focus for the second point of view. The writer uses this surface as a transition to get from the outside to the inside. Once the focal point is inside the tube, the surface is further described; then the action of the electron gun at the other end of the tube is related by way of its effect on our focal point. The result is a complete, orderly picture. We can see the whole tube, outside and in, as if all at once. By using the details already described as a base for new details, the writer accumulates the description and gives it a sense of movement.

Effective descriptions can be created at all points along the spectrum of rhetoric by selecting an advantageous point of view, focusing on the core of interest, and accumulating details along a line of development that relates them to the core.

Selection of Detail

The description of the PPI tube above could include many more details — for example, the color, size, and material of the electron gun or the kind and color of the paint on the inside surface or screen. But these irrelevant details are like too many knickknacks in your grandmother's parlor. They impart a sense of chaos and leave the reader with the weary job of sorting out the significant from the trivial. The painter does not reproduce every blade of grass or every twig of a tree but selects the details that will give the viewer the impression of grass, bush, and tree, whether the description is a detailed view, as in the first paragraph below, or a generalized one, as in the second paragraph.

> I still kept in mind a certain wonderful sunset which I witnessed when steamboating was new to me. A broad expanse of the river was turned to blood; in the middle distance the red hue brightened into gold, through which a solitary log came floating, black and conspicuous; in one place a long, slanting mark lay sparkling upon the water; in another the surface was broken by boiling, tumbling rings, that were as many-tinted as an opal; where the ruddy flush was faintest, was a smooth spot that was covered with graceful circles and radiating lines, ever so delicately traced; the shore on our left was densely wooded and the somber shadow that fell from this forest was broken in one place by a long, ruffled trail that shone like silver; and high above the forest wall a clean-stemmed dead tree waved a single leafy bough that glowed like a flame in the unobstructed splendor that was flowing from the sun. There were graceful curves, reflected images, woody heights, soft distances, and over the whole scene, far and near, the dissolving lights drifted steadily, enriching it every passing moment with new marvels of coloring.
>
> Mark Twain, *Old Times on the Mississippi*

> A casual traveler topping the hill where the highway swings up from the south can take in the entire community at a glance, from St. Ignatius' Catholic church at one end of town, past the wooden row houses and empty storefronts in the center, to onion-domed St. Mary's Russian Orthodox church at the other. But a more careful look reveals something else. . . .

The proper amount of detail depends upon the writer's purpose and scope. Descriptions may vary from a simple statement of how a mechanism works or a group of roses is arranged to a finely wrought totality that a reader might replicate. The level of generality and the structure that the writer perceives in the subject to be described determine which details are selected. In technical descriptions, all major parts of the perceived structure should be represented. We must remember the denotative aim of such objective discourse. In impressionistic descriptions, however, details are chosen to represent more than themselves. They should be capable of connotative expansion in the reader's mind. In the opening paragraph of Hemingway's *A Farewell to Arms,* for example, the details all contribute to a single dominant impression of dusty weariness. It seems a whole scene is spread before us, yet we find only a few details described: the riverbed; the pebbles, boulders, and water; the troops; the trees and their leaves; the road. Hemingway concentrates on these few details until he renders a dominant impression:

> In the late summer of that year we lived in a house in a village that looked across the river and the plain to the mountains. In the bed of the river there were pebbles and boulders, dry and white in the sun, and the water was clear and swiftly moving and blue in channels. Troops went by the house and down the road and the dust they raised powdered the leaves of the trees. The trunks of the trees too were dusty and the leaves fell early that year and we saw the troops marching along the road and the dust rising and leaves, stirred by the breeze, falling, and the soldiers marching and afterward the road bare and white except for the leaves.

The next paragraph focuses on the plain across the river and on the mountains, still from the point of view within the house. The succeeding paragraph turns to the troops, giving a close-up as they march under the windows of the house, their "guns going past pulled by motor tractors." Each focus is a separate description, its effect depending upon the selection of detail that suggests the whole.

After choosing the significant details, writers arrange them in some effective order, emphasizing some and subordinating others, according to some function or emotive importance, as Hemingway has done.

EXERCISES

1. Read the following, part of a description of a barrio from "The Barrio" by Robert Ramirez:

   > Members of the barrio describe the entire area as their home. It is a home, but it is more than this. The barrio is a refuge from the harshness and coldness of the Anglo world. It is a forced refuge. The leprous people are isolated from the rest of the community and contained in their section of town. The stoical pariahs of the barrio accept their fate, and from the angry seeds of rejection grow the flowers of closeness between

outcasts, not the thorns of bitterness and the mad desire to flee. There is no want to escape, for the feeling of the barrio is known only to its inhabitants, and the material needs of life can also be found here.

The *tortilleria* fires up its machinery three times a day, producing steaming, round, flat slices of barrio bread. In the winter, the warmth of the tortilla factory is a wool *serape* in the chilly morning hours, but in the summer, it unbearably toasts every noontime customer.

The *panderia* sends its sweet messenger aroma down the dimly lit street, announcing the arrival of fresh, hot sugary *pan dulce*.

The small corner grocery serves the meal-to-meal needs of customers, and the owner, a part of the neighborhood, willingly gives credit to people unable to pay cash for foodstuffs.

The barbershop is a living room with hydraulic chairs, radio, and television, where old friends meet and speak of life as their salted hair falls aimlessly about them.

The pool hall is a junior level country club where 'chucos, strangers in their own land, get together to shoot pool and rap, while veterans, unaware of the cracking, popping balls on the green felt, complacently play dominoes beneath rudely hung *Playboy* foldouts.

The *cantina* is the night spot of the barrio. It is the country club and the den where the rites of puberty are enacted. Here the young become men. It is in the taverns that a young dude shows his *machismo* through the quantity of beer he can hold, the stories of *ruchas* he has had, and his willingness and ability to defend his image against hardened and scarred old lions.

What is the dominant impression? What are some of the notable words and phrases that contribute to the dominant impression? Where does the focus shift? How does Ramirez accomplish any shifts in focus? Can you detect different levels of generality? Write a short impressionistic description of a place familiar to you, imitating this one of the barrio.

2. Select a picture from a magazine or a photograph of a painting from a magazine. Describe it first in a technical way and then in an impressionistic way. Explain in a brief paragraph what detail you excluded in the impressionistic description and why. Also state your point of view, focus, and line of development in each description.

3. Describe impressionistically a scene by day and by night, or in the sun and in the rain. Note how your focus and line of development change.

4. Describe one of the following, first as it appears from the outside, then as it appears from the inside: a boat, a house, a desk, a car.

5. Describe the state of your mind. Perhaps simile, metaphor, and analogy may help.

6. Using description as the major rhetorical operation for developing your ideas, explain the importance of one of the following: the layout of the college you are attending, a certain type of house, an ideal workshop for a particular hobby, the layout of a town.

Chapter 2

Narration

Narration is a chronological or temporal operation. It tells about actions or events taking place in time. Reports of experiments, tests, air disasters, circus performances, and love affairs are all narratives. So are biographies, journals, memoirs, histories, tales, novels, myths, anecdotes, and obituaries. All along the spectrum of rhetoric the narrator answers the question, "What happens?"

If we look upon description as a photograph, a picture of something at a given moment, then we can see narration as a motion picture, a presentation not only of the thing in motion but the motion of the thing. In most discourse, description and narration occur together, one dominating, the other supporting. Writers frequently stop the chronological movement of narration to render a picture spatially, frozen in time; conversely, they may enliven a description with a touch of movement. Description is static, narration dynamic. Instead of saying, "The drive shaft is connected to the wheels, and its rotation imparts movement to the vehicle," a writer can employ a sequential line of development: "The drive shaft rotates, turning the wheels, which move the vehicle."

Narration also enlivens impressionistic descriptions. In the following paragraph from the introductory chapter of *The Tragedy of Pudd'nhead Wilson,* notice how Mark Twain injects action into a still picture:

> The hamlet's front was washed by the clear water of the great river; its body stretched itself rearward up a gentle decline; its most rearward border fringed itself out and scattered its houses about the base line of the hills; the hills rose high, enclosing the town in a half moon curve, clothed with forests from foot to summit.

The paragraph focuses on the quality of relaxation, on stillness, yet the parts related to this focus are suffused with a dynamic quality — the river washes, the hamlet stretches, the rearward border fringes itself out and scatters houses, the hills rise and enclose, the forests clothe.

Narrative Pattern

In narrative patterns, the line of development is always sequential; the point of view focuses on the object, concept, person, or form of energy going through some series of actions, events, stages, steps, or changes. In explaining how radar works, a writer would first assume a panoramic point of view to observe the entire process, the flow of energy as it is fed into the transmitter, shaped into a signal, transmitted, strikes a target, and finally returns in the form of an echo. The writer might then shift the point of view to specifically narrate each major component of the system, pausing to describe the qualities and features of key pieces of equipment: the transmitter, the antenna, the receiver, and the picture tube displaying the information.

Narrating the process of manufacturing an automobile would be more complex because a simultaneous series of processes would have to be narrated. The writer would have to determine major and minor processes, then treat the major processes equally in turn while properly subordinating the minor processes. Those that produce the upholstery, instruments, fittings, and so on would be subordinated, say, to the major sequences that produce the chassis, the body, and the engine. The reader would be informed directly or by implication that all sequences of action occur at once, although they are being narrated one at a time. When the engine is fitted to the chassis, the major lines of development shrink from three to two; and after the body is attached to complete the assembly of major parts, the narrative proceeds along a single line until it shows the completed automobile being driven off the assembly line.

Organizational charts presenting the lines of command are essentially narratives, as are flow charts that show the passage of information, product, or energy through a series of stations, machines, or hierarchical offices. At each stage or step in the narrative the writer may pause to elaborate by describing qualities, characteristics, duties, conditions, or requirements — whatever the narrative purpose dictates. Writers also follow narrative patterns in manuals and all kinds of instructions, whether the reader will operate a lawnmower, construction crane, or space capsule. How-to books and articles are essentially narratives giving step-by-step directions. So are recipes. The narrative pattern can also structure and support an argument. For example, a flow chart can be used to point out efficient or inefficient arrangements or even incompetence in an organization.

Usually we think of stories when the word *narration* is mentioned — stories about persons. Processes, on the other hand, whether natural, social, technological, or psychological, are usually considered the subjects of descriptions. However, stories and processes share the sequential line of development. All are essentially narrative, and therefore we can simplify the task of writing processes and stories by envisioning them in terms of flow, as action following an orderly path from beginning to ending, source to outcome. The writer may rearrange the chronology of events in the narrative — that is, put the ending first or begin in the middle of the action and then go back to the time when the action began — but the reader must be able to put the events back together again in the natural time sequence.

Narrative Source

The narrative source is the generator of the narrative flow. In reports of processes, procedures, and operations, the narrative source is the purpose of the process and its significance, usually the production of a service or object. All the steps or stages are generated in sequence with that singular aim. In a typical "hot" newspaper story, the source is the lead (the opening sentence or sentences) that summarizes what happened, where, when, how, why. The rest of the story elaborates upon the answers to these questions with specific details. In essay and fiction, the theme is the source of narration, generating choices of events and characters, and details about them.

Whether the narrative is the whole discourse or part of it, the source must be implied or stated in order to generate flow:

> Man, by his unique nature — his ability to calculate, stand upright, use his arms, and put his thumb over his palm to hold a tool — is an industrial animal. The story of inventions through eight thousand years is virtually a prolonged industrial revolution.
>
> Robert Furneaux Jordan, *Victorian Architecture*

These sentences introduce a story of industrial development, a narrative within a larger framework, a book about architecture. The purpose of the narrative in this section of the book is to show human beings as industrial animals. From that source the writer will generate the historical events that comprise man's development as a maker and user of tools. Jordan's point of view is distant enough to allow a vision of the entire industrial revolution; he promises a good deal of knowledge, a flow of considerable magnitude.

With fiction that begins in the midst of things, chronology has been rearranged, and two narratives are actually generated, that of the physical events and that of the mental or internal events. The reader is led through a straight chronology of the internal events — that is, as they occur in the mind of a character or the narrator — but the reader must reorder the external events in sequence in order to understand what happened. Nevertheless, the source still establishes flow for both external and internal events. It sets theme, the fictional equivalent of purpose, as well as time and place, and it introduces characters and initial relationships. Here, for example, are the opening paragraphs of Hemingway's "The Battler":

> Nick stood up. He was all right. He looked up the track at the lights of the caboose going out of sight around the curve. There was water on both sides of the track, then tamarack swamp.
>
> He felt of his knee. The pants were torn and the skin was barked. His hands were scraped and there were sand and cinders driven up under his nails. He went over the edge of the track down the little slope to the water and washed his hands. He washed them carefully in the cold water, getting the dirt out from the nails. He squatted down and bathed his knee.

Nick's bruise, not the event that caused it, generates the story. Actually he has been tossed off a freight train. Down the road he meets Ad, "the battler," who is so bruised by similar incidents that his face is permanently misshapen. "They couldn't hurt me," he says. Most of the physical narrative focuses upon this extremely pugnacious fellow, who even attacks Nick at the climactic moment. However, this external flow of events is accompanied by the internal one with which the story opened. Nick's lesson accumulates steadily: bruises in life are inevitable, and the individual's response of bravado is futile but admirable.

Narrative Flow

After narrative flow is generated, it should guide the reader through the narrative.

For processes, flow is the sequence of steps. Some processes move simply through consecutive steps, but many processes are so complicated with simultaneous steps, and with substeps and subsubsteps, that writers can easily lose control. In such situations writers must consciously adhere to the level of generality they are covering to avoid writing on more than one level at once. In narrating the process of assembling an automobile, for example, a writer would exhaust first the general level of major steps in assembling the chassis, engine, and body before turning to the next narrower level, say, assembling the parts of the engine. The writer must decide just how specific the narration must be and maintain consistency on that chosen level. In narrating the automobile assembly line, the level at which nuts and bolts are inserted might be omitted. Once the flow is established, writers should ask these questions as they proceed: "Is this step necessary?" "Have I presented material that does not bear directly on the process?" "Do I blur the point by extending even relevant material?" "Have I shown the relationships between steps?" "Does the reader still know where we're going?" Note the consistency and care Benjamin Franklin devotes to the level of generality and the relationships between steps as he narrates the way he learned to write. We have numbered the steps:

> I took some of the [*Spectator*] and, [1] making short hints of the senti-ments in each sentence, laid them by a few days, and then, [2] without looking at [them] tried to complete the papers again, by expressing each hinted sentiment at length, and as fully as it had been expressed before, in any suitable words that should come to hand. [3] Then I compared my Spectator with the original, discovered some of my faults, and corrected them. But I found I wanted a stock of words, or a readiness in recollect-ing and using them. . . . [4] Therefore I took some of the tales and turned them into verse; and, after a time, when I had pretty well forgotten the prose, turned them back again. [5] I also sometimes jumbled my recollec-tions of hints into confusion, and after some weeks endeavored to reduce them in [the] best order, before I began to form the full sentences and complete the paper. This was to teach me method and arrangement of thoughts. [6] By comparing my work afterwards with the original, I dis-covered many faults and amended them; but I sometimes had the plea-sure of fancying that, in certain particulars of small import, I had been lucky enough to improve. . . .
>
> Benjamin Franklin, *Autobiography*

In fiction and rearranged accounts of history or personality, the narrative is a sequence of situations or scenes rather than steps or stages. And rather than a straight flow to an outcome, situations de-velop into conflicts, snags in the stream, which impede and ultimately change the direction of the flow. Tension is created and maintained throughout the flow of events. The tension is aroused at the source: Priscilla loves Henry and does not believe he is uninterested, although he has said so. The flow proceeds as she acts to create more situations that bring about Henry's reactions, to which she reacts in turn. The narrative flows through these "rising actions" until a "climax" is reached in which the conflict is resolved. This decisive moment occurs near the end, but each scene leading to it contains its own conflict and tentative resolution until the final one where Priscilla either gives up on Henry, gains his love, or shoots him, among other ultimate possibilities.

A narrative of a process pauses frequently for description, and so does the narrative of a story. It describes scene, atmosphere, and char-acters (their interests, tastes, histories, and thoughts). These descriptive details are the means of delineating the conflicting forces. A narrative that excludes them is merely a skeleton, a bare statement of steps, void of experience. Just as in the flow of a process, however, the writer must arrange the details in an order, in this case an order that allows the reader to realize the conflict and absorb its meaning.

Although writers of nonfiction prose usually narrate on more gen-eral levels than fiction writers, they can seek moments of particulariza-tion as much as possible. Consider this example:

It took four days for the troops recruited by Arnold and his aides to arm themselves and reach Ticonderoga, and their arrival did much to restore order in the fort. Arnold's men had commandeered a schooner, and Arnold . . . rapidly loaded the schooner with some captured artillery and set sail for the North to capture the armed British ship reported to be around the Northern end of Lake Champlain.

> Brian Richard Boylan, *Benedict Arnold: The Dark Eagle*

The writer of the preceding generalized account follows it with this particularized bit of narrative:

As the Boys ransacked the fort, stealing whatever was not nailed down, Arnold protested strongly and quoted military law forbidding such practices to the looters; most of whom ignored him or replied by spitting at his feet.

But this level of narration is still more general than the fiction writer's:

The din in front swelled to a tremendous chorus. The youth and his fellows were frozen in silence. They could see a flag that tossed in the smoke angrily. Near it were the blurred and agitated forms of troops. There came a turbulent stream of men across the fields. A battery changing position at a frantic gallop scattered the stragglers right and left.

> Stephen Crane, *The Red Badge of Courage*

Narrative Outcome

Since there was some purpose for the action to begin with, the flow ends in a fulfillment of that purpose, whether it is a tragic or happy outcome of conflicting forces, the product of a manufacturing process or how-to article, or the interpretation of data from a test or experiment. In explaining outstanding characteristics of a lengthy process, the writer may summarize major steps in the process or procedure, especially those responsible for important characteristics — for example, the particular way cheddar cheese is stored for aging. The ending satisfies the reader's interest about the process or procedure.

The resolutions of the conflicts in history, fiction, and biography forecast the ending, the outcome. If the forces are not reconcilable, their tension is broken. If they are reconcilable, the tension is relieved in joining. The lovers marry. Often endings are ironical. They say one thing but mean another. The ending of Stephen Crane's *Red Badge of Courage,* for instance, states that the young soldier has learned to face death and be courageous, but the whole story indicates that he only thinks so, that more complex battles of life still await him.

EXERCISES

1. One of the following paragraphs lists actions; the other traces the derivation of a word. Are both narratives? Is neither a narrative? Is one a narrative but not the other? Give reasons for your answers.

> Ants are so much like human beings as to be an embarrassment. They farm fungi, raise aphids as livestock, launch armies into wars, use chemical sprays to alarm and confuse enemies, capture slaves. The families of weaver ants engage in child labor, holding their larvae like shuttles to spin out the thread that sews the leaves together for their fungus gardens. They exchange information ceaselessly. They do everything but watch television.
>
> Lewis Thomas, *The Lives of a Cell*

> It [comparative linguistics] is a field in which the irresponsible amateur can have a continually mystifying sort of fun. Whenever you get the available answer to a straight question, like, say, where does the most famous and worst of the four-letter Anglo-Saxon unprintable words come from, the answer raises new and discomfiting questions. Take that particular word. It comes from *peig,* a crawling, wicked Indo-European word meaning evil and hostile, the sure makings of a curse. It becomes *poikos,* then *gafaihaz* in Germanic and *gefay* in Old English, signifying "foe." It turned from *poik-vos* into *faigjaz* in Germanic, and *faege* in Old English, meaning "fated to die," leading to *fey.* It went on from *fehida* in Old English to become *feud* and *fokken* in Old Dutch. Somehow, from these beginnings, it transformed itself into one of the most powerful English expletives, meaning something like "Die before your time!" The unspeakable malevolence of the message is now buried deep inside the word, and out on the surface it presents itself as merely an obscenity.
>
> Lewis Thomas, *The Lives of a Cell*

2. Write a how-to essay about some process or procedure familiar to you but probably unfamiliar to many other people (for example, blousing trousers on military fatigues or phototypesetting). Be sure to stop the narrative for descriptive passages. In your descriptive efforts, try to use metaphor, simile, and analogy whenever appropriate, chiefly to clarify.

3. Write a how-to essay about some process or procedure familiar to you and also familiar to many other people (for example, registering for classes at your college or roller skating). Be sure to stop the narrative for descriptive passages. In your descriptive efforts, try to use metaphor, simile, and analogy whenever appropriate, principally to create interest.

4. Write a brief biographical sketch of a friend or a sketch of your own life in 250 words. Then expand the sketch into a narrative twice as long by elaborating on one or two incidents to illustrate a point such as a painful lesson learned over a long time.

5. Trace your genealogy — parents, grandparents, and so on — as far back as you can. Include dates of births, marriages, deaths, and places of residence and major events. Check available records and photographs. Interview relatives and their friends. Put the gathered information into some coherent, meaningful order.

6. With the gathered, ordered information from exercise 5, write a narrative of interest to family members.

7. With the gathered, ordered information from exercise 5, write a narrative of interest to a stranger.

8. Write a brief eulogy for yourself, speaking of yourself in third person from the point of view of a friend who knew you well in one particular area of your life (for example, childhood years or high school). Assume that you are one speaker of several and so have no need to include the cliché "dearly beloved" or similar expressions. Focus rather on a full survey of events that support a point.

Chapter 3

Comparison

The basic operations of a computer are comparison, by which the machine identifies, and generalization, by which it classifies. These operations mirror the fundamental workings of the human mind. All our lives we learn by comparing and contrasting (also comparison). A child says, "I'm taller than you"; "My father can lick your father." In high school, someone observes, "Mary is prettier than Susy, but Susy is smarter." Another student remarks, "That bike has better tires, but it's got rust spots, yet it seems to be stronger than the other"; and another, "I don't love him the way you do." In college, we compare governmental, cultural, religious, biological, and philosophical systems, and social conditions of classes and races. In our professional lives we compare profits and losses year to year, personnel, equipment, procedures, operations, and our merits and personalities. We compare even when we are not aware of it. Comparison is so fundamental an operation that it seems automatic. Comparisons underlie most of our judgments:

> The Concorde, a spectacular fuel guzzler, may be a victim of oil prices not foreseen when its engineering got under way two decades ago. Its shock wave prohibits flying over land, and its passenger capacity is relatively small.

The implied comparison here is against the standard of other transport planes in similar service.

Language itself grows by means of comparison. We draw analogies, create metaphors. We perceive similarities, for example, between an anatomy, a corporation, and a river: *heads* rest upon shoulders, command operations in places called *head*quarters, and comprise the source of a river's flow, the *head*waters. Like trees, rivers are said to have branches. So do commercial banks and libraries. Electricity has *current*. Identifying one thing by comparing it with another, more familiar thing is a valuable aid in the rhetorical operation of definition. Comparison is also at the root of classification and analysis. In classifying we group items by comparison — apples in one bin, tomatoes in another — according to similar characteristics. In analysis we separate one part from another by contrast — the leaves from the branches, the branches from the trunk, the trunk from the roots of a tree.

Literal Comparison

Analogies and metaphors are figurative comparisons. They give striking images to thoughts and lead to a more profound sense or feeling about something. They are used throughout the spectrum of rhetoric. Literal comparisons are direct and usually confined to identification at the more factual end of the spectrum: "The radar is like a radio except that both transmitter and receiver are in the same place and use a common antenna." Here the comparison is made to point out the differences, that is, to contrast. The interest is focused on one of the items, the unfamiliar one.

Writers interested in both items extend the literal comparison into paragraphs that show likenesses and differences point by point or item by item. Rather than use one of the items to explain the other, they focus on the similarities or the differences: "Although A is similar to B in these ways, it differs more importantly in these ways." Often the writer will emphasize similarities in things commonly seen as different, for example, President Reagan's own comparisons between himself and President Roosevelt. Or the writer will emphasize differences between things usually seen as similar, for example, television advertisements on competing pain relievers. How alike was totalitarianism in two different states, Mussolini's Italy and Stalin's Russia? Or how different is communism in present-day Yugoslavia and China? In the comparison below, the similarities are minimized and the differences emphasized:

Bing Crosby and Elvis Presley were creations of the microphone. It made it possible for people with frail voices not only to be heard beyond the third row but also to caress millions. Crosby was among the first to understand that the microphone made it possible to sing to multitudes by singing to a single person in a small room.

Presley cuddled his microphone like a lover. With Crosby the microphone was usually concealed, but Presley brought it out on stage, detached it form its fitting, stroked it, pressed it to his mouth. It was a surrogate for his listener, and he made love to it unashamedly.

The difference between Presley and Crosby, however, reflected generational differences which spoke of changing values in American life. Crosby's music was soothing; Presley's was disturbing. It is too easy to be glib about this, to say that Crosby was singing to, first, depression America and then to wartime America, and that his audiences had all the disturbance they could handle in their daily lives without buying more at the record shop and movie theater. . . .

To explain each man in terms of changes in economic and political life probably oversimplifies the matter. Something in the culture was also changing. Crosby's music, for example, paid great attention to the importance of lyrics. The "message" of the song was as essential to the audience as the tune. The words were usually inane and witless, but Crosby — like Sinatra a little later — made them vital. People remembered them, sang them. Words still had meaning.

Although many of Presley's songs were highly lyrical, in most it wasn't the words that moved audiences; it was the "sound." Rock 'n' roll, of which he was the great popularizer, was a "sound" event. Song stopped being song and turned into "sound," at least until the Beatles came along and solved the problem of making words sing to the new beat.

Russell Baker, "From Song to Sound: Bing and Elvis," *New York Times,* October 18, 1977

After touching upon the similarities (both singers were creations of the microphone, had frail voices, and caressed their audiences), this excerpt focuses on differences. The major points of the comparison are (1) Presley's hugging the microphone as opposed to Crosby's concealing it, (2) Presley's disturbing effect as opposed to Crosby's soothing effect, and (3) Presley's emphasis on sound as opposed to Crosby's emphasis on lyrics. The essay develops by examining each of the points of difference between Presley and Crosby, after confining all the points of similarity to the short first paragraph. We notice that the paragraphs also contain other material that relates to another set of differences, those in American values. These differences bring out the theme of the article: changing American values as revealed by the different styles of two famous singers.

Essentially, in the excerpt above, Russell Baker employs literal comparison as evidence for his insight into change in American values, but he does not take a position favoring one set of values over the other. Such a preferential point of view, however, is common in literal comparisons, in the popular "now and then" article, for instance, where the writer prefers either the old ways or the new, the relaxed pace and moral security compared with the convenience and variety of modern appliances. Emphasis, as in all writing, directs the meaning in literal comparisons. Unless the writer undertakes a complete comparative analysis for the purpose of selecting one item over another or judging one better than another — that is, to reach a conclusion in a problem-solving situation — the comparison will turn bland and dull without emphasis, a mere exercise either in the obvious or the obscure. (See Chapter 5 for comparative analysis.)

Whether emphasizing similarities or differences, the objects, processes, concepts, or personalities compared must possess common qualities. It would not be profitable to compare General Patton's behavior in World War II with General Eisenhower's because one was a field commander and the other a headquarters general. Patton's behavior could be compared more fruitfully with another field general's, say Field Marshal Rommel of the German army or Field Marshal Montgomery of the British, or closer to home, General Bradley; and General Eisenhower's wartime behavior could be compared profitably with that of another headquarters general, say General MacArthur.

Although the similarities may be residual in the things compared, it is the writer's vision that perceives and renders them. In the following excerpt comparing two Civil War generals, the author not only emphasizes the similarities in essentially dissimilar personalities but envisions these personalities as having the basic qualities needed for reconciliation and the healing of the divided nation:

> Grant and Lee were in complete contrast, representing two diametrically opposed elements in American life. Grant was the modern man emerging; beyond him ready to come on the stage was the great age of steel and machinery, of cities, and a restless, burgeoning vitality. Lee might have ridden down from the old age of chivalry, lance in hand, silken banner fluttering over his head. Each man was the perfect champion of his cause, drawing both his strengths and his weaknesses from the people he led.
>
> Yet it was not all contrast, after all. Different as they were — in background, in personality, in underlying aspiration — these two great soldiers had much in common. Under everything else, they were marvelous fighters. Furthermore, their fighting qualities were really very much alike.
>
> Each man had, to begin with, the great virtue of utter tenacity and fidelity. Grant fought his way down the Mississippi Valley in spite of acute personal discouragement and profound military handicaps. Lee hung in the trenches at Petersburg after hope itself had died. In each man there was an indomitable quality . . . the born fighter's refusal to give up as long as he can still remain on his feet and lift his two fists.
>
> Daring and resourcefulness they had, too, the ability to think faster and move faster than the enemy. These were the qualities which gave Lee the dazzling campaigns of Second Manassas and Chancellorsville and won Vicksburg for Grant.
>
> Lastly, and perhaps greatest of all, there was the ability, at the end, to turn quickly from war to peace once the fighting was over. Out of the way these two men behaved at Appomattox came the possibility of a peace of reconciliation. It was a possibility not wholly realized in the years to come, but which did, in the end, help the two sections to become one nation again . . . after a war whose bitterness might have seemed to make such a reunion wholly impossible. No part of either man's life became him more than the part he played in their brief meeting in the McLean house at Appomattox. Their behavior there put all succeeding generations of Americans in their debt. Two great Americans, Grant and Lee — very different, yet under everything very much alike. Their encounter at Appomattox was one of the great moments of American history.
>
> Bruce Catton, "Appomattox," *This Hallowed Ground*

Analogy

Analogies are figurative comparisons that focus attention on the similar qualities of things that are essentially different. If we examine similar and contrasting features of two automobiles, we are writing a literal comparison. However, if we compare one of the automobiles with a workhorse for several similar points, we are writing an analogy. In analogy, we are not really interested in the familiar item, only the unfamiliar one to which it is compared. Deposits of oil can be visualized by comparison with water in a sponge, although the water differs from the oil in almost every way, and oil cannot be extracted by squeezing rock. The qualities of water in a sponge are of no interest except as they help illustrate the qualities of oil in the rock. And in this analogical comparison of a summer's day with a beautiful woman, Shakespeare is quite obviously focused on the woman:

> Shall I compare thee to a summer's day?
> Thou art more lovely and more temperate:
> Rough winds do shake the darling buds of May
> And summer's lease hath all too short a date:
> Sometimes too hot the eye of heaven shines,
> And often is his gold complexion dimm'd;
> And every fair from fair sometime declines,
> By chance or nature's changing course untrimm'd:
> But thy eternal summer shall not fade
> Nor lose possession of that fair thou ow'st,
> Nor shall Death brag thou wand'rest in his shade,
> When in eternal lines to time thou grow'st;
> So long as men can breathe or eyes can see
> So long lives this and this gives life to thee.
>
> William Shakespeare, Sonnet 18

Shakespeare's purpose in this sonnet is to assert on the basis of his analogy that his art, his poem, will defeat the ravages of time, which erode the beauties of the woman he is comparing to the day.

Shakespeare has employed an extended analogy, not to clarify something difficult to visualize, but to create a new and unusual perspective on the old and familiar. When scientists use extended analogies, it is to explain and clarify complex ideas. Here, for example, is Richard P. Feynman using the motion of corks in water to explain electromagnetic fields, a phenomenon we cannot see:

> Here is an analogy: If we are in a pool of water and there is a floating cork very close by, we can move it "directly" by pushing the water with another cork. If you looked only at the two *corks,* all you would see would be that one moved immediately in response to the motion of the other—there is some kind of "*interaction*" between them. Of course, what we really do is to disturb *water;* the *water* then disturbs the other

cork. We could make up a "law" that if you pushed the water a little bit, an object close by in the water would move. If it were farther away, of course, the second cork would scarcely move, for we move the water *locally*. On the other hand, if we jiggle the cork, a new phenomenon is involved, in which the motion of the water moves the water there, etc. and *waves* travel away, so that by jiggling, there is an influence *very much farther out*, an oscillatory influence, that cannot be understood from the direct interaction. Therefore, the idea of direct interaction must be replaced with the existence of the water, or in the electrical case, with what we call the electromagnetic field.

> Richard P. Feynman, *The Feynman
> Lectures on Physics*

In the following passage, Tom Wolfe extends an analogy between two dissimilar kinds of living beings — New Yorkers and animals — through several paragraphs, elaborating on the similarities that contribute to his point, which is neither affective like Shakespeare's nor factual like Feynman's. It is an attitude, and not about the animals but the New Yorkers:

> It got to be easy to look at New Yorkers as animals, especially looking down from some place like a balcony at Grand Central at the rush hour Friday afternoon. The floor was filled with the poor white humans, running around, dodging, blinking their eyes, making a sound like a pen full of starlings or rats.
>
> They stop short to keep from hitting somebody or because they are disoriented and they suddenly stop and look around, and they skid on their rubber-soled shoes and a screech goes up. They pour out of the floor down the escalators. . . .
>
> We inhaled those nice fluffy fumes of human sweat, urine, effluvia, and sebaceous secretions. One old female human was already stroked out on the upper level, on a stretcher, with two policemen standing by. The other humans barely looked at her. They rushed into line. They bellied each other, haunch to paunch, down the stairs. Human heads shone through the gratings. The species North European tried to create bubbles of space around themselves, about a foot and a half in diameter. . . .
>
> Tom Wolfe, *The Pump House Gang*

The analogy certainly helps Tom Wolfe impart his attitude toward New Yorkers. But people, of course, are unlike animals in many ways that he has suppressed in order to make his point. If the human beings in New York City behave at times like animals, they also produce and appreciate drama, painting, music, and other fine arts and manage enormous enterprises quite unlike animals. Because analogies select the points of similarity, they can be easily used to mislead or emotionally charge the reader. Analogies should always be written cautiously so that the writer does not emotionally bias or mislead a reader unintentionally. The writer should indicate that similarity on one or two points does not imply that the compared items are actually alike. Basically, an analogy is effective because the compared items are essentially unalike: "Just as the ear cannot hear sounds beyond a certain pitch, so the human cannot perceive phenomena beyond a certain range."

Extended analogies are most prone to mislead in the center of the spectrum of rhetoric where arguments dominate, either indirectly as in the Tom Wolfe excerpt or more directly as in the following excerpt from "Letter from Birmingham Jail." Here Martin Luther King, Jr., selects only the quality of extremism in known heroes, and by means of analogy on that point, he implies that he and those who follow him will also be heroes.

> But though I was initially disappointed at being categorized as an extremist, as I continued to think about the matter I gradually gained a measure of satisfaction from the label. Was not Jesus an extremist for love: "Love your enemies, bless them that curse you, do good to them that hate you, and pray for them which despitefully use you, and persecute you." Was not Amos an extremist for justice: "Let justice roll down like waters and righteousness like an overflowing stream." Was not Paul an extremist for the Christian gospel: "I bear in my body the marks of the Lord Jesus." Was not Martin Luther an extremist: "Here I stand; I cannot do otherwise, so help me God." And John Bunyan: "I will stay in jail to the end of my days before I make a butchery of my conscience." And Abraham Lincoln: "This nation cannot survive half slave and half free." And Thomas Jefferson: "We hold these truths to be self-evident, that all men are created equal. . . . " So the question is not whether we will be extremists, but what kind of extremists we will be. Will we be extremists for hate or for love? Will we be extremists for the preservation of injustice or for the extension of justice? In that dramatic scene on Calvary's hill three men were crucified. We must never forget that all three were crucified for the same crime — the crime of extremism. Two were extremists for immorality, and thus fell below their environment. The other, Jesus Christ, was an extremist for love, truth and goodness, and thereby rose above his environment. Perhaps the South, the nation and the world are in dire need of creative extremists.

King, of course, is spellbinding. He moves his audience, as he intended, regardless of his logical leaps; for instance, he merely assumes that the two other condemned men on Calvary Hill were immoral, and he fails to show that Abe Lincoln's extremism really was extremism at all. What, after all, does King mean by extremism? King follows the practice of those named, leaders of the people whose emotional motives carry the argument over the illogicalities. He is able to succeed partly because he has carefully avoided offending anyone. Here is a student's analogy attempting much the same approach as King's, but it falls prey to the inherent dangers of argumentative analogy. It unnecessarily offends people, and the stated similarities are too simplistic to ring true.

Believing in God is like playing the lottery. Both require a relatively small initial investment. A lottery ticket is cheap and readily available; belief is easily adopted. Yet in each case, the gambler's action secures a chance of final reward. You can t win the jackpot if you don't buy a ticket. Likewise, you won't go to heaven if you don't believe in God. It makes sense to gamble in both cases, not only because of the enticing end reward, but also for the benefit you get from the means itself. The acts of playing or believing themselves can color your world with hope, making pre-reward poverty or earthly existence more bearable.

Metaphor and Simile

A metaphor is a figure of speech that implies a comparison; a simile is a figure of speech that expresses the implied comparison. The term *metaphor* means to carry beyond or over and is often used as an umbrella term for figurative language in general. Specifically, however, the form of a metaphor identifies the compared items so closely that they appear to be joined. The metaphor gives to one the quality of another by fusing the compared items into a single figure of speech. To say a Ferrari is like a Maserati makes a literal comparison. To say a Ferrari is like a winged chariot creates a simile. To say a Ferrari is a winged chariot creates a metaphor. Shakespeare's comparison, "If hairs be wires, black wires grow on her head," is reduced to metaphor by simply omitting the first phrase. The comparison in the metaphor could be made more obvious by using the words *like* or *as:* "Her hair is like black wire," changing the metaphor to a simile, which stems from the same word root as *similar.* "His nose is like a marshmallow" is a simile; "His nose is a marshmallow" is a metaphor. The implicit comparison in the metaphor can be concealed further for a more dramatic effect: "his marshmallow nose"; "her wiry hair."

In the form of a simile, the two components of metaphor are easy to identify. These are the tenor, the literal part, such as the nose and the hair, and the vehicle, the part that carries over to the thing compared, such as the marshmallow or the wire. In "My love is a red, red rose," the tenor is *love* and the vehicle is *rose.* In "The government is an octopus," the tenor is *government* and the vehicle is *octopus.* In these straightforward metaphors the tenor and vehicle are distinct. In condensed or concealed metaphors, however, the tenor may be totally suppressed if the vehicle is a noun or verb:

The *witch* kept him after school.

He *clawed* his way to the top.

The ship *plowed* the seas.

He listened to the *music of the spheres.*

When the tenor is added, as in "the glassy eye" or "the fiery mind," or "the fat moon," the vehicle becomes a modifier:

> The *witch* of a teacher kept him after school.
>
> He used his wits like *claws* to reach the top.
>
> The ship made its way through the seas *like a plow.*
>
> He listened to the noise *as if it were the music of the spheres.*

Although metaphors occur less frequently in reports than in poetry and essays, they are employed everywhere along the spectrum of rhetoric. Metaphors enliven our prose by adding dramatic effect to our explanations and descriptions. By cutting verbiage and fusing images, these figures of speech join similarities in basically dissimilar things. Not only do they clarify with color and vigor, but often they inspire flashes of insight, showing relationships of things never seen together before. Like too much of anything, of course, excessive use of metaphor defeats its purpose: "His head was a beachball, his neck a great trunk, his torso a tank." Trite metaphors are also self-defeating: "ship of state"; "rat race"; "bottom line"; "one for the road"; "bitter end"; "lock, stock, and barrel." These metaphors are stale. They have negative effects because they are still recognizable, as opposed to dead metaphors, which have become literal language to us through long usage: "the legs of a table"; "the leaves of a book"; "the trunk of a tree"; "the hotness of spice"; "the current of electricity"; "the flow of thought." Dead metaphors have entered ordinary language, but stale metaphors have not.

A metaphor is extended by making more than one point of comparison between the same tenor and vehicle. The extended metaphor is as much descriptive as explanatory and appeals as much to the senses as to the reasoning powers. In the following excerpt, Lewis Thomas extends a metaphor by comparing the sounds of a bird (tenor) with human song (vehicle):

> The thrush in my backyard sings down his nose in meditative, liquid runs of melody, over and over again, and I have the strongest impression that he does this for his own pleasure. Some of the time he seems to be practicing like a virtuoso in his apartment. He starts a run, reaches a midpoint in the second bar where there should be a set of complex harmonics, stops, and goes back to begin over, dissatisfied. Sometimes, he changes his notation so conspicuously that he seems to be improvising sets of variations. It is a meditative, questioning kind of music, and I cannot believe that he is simply saying, "thrush here."
>
> Lewis Thomas, *The Lives of a Cell*

Metaphors can also be extended by attaching a number of vehicles to a single tenor. In effect, the writer presents a series of metaphors as examples to make a vague abstraction concrete and clear. In the following example, a number of vehicles are applied to explain a single abstract tenor, the nature of words:

> A word is a many-headed hydra. Its meanings are always multiple, and one may bite into another. They are also birds seeking free air, hating confinement. Words are as sensitive and self-conscious as shy children, as fathomless as bottomless pools, as old and historical as monuments and relics.

Perhaps the most humorous misuse of metaphor is the incongruous combination of two or more vehicles for one tenor, called a mixed metaphor: "She hurled abuse at him with deliberate speed"; "His back to the wall, he turned her off by retreating into the memory of her younger more angelic self." Politicians seem exceptionally prone to mixed metaphors, "We are operating in the teeth of an inadequate purse," said a presidential aide; and from a senator, "We need this bill like a horse needs a fifth wheel."

The Organization of Comparisons

Whether figurative or literal the extended comparison needs to be organized. Otherwise, we produce only a list of similarities and differences. The introduction should include the purpose of the comparison, either stated or implied, along with some overview of the items to be compared and some indication of the basis for comparison. Actually all plans of comparison are variations of two basic schemes, which may be used in combination:

1. the block-by-block plan, in which all points of comparison are presented first in paragraphs about one of the subjects and then applied in paragraphs about the other, and
2. the point-by-point plan, in which the comparative points of each subject are presented side by side.

For shorter comparisons the block-by-block arrangement is preferable because the reader can hold in mind the comparative points, while a point-by-point presentation would tend to be disjointed. When the writer does not have an equal number of points, the block-by-block method must be used. For longer presentations, the point-by-point arrangement is preferable because it saves the reader from having to hold in mind all the points cited earlier as he or she reads the second part, in order to make the comparison. In general, the block-by-block method is easier to write and more difficult to read. Frequently the reader gets the feeling of reading two distinct pieces; that is, the block-by-block method has a tendency to split down the middle. Though the point-by-point method requires more control to write, it often allows the writer to make the comparisons in balanced sentences that impose a pleasing rhythm and aid coherence.

Good writers often combine these arrangements. They may present all the points of similarity first, then follow with differences point by point. Or the comparative points may be arranged by degree of significance in a climactic pattern, as we found Bruce Catton doing in his study of Grant and Lee. Russell Baker in the excerpt on Crosby and Presley starts out on a point-by-point pattern but then devotes a whole paragraph to Crosby's lyrical emphasis and another whole paragraph to Presley's sound emphasis. This arrangement is a modification of the block-by-block method. The effect, actually, is the same as Catton's in the Grant and Lee excerpt—a climactic emphasis on the most significant of all the points.

In the conclusion the writer either summarizes the similarities and differences with an emphasis appropriate to the purpose, or he extends the comparison to the point he set out to establish. Shakespeare states his conclusion in the last two lines of his sonnet, to the effect that art lives on beyond life and so gives life to its subject; by means of his art, that is, the woman will outlast by far the summer's day to which she is compared. The conclusion of Bruce Catton's comparison of Grant and Lee imparts value to their similarities in spite of the differences: "Two great Americans, Grant and Lee—very different, yet under everything very much alike. Their encounter at Appomattox was one of the great moments of American history." Russell Baker's comparison between Crosby and Presley concludes:

> The Crosby generation has trouble hearing rock because it makes the mistake of trying to understand the words. The Presley generation has trouble with Crosby because it finds the sound unstimulating and cannot be touched by the inanity of the words. The mutual deafness may be a measure of how far we have come from really troubled times and of how deeply we have come to mistrust the value of words.

The conclusion weighs the similarities and differences in summary, synthesizes their meaning, and then applies that meaning to fulfill the purpose given or implied in the introduction.

EXERCISES

1. Identify metaphors in the excerpts from Russell Baker and Bruce Catton. Does one writer use more than the other? Does one writer use these figurative comparisons more descriptively than another? If so, what effect do the differences have on readers?
2. Write a simile, then a metaphor, for each of the following:

going to college	a fine watch
a book	the U.S. Army

a supermarket	church
a professor you know	air controllers
blindness	a used car salesman
psychiatrists	the national debt
bureaucrats	dentists

3. Extend one of the metaphors or similes created in exercise 2 into an analogy. Be sure your extended metaphor or simile offers four or five points of comparison that will make the less familiar more understandable.

4. What are the problems with the first analogy? How does the second analogy improve on the first one? What problems remain in the second analogy? What can be done to make the second analogy work?

The Young in Society

A change has transpired in society where the young people are clinging to the social welfare system for security as baby birds cling to the nest. By seeking safety and security, just like the security their parents provided when they were young, the recipients receive money for their nourishment and protection. Just like humans, the baby birds fear the world away from the nest. Once away from the security of their home, young people seek protection from the next best source, welfare. The baby birds also run for cover, at first, fearing the slightest activity. Young people have not learned to come out from behind this protective shield to stand on their own two feet, whereas baby birds either mature quickly and fight for their survival or they die. If young people are to survive they must be made to see that welfare is not the answer and that hard work is one answer for their survival.

The Young in Society

There is a phenomenon presently occurring in our society in which young people are clinging to a social welfare system for security as baby birds cling to the nest. Newborn baby birds fear the world away from the nest by cowering beneath their mothers' wings for the safety and security their parents provide. Unfortunately, parents no longer want the burden of supporting and feeding their young; so young people search for an alternate means of providing for nourishment and protection. They become recipients of the social welfare system. The difference between young people and baby birds is that baby birds get pushed from the nest and forced to survive on their own. In contrast, young people are never forced to become independent. They are allowed to exchange the security their parents offered for the security of the social welfare system. There is no security system for baby birds. If baby birds have not learned to fend for themselves, they will die. Baby birds must work hard to learn how to survive. Our society encourages young people to remain dependent by not "pushing them out of the nest" to live on their own. Young people must learn to fend for themselves, to be independent, to survive on their own.

5. Compare two paintings in a museum or pictures of paintings in a magazine. Make sure that they are comparable, that is, of similar things, such as street scenes, still lifes, countrysides, ocean and sky, personal portraits. List comparative points, establish a principle of comparison, and then seek a central idea or theme that these points suggest. Outline the comparison first block by block, then point by point. Choose the more appropriate arrangement and rewrite the comparison, including suitable introduction and conclusion.

6. Make a literal comparison of two people, historical or contemporary, so that some central idea emerges, from either their similarities or their differences. The Bruce Catton excerpt should be a useful model. Be sure to include proper introduction and conclusion. Use metaphor and simile in your explanation and description, but do not overuse them.

Chapter 4

Classification

What is it like? To what does it belong? Astronomers pursue these questions in their studies of light and other forms of energy in the universe just as we pursue them upon meeting an intriguing person, although we do it less systematically. Where does she come from? Does she have a family? Is she a worker? A professional? These questions lead to the generalizing process we call classification.

Classification is the operation of grouping or sorting things — concepts, systems, and objects as well as personalities — into categories according to common characteristics. The word comes from the Latin *classis,* meaning "collection." Writers classify by comparing items for likenesses and grouping them accordingly. They either place an item in an established group of similar items, or, confronted with a disordered array of things, they order the items into groups they conceive. The classifier always deals with more than one thing. A classification is a collection, a plural concept.

On the simplest level, classifying is like the act of replacing an apple fallen from its pile. Does it resemble the pyramid of apples marked Jonathan? Delicious? Rome Beauty? Winesap? Or imagine all the apples in all the piles tossed together in one disordered mess on the floor of the fruit stand. Now the classifier separates and categorizes them into their groups according to genetic shape. They could also be classified according to size, if this criterion were useful, say, if large apples were selling for more per pound. Or other criteria might be used.

A Process of Generalization

To classify we must generalize. Generalization is basic to all thought. From the moment we are born we classify: mother here, everyone else there; family here, strangers there. We generalize constantly, classifying our experiences. Breakfast is tasty or bland. The weather is cold, hot, fair, foul. The people we meet are strangers, friends, fellow employees, bosses. Such generalization is unsystematic and imprecise because it does not stem from completely unbiased observation. "Latins

Are Lousy Lovers" was an article written in *Esquire* magazine many years ago to correct the equally unfounded generalization that Latins were exceptionally good lovers. Careless generalization often leads to harmful prejudices and sometimes to cruel judgments on the basis of traits arbitrarily assigned to all members of a race, sex, or nationality: "Jews are greedy"; "Japs are sneaky"; "Blacks are lazy." It is quite important, therefore, that we generalize cautiously, whether creating formal classifications that are systematic, impersonal, and objective or informal classifications that serve the purposes of the moment and do not require completeness or rigorous precision. Informally, we may classify a collection of automobiles into such categories as roomy, ugly, and stiff, but a formal classification would have to establish these classes systematically according to a criterion, such as comfort. This criterion could account for two of the classes, roomy and stiff, but not the third, ugly.

Formal Classification

Formal classification achieves precision by limiting the collection of things to be included, then selecting and following a useful criterion for grouping the items into classes.

The more unlimited the collection of things to be classified, the more difficult the classifying process. Setting out to classify automobiles without placing limits on the collection imposes the impossible burden of dealing with all automobiles that ever existed. To make useful classification, the collection would have to be limited to time or place of manufacture or even according to some characteristic: "automobiles built before World War I"; "automobiles built in Spain since 1980"; "convertible automobiles built in 1981."

The other major requirement of formal classification is the selection of a criterion for separating the items into classes. The criterion must fit the needs of the classifier. In classifying college applicants, the admissions director might sort them into groups according to their entrance examination scores or the region of the country they come from; a financial aid officer might classify them according to their family income or requested funding; a director of student activities would sort prospective students according to their extracurricular activities in high school. The interest of the classifier determines the criterion or principle to use in establishing classes.

A single classification does not employ more than one criterion or principle at a time. A city block of dwellings, for example, could be classified according to accommodations provided: one-family, duplex, apartment house. Or according to materials of construction: stone, brick, wood, brick and glass, wood and stone. Or style: French provincial, colonial, modern. The collection could not be classified into these groups: apartment, brick, colonial. These terms cut across all three classes and tend to identify or describe a single structure. An apartment house, for example, could be built of brick in a colonial style.

A second principle can be applied in the system only after the first is exhausted. After we have classified dwellings according to type of accommodation, we can apply a more narrow classification within the system, according to material, and then a third within that system, according to style:

    Single dwellings
      Brick
          French provincial
          Colonial
          Modern
      Wood
          French provincial
          Colonial
          Modern
      Stone
          French provincial
          Colonial
          Modern
    Duplexes
      Brick
          French provincial
          Colonial
          Modern
      Wood
    Apartment houses
      . . .

The classifier's purpose determines the level of detail, whether one or more criteria should be applied, and which one should come first. In classifying the books we own for the purpose of shelving them in a given room with bookcases in place, the first level of classification might very well be size, if some books are oversized and our space for these books is limited. Otherwise, the first criterion is more likely to be subject matter. Suppose most of the books in this collection deal with economics, politics, astronomy, algebra, calculus, the Roman Empire, history of art, political history, physics, psychology, trigonometry, and literary history. Others appear at first not to fit the groups according to subject: drama, verse, short stories, and novels. We ordinarily group these books in terms of form rather than subject, but to make a classification system one level at a time, they must be classified along with the others, according to subject. Although several forms are represented, all of those books are literature, and we can look upon that as their subject. The classification could look like this:

I. Science
    A. Physical
        1. Astronomy
        2. Mathematics
            a. Calculus
            b. Trigonometry
    B. Social
        1. Economics
        2. Politics
        3. Psychology
II. History
    A. Political
    B. Civilization
    C. Cultural
        1. Art
        2. Literary
III. Literature
    A. Fiction
        1. Short story
        2. Novel
    B. Drama
    C. Poetry

This system adheres to one criterion on each class level. The books in this collection have been classified according to their subjects: science, history, and literature. All subclasses maintain the same criterion until we come to literature. Here the criterion of subject is exhausted at the first level, and so the classification proceeds according to the criterion of form, a second criterion within the level established by the first.

Classification outlines are developed into discourse by defining, exemplifying, describing, and comparing one class with another. When the meaning of the classes is obvious, as in the classification of books above, it is unnecessary to expand. The outline itself could be inserted at the appropriate place in a discourse such as a report. If, however, a classification outline as complex as the one above were developed, the descriptions and examples could involve the writer in a book-length discourse. Writers determine a scale to suit their purpose. Introducing *Myths and Legends of All Nations,* the authors H. S. Robinson and K. Wilson give an overall view of their complex subject with this classification:

> The mythologies which have had the greatest influence on our literature and art and on our thinking have of course been presented most fully,

since there are frequent occasions for acquainting or reacquainting one's self with their perennially fascinating characters and episodes, but the reader will also find much that is intriguing in the tales and themes from the less familiar sources. . . .

We take up first the Egyptians and then the Babylonians, two peoples whose civilizations go back to the very beginnings of recorded history. Next we give some of the ancient legends of the Hebrews which stand apart from the Old Testament yet have their place in the great tradition which molds the work of writers and artists and thinkers of many countries. Next we turn to the rich and varied myths and legends of the ancient Persians and of the peoples of India. And following these we give early beliefs and stories of the Chinese and then of the Japanese.

The mythology of Greece has through the ages provided inspiration and theme, character and plot, to every people who have come into touch with its myriad enchantments. We inevitably give the largest section of the book to this vast treasure of the Greeks. The lore of the Romans is closely connected to them, and we make clear in our section on the Romans just what the relationship is; also telling something of the Etruscans who preceded the Romans in Italy.

The first sentence of this excerpt limits the classification. Because the criterion is so obvious, according to cultural or ethnic origin, it need only be implied. The book itself will elaborate on each class, but the burden of this overview is to relate the classes. Subclasses are not included, although we anticipate them in the chapters that follow, probably classified according to the criterion of theme—myths of birth, of initiation, of transfiguration—and after that, a third level, perhaps according to character—the hero, the tempter, the mother. In the last paragraph the author stresses the more significant myths and their concern for relationships.

The Essentials of Formal Classification

Formal classification is a precise way of thinking. It is employed when the writing occasion requires complete information. However, even in less formal situations—essays, articles, letters, and memoranda—writers are wise to follow as much as possible the essentials of formal classification. We have already seen that a classification must be limited to be useful and must have only one criterion applied at a time. Other essentials are the following:

1. *The criterion should be unbiased and sensible.* A classification of books according to their greatness begs the question. Probably no two persons would agree on the greatness of books. It is not a quality but an opinion. A classification "according to type" also begs the question. It is senseless because the product of all classification is the creation of types. Classes are types, and therefore the statement is sheer redundancy, "classification according to classes."

2. *Every classification or subclassification must have at least two groups; otherwise, no classification has taken place.* Instead, the writer has listed a quality or an item but not a class. A roster of a football or baseball team is classification on only one level, together with a listing under each class. The positions are the classes, and the names of the players under each position are the lists. Only one name may appear under any class, because it may be that a team has only one fullback or tight end.

3. *Avoid overlapping.* Individual items should be classified under only one heading. Often this requirement must be waived because of the nature of things. Some hybrid members of a collection defy single classification, such as amphibious military vehicles or a car that also flies. In a classification of football players according to position, one player may play several positions. The most famous case of natural overlapping is the duckbilled platypus, a zoological curiosity. It has a beak and webbed feet, and it lays eggs like a fowl. It also has poisoned spurs like the fangs of a snake. Because it suckles its young, however, zoologists have chosen to classify the duckbilled platypus as a mammal.

4. *The classes and subclasses should be arranged in some logical order.* Classification, along with analysis, provides the basic scheme of outlining. Any collection of materials to be shaped into a composition can be considered a collection for classification, according to the theme or central idea. Whether writers are constructing a formal arrangement of classes or an informal set of related points, they place similar materials into groups. This is the basic step in the organization of all discourse. The outline should have some conventional form. The most common looks like this:

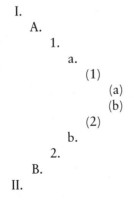

The classes are presented in order of importance, relationship, chronology, or any other logic. The terms of the headings in each level should be parallel, grammatically as well as logically. For example, the headings "Holding student conferences" and "Grading themes" are parallel, but the headings "Student conferences" and "Grading themes" are not.

Informal Classification

The essential guidelines of formal classification are also followed in making informal classifications, but limitations and the criterion of classification are implied rather than stated explicitly. Often the reader must infer the whole collection from the classes mentioned. In writing of religious denominations, for instance, we might specify Protestant, Catholic, and Jewish and suggest the inclusion of more with the phrase "among others" or "such as." If we name one or two others, Hindu and Buddhist, say, we would imply that our collection extends beyond Western religions, and if we also included African religions, the limits of our collection would be understood to include all religions of the world, even though they are not mentioned.

Informal classification sometimes masquerades as formal classification, as in literary criticism. Literature is often classed into various genres that overlap. The poetic, fictional, and dramatic categories slide into each other, as do the modes — realistic, romantic, lyric. Or again, the satiric, tragic, historic, comedic, and so on. Yet, in order to think, we must generalize, categorize, and classify. We do so by following our essential guides to the extent we can. For example, if we attempt to write about the problems of the city, not in a report but informally in an essay, we must begin by limitation. Casually, we write "major problems," then proceed to list a number of them: transportation, housing, crime, welfare, slums, education, recreation, and industry, even though slums overlaps with housing, welfare, and crime, housing overlaps with welfare, and so on. We could attempt to find more order by superimposing larger categories upon these, such as economic, political, social. Then we could place housing, crime, transportation, and the like in the appropriate superclass. Again, however, we find our categories overlapping. Transportation is a social and political problem as well as an economic one. Although our superimposed classes appear to be inseparable, we must proceed to organize our thoughts, and we do so by casually or informally following our essentials of formal classification. If we must let things overlap, then we do.

The following excerpt informally classifies words, not according to the usual grammatical functions — nouns, verbs, modifiers, and so on — but according to the effects they produce in the reader. This criterion is implied. There are three major classes — colorful, colored, and colorless — and knowing what we do about the connotative nature of language, the classification is bound to overlap; that is, a word may fit into more than one category, depending on context. Nevertheless, the classification adheres to the essentials of formal classification to the extent it can:

> Some words are what we call "colorful." By this we mean that they are
> calculated to produce a picture or induce an emotion. They are dressy

instead of plain, specific instead of general, loud instead of soft. Thus, in place of "Her heart beat," we may write "Her heart *pounded, throbbed, fluttered, danced.*" Instead of "He sat in his chair," we may say, "He *lounged, sprawled, coiled.*" Instead of "it was hot," we may say, "It was *blistering, sultry, muggy, suffocating, steamy, wilting.*"

Some words we would call not so much colorful as colored — that is, loaded with associations, good or bad. All words — except perhaps structure words — have associations of some sort. We have said that the meaning of a word is the sum of the contexts in which it occurs. When we hear a word, we hear with it an echo of all the situations in which we have heard it before.

So also with such words as *home, liberty, fireside, contentment, patriot, tenderness, sacrifice, childlike, manly, bluff, limpid.* All of these words are loaded with favorable associations that would be rather hard to indicate in a straightforward definition. There is more than a literal difference between "They sat around the fireside" and "They sat around the stove." They might have been equally warm and happy around the stove, but the *fireside* suggests leisure, grace, quiet tradition, congenial company, and *stove* does not.

Conversely some words have bad associations. *Mother* suggests pleasant things, but *mother-in-law* does not. Many mother-in-laws are heroically loveable and some mothers drink gin all day and beat their children insensible, but these facts of life are beside the point. The thing is that *mother* sounds good and *mother-in-law* does not.

Probably most student writers come to grief not with words that are colorful or those that are colored but with those that have no color at all. A pet example is *nice,* a word we would find it hard to dispense with in casual conversation but which is no longer capable of adding much to a description. Colorless words are those of such general meaning that in particular sentences they mean nothing. Slang adjectives, like *cool* (That's real cool), tend to explode all over the language. They are applied to everything, lose their original force, and quickly die.

Paul Roberts, *Understanding English*

Classification is most useful in combination with other operations. Paragraphs can be composed from each class by defining, describing, and exemplifying each one and by explaining the relationships between members of each class and between classes, as in the excerpt above. Often informal classification is used to expand upon an insight: "Changes in the technological work of this century are structural, methodological, and systematic." This assertion could be used as the topic sentence of a paragraph within a paper about the problems of a city and expanded by identification of each class, or it could become the basis for a section of paragraphs or even the theme statement of an essay in itself.

EXERCISES

1. Is the following excerpt a formal or informal classification? To what extent does it adhere to the essentials of a formal classification? To what extent does it violate them?

   How are the classes ordered? What effect would be created if the classes were ordered differently, say nonviolent resistance first?

   Where would you place King's discourse along the spectrum of rhetoric?

   Oppressed people deal with their oppression in three characteristic ways. One way is acquiescence: The oppressed resign themselves to their doom. They tacitly adjust themselves to oppression, and thereby become conditioned to it. In every movement toward freedom some of the oppressed prefer to remain oppressed. Almost 2800 years ago Moses set out to lead the children of Israel from the slavery of Egypt to the freedom of the promised land. He soon discovered that slaves do not always welcome deliverers. They become accustomed to being slaves. They would rather bear those ills they have, as Shakespeare pointed out, than flee to others that they know not of. They prefer the "fleshpots of Egypt" to the ordeals of emancipation.

   There is such a thing as the freedom of exhaustion. Some people are so worn down by the yoke of oppression that they give up. A few years ago in the slum areas of Atlanta, a Negro guitarist used to sing almost daily: "Been down so long that down don't bother me." This is the type of negative freedom and resignation that often engulfs the life of the oppressed. . . .

   A second way that oppressed people sometimes deal with oppression is to resort to physical violence and corroding hatred. Violence often brings about momentary results. Nations have frequently won their independence in battle. But in spite of temporary victories, violence never brings permanent peace. It solves no social problem; it merely creates new and more complicated ones. . . .

   The third way open to oppressed people in their quest for freedom is the way of nonviolent resistance. Like the synthesis in Hegelian philosophy, the principle of nonviolent resistance seeks to reconcile the truths of two opposites — acquiescence and violence — while avoiding the extremes and immoralities of both. The nonviolent resister agrees with the person who acquiesces that one should not be physically aggressive toward his opponent; but he balances the equation by agreeing with the person of violence that evil must be resisted. He avoids the nonresistance of the former and the violent resistance of the latter. With nonviolent resistance, no individual or group need submit to any wrong, nor need anyone resort to violence in order to right a wrong.

   Martin Luther King, Jr., Stride
Toward Freedom

2. According to the essentials of formal classification, what are the faults of the following statement of classification and outline?
   Classification of roads according to type:

   I. Primary
      A. Interstate
      B. Intrastate
      C. Multiple lane
      D. Double lane
      E. Improved
   II. Secondary
      A. Intercity
      B. Double lane
      C. Single lane
      D. Unimproved

   Rewrite both the statement of what will be classified and the outline according to the essentials of formal classification.

3. College catalogs list courses according to academic discipline because the college is organized into departments according to the training of professors. Take your college catalog and come up with at least two other ways of classifying courses; state the purpose for each classification.

4. Classify restaurants in the city or town where you live or attend college. Your first basis of classification might be the type of food served. Determine second and third levels of classification on some other bases. Write a discourse with these classes as your major mode of development. Use description, narration, and other rhetorical operations as needed to develop your classes.

5. Classify the towns and cities in the state you are from at a high level of generality appropriately for a general audience, with subclasses as necessary. Then reclassify the towns and cities, this time for a specific audience, say, college seniors who are beginning to look for jobs. Outline each classification. Develop one or the other into a useful discourse.

6. Write a discourse developed mainly by classification explaining any collection of things of value to you — rock bands, students on campus, religious sects, unfair laws, airplanes, dogs, lovers, whatever. Make sure that you follow the essentials of formal classification to the extent you can to produce a useful classification. Make sure the paper at some point clearly expresses why this collection of things has value to you.

Chapter 5

Analysis

What are its parts? Its causes? Its value? How does it work? These are the questions of analysis, the rhetorical operation that resolves a structure — of idea or material — into components. Analysis comes from the Greek *ana* + *lyein*, which means "loosen up." It is the opposite of classification. Instead of generalizing, as in classification, we particularize. The concept of classification is plural; the concept of analysis is singular. Rather than place numbers of things together in classes, the writer of analysis breaks one thing or idea into its elements. The parts of an analysis always add up to a single structure, and the categories of a classification add up to a collection. Analysis is often used together with classification. A motor scooter, for example, could be analyzed by mechanical parts and then the parts categorized into classes of wheels, motors, chassis, and so on. When the subject is seen as a member of a collection or as a collection that needs sorting, the writer classifies; when the subject is seen as an individual item consisting of components, the writer analyzes.

A Process of Particularization

Anything a writer can visualize as a structured whole can be analyzed. The process of analysis allows the writer to examine the particulars of a structure, whether an object, process, place, person, or concept. Examples also particularize, but not systematically, not according to structural elements. A structure is a concept of mutually supportive components that function together or bear other relationships, one to the other. The pile of debris that a wrecker's ball leaves after hitting a building is not a structure, but the building could have been analyzed as a structure before the wrecker swung the ball. A human being, a science, a religion, a textbook, a technical report, a chemical procedure, a truck, a law, and an educational institution all have structure. They can all be analyzed because in each of them some principle can be found to explain the relationship of parts.

Concepts, of course, cannot be divided into parts as easily as a physical mechanism or place. Separating the individual chairs, desks, computing machines, and other equipment of an office would break it down physically but not conceptually. As a concept, the office would have to be analyzed according to some other principle, such as work produced, or as a process for handling business papers.

Like classifications, most analyses are informal. They appear in essays, editorials, business memos, and literary criticism. In these informal analyses the writer presents only those parts that are significant for the purposes of the discussion. However, in formal situations — say when someone evaluates a piece of real estate, investigates a crashed airliner, or argues to establish a thesis or theory — the analysis must be as complete and unbiased as a trusted physician's diagnosis (which is an analysis), and its principle of division clearly understood. And, like classifications, informal analyses follow as closely as possible the essentials of formal analysis.

Formal Analysis

In formal, precise analysis, the principle for breaking the whole into parts is chosen according to the writer's interest, just as the criterion is chosen in classification. A botanist sees a structure in a tree that is different from what a poet or a painter sees. The particular interest of each determines the structure, and this interest suggests the principle of analysis. If various analyses can be made of a structure, each analysis implies a different relationship among the parts, and indeed each analysis concerns itself with different parts. A university may be analyzed as an educational structure, an economic structure, a social structure, or even a moral structure, but it could not be analyzed according to all principles simultaneously. Each principle would illuminate different parts. By applying each principle in turn, the writer could produce a complex analysis, consisting actually of several smaller analyses.

A formal analysis does not merely specify the various parts of the structure analyzed, but indicates the relations among them. The way each part or point functions in association with the other parts or points and in relation to the whole is the very essence of analysis. In analyzing an automobile engine, for example, when the writer comes to the carburetor, he shows how this mechanism fulfills its function, how it works together with the other parts, and how it contributes to the whole purpose of the engine. The writer is concerned only with necessary details of the carburetor's function in the engine, component by component, but not with details like its color or material unless they are vital aspects of its function. In such physical analyses, the writer can follow a model; in a conceptual analysis, the writer must conceive a good deal more. In the following analysis of the design of an incinerator, notice how the writer has to substitute phrases for parts that have no name and then has to define them. Although the subject is certainly material, the structure analyzed is conceptual, a design:

> The design of an incinerator comprises the following four parts:
>
> 1. General aspects such as the quantity and character of refuse, the location of the plant, and the characteristics of the receiving airway. It is assumed that such general parts will have been covered by an adequate engineering investigation and report.
>
> 2. General arrangements, such as the approaches, the yard, the scales, the storage bin, the building, the clearances within the building, the cranes, and the ash removal facilities.
>
> 3. The part which comprises the furnaces and their appurtenances, grate areas, dampers, flues, and subsidence (or expansion) chambers for the removal of fly ash or particulate matter. This part constitutes the structures and the equipment which have to do with combustion.
>
> 4. The chimney.

Analyzing a concept requires the writer to conceive of the parts, which are not ready in place for the writer's convenience. Parts are abstractions in a structure envisioned by the writer. For example, the structure of a political or economic idea is a vision the writer sees. It is a concept stemming from observation and thought. Analyses of such abstractions are highly conceptual in comparison to those of a mechanism. If we wished to evaluate the condition of our national transportation system, we could not point to an existing structure but would have to pull together the numerous parts that make up our concept of it. The parts would not be the single road, bridge, or airplane we might observe but concepts based on these observations: roads, bridges, railroads, airports, harbors, and the various kinds of vehicles that use them. We could proceed by breaking apart these structures, airports into runways, towers, terminals, weather facilities, approach and departing systems, operating personnel, and so on. The description of each part would be composed from statistical data. Such a conceptual analysis would be of enormous extent, requiring teams of analysts and millions of dollars. No matter how extensive, however, the details gathered about each part or subpart would not only describe that part in itself but show the way it functions with the other parts and with the whole. Finally, the major systems or structures — the railroad system, the harbor system, the airport system — would be related to show the condition of the entire concept, the national transportation system. Classification, of course, would be an indispensable aid in organizing such an analysis. That is, each major part, or system, would have to be envisioned from groupings of railroads, harbors, airports, and so on.

To put flesh on any analysis, writers use other rhetorical operations, particularly description and narration. Explaining how a thing is put together, the writer describes it as a whole structure and part by part. In this example the structure is mechanistic:

> The gathering system in the Alaskan energy fields is composed of five distinct pipeline systems, consisting of the oil gathering system, the gas gathering system, the fuel gas distribution system, the gas injection system and the flow line system. All of the pipelines are above ground, supported on bents constructed of steel pipe piles and structural sap beams. In general, the pipes are supported at fifty to sixty-nine foot intervals.

In contrast, here is an analysis of a literary structure:

> To speak of tone is to speak also of point of view, and of details, of symbols and images and style and character. In literature as in all other views of existence, there are no isolated phenomena. We have chosen tone as the main indicator of conflict because it informs us about all the other elements, beyond their denotations; because it points to the meanings below the singular surfaces of things. It is tone which directs us to meanings. The sunshine, for example, in Mark Shorer's "Boy in the Summer Sun" comes to represent the golden past that is being produced at the very moment of the story. How do we know? From the boy's tone, rendered not only in his dialogue but in the restricted point of view which allows us to get inside his mind:
>
> > He thought he must cry. All his youth gathered into a knot of pain that choked him, that, dull and heavy, pressed against his heart. He thought of going back to the city, to the hot office, to stupid work sweating over accounts, of the years he had ahead of him in which to slave there. And he knew as he lay in the sand, really knew for the time, that all of that was no mere interlude.
>
> The words he employs, the rhythms of his speech, the detail and symbols — such as the sand — reveal his conflict, his resistence to the pressures of growing up, represented by Max who has invaded the sunshine, as stated a few lines later:
>
> > Then they went up the shore, back to the raft where Max still lay in the lessening glare of the sun.
>
> Here we notice that the sun glares, hardly the tone for the golden past — the sun on the sand — but rather the harsh present, the current problem.

To explain how something works, the writer analyzes it as a process, in a time sequence:

> In the manufacture of an earth's satellite's shell and frame the first operation is the molding of a deep drawn hemisphere. The magnesium is heated in an oven to 650 degrees F, and the die is heated to the same temperature. The draw die consists of a punch and two rings. The flat metal blank is placed between the draw rings, and the stamping is accomplished by pulling the magnesium over the heated punch. After the metal has cooled to room temperature; the stamping is trimmed. The next operation is placing the hemispherical stamping over a spinning-lathe tool,

where certain contours are formed manually. This operation consists primarily of adding a pressure-ring area to the concave side of the stamping. Again the spinning operation. . . .

Covers are then welded into the depressions which have been spun on the lathe. Each hemisphere is placed on the lathe, and the gauge of the metal is machined. . . .

After the internal framework and equipment have been completed and assembled, the two hemispheres are brought together at the equator and fastened.

To explain how one thing differs from another, the writer compares by dividing each structure into parts or steps in a parallel fashion, then describing or narrating the similarities and differences. To explain what causes things or what effects are caused, the writer analyzes by using chains of induction and deduction. Analyses of mechanisms and processes have already been discussed in the chapters on description and narration. Comparative and causal analyses are special cases that will be discussed later in this chapter. All of these types of analyses are made useful and effective by following essential guidelines.

Essentials of Formal Analysis

1. The writer *examines the subject to determine its structure.* If the writer cannot conceive a structure in, say, a heap of trash or an ocean, the subject cannot be analyzed. If the writer were to see the heap as having a shape, however, the shape could be analyzed, perhaps for the forces that caused it or for its contours, and the ocean, of course, could be seen as having layers or chemical structure.

2. The writer *adopts a principle of division according to his or her interest.* A bank could be analyzed according to its financial condition, physical condition of the building, employees' morale, and so on, depending on the interests of the analyzer.

3. The writer *accounts for all parts of a structure and tries to avoid overlapping.* In the analysis of the bank according to financial condition, the writer who neglects any part would obviously be suspect. As in classification, overlapping cannot always be avoided. One part may perform two or more functions.

4. The writer *divides the subject into at least two parts on any level.* A structure cannot be analyzed according to its materials if it is made of only one material; but the material itself can be analyzed according to some selected principle of division such as its chemical constituents. Then at least two subdivisions result.

5. The writer *presents divisions and subdivisions in some logical order.* As in classification, an outline is helpful. It indicates to the writer whether or not the parts of the whole are being systematically presented, that is, how the parts are arranged and related.

The following excerpt follows the essentials of formal analysis. The civilized mind is the subject, divided into four parts according to historical development. Each part is introduced with a short identifying phrase, which we assume is elaborated with descriptive detail throughout the rest of the essay. Overlapping is not apparent in the excerpt but may occur inevitably in the effort to distinguish the savage mind from the child mind or animal mind. The order of presentation is chronological in keeping with the principle of division:

> There are four historical layers underlying the minds of civilized men — the animal mind, the child mind, the savage mind, and the traditional civilized mind. We are all animals and never can cease to be; we are all children at our most impressionable age and can never get over the effects of that; our human ancestors have lived in slavery during practically the whole existence of the race, say five hundred thousand or a million years, and the primitive human mind is ever with us; finally we are all born into an elaborate civilization, the constant pressure of which we can by no means escape.
>
> James Henty Robinson, *The Mind in the Making*

Comparative Analysis

We have already examined the uses of comparison in informal ways. A transistor, for example, might be explained by pointing out its functional similarities to the vacuum tube and then delineating its differences. When the writer's intention is to present a full body of information about two whole structures in a precise way, then comparison becomes a special type of analysis. The analysis proceeds after the writer introduces some principle for dividing both items into their corresponding parts. The specific purpose guides the writer in establishing the principle of analysis.

Judgment

Some comparative analyses are motivated by sheer curiosity — that is, a desire to find out how one thing differs from another — while others are undertaken to provide the basis of some judgment. Two things are analyzed together so that likenesses and differences and merits and faults can be paralleled. Judgment is made on the basis of the comparative data, that is, at the end. Too often, however, it enters the comparative analysis before the conclusion is reached. Often it enters at the start because the writer has not controlled bias. Biased writers tend to omit comparative points that bring out more merits or faults for one of the items than for the other, or they may devote more detail to the merits of one item and less to its faults. Although bias can never be completely eliminated, it can be largely neutralized by making a complete analysis, including all points and treating both items equally, that is, giving all essential data on each comparative point. The merits and faults accumulate as the reader proceeds, and the conclusion is usually evident even before it is presented in summary.

Judgments are either relative or absolute. Relative judgments occur as a result of comparing similar items, as in the analyses we have been discussing. Absolute judgments result from a comparison of one item with a standard such as a building code. Inspections and examinations of every kind result in absolute judgments. Medical examinations as well as car inspections are matters of absolute judgment. So are scientific investigations that compare experimental results with theory, or social observations that match behavior with a moral code or other sets of criteria. Relative judgments are expressed as matters of degree, and absolute judgments are expressed absolutely. After a comparative analysis of two restaurants, one may be judged better in service and food but less comfortable than the other. However, after a comparison of the health conditions with health regulations, one or the other or both may be shut down. Either they passed or failed. (Bribeless inspectors assumed.)

Whether relative or absolute, unbiased judgment does not result from singular observation, such as, "John is a better football player than Jack because he runs faster." Instead, a complete analysis, conceiving of the whole structure and examining all the parts, is necessary.

Organization

The methods of organizing comparative analyses are the same as those of informal comparisons. In the divided method, the writer makes a full analysis of the first item, part by part, and then a full analysis of the second. In the second method, let us call it the alternating analysis, the writer presents a part of one, compares it to the similar part of the other, then goes to the next parallel set of parts until all the parts of both are treated. With either method, the comparative analysis is completed by summing the likenesses and differences or the merits and faults, and making judgments or selections according to the writer's purposes in undertaking the analysis.

If we wished to determine the most feasible form of alternative energy to be developed and the choices had been narrowed to solar and wind power, our outline for the divided method might be as follows:

I. Introduction
   A. Background and purpose
   B. General description of solar and wind processes
   C. Principle of analysis (feasibility)

    II. Analysis of data
      A. Solar process
        1. Availability
          a. State of development
          b. Convenience of use
          c. Extensiveness of supply
        2. Efficiency
          a. Output versus input
          b. Operational stability
        3. Costs
          a. Research and development
          b. System construction
          c. Operations
          d. Maintenance
          e. Depreciation
      B. Wind process
        (Repeat all subdivisions.)
   III. Conclusions
      (The merits and faults are summed and compared in general terms, and the selection is made.)

In the divided method, the reader must wait for the presentation of the second item to begin estimating differences as well as merits and faults. In the alternating method, where the two are compared point for point, the differences, merits, and faults can be discerned without waiting for a concluding section. The merits and faults in fact conclude the discussion of each comparative part, and the conclusion is a summary of these smaller or accumulating conclusions, an addition and subtraction of them:

    I. Introduction
      (Same as divided method)
    II. Analysis of data
      A. Availability
        1. State of development
          a. Solar
          b. Wind
          c. Merits and faults
        2. Convenience of use
          a. Solar
          b. Wind
          c. Merits and faults
        3. Extensiveness of supply
          . . .
      B. Efficiency
        . . .

C. Costs
   . . .

III. Conclusions
(Likenesses and differences or merits and faults are summed and judgment made.)

Use of the divided method often breaks the material down the middle and fails to bring together the related facts. The job of relating is still to be done and usually shows up in the concluding section. This method is appropriate and perhaps advantageous when the two items compared are simple. In a comparison of complicated things, the reader cannot be expected to carry in mind all the details of the first item and then apply them when the same points are analyzed in the second item.

In the following excerpt from a student paper, a specific make of hunting knife is compared with a standard. The analysis is short enough to employ the divided method. The principle of division is performance in camp and field:

To meet the requirements of camp and field, a hunting knife should possess certain qualities. First, since too long a blade tends to snap, and one too short is inadequate for many operations, the blade should not be less than five nor more than eight inches long and about a quarter of an inch at its widest. Whether curved or straight, double or single-edged are matters of personal preference and need not be considered here.

The steel should be of high carbon content (upwards of three-quarters of one percent) so that the knife will hold its edge without resharpening for at least three days of normal field activity.

For ease of employment, the handle and blade should be so proportioned that the knife will balance when the index finger is placed at a point an inch to the rear of the guard. The safest guard is the cross type, which protects both thumb and finger of the user. As to the handle, since bone and staghorn chip easily, a five and one-half inch handle made up of a series of rubber or leather washers ringing the central steel shaft and secured at the end by a metal knob will give the best service. The entire knife should weigh about five ounces.

Now let us see how the Boone hunting and fishing knife meets these standards. Available either curved or straight, the Boone blade measures six inches and is apparently of good carbon steel. It has consistently been tested in all kinds of field work for seven days at a time without resharpening. Equipped with cross-type guard and handle of leather washers, the knife balances, however, only fairly well. The handle apparently is too heavy for the blade, and the washers have a tendency to separate, especially in dry weather. The complete knife weighs four and a half ounces. In the light of this evidence, the Boone knife is acceptable but needs to be improved for better balance.

In comparative analysis of two concepts, the details are usually statistical data. The two concepts compared in the following analysis are two groups of people, one least likely to move their residence and the other most likely. The information for the comparative points was gathered in two surveys, one in 1977 and the other in 1981, and it would seem that the comparison is between these sets of data. But they proved so much alike that one corroborates the other and gives the reporter more confidence in delineating the characteristics, the comparative points, of the two types of residents:

> Little change has occurred since a 1977 survey in the proportion of urban residents reporting they would like to move. Nor was any major change in the demographic background of those wishing to leave noted. Those residents expressing a desire to leave their cities represent essentially the same socioeconomic groups who have been moving away for the last three decades — and whom the cities can least afford to lose. These are the younger, better educated, more affluent residents, who provide the largest share of tax revenues as well as most of the people needed to fill public and private leadership roles.
>
> Conversely, those least likely to want to move away are the older, less well-educated, less affluent population segments, including the so-called public service dependent groups, such as the retired and the unemployed.
>
> The two main reasons for wanting to leave urban areas mentioned in 1981 were also the key reasons given in 1977. However, the proportion currently mentioning crime has increased since 1977, while overcrowding, the number one reason in 1977, has declined. Furthermore, high crime rates are of more concern in central cities than they were in 1977.
>
> Central city residents of urban areas with a population of one million or more are more likely than others to mention the high crime rate and pollution as reasons for wanting to move away. Residents of the smaller metropolitan areas mention pollution or the housing situation more frequently. Undoubtedly, those least able to leave the cities express the least desire to leave, and those who find the city an undesirable place to live do not see it as likely to improve in the future.

The first principle of analysis is socioeconomic condition. After the analysis is exhausted according to this principle, a second principle is applied to further analyze one of the groups; the writer investigates those wanting to move according to their reasons, and we notice that he now classifies them into central city and smaller metropolitan residents. The points of this analysis within the analysis are crime, overcrowding, pollution, and the housing situation. These reasons are, of course, causes, and so we have a causal analysis within the comparative analysis. Causal analysis is another special type of analysis.

Causal Analysis

"How did it happen?" "What will happen?" Immediate answers can be given without analysis:

Already gentrification — middle-class renovation of the slums — has
started on the Lower East Side, where speculators are buying up property. They are encouraged by the communities' own renovation efforts as
well as rising rents and co-op conversions in the neighboring East Village.

The cause of "gentrification" given in the second sentence is merely an
assumption. It is an apparent cause, which is the way we usually treat
causation. However, the speculators could have given other reasons for
buying the property. Perhaps they mean to tear down the buildings and
put up commercial structures, or just hold the property until the scar-
city of land commands higher prices and then profit through resale.
Quick attribution of causes for effects (clouds are in the sky; rain coming) or effects to causes (car won't start; battery's worn out) often prove
to be poor logic, as analysis will show. To find dependable answers to
the basic question, "Why?" we ask further questions: "What caused
it?" or "What will happen as a result?" The answers are pursued
through causal analysis.

If we consider effects as a whole, causes become the parts, and the
factors contributing to each cause become the subparts:

EFFECT: The future of the world oil supply is dim.

CAUSES: Even if the government limits on production were absent, we
           could not be optimistic about additions to our oil reserves,
           those that can be readily tapped and those requiring technologi-
           cal innovation such as deposits in shale. Another constraining
           cause, of course, is the level of production set by countries with
           large reserves and low consumption rates, such as the OPEC
           nations. This factor depends largely upon political and eco-
           nomic relations.

If we consider the causes as a whole, major effects become the parts:

CAUSE: The United States lost a great deal because of the hostage crisis
           in Iran.

EFFECTS: The United States showed itself and the rest of the world that
           its defenses and foreign policies could be confounded by a street
           gang. It demonstrated that the United States was willing to deal
           with kidnappers, that its military and covert forces were faulty
           and impotent, that its political intelligence was porous. Beyond
           these, the United States lost clarity in its foreign policy when
           clarity was needed most.

Both of these examples are analytic but informal, still incomplete, and
unsubstantiated with evidence. They are only partially convincing to the
careful reader, who can easily find other causes for the dim future of
oil, such as the high interest rates on money for investment, and who
can readily add other losses from the Iranian crisis, such as the embassy
itself, lives, and equipment.

As we will see below, informal analysis is sufficient when facts are not questionable and evidence is superfluous. A complete causal analysis establishes immediate and ultimate connections, as well as the conditions or situations in which events occur or reasons apply. Of course, no causal analysis can really be complete since the trail of ultimate connections heads to infinite regression.

Immediate and Ultimate Connection

"I can't go shopping today because I have no money and no credit." This pauper's situation could be investigated analytically. The analysis would begin with the realization that we have been given only the immediate cause, "I have no money and no credit." The first question in analyzing this situation would be "Why?" That is, we would take the cause as effect and seek its cause in turn. "Lost my job." "Why?" "General layoff." "Why?" "Our sales fell off." "Why?" The chain of cause and effect continues until we reach some ultimate cause, most often obscure or hidden and taken as ultimate only because our means of inquiry can go no further. The most ultimate of ultimate causes is a mystery for mankind, Aristotle's prime mover, or the idea of God. The chain of cause and effect is the formal way causal analysis seeks complete and valid answers. It is the way to explain why astronauts must travel curved rather than straight paths or why wars, depressions, and divorces occur, why machinery breaks down, and why the earth goes around the sun exactly as it does. Nothing less than a complete causal analysis would be acceptable in the investigation of an airplane crash, the planning of a new airport, or the design of aircraft.

Writers avoid analysis when they do not ask questions of immediate causes or effects, but they usurp analysis when they leap to the ultimate causes or effects. A statement, for example, that plants grow because of the sun's energy is really a conclusion of an analysis. The analysis itself would be the chain of immediate causes and effects, which one by one work to transform the sun's energy into the plant.

Multiple Causes and Effects

Causal analysis becomes complex when the writer discovers multiple causes for one effect and multiple effects from one cause. Following a chain in such a situation is extremely difficult. For example, we can hardly trace the multiple effects of the launching of the first Soviet satellite in 1957 upon American society. One of them is the United States' own landing on the moon twelve years later, but this is not an immediate effect. Increased research expenditures were more immediate, along with a system of National Defense Scholarships to the colleges and universities, and rearrangement of priorities in the national budget. Another example would be a tracing of chains of causes and effects leading to the Vietnam War and leading away from it. The first chain would emphasize cause; the second would emphasize effects. That is, we would look for cause in the chain before the war and effects after. However, for each major cause we could isolate we would have to make a separate chain, one for economic causes, another for psychological causes, another for historical causes, and so on. Such complex analyses exceed the scale that can be accommodated by a newspaper editorial, magazine article, or classroom report. They require the space of a book or two.

Whenever we present groups of causes for effects or effects of causes, we should recognize them as summary statements of analytical chains:

> The irritation that causes sneezing may be due to a swelling of the mucous membrane of the nose, as happens when we have a cold. It also may be due to foreign bodies that somehow got into the nose. And it may be caused by an allergy. But all that sneezing is an attempt by the body to expel air to get rid of irritating bodies.

If we questioned each of these causes — why does the mucous membrane swell? — we would discover an analytical chain. Along the reportorial portion of the spectrum of rhetoric, which tends to be formal, a source reference should be given as evidence when the analytical chain is not presented. In the more informal situations along the spectrum of rhetoric, where argument or representation is paramount, the writer's logic, artistry, or authority provides the validity for the missing chain of cause-and-effect analysis. Personal authority is convincing in this listing of causes for an effect: "I was shocked when I saw his beard, dirty clothing, thinness, the gash on his head, and the vacancy in his eyes." Artistry and logic validate this informal causal analysis:

> . . . a strange blight crept over the area and everything began to change. Some evil spell had settled on the community; mysterious maladies swept the flock of chickens; the cattle and sheep sickened and died. Everywhere was a shadow of death. The farmers spoke of much illness among their families. In the town the doctors had become more and more puzzled by new kinds of sickness appearing among their patients. There had been several sudden and unexplained deaths, not only among adults but even among children, who would be stricken suddenly while at play and would die within a few hours. . . .
>
> The roadsides, once so attractive, were now lined with browned and withered vegetation as though swept by fire. These, too, were silent, deserted by all living things. Even the streams were now lifeless. Anglers no longer visited them, for all the fish had died.
>
> Rachel Carson, *The Silent Spring*

For emotional impact, these effects are artistically arranged before the cause in a pattern of inductive logic. Rachel Carson supplies the cause as though she were releasing the suspense at the end of a mystery story, and even then she does not name it:

> In the gutters under the eaves and between the shingles of the roofs, a white granular powder still showed a few patches; some weeks before it had fallen like snow upon the roofs and the lawns, the fields and streams. No witchcraft, no enemy action had silenced the rebirth of new life in this stricken world. The people had done it themselves.

For the reader who does not recognize DDT and other poisons as the causes of the effects, the author fully identifies them later.

Condition

All events take place under circumstances. When the circumstances change, the same causes may produce varying effects. The factors existing in a situation that permit causes to have effects are called *conditions*. Air is a condition for transmitting sound waves. Fuel is a condition for firing a furnace. But these are not the only conditions for each of these events. Sound waves can also be transmitted through gas mixtures other than air, even through liquids and solids; and the furnace may not function with the fuel if the oxygen is deficient. Since many other substances could be substituted for air to transmit sound waves, the air is not a *necessary* but a *sufficient condition*. The furnace, on the other hand, could not function without fuel. The fuel, therefore, is a necessary condition, just as some medium is a necessary condition for the transmission of sound waves.

An event takes place only when the necessary conditions are present. Causal analysis often becomes confused or dubious when conditions are not stated at all or not stated clearly: "Obesity results when food intake is greater than the body's use of energy." The omitted conditions here are complex. Food intake is a necessary condition for obesity, but not the only one. Obesity may occur when the intake of food does not exceed bodily expense of energy. Much depends on the condition of the bodily organs, grandular secretions, and metabolic rates. Some people who eat little and exercise much remain fat.

Often one event that precedes another is taken as cause and the following event as effect, although the two events may not be connected. This mistake is a *faulty connection* or *non sequitur*. It is frequently found in political and religious arguments:

> America fought no wars during the Eisenhower administration. Eisenhower's policies produced peace.

> The storm demolished the boatload of dope smugglers. It was God's punishment.

Informal Analysis

It is ironical that formal analyses are so rigid, so tight, when the word itself means "loosen up." Although formal analyses are essential when the occasion warrants, most writing occasions in the modern world are informal, and so are the analyses. Basically, informality means that all the parts are not accounted for and all the relationships are not stated, although they are all implied. The tone may also differ because the audience is usually broader than the readers of formal analyses (who are usually members of a profession). Informal analyses are lightened more often than formal analyses with figures of speech, metaphors, and analogies. They may be argumentative, humorous, or pugnacious. Nevertheless, the essential framework of formal analysis should be pursued. Informal analyses must also be logical, if not complete, and the facts should not be distorted, even though the rendering of opinion may be the purpose. In an informal analysis, the writer selects the parts important to the theme, which would include the writer's attitude toward the subject. Such biased analysis, however, is not useful unless it follows to the extent possible the guidelines of formal analysis. Here is a piece of informal analysis from an editorial on the national transportation system discussed above:

> Roads will continue to deteriorate. Bridges will continue to shake and settle. Small city airports will keep on losing service and be forced to close. More towns and cities will lose rail service. More and more big city subway lines and even train stations will close down or become too dangerous to use. . . .
>
> The conferees . . . did agree that a planned redevelopment policy was already needed to restore the nation's obsolescent transportation system. So far, however, there's precious little evidence that any such redevelopment is at hand. On the contrary, the administration seems to be walking away from the problem. Federal mass transit subsidies are to be cut; airport subsidies are to be reduced; highway programs are to be curtailed. Conrail is to be sold off, threatening a massive shrinkage in Eastern railroad service.

Selected parts of the system are simply enumerated, but they are enough to suggest the whole system. Even though the parts not mentioned, such as port facilities, may not easily float into mind, they would fit in if they were mentioned. The logic of the analysis accommodates the parts not mentioned and thus preserves the aura of a system. Moreover, the facts are not violated, we notice, in spite of the author's apparent bias.

At times, however, enumerations of undeveloped points in an informal analysis may be so excessive that they appear ridiculous. The following paragraph is an anonymous parody of an analysis in which enumeration has outstripped reason; the effect is ironical:

> The farmer's wife has no excuse for not being cultured and up-to-date. All she has to do is to cook the meals and wash the clothes and mend the

linen and darn the socks and milk the cows and churn the butter and feed the chickens and bathe the children and can the fruit and cut the children's hair and set the dog on tramps and chase the cat out of the milk house and polish the silver and black the stove and straighten the shades and settle the children's scraps and shoo the hens off the porch and wipe up the mud father and the boys track in and bake the bread and make the cake and chase the pigs out of the garden and answer the telephone and sift the ants out of the sugar and air the feather beds and heat the water for father to wash his feet and watch out for bed bugs and get the men up in the morning and gather the eggs and set the hens and keep the neighbor's baby while she goes to town and get the children off to school and get rid of the insurance agents and spray the fruit trees and gather the berries and trim the lamps and swat the flies and empty the ashes and slop the pigs and peel the peaches and rake the lawn and feed the pet lambs and string the beans and fill the lantern and sort the apples and find the men's collar buttons and carry in the wood and pick the geese and answer the door and tell the men what they did with the axe the last time they used it and write a letter to mother. Then in the afternoon she can go to the missionary meeting and work her head off for the heathen.

The humor overwhelms any tendency for sobersided examination of this analysis. Instead, we may appreciate some of the artistic touches, for example, the associative arrangement of the insurance agent next to the spray that will kill insects on the fruit trees, and the excessive understatement and irony of the short last sentence, which matches the first one. All the rest of the paragraph, also one sentence, amply renders the opposite meaning of the short opening and closing sentences.

A Way of Thinking

We have considered analysis both formally and informally and have examined two fundamental types, comparative and causal analyses. These analyses are not rigid specifications but operations of rhetoric, of thought, like classification. Writers use different kinds of thinking to bring about full understanding. Telling how something fits into the scheme of things, they classify; then by showing how it is put together, or taken apart, how it works, what causes it, what effects it produces, and how it is like or unlike similar things, they analyze. The various forms of analysis are among the most important rhetorical operations the writer performs.

EXERCISES

1. Fit particulars of the informal analysis of the farmer's wife into the following classes:

cleaning	rearing
cooking	tending
protecting	socializing

This classification generalizes the activities of farm wives, but the same categories could also be seen as parts of a single day in the life of a particular farm wife. In other words, these items could be viewed as particulars in a single structure and could therefore serve as a framework for analysis. Outline the analysis, let us say, of the day in the working life of Mrs. Arbor on the farm.

2. Read the following opening scene from D. H. Lawrence's "The Prussian Officer":

> They had marched more than thirty kilometers since dawn, along the white hot road where occasional thickets of trees threw a moment of shade, then out into the glare again. On either hand, the valley, wide and shallow, glittered with heat; dark green patches of rye, pale young corn, fallow and meadow and black pine woods spread in a dull, hot diagram under a glistening sky. But right in front the mountains ranged across, pale blue and very still, snow gleaming gently out of the deep atmosphere. And towards the mountains, on and on, the regiment marched between the rye fields and the meadows, between the scraggy fruit trees set regularly on either side of the high road. The burnished, dark-green rye threw off a suffocating heat, the mountains drew gradually nearer and more distinct. While the feet of the soldiers grew hotter, sweat ran though their hair under their helmets, and their knapsacks could burn no more in contact with their shoulders, but seemed instead to give off a cold, prickly sensation.

The dominant impression from this description is merciless heat. Write an informal analysis of the elements that contribute to creating this dominant impression.

3. A financial statement is a comparative analysis of an organization's financial condition for one year as opposed to another. Obtain a financial statement from any annual report of a corporation, outline its comparative parts, and then summarize the outline in two paragraphs.

4. Find pictures of two paintings that render similar scenes. Write a comparative analysis of them, and underline the statement that presents your principle of analysis.

5. Bring the pictures of the paintings you analyzed to class along with your analysis. Exchange them with a fellow student. Write a paragraph evaluating your fellow student's analysis with these questions in mind:
   a. Is the principle of analysis stated?
   b. Is the principle of analysis followed?

    c. Are any points of comparison missing?

    d. Is the conclusion justified by the presentation? If not, why not?

6. List up to five possible causes for the following events:

a quarrel	Homecoming Day
a car wreck	alcoholism
a marriage	a divorce
a layoff	a dinner party

In each list, identify immediate and ultimate causes, and then construct analytical chains of cause and effect, moving from immediate to ultimate cause.

Write a paper based on the list that presents the best prospect for being developed into a full-fledged analysis.

7. Think of some sport or activity that you enjoy or know a lot about (for example, swimming or public speaking). Analyze the sport or activity to identify the qualities needed to make someone a very good performer of it. Choose the qualities that would be particularly interesting and convincing to others who also enjoy the sport or activity. With this audience in mind, write an analysis of the key qualities that lead to excellence.

Chapter 6

Induction and Deduction

The major movements of reasoning are induction and deduction. Movement from the general to particulars is deductive; movement from particulars to the general is inductive. Whenever we start to think and write with a generalization and point to examples or evidence in support, we are operating deductively. Whenever we draw a general conclusion from evidence or a number of examples, we are operating inductively.

Most of our rhetorical operations are used both inductively and deductively. The categories we make in classification are generalizations drawn from particulars, as we have seen. A particular item, however, is placed in an existing category by induction according to its typical characteristics. In analysis we deduce parts from the whole and from these arrive at judgments through induction. In definition, as we shall see, we use induction to classify and deduction to differentiate the term we are defining from all other members of the class. Every time we read and write, we process information both inductively and deductively. In reading descriptions and narrations, we pull together the specific details into generalizations and check them against our memory of experience or the generalizations we have made about the way things are. In writing, we organize first by pulling together the details of our experiences into generalizations and then by seeking specific examples and incidents to represent these generalizations.

Although induction and deduction operate in all reasoning, most people think of these operations primarily as the basis of argument and persuasion, of bringing about agreement. The terms *argument* and *persuasion* are sometimes used interchangeably, but each one has a distinct reference, the former to type of discourse, the latter to aim; that is, we write an argument in order to persuade someone about something. It has also become customary to base the distinction between argument and persuasion on the notion of truth. According to this understanding, an argument presents reasons that show the truth of a proposition, which is a generalization or conclusion drawn from evidence. If the argument has been convincing, that is, if it appears true, it is said to be persuasive. But an argument can be persuasive without being true. Advertisements, for instance, may convince with less than truth. Arguments may be persuasive whether they are true or false. False arguments usually persuade by means of faulty or tricky generalizations and specifications, omission of certain details, and appeals to insecurities and desires. An understanding of the inductive and deductive processes, therefore, should guide not only the writer but also the reader and listener in determining the validity of all propositions, the pitchman's as well as the teacher's. (*Validity* is a better word for us than *truth*, which is too mystical and absolute a concept for practical use.)

Valid and Invalid Generalization

Rhetorical generalizations are based on evidence, which includes previously accepted generalizations. Writers generalize from specific observations, data, statistics, testimony, authority of law or position, or moral codes. From these particulars they form opinions, attitudes, sentiments, judgments, convictions, and beliefs. In a famous essay, "The Method of Scientific Investigation," Thomas H. Huxley defines scientific method as induction and deduction. The generalization is achieved by induction and then strengthened by deductive verifications. First, the induction:

> Suppose you go into a fruiter's shop, wanting an apple—you take one up, and, on biting, you find it sour; you look at it, and see that it is hard and green. You take up another one and that too is hard, green, and sour. The shop man offers you a third; but, before biting it, you examine it, and find that it is hard and green, and you immediately say that you will not have it, as it must be sour, like those that you have already tried. . . . You have performed the operation of induction. . . . You generalize the facts, and you expect to find sourness in apples where you get hardness and greenness.

In the deductive process, the experimenter gathers more evidence to validate the generalization:

> "It is a very curious thing—but I find that all hard and green apples are sour!" Your friend says to you, "But how do you know that?" You at once reply, "Oh, because I have tried them over and over again, and have always found them to be so. . . . I have heard from the people in Somersetshire and Devonshire, where a large number of apples are grown, that they have observed the same thing. It is also found to be the case in Normandy, and in North America. In short, I find it to be the universal experience of mankind, wherever attention has been directed to the subject." Whereupon your friend, unless he is a very unreasonable man, agrees with you. . . . He sees that the experiment has been tried under all sorts of conditions, as to time, place, and people, with the same result; and he says with you, therefore, that the law you have laid down must be a good one, and he must believe it.

Huxley's mental movement leaps from bits of evidence to a generalization that accounts for all the specifics in the case, even those not sampled. As the experimenter seeks more and more verifying evidence, the leap to generalization narrows to a step and ultimately seems to disappear. The statement, "Capitalists are motivated by profit," like "Hard, green apples are sour," hardly needs further proving because the evidence everywhere in the world where capitalists operate verifies it.

No precise number of examples or specifics exists that will validate a generalization. The smaller the population the generalization covers, the greater the proportion of examples needed. For instance, if we were trying to generalize about the attitude toward birth control in a village of 1,000 people, each person's attitude would be more significant than in a city of 100,000. In the larger population, individual differences tend to level out. People en masse, apparently, act much like contained gas molecules. One cannot know how any particular molecule will move, but we can trace the general behavior of huge numbers of them.

Hasty or Sweeping Generalization

In the leap to generalization, the danger of invalid statement diminishes as we increase our evidence and examples. Writers, however, do not usually go about counting their particulars. They intuitively gauge the necessary amount of evidence from general experience. "They must be living together," the town gossip says, having seen the couple entering the apartment several times. To the careful writer, these observations would be insufficient for the generalization. Most rumors are based on such invalid leaps, on hasty or sweeping generalizations. The leap to generalization would be reduced and the rumor would become more factual if the couple were observed entering each evening and emerging each morning. One of the causes that contributed to the emergence of the women's independence movement was the fact some men make hasty generalizations about the other half of the human race: "Women are less rational and more emotional than men"; "Women want it both ways, equal opportunity and deferential treatment." These generalizations ignore sufficient sampling. Circumstances of time, place, and condition make the behavior of one woman differ from that of another as much as it differs from any man's behavior. Poor peasant women in earlier times acted much more like their husbands than like genteel ladies.

In his *Autobiography,* Benjamin Franklin attributed much of his success to the way he skirted hasty or sweeping generalizations. Most generalizations were probable to him, few factual. "Perhaps" and "it seems" and "it may be" were among his guardians. Careful writers usually follow Franklin's way. Their generalizations are only as strong as the evidence will allow. When the evidence is not indisputable, the judicious hedge will enhance the reader's confidence in the writer. Instead of saying, "Young people aren't going to college these days," the writer might try, "More young people are tending to skip college nowadays." Instead of "Women still prefer lives as housewives and mothers," we might try, "Many women still prefer lives as housewives and mothers"; and rather than "Manners are changing more rapidly," we would write, "Manners appear to be changing more rapidly."

A Priori Generalization

Although specifics may be representative, generalizations may still be skewed, often to confirm a writer's bias. In the eighteenth and early nineteenth centuries, the European middle and upper classes commonly concluded that peasants were happy in their poverty because they were outwardly good-natured. The same skewed generalization was applied to the American blacks during slavery and after; they were "darkies" singing as they sweated in the sunshine. Although writers may display all the signs of objective observation — that is, select representative samples at random — they may still draw generalizations that are preconceived, *a priori*. A priori induction is a common trick of comparative advertising or political promotions. The points of comparison are selected beforehand to show that the coffee Mrs. Swenson uses is better than others. Most Americans judge economic action taken by a communist country as a priori against the good and even the will of the majority. Of course, any economic action taken by a capitalist country, in the eyes of communists, is also a priori against the good and the will of the majority.

A priori induction may also occur when scientists hypothesize. By definition, hypotheses are propositions set up for testing or approving. They are suppositions, temporary theses that guide the search for substantiating evidence. However, a scientist who is committed to a hypothesis beforehand will tend to find the evidence that supports it and suppress the evidence that denies it.

Analogical Generalization

Induction by extended analogy is perhaps more striking than induction from examples, but it is more risky. As we have seen, analogy shows that one thing is like another in a particular way. By implication or outright argument, the writer may then generalize that the two items are therefore similar in other ways. To be valid, the extended analogy must offer a true parallel. If the differences are greater than the resemblances, the extended analogy is invalid. In the first half of the twentieth century, the labor movement in both England and America was often attacked by analogy with the communist movement. The point of similarity was the unification of workers, but unionization in England and America was not enforced by government, and unions could not legally impose themselves upon workers. Although the analogy was obviously invalid, many people identified the union movement with communism. In the first half of the century, automobiles and horses were also analogous, but no one mistook one for the other.

Induction and Interpretation

Interpretations of events, poems and stories, and scientific and statistical data are all formed inductively. Through the presentation of details, the writer guides the reader of a story to induce a generalization that is the theme, a dominant idea or mood. The details of Edgar Allan Poe's "The Fall of the House of Usher" create an atmosphere of desolation and decay. Readers are led to equate the condition of Roderick Usher with the condition of his house; his soul is likewise desolate and decayed. He becomes enervated when he imagines that his sister is dead. He plays a musical instrument and sings. Then his sister appears, or at least her body. Her body falls upon him, taking Usher into death with her, and the House of Usher crumbles. From these signs, the reader may infer this interpretation: The earthly flesh (the sister) cannot be separated from the ethereal and aesthetic soul (Usher who plays the music in the momentary freedom from the flesh when his sister is presumed dead). Because she returns to take her brother with her, we generalize that body and soul cannot be separated. We can further induce the author's attitude toward that generalization: He yearns to separate the soul from the body, in spite of the impossibility. If any facts of the story contradict this interpretation, it is not valid.

We can induce an interpretation very much like the one from Poe's story out of these often-quoted lines of Yeats that end "Among School Children":

O body swayed to music, O brightening glance,
How can we know the dancer from the dance?

Form and substance, act and being are one; body and soul are inseparable. From these interpretations, one from the writing of a nineteenth-century American and the other from a twentieth-century Irishman, we can induce a further generalization. We can conclude that all things form one organic unity. One thing cannot be separated from another. Roughly speaking, this is the theory of organicism, which ran through the nineteenth century and is still with us.

History is also a series of interpretations induced from specifics. We generalize meaning even though we cannot account for all the events; and even if we could, the countless number of specifics would overwhelm all efforts to form a pattern of meaning. The specifics must be selected from masses of detail according to some principle. As the selection of details proceeds according to a preconceived notion, the chosen details verify and thus strengthen the notion until we induce from them the generalization we call a hypothesis. Differing interpretations of history result from differing hypotheses that guide the selection of evidence or "facts."

Most scientific generalizations are induced from statistics or other sets of data. The heart of any investigative report is the interpretation of data, whether it is called analysis, evaluation, or discussion of results. Our study of comparative analysis showed that various conclusions or interpretations are possible, depending on the writer's purpose. This observation holds for all data. In the following set of hypothetical statistics about accidents that two groups of drivers were involved in within the limits of a certain city in a certain month, we may infer (deduce) that older drivers are utterly reckless compared with younger drivers:

Group	Accidents	Percent of Total
Over 50	33,800	92.6
Under 50	2,700	7.4
Total	36,500	100.0

However, if we added the information that there are three younger drivers to every ten older drivers in that city, our percentages of accidents per driver would tend to even out between the groups. If we added the further information that the older drivers average ten times as much driving as the younger, our initial interpretations would begin to look skewed; the older drivers would now seem the more careful of the two. To make valid interpretations of data, the writer must be sure the data are complete.

Another common error is using misleading and inconsistent units of measurement. Let us assume a table showing the unemployed, month by month, with four sets of figures provided by four different agencies. None of the figures agree. One agency excluded part-time workers. Another included nonworking students home for summer. And a third included the physically handicapped. Even when the units of measurement are consistent, they may be misleading. We may read that housing starts in Cowtown increased by 100 percent and then discover that only two houses were started compared with one the previous year.

Deduction and the Syllogism

Induction is generalization; deduction is specification. The two work together in logical thought, the specifics leading to the generalization and the generalization leading to the applications or specifications.

When we apply the generalizations that result from our inductive thinking to specifics, we reason deductively. In classical logic, deductive reasoning is identified with the syllogism. It is a formal way of specifying that we can use to test deductive validity.

Categorical Syllogism

A syllogism contains three parts: major premise, minor premise, and conclusion. The major premise is a generalization taken as true; the minor premise is a specific instance covered by the generalization; and the conclusion is the logical connection between the major and minor premises:

MAJOR PREMISE: All graduates of XYZ University are people who have taken at least one writing course.

MINOR PREMISE: Tom Jones is a graduate of XYZ University.

CONCLUSION: Tom Jones is a person who has taken at least one writing course.

To test for validity, we first examine the truthfulness of the major and minor premises and then find the common term between them, "graduate of XYZ University." The common term is then dropped and the conclusion is composed of the remaining terms: "Tom Jones has taken at least one writing course." The reasoning in this syllogism appears valid. However, if there were an exception—if some students were exempt from the writing course—the syllogism would be invalid. The writer would have to adjust with "most" or "many" depending on the proportion of exempt students:

Most graduates of XYZ University are people who have taken at least one writing course.
Tom Jones is a graduate of XYZ University.
Tom Jones is a person who has probably taken a writing course.

Notice that the conclusion has also changed with the hedge word "probably." However, even if hedge words were applied to the following syllogism, the reasoning would remain invalid:

All educated people write adequately.
Tom Jones is educated.
Tom Jones writes adequately.

Logicians who distinguish between "valid" and "true" would consider this syllogism valid since it adheres to the following logical form:

$$A = B$$
$$C = A$$
$$C = B$$

Nevertheless, they would find the syllogism untrue because the major premise is untrue. If we substituted "most" for "all" in the major premise and added "probably" to the conclusion, our syllogism would still be invalid because the major premise would still be untrue. Most educated people do not write adequately, according to the popular criticism of today's "illiterate" college graduates. Perhaps the syllogism could be made valid if the major premise associated writing with our expectations for an educated person:

> An educated person should write at least adequately.
> Tom Jones is an educated person.
> We expect Tom Jones to write at least adequately.

Rules for valid syllogisms are not universally applicable. The writer must be guided by experience of the way things are and by common sense.

Hypothetical Syllogism

When the major premise is a conditional or conjectural proposition, the syllogism is considered hypothetical. The major premise asserts that if one event occurs or one condition exists, another will follow:

> If it snows less than six inches, schools will remain open.

The minor premise asserts or implies that the first condition or event did or did not come about:

> It snowed two inches.

The conclusion gives the outcome as promised by the major premise:

> Schools remained open.

The first part of the major premise in a hypothetical syllogism is called the *antecedent* and the second part is called the *consequent*. For validity, the minor premise must either affirm the antecedent, in which case the consequent occurs, or it must deny the consequent:

> It snowed eight inches.
> The schools closed.

Upon careful scrutiny, the logic of the syllogism may appear faulty. Perhaps there was another reason for the schools to close. If so, it would not be in the context given. Cause and effect are quite clear; the school closed because of the snow. Observe the following hypothetical syllogism:

> If Danya crosses the street, she will be spanked.
> Danya did not cross the street.

From this syllogism we may conclude, "Danya was not spanked." Yet she could have been spanked anyway, but not for crossing the street—perhaps for poking a finger in the dog's eye. (The conclusion to this syllogism is too obvious to state. The writer could merely allow the reader to infer the conclusion or provide it with a more interesting statement: "Danya was given a lollipop.")

Disjunctive Syllogism

When the major premise presents choices or alternative possibilities as in either/or thinking and dilemmas, the syllogism is disjunctive:

> You are either with us or against us.

The minor premise declares an alternative:

> You are against us.

And the conclusion is the remaining alternative, which common sense tells us to omit. Conclusions of disjunctive syllogisms are most often implied because they are so obvious:

> No tie games, we either win or lose.
> We won.

The alternatives must include all possibilities:

> If not an actress, she must be a model.
> She's no model.

Do we conclude therefore she is an actress? Perhaps she is a singer with a rock band. The major premise is invalid because it excludes possibilities. A valid premise would say less and no doubt be less interesting, but it would offer stricter logic:

> Either she's an actress or not.

A second syllogism could begin with this major premise:

> Either she's a model or not.

Often in cause-and-effect analysis, disjunctive deductions fail to include all the possibilities:

> The car stopped because it was out of gas, or else the engine overheated.

There could be many other possibilities, spark plug failure, faulty gas pump, or burned out generator or alternator.

The alternatives of the major premise must also be mutually exclusive:

> The duckbill platypus is either a bird or a mammal.

A syllogism can't be formed on this premise. Dilemmas usually present difficulties of exclusiveness. Patients on life-sustaining machines, for example, are both alive and dead, depending on the definition. According to some experts, if brains still produce waves, people are alive, even though machines are required to keep all the fluids flowing through the flesh and to work the lungs.

The Enthymeme

In practice we seldom follow the precise form of the syllogism. Rather we employ the shortcut that the Greeks called the *enthymeme,* meaning "in mind." The enthymeme expresses two parts of the syllogism and implies the third, putting it "in mind" but not on paper. An enthymeme may begin with a conclusion and follow with one premise while omitting the other:

> The school closed because it snowed more than six inches.
> Tom Jones is eligible to be hired because he has no jail record.

These enthymemes imply the major premises. The following enthymeme implies the conclusion:

> An educated person should write at least adequately, and Tom Jones is an educated person.

In the next enthymeme, the minor premise is implied:

> A writer who plagiarizes is a thief. Tom Jones is a thief.

The validity of an enthymeme can be determined by rewriting it as a syllogism and testing it as such:

> A writer who plagiarizes is a thief.
> Tom Jones is a writer who plagiarizes.
> Tom Jones is a thief.

Faults most often occur when the writer implies the major premise:

> Ralph Waldo Emerson is a plagiarist because he borrowed from Hindu writers without giving them credit.

The major premise implied here is incomplete:

> A plagiarist is a person who borrows without acknowledgment.

Actually Emerson only borrowed from Hindu writers in the narrowest sense; he used them as a point of departure for his own ideas, and although he did not often specify them individually, he alluded to them. Incomplete major premises implied in enthymemes usually result from fuzzy or prejudicial thinking:

> Sure, Jack got the job. He had influence.

The implied premise is: "Those with influence get the jobs."

He knows a lot about Marx. Must be a communist.

The implied premise is, "Communists know a lot about Karl Marx." Many people get jobs without influence, and staunch Democrats and Republicans who are also educated may know a good deal about Karl Marx.

When politicians give reasons for soliciting votes they usually create chains of enthymemes, the implied conclusions of them all being "Vote for me":

> I will stop the waste in Washington. (Vote for me.)
> I will cut taxes. (Vote for me.)
> I will strengthen our defenses. (Vote for me.)
> I will guard our social benefits. (Vote for me.)

The implied premise is that the voter desires each of these. The more credible politicians will go on to subordinate chains of enthymemes, showing, for example, how they would go about eliminating waste. The structure of all reasoned discourse consists of chains of enthymemes, each supported by a string of subordinate reasons and various kinds of evidence:

> Anyone with heavy debts benefits from inflation, which is why Americans no longer heed the warning in *Hamlet:* "Neither a borrower nor a lender be." People take out loans expecting to be able to pay them off later with cheaper dollars, and in recent years they have been right. Borrowers can now repay their debts with dollars worth just 63 cents in 1975 terms. That view is an important factor behind the sharp increase in consumer installment debt, which since 1975 has gone from $172.4 billion to $305.5 billion by the end of last October.

The two parts of the enthymeme that begin this essay are these: (1) "Anyone with heavy debts benefits from inflation" and (2) "Americans have heavy debts" (they no longer heed the warning in *Hamlet*). This enthymeme is followed by another, "People take out loans in the expectation that . . . ." The writer validates the whole with heavy statistical evidence in the rest of the paragraph. The opening enthymeme continues into succeeding paragraphs, each beginning with a second part:

> Homeowners are among the biggest gainers. . . .
>
> Inflation also benefits millions of unionized workers, government pensioners, and Social Security recipients whose incomes rise automatically. . . .
>
> One clear gainer from inflation is the government. . . .

Each paragraph, completing the same enthymeme, is developed with further enthymemes and supporting evidence.

Fallacious Reasoning

Invalid generalizations and syllogisms are among the most common faults of inductive and deductive reasoning, but there are more. Often they may occur thoughtlessly, although often they are deliberately staged to win arguments, as in various advertisements and political campaigns. An astute reasoner, however, will be able to recognize the falseness. Fallacious reasoning is examined in Chapter 15, The Argumentative Essay or Article.

EXERCISES

1. Identify the flaws in these generalizations:

   a. The price of oranges went up today. So did the price of eggs. Inflation is never ending.

   b. My car broke down again. They don't make cars the way they used to.

   c. Two hundred million Americans can't be wrong.

   d. Aren't you glad you use Dial [soap]? Don't you wish everyone did?

   e. The army is full of fascists.

   f. His face is red, he walks unsteadily, and his speech is slurred. He's drunk.

   g. She's psychotic. She spent two months in a mental hospital.

   h. All the ladies of that day loved Rudolph Valentino. My mother was no exception.

2. Identify the valid syllogisms among the following. Identify the flaws or fallacies in the others and take whatever liberty is necessary in rewriting them into valid syllogisms.

   a. Life is the same for everyone.
      Old man Saunders is still alive.
      His life is like everyone's.

   b. If you work hard, you succeed.
      James is a success.
      He worked hard.

   c. Love is sacrifice.
      You won't give up your beer buddies.
      You don't love me.

   d. Ministers are people of God.
      People of God are good.
      Ministers are good.

   e. Mothers protect their babies.
      James protected his infant son.
      James is a mother.

f. No respectable person would allow herself to get thirty pounds over-weight.
But Linda, the streetwalker, is not at all overweight.
Linda is a respectable person.

g. I asked you to give up that nasty job if you loved me.
You gave it up.
Now I know you love me.

h. This boy is either very tired, or he's sick.
He's not sick.
He must be tired.

i. Almost every woman in the liberation movement wants the Equal
Rights Amendment to pass.
Amanda Black is a member of NOW.
You can bet she wants that amendment to pass.

3. Convert the valid versions of the syllogisms in exercise 2 into enthymemes.

4. Test the validity of the following enthymemes by converting them into syllogisms. Supply the missing premise or conclusion:

a. He lives abroad. He must be rich.

b. She's no professor, but quite an actress.

c. Certainly she loves opera. She was born and raised in Italy.

d. Drugs are habit-forming, and alcohol is a drug.

e. Carol is a psychotic. Psychiatrists can't do much for her.

f. I can't afford to see Dr. Menninger. His office is in the Plaza Building.

g. Everyone who kills is a murderer. Murderers should be executed.

h. No one ever caught him cheating, so he must be honest.

i. If that painting is by Helmholtz, it's great art.

5. Choose an event reported in your newspaper and connect it to previous events. How can you connect it? By cause and effect? Comparison? Contrast? Can you foresee any future developments, possible events that might now occur as a result? For example, you might look into current news of events in the Near East or Wall Street, or of some scientific or medical discovery or some political action or legislation. Write your interpretation with supporting evidence.

6. Give your interpretation of the following poem by A. E. Housman and show how the evidence — the words, images, rhythms, metaphors, structure, thoughts — lead to that interpretation, that is, how they substantiate it.

With rue my heart is laden
For laughing friends I had,
For many a rose-lipt maiden
And many a light-foot lad.

By brooks too broad for leaping
The light-foot lads are laid.
And rose-lipt girls are sleeping
In fields where roses fade.

7. According to these invented statistics, are you safer riding a private car, taxi, bus, or motorcycle?

	Deaths in Accidents per Year	Accidents per Year	Vehicles in Operation per Year
Private car	28,000	1,500,000	50,000,000
Taxi	350	90,000	1,500,000
Bus	380	1,000	800,000
Motorcycle	11,800	180,000	1,100,000

How could you use further information to improve your interpretation, such as miles traveled per year and number of passengers per year? Write an interpretation of the statistics you do have.

8. Play Abby:

Dear Abby:

I am a 60-year-old nurse widowed for 10 years. I took care of a very attractive, well-to-do widower, age 69. Recuperating, he asked if he could see me again so we could get better acquainted. I agreed, but it took him nearly six months to call me, still — I was on cloud nine! We've been going out for over a year now, and he proposed marriage.

My problem is that he admits that he is still seeing several other women and says that until he has my answer, he will continue to date others.

Abby, this has made me skeptical of his so-called marriage proposal. If a man thinks enough of a woman to want to marry her, why would he want to date other women? How can I say yes tonight when I know he had another woman in his arms last night?

Frustrated at 60

Make one or more syllogisms of Frustrated's logic, evaluate, and then respond.

9. Trace the chain of induction and deduction in the following selections, noting those that are valid and those that are invalid. Name specific errors.

a. To hold fast in the Caribbean is going to require a toe-to-toe slugfest with academicians who, though they profess to teach history, have lamentably failed to read it. The heckling that greeted the secretary of state at the university was accompanied by a faculty walkout organized by members of the history department. The Keynesians may have been routed in most economics faculties, giving way to Friedman monetarists and Jack Kemp supply-siders, but in history and the social sciences the left still maintains its strong position.

If the President had been bloodied a long time ago in his fight against the communists and fellow travelers in the Screen Actors Guild, we might have to worry about his knuckling under to the left in the manner of Lyndon Johnson. But we have a man in the White House who knows history because he has lived it in labor-front confrontations.

b. The corn standard? Somehow that doesn't sound stately enough for a monetary system. It is difficult to visualize some future William Jennings Bryan declaiming against crucifying mankind "upon a cross of corn." However, that doesn't mean we don't need a better system.

As frequently happens when retrospective issues arise, I betook myself down to the Future-Is-Yesterday Foundation, a privately endowed think tank and research center. There I asked Sam Harkenback, the executive director, whether there was any erstwhile monetary standard other than gold that the United States might feasibly return to.

"Indeed, yes, dear boy," Harkenback replied, leading me into a tanning room whose walls were covered with hides.

"Land o' Goshen!" I exclaimed. "Whatever are those?"

"Beaver pelts," Harkenback replied portentously. "We here at Future-Is-Yesterday Foundation have devoted a great deal of study to the question of what monetary standard would be best to return to and we have concluded that beaver pelts are the answer."

Warming to his subject, Harkenback reminded me that America has used many different mediums of exchange over its span of history. One of the first was wampum, clamshells strung together like beads. "From a pure nostalgia standpoint, wampum was clearly the favorite as the currency of the future," he said. "Even today, its terminology remains a part of our language. For instance we still speak of something as costing '10 clams.' "

I said, "Could this be where the term 'strung out' originated?"

"Could be," Harkenback acknowledged. "Many colonial areas had laws requiring that wampum be 'well strung.' "

But other considerations caused the foundation to recommend against reviving wampum as our currency standard. "It would discriminate against some of the inland states," he said. "Iowa, for example, has hardly any clams."

Another former monetary standard rejected by the foundation was the musket ball. "We were afraid it might cause monetary policy to get mixed up in the gun control issue," Harkenback said.

Finally, it boiled down to a choice between beaver pelts and tobacco. The foundation opted for the former. "We feared the latter would lead to demands for health warning on dollar bills." Harkenback said.

Dick West, "The Lighter Side,"
Tulsa Tribune, June 2, 1981

10. Complete the following statements by giving several reasons.

   a. I go to college because . . .

   b. Wars are necessary because . . .

   c. Wars are unnecessary because . . .

   d. A personal sense of morality is essential because . . .

   What supporting evidence could you bring to bear on each of these theses?

11. Write an essay on any of the above theses or one of your own, using inductive and deductive reasoning with substantiating evidence.

Chapter 7

Definition

What is it? What does it mean? These questions subsume those of all the other rhetorical operations. (To what does it belong? What are its parts? What is it like? How does it work?) The questions of definition are at the root of our understanding. The answers lead us to the essential nature of a thing, idea, or quality. When we extend our definitions beyond a synonym or brief example, we expose our subject, lay it out to full view. Consequently, definition is often equated with exposition. Exposition of a topic ultimately answers the question "What is it?" The words *definition* and *exposition* are sometimes used interchangeably, as in this excerpt from a review of the movie *Excalibur:* "There is a touch of humor through the film's first half, especially as Merlin is defined — exposed — as part magician, part con man." We can view a college text as a lengthy definition or collection of definitions, or a financial statement as a definition of a corporation's condition.

The concept of definition, however, is not confined to one side of our spectrum of rhetoric. Narratives at the affective end of our spectrum can be seen as definitions of character and relationship, and the lyric poem as a definition of an emotion. Logical definitions, however, are naturally restricted to the factual and the reasoning portions of the rhetorical spectrum. Like the other rhetorical operations, logical definition may provide the dominant pattern of a discourse or may be used as support for other dominating operations, such as classification or analysis.

Definition and Context

Language is a system of symbols that we agree upon to represent objects, ideas, and action. The definitions of these symbols tell readers how to use them if they don't already know. We also use other systems of symbols, such as mathematical systems in which definitions are given in a legend and each symbol stands for only one thing. If this one-to-one relationship between a signifier and the thing signified existed in verbal language, problems of communication would be greatly simplified, but so would the ideas being communicated. Our use of language would be so limited that we would be unable to express ourselves. Unlike mathematical symbols, verbal symbols constantly shift with use and time so that each word contains several possible meanings. The word *distemper*, for example, could mean "ill-humor" in one place and "a fatal disease of dogs" in another. It could also refer to "a particular process of painting" or "a state of civil tumult." Many years ago *distemper* was used as a technical term meaning "to dilute." A word is aligned with one of its particular meanings when the reader is led into that particular meaning by its neighboring words, its *context*.

A reader's experience with a word contributes to its field of possible meaning. These possibilities are the word's *connotations*, the associations the word may arouse. *Home*, for example, may carry the connotation of comfort to one reader but sloth to another. Connotations are also controlled by the context. Fifty years ago, a person could refer to a roommate of the same sex as "friend," but for readers experienced in today's society, the context would have to guide the meaning away from the possibility of homosexuality unless that meaning were intended. Today Americans who oppose gun control point to the Second Amendment of the Constitution, which states the right to bear arms. However, the reference at the time was to the right of raising a militia, not of buying a gun. Obviously, to control connotations, writers must anticipate the possible interpretations of their words. When context fails to control connotations and guide the reader to the intended meaning, that is, the proper, *denotative* meaning — whether "yellow stripe" refers to cowardice or the pattern of a sofa — then informal or formal definition is employed.

The definition may be a brief identification, a mere example, a formal statement that isolates one meaning from all others, a series of statements that stipulate one meaning through specific uses of the term (stipulative definition), or an essay using all rhetorical operations needed to penetrate to the essence of meaning.

Exemplification and Other Informal Definition

Often in the midst of discourse, it is necessary to identify an uncommon term or idea. Such identification is informal and incomplete. It is extremely useful, however, when we wish to suggest a meaning without digressing from the main thrust of thought. The simplest way to identify is to exemplify. We usually make our abstract ideas and propositions concrete through examples:

> A rational government is not possible in democracy. At best we can offer
> incentives or discouragements and hope they will work: free the rich
> from taxes and perhaps they will invest; restore the electric chair and
> killers may think twice; ban abortions and maybe we won't see so much
> open sex.

The examples in this excerpt certainly identify or help to define the proposition, but they do not support or substantiate it. Each example would have to be reasoned further with logic and evidence before an intelligent reader would agree with it. Examples are never sufficient to establish an idea or proposition, and definitions that establish meanings are essentially ideas or propositions. The example is useful only when quick identification is sufficient; examples gracefully and efficiently reduce abstract terms to their concrete foundations.

If we wished to exemplify the abstraction "modes of production" in the following statement, we would have to employ more than one example: "As modes of production have developed throughout history, people have adapted to their presence." If we stopped with a single example, "Where students once wrote essays, they now attune their minds to machine-graded examinations," the abstraction would remain vague because we do not ordinarily think of examinations as "modes of production." To establish the meaning, we would have to associate this example with others. Together the examples would direct us to the meaning:

> Earlier generations of family doctors diagnosed largely by human intui-
> tion, but today's physicians tend to see their patients as computer print-
> outs. Consumers hardly distinguish between food that is fresh and food
> that comes in frozen form. Many prefer music that is electronically medi-
> ated. Where students once wrote essays, they now attune their minds to
> machine-graded examinations.

Analogical comparison can be seen as a special kind of example in which the unknown is partially exemplified by the known, and the differences lead the reader to understanding. A space shuttle could be compared with an airplane in having wings and airlift characteristics, and also with a space capsule in having orbiting capabilities. The features that distinguish it from either, such as its gliderlike landing ability, lead the reader to a rudimentary understanding of this object. The analogy could be extended by comparison and contrast through analysis and description of the shuttle's generic parts with those of the airplane and space capsule.

We use identification also to attach special meanings to a term for the duration of our discourse. Such identifications are called *stipulative* definitions. In "Wages," for example, Henry George stipulates that for his purpose, in the political-economic sense *wages* are not to be distinguished from *salary;* that is, payment for manual labor is not distinct from remuneration for professional labor. Wages, rather, are all returns received from the exertion of any kind of labor as distinct from returns received from the use of capital. Stipulative definitions may also identify meanings geographically or historically, in terms of other cultures and times:

By "relics" in his eighteenth-century *Epochs of Nature*, Buffon means such things as fossils, shells, and mammoth bones.

Synonyms are also informal identifications, offering familiar words for unfamiliar ones: "Patronizing is being snobbish or high-hatted"; "Sludge is mud"; "To be sly is to be cunning, foxy." We notice that synonyms are nearly the same in meaning, never identical.

All informal definitions, whether a clause — "mauve is a mixture of colors somewhat like purple" — or a paragraph of examples, give readers their bearings, substituting familiar words, phrases, and images for unfamiliar ones. Informal definitions are brief, partial identifiers that should be used (1) when the writer wishes to limit a meaning rather than let the reader choose any one of several meanings, or (2) when the writer needs some identification in the midst of a long discussion and does not wish to break into the reader's main line of thought for too long. Informal definitions merely point to the general direction in which the meaning may be found. Mauve is purplish in color but so is lavender. Other words and meanings lie in the same direction, and, therefore, ambiguity and obscurity may result.

Formal Definition

To attain precise meanings, an equation-like statement called formal definition is employed. It is achieved through a logical process of setting limits or boundaries to the meaning of a word and then narrowing those boundaries until a single meaning becomes evident. (The word *definition* stems from the Latin *definire,* which means "to limit.") This process is called formal because it follows a prescribed form composed of three parts: the *species,* the *genus,* and the *differentiae.* The *species* is the word or term being defined. The *genus* is the class of things to which the term belongs. The *differentiae* are the differences which isolate the species from all other members of its class, or genus. The elements of a formal definition can be seen as an equation:

term (species) = class (genus) + sum of differences (differentiae)

Two logical steps, then, are required to define a word formally: classification, in which the term is placed in the general group of things similar to it, and differentiation, in which the term is isolated from all other members of its class by indicating its distinguishing characteristics. To define *coat,* the writer would first find a suitable genus. In this case "clothing" appears appropriate. Next, the coat is differentiated from all other clothing. Differences that present themselves immediately are (1) that it is worn as an outer garment and (2) that it covers torso and arms. The definition needs both differentiae; otherwise, the writer might be defining a skirt or pajamas. But have we exclusively defined *coat?* Or does a shirt also fit our definition? Perhaps we could be more precise if we stressed the term "outer garment" as a covering over other clothing. Our definition, put into a graceful sentence, might assume that a reader will understand that the genus "clothing" has been implied in the word "garment." We might write, "A coat is an outer garment covering the torso and arms and also covering other clothing." A sleeveless coat would be a special case of this definition.

A coat, however, can be other things as well as a garment. There are coats of paint and, in heraldry, coats of arms. The word is also a transitive verb. We coat pills. We insulate electric wires by coating them. A class that would cover all these cases — "a coat is any kind of covering" — would be too general for any one. It would cover too much. The writer must limit the class in which the term or concept is to be placed. As in all choices, writers determine class according to intentions. For instance, several classes are possible in defining a simple term like *set*. As a verb, some of the possibilities are "to seat" (to set a king on a throne or a boy on a horse), "to put in place" (to set a tree), "to establish" (to set a meeting time), and "to cause" (to set a house on fire, a ship afloat, or another person at ease). As a noun or adjective *set* is a position (the set of one's mind), a form (the concrete was poured into a set), a pose or carriage (the set of her head), a direction or course (the set of the wind or the sails), a fixed position (set in his ways), the act of hardening or the hardened condition (the paint was set), a collection of things (a set of laws or numbers), or a theatrical scene (the audience applauded the set).

Good writers have learned to follow these general guides in constructing formal definitions:

1. *The narrower the class, the fewer the differences.* A class that is too broad imposes too great a burden on the differentiae: "A clock is a device that keeps time." Because there are all kinds of devices, this class is too broad. The differentiae are insufficient. They do not show the differences between clocks and sundials. However, if the clock were defined as a "mechanism" for keeping time, the limited differentiae would sufficiently isolate *clock* from all other members of its class.

2. *The term is never used as the root of the definition.* To say that a *statistician* is a person who makes a profession of *statistics* is talking in circles. In the depths of philosophy even so fine a mind as Bertrand Russell's may turn circular. Notice his effort to define the term *number:* "It is clear that *number* is a way of bringing together certain collections, namely, those that have a given *number* of terms."

3. *The formal definition is negative only if the term is negative in essence.* Nirvana could be defined as the absence of earthly matters and materials. It is negative in its essence, like *widow* or *widower*. However, if we defined democracy as the absence of dictatorship, we would certainly miss its essential meaning.

4. *The formal definition is not a mere statement about the term.* Statements about terms may informally define, that is, identify. In formal definition, however, the writer must guard against mere statements. Love may be a "many-splendored thing," but that does not define the term. Such phrases as "is what" or "is when" do not provide classes for definition: "A handbook is what we use for reference in writing courses," or, "Communication is when we speak or write or signal to each other." Actually these terms have not been classed. Instead of limitations on the term, these statements have only given instances of use.

5. *The formal definition is more familiar than the term being defined.* Vague, abstract words that are as unfamiliar to the reader as the term being defined can hardly do the job of definition. Considerate writers aim to familiarize readers with the strange, so they use familiar language in their definitions. Often, however, a word stands for a concept so complex that abstract terms cannot be avoided. The writer is defining the term for himself as much as for the reader. That is the situation in which Bertrand Russell employed the term *number* in its own definition. In such a situation, the writer should first define for himself and then for the reader. The first effort may emphasize logic at the expense of rhetoric, but the second effort must be rhetorical, which means it must appeal to the reader's understanding. If a writer, for example, settles upon the meaning of *oscillation* as "a vibration or fluctuation back and forth," the reader who does not know what oscillation is may also not know what fluctuation is.

Expanded Definition

The definition of *oscillation* becomes clear when we add "like the motion of a pendulum on a grandfather's clock." The writer could go on with further analogies, extending the definition to cover all instances of "oscillation," such as those in a transistor, which perhaps can be envisioned as a shivering motion. Expanded definitions are used not only in this way, to supplement the information of short definitions, but also to fully answer the question, What is it? The full answer to this huge question requires the reader to work through complicated relations and discover answers to the other rhetorical questions concerning components, processes, similarities, history. To lead the reader toward the essential meaning of a complex subject, the writer describes major characteristics, shows how one affects the other, and demonstrates how they combine to form a recognizable whole. The writer may also show pertinent aspects of its history as well as its wider implications and ramifications. Such definitions result in systems of paragraphs, chapters, sections of reports, essays, and even whole volumes.

We have already seen how examples, comparisons, and analogies provide informal definition. They are also means of expanding the definition, along with the rhetorical operations of analysis, description, and narration. Explications, history, origins, and derivations of things also help reveal the essence of terms. Explication is always a strong way to begin the expansion.

Explication

The writer can explain unfamiliar terms that are necessary in a formal definition by applying more definition. The process is similar to the old pedant's approach to his subject, *explication de texte,* where the instructor ponders over the text in class, defining for students each difficult term in turn. The authors of the excerpt below introduce a new concept with this definition: "Operations research is a scientific method of providing executive departments with a quantitative basis for decisions regarding the operations under their control." The following is the way they began the expansion, which became the whole book:

> First of all operations research is a "scientific method." It is an organized activity with a more or less definite methodology of attacking new problems and finding definite solutions. Executives have often in the past used some of the techniques to be explained herein to help themselves arrive at decisions; military staff have used some of the techniques and "efficiency experts" have exploited some of its methods. But the term scientific method implies more than recognized and organized activity amenable to application to a variety of problems and capable of being taught.
>
> Next we see that operations research is of service to executive departments. . . .
>
> F. M. Morse and G. E. Kimball,
Methods of Operations Research

The definition goes on to explicate each term in the formal definition. After service to "executive departments," it explains "quantitative basis for decision," and "operations under their control." Within this framework of explication, the authors proceed to define further by means of example. In the quoted material they point to executives who employ operations research, military staffs, and "efficiency experts."

Analysis, Description, and Narration

When analysis is used to tell what steps comprise a process, it is the basis for narration. When it is employed to show what parts make up a whole, what constituents make up a substance, or what characteristics comprise an entity, it is the basis for description. It is also the basis for explaining the causes of an effect or the effects stemming from a cause. As means of expanding definition, these rhetorical operations are never applied extensively. (When they are, we tend to call the results analysis, description, or narration.) For relatively simple subjects, components may simply be named and qualities quickly described:

> Pure water consists of hydrogen and oxygen in the proportion of two atoms of hydrogen to one of oxygen . . . an odorless, tasteless, transparent liquid which is very slightly compressible.

Steps in a process may be named and narrated as an action:

> Primary production occurs when a well releases the natural pressure and allows the oil to flow. It gathers in the well and is pumped to the surface.

Some concepts can be only indirectly defined by analysis of their causes and effects because so little is actually known about them. Most dictionaries still define gravity, for example, as a force between terrestrial bodies, a force that accelerates toward the center of those bodies. Cause-and-effect analysis is also useful in probing the deeper meanings of familiar terms. *Technology,* for example, can be understood more fully by stating its effects in creating the first worldwide human civilization. The expanded definition might cite the role of technology in causing the reexamination of old concepts, such as the social position of women, or of attitudes toward work, education, and welfare. The definition might go on to describe changes in the physical environment, from one of nature to one of industry, and changes in human spirit, from hope for a utopia to fear for the ultimate destruction of humanity.

Example, Comparison, and Analogy

The use of analysis in definition is usually enhanced by examples, comparisons, or analogies. These identifiers are the most prominent means of rendering any definition, whether a brief pause or a full essay. Notice how large a proportion of the following definition, which has an analytic framework, is given over to example and comparison:

> What do people mean when they use the word "grammar"? Actually, the word is used to refer to three different things, and much of the emotional thinking about matters grammatical arises from confusion among these different meanings.
>
> The first thing we mean by "grammar" is "the set of formal patterns in which the words of a language are arranged in order to convey larger meanings." It is necessary that we are able to discuss these patterns self-consciously in order to be able to use them. In fact, all speakers of a language above the age of five or six know how to use its complex forms of organization with considerable skill; in this sense of the word—call it "Grammar 1"—they are thoroughly familiar with its grammar.
>
> The second meaning of "grammar"—call it "Grammar 2"—is the "branch of linguistic science which is concerned with the description,

analysis, and formulization of formal language patterns." Just as gravity was in full operation before Newton's apple fell, so grammar in the first sense was in full operation before anyone formulated the first rule that began the history of grammar as a study.

The third sense in which people use the word "grammar" is "linguistic etiquette." This we may call "Grammar 3." The word in this sense is often coupled with a derogatory adjective: we say that the expression "he ain't here" is "bad grammar." What we mean is that such an expression is bad linguistic manners in certain circles. From the point of view of "Grammar 1" it is faultless; it conforms as completely to the structural patterns of English as does "he isn't here." The trouble with it is like the trouble with Prince Hal in Shakespeare's play—it is "bad," not in itself, but in the company it keeps.

> W. Nelson Francis, "Revolutions in
> Grammar," *Quarterly Journal of
> Speech* 40 (1954)

Elimination

Sometimes called obverse iteration, elimination is actually a form of contrast. By telling what something is not before telling what it is, the writer often clears the air of misconceptions at the outset and eases the following burden of positive definition: "Economy no more means saving money than it means spending money. It means the administration of a house; its stewardship; spending or saving, that is, whether money or time, or anything else, to the best advantage" (John Ruskin, "A Joy Forever"). In the following example from Carl L. Becker's *Modern Democracy,* the technique of elimination separates a gross understanding of a term (which may be socially harmful) from the understanding that democrats probably have in their hearts if not on their tongues:

> All human institutions, we are told, have their ideal forms laid away in heaven, and we do not need to be told that the actual institutions conform but indifferently to these ideal counterparts. It would be possible then to define democracy either in terms of the idea or in terms of the real form—to define it as government of the people, by the politicians, for whatever pressure groups can get their interests taken care of. But as a historian I am naturally disposed to be satisfied with the meaning which, in the history of politics, men have commonly attributed to the word—a meaning, needless to say, which derives partly from the experience and partly from the aspirations of mankind. So regarded, the term democracy refers primarily to a form of government, and it has always meant government by the people as opposed to government by a tyrant, a dictator, or an absolute monarch. This is the most general meaning of the word as men have commonly understood it.

History, Origin, and Etymology

We can know better what something is by knowing what it was or what it came from. Original meaning, roots, help define by suggesting histories, expansion, and changes through time. A popular conception in medieval times was the enchantment of Latin grammar. It was thought to cast spells upon listeners. The word *grammar* was then corrupted or changed into *glamour,* which retained its association with mysterious enchantment. Early in our discussion of definition we referred to the Latin root word *definire,* which means "to set the limits or bounds of," and we are still expanding on that root meaning.

Etymology, the derivation of words, is often combined with explication. In "The Idea of a University" John Henry Newman derives his formal definition from the implications of its "ancient designation" as "Stadium Generale, or School of Universal Learning," and then explicates the terms in the formal definition so derived:

> I should draw my answer from its ancient designation of a Stadium Generale, or "School of Universal Learning." This description implies the assemblage of strangers *from all parts* in one spot — from all parts; else, how will you find professors and students for every department of knowledge? And *in one spot;* else, how can there be any school at all? Accordingly, in its simple and rudimental form, it is a school of knowledge of every kind, consisting of teachers and learners from every quarter. Many things are requisite to complete and satisfy the idea embodied in this description, but such as this a University seems to be in its essence, a place for the communication and circulation of thought, by means of personal intercourse, through a wide extent of country.

Through etymology, Newman arrives at the terms for his explication, *from all parts* and *in one spot.* We notice that he is concerned with the heart of definition, the essence of the thing. Arriving at the understanding of what a university is in essence, he can proceed to a formal definition in the last sentence. However, as Newman himself points out, his definition is not complete. "Many things are requisite to complete and satisfy the idea. . . ." Completion would involve the whole process of a university's workings and more.

A term's history, however, is more than etymology. Uses of a term whose form has not changed significantly through the ages can be an incisive way to essential meaning. For example, Carl Becker's paragraph defining democracy above is followed by this paragraph, in which history is combined with the technique of elimination:

> In this antithesis there are, however, certain implications, always tacitly understood, which give a more precise meaning to the term. Peisistratus, for example, was supported by a majority of the people, but his government was never regarded as a democracy for all that. Caesar's power derived from a popular mandate, conveyed through established republi-

can forms, but that did not make his government any the less a dictator-ship. Napoleon called his government a democratic empire, but no one, least of all Napoleon himself, doubted that he had destroyed the last vestiges of the democratic republic. Since the Greeks first used the term, the essential test of democratic government has always been this: the source of political authority must be and remain in the people and not in the ruler. A democratic government has always meant one in which the citizens, or a sufficient number of them to represent more or less effec-tively the common will, freely act from time to time, and according to established forms, to appoint or recall the magistrates and to enact or revoke the laws by which the community is governed. This I take to be the meaning which history has impressed upon the term democracy as a form of government.

Definitions as Paragraphs

The structure of Becker's paragraph resembles that of Newman's, although one combines history with elimination and the other combines etymology with explication. Like Newman's paragraph, Becker's also drives toward essential meaning: "... the essential test of democratic government has always been this. ..." We notice also that Becker ar-rives at his formal definition inductively, at the end, just as Newman does.

An expanded definition may proceed from the formal definition, which would be a general statement of meaning. It would then render this generalization by explication, analysis, description, exemplification, comparison, and elimination. This procedure corresponds to deductive reasoning. The paragraph we read on operations research, for example, is deductive. The formal definition is given at the outset, and each part of the definition becomes a topic for a paragraph of explication. The first paragraph of explication discusses "scientific method." The re-maining paragraphs explicate the terms "executive department," "quantitative basis for decision," and so on.

A paragraph that is developed inductively reverses the procedure. Beginning with an example, comparison, analogy, or some other method of expansion, the writer works toward a conclusive generalization that is the formal definition. This procedure is more dramatic than the other and involves the reader more in its process of discovery because the reader anticipates the outcome, which is the formal definition.

Whether the structure is deductive or inductive, a formal definition appearing within the paragraph serves as a core statement. When a definition extending to several paragraphs is approached deductively, the formal statement of definition appears in an introductory para-graph. When it is extended with an inductive approach, the formal statement of definition appears in a concluding paragraph.

EXERCISES

1. Compose sentences which incorporate informal definitions for each of the following terms:

aerobics	dancercise	colon (in grammar)
semicolon	sentence fragment	physics
chemistry	a soldier	humanities
experiment	love	adoration
a word	subjective	hurricane

2. Compose formal definitions for the terms in exercise 1, indicating class and adequate differentiae.
3. Compose an extended definition of any term in exercise 1 or another term that interests you and that you know something about. Write it as a complete essay, remembering that your intention throughout is to explain the term so that readers clearly understand your perspective on it.
4. Read the following extended definition:

   Greek architecture of the great age is the expression of men who were, first of all, intellectual artists, kept firmly within the visible world by their mind, but, only second to that, lovers of the human world. The Greek temple is the perfect expression of the pure intellect illumined by the spirit. No other great buildings anywhere approach its simplicity. In the Parthenon straight columns rise to plain capitals; a pediment is sculptured in bold relief; there is nothing more. And yet — here is the Greek miracle — this absolute simplicity of structure is alone in majesty of beauty among all the temples and cathedrals and palaces of the world. Majestic but human, truly Greek. No superhuman force as in Egypt; no strange supernatural shapes as in India; the Parthenon is the home of humanity at ease, calm, ordered, sure of itself and the world. The Greeks flung a challenge to nature in the fullness of their joyous strength. They set their temples on the summit of a hill overlooking the wide sea, outlined against the circle of the sky. They would build what was more beautiful than hill and sea and sky and greater than all these. It matters not at all if the temple is large or small; one never thinks of the size. It matters not — really — how much it is in ruins. A few white columns dominate the lofty height at Sunion as securely as the great mass of the Parthenon dominates all the sweep of sea and land around Athens.

   Edith Hamilton, *The Greek Way*

   Identify all the formal and informal definitions in this discourse, determine whether the piece is composed inductively or deductively, and note the rhetorical operations used to develop the definition.
5. Expand the following information to make a more detailed definition of what an urbanized area is:

This country is basically an urban society. More than six of every ten Americans (61.4 percent) live in urbanized areas. An urbanized area according to the Census Bureau is composed of an incorporated place and densely settled adjacent areas that have a combined population of at least 50,000.

The ten most highly populated urbanized areas, as listed in provisional data from the 1980 U.S. Census, are:

1.	New York	15,588,985
2.	Los Angeles–Long Beach, CA	9,477,926
3.	Chicago, IL	6,711,391
4.	Philadelphia, PA	4,114,354
5.	Detroit, MI	3,808,676
6.	San Francisco–Oakland, CA	3,191,913
7.	Washington, D.C.	2,762,423
8.	Boston, MA	2,678,473
9.	Dallas–Fort Worth, TX	2,451,555
10.	St. Louis, MO	1,848,363

Parade, September, 20, 1981

6. Look back over the assignments you have written in this course so far. Select a term where a definition is most needed (either a specialized term or one you used in an unusual or not widely accepted way) and revise the discourse. Include an extended definition of one well-developed paragraph in the new version.

7. Expand the following definition by focusing particularly on development of the differentiae:

A buyers' market is a market condition characterized by prices being at or near cost that occurs when the supply of commodities exceeds market demands.

SECTION TWO

Rhetorical Structure

Successful writers structure their discourse according to topic, audience, and aim in order to gain agreement from their readers. The aim in any discourse is usually not singular, but typically one aim dominates. The writer primarily wishes to inform, to persuade, to entertain or please, or to express personal emotions and opinions. Writing that emphasizes the subject, the giving of information about it, falls at the reportorial end of the rhetorical spectrum. Self-expressive writing falls at the affective end of the spectrum with its emphasis on the writer's hopes, fears, beliefs, opinions — the feelings of experience, we might say. Writing to entertain or please can fall anywhere between these poles, but usually falls toward the self-expressive pole. It emphasizes the aesthetic quality of language and story in essay, fiction, drama, and poetry. Writing to persuade falls in the middle of the spectrum, but usually closer to the factual pole. In all except the most self-expressive writing, an audience other than self is in mind. Persuasive writing particularly emphasizes the audience because the writer desires to get others to believe or act in some way. Most of the writing we do in the various college disciplines is like the writing produced in business and industry. It aims to be informative or persuasive.

Whatever the aim or consequent type of discourse, however, an effective rhetorical structure is necessary — a suitable beginning, middle, and ending for the whole discourse and for the units of its structure, its paragraphs and sentences. Well-structured, well-developed, and well-styled discourse brings to the writer at least a partial stay against confusion and at most the pleasure of understanding and of communicating.

In Section One we have seen how rhetorical operations can help a writer question the subject to discover a topic. From the answers, as we shall see in this section, writers formulate a core statement that launches the discourse and controls it. The core statement presents the topic in appropriate form, arouses the reader's curiosity, and makes a promise to fulfill that curiosity.

The middle elaborates, supports, or substantiates the topic by ordering the writer's thought into a coherent, consistent whole. Material is developed through the rhetorical operations — describing, narrating, comparing, classifying, analyzing, reasoning, and defining.

An ending brings to the discourse a sense of the promise fulfilled, a sense of completion.

Chapter 8 treats in detail ways to gain conscious control over good beginnings and how to formulate core statements, whether a proposition or thesis for an argument, a theme for an informative article or essay, or a statement of problem or purpose for a report. Chapter 9 discusses ways to bring a discourse to an appropriate end. Chapter 10 presents ways that words contribute to the whole stream of meaning in a discourse. Chapters 11 and 12 offer the means of constructing effective sentences and paragraphs to produce unity, coherence, emphasis, and variety in the whole discourse.

Chapter 8

Beginning

The structure of an effective piece of writing follows a basic pattern: beginning, middle, ending. Although a beginning may not be completed until ideas have been developed and concluded, nonetheless, the writer needs to have a starting place, a subject honed so that it is focused and manageable. To reach a starting place, you might ask questions of a general subject area, such as language. What aspect of language? Its use? Its structure? What type? Euphemisms? Idioms? Slang? What about college slang? You try to recall everything you know about college slang, and remember laughing when someone explained to you that "Jock Rocks" referred to "Comparative Geology," supposedly a supereasy course for athletes, and that "VD" was another name for "Voice and Diction." You further sharpen your subject by making a statement about it: "Nicknames for official course titles are a form of college slang." Through a series of focusing questions you have refined your subject and arrived at a core statement.

A core statement asserts something about a limited subject. In making this statement, you also make promises to the reader, even if that reader is only yourself when you begin, as is often the case. The most immediate promise in the statement about alternative course titles is to fulfill the reader's curiosity about the humorously descriptive names. However, there is at least one more promise implicit in the core statement. How were the names formed? "Con Law" is a shortened form for "Constitutional Law"; "PR" is an acronym for "Professional Responsibility"; "Star Wars" for "Introductory Astronomy" comes from borrowing. Such explicit and implicit promises attach to all core statements of written discourse, and it is the discourse itself that fulfills them. The statement is called "core" because the assertion it makes unifies the entire piece of writing, and everything written in the discourse can be related to it.

A central task of the beginning section is to catch the reader's interest and establish the core statement, but fulfillment of these tasks does not complete the beginning section. It is completed by asking other questions: "What am I doing with this statement?" "Why am I doing it?" "How am I doing it?" Thinking about these questions will lead to the significance of the statement, its background, and the means of developing it. Once you have gathered material in answer to these questions, you will need to choose the best way to present it to your reader. The core statement, for example, may be delayed until after its background and significance have been presented. Or in mulling over the questions, you might find a deeper possibility for the topic, choose to penetrate it, and find a core statement on another level. The forming of nicknames for courses might be seen as evidence of students' attitudes toward the courses and even education in general.

The core statement about nicknames for official course titles is an announcement of theme, which the rest of the paper will elaborate. Core statements may also be a thesis to be supported or proved, a statement of purpose, an announcement of what the writer hopes to accomplish, or a statement of problem, the definition of a limited subject to be investigated.

A good beginning helps both reader and writer. Whether the first sentence of a paragraph, the first paragraph of a paper, or the first chapter of a book, the beginning should tell readers what to expect and should indicate where the reading journey will take them. Often the beginning shows the way the promise will be fulfilled, giving an overview or plan of the paper. A good beginning also serves the writer as a checkpoint for later self-questioning. Each step of the way you will want to ask youself if everything you have written directly develops your core statement.

Writing a Core Statement

Some pieces of writing do not actually have a core statement, an explicitly stated idea that launches the discourse and controls it. Such an explicit statement is missing in the first few paragraphs taken from Lance Morrow's "The Weakness That Starts at Home" (*Time,* June 4, 1979):

> Toward dusk, their small boats go whumping across lakes and bays, rooster-tailing on fierce twin-100 outboards. Caravans of eight-miles-to-the-gallon RVs start homing off the interstates, their occupants damply chilled in the air conditioning, bathed in Dolly Parton from the tape deck. In shopping malls, supermarkets the size of National Guard armories feel as cold as meat lockers; housewives in pedal pushers go *Brr* as they load their carts with food incased in a wealth of nonreturnable glass, metal and paper. They shake their heads as they pay what the check-out computer demands of them, and pile the groceries into broad-beamed station wagons. At home, the automatic icemaker sighs and clatters in the kitchen; the automatic washer discos through the spin cycle. The microwave starts dinner.

Meantime, in winding ropes of bright capillaries, the slow and over-powered commuting cars poof home. From above, at night, American cities look like garishly jumbled jewelry strewn up and down the land-scape; in the centers, empty highrises of piled diamonds glow, great spar-klers kept alight for the cleaning women, for the admiration of passing planes.

For years foreigners have regarded America (enviously, contemptu-ously) as a shocking wastrel, besotted with its own resources, lighting its cigars with $1,000 bills. In winter, visitors remark, the U.S. is always too warm indoors, and in summer always too cold; in a flawless little Amer-ican parable, Richard Nixon used to turn up the White House air condi-tioning full blast and then start a cozy blaze in the fireplace.

Although a core statement is missing here, we have a strong sense of a controlling idea, which emerges more clearly through accumulating details in the essay. Because Morrow wrote the essay fully aware of his controlling idea and all the elements that bear upon it, his repeated documentation of the mindless wasting of resources leads readers to formulate their own core statement. Here is one possibility: "A certain slackness in the character of today's Americans, the fault of Americans themselves and their leaders, can be cured only when they assume re-sponsibility for conducting their lives."

Omission of a core statement is usually poor practice for all but the most skillful and experienced writers. For the inexperienced, discourse without a core statement usually suffers from randomness. Thoughts just wander about, seeking attachment.

Even after inexperienced writers narrow a subject to a manageable focus, they may simply start to write without knowing exactly what point they will demonstrate. The result can read like this:

> The English language is deteriorating because the percentage of children
> watching television is increasing. Many children have watched hundreds
> of hours of TV before they have learned to read. They want to watch
> *Walt Disney* or *Family Classics* instead of reading the very same story.
> All they do is sit and listen. While watching TV, the children are becom-
> ing ignorant and lazy. They are being trained to accept violence too.
> There is far too much violence on TV. . . .

The paragraph begins with a statement about the deteriorating language and ends with a statement about violence on television. There is no connection between the two within the paragraph. This writer is foundering in a sea of ideas, and consequently drowns the reader. Al-though writers with years of professional experience can select and organize material without the guidance of an explicit core statement, they usually include it early in their discourse. They know the core statement acts as a directional signal for them and their readers.

A core statement is often a single sentence, but it may be part of a sentence, or more than one sentence. It may be a thesis that will be supported, argued, or proved: "Sharks are really loving creatures." Or it may merely state the theme of a description or sketch: "I became fascinated with sharks one afternoon at the aquarium." It may state a problem under investigation: "Our curriculum was compared with that of similar programs abroad to determine the possibility of student exchanges." Whatever the type of core statement, it obligates the writer to a restricted point about a subject and serves as a guide for selecting and relating material as the discourse is developed. Directly or indirectly, everything must develop the core statement, advancing it in some way.

A good core statement tells the reader something new or significant; or it provides a new slant on a familiar subject; or it may introduce a new explanation, definition, analysis, or description not before available. It helps answer the reader's question, "Why am I reading this?" If the core statement fails to raise expectations of learning or experiencing something beyond the old and familiar, the reader will be inclined to stop reading. If you say, "Integrated circuits are the hottest and most competitive field of advanced industrial technology," not many readers who are abreast of current news will read on. The statement would be news to very few of them. Instead of repeating what the reader knows, the writer may provide significance to the established facts by asserting a point about the facts: "In order to counteract the Japanese challenge to American leadership in the semiconductor field, American companies must increase their current 10 percent reinvestment in research and development." This thesis not only promises something the reader does not know, it has an argumentative edge. You may not gain your readers' affection with statements that take a stand, but at least you will not bore them. Perhaps a colloquial example would be more familiar: "My last summer job was clerking nine to five at Smith's Sporting Goods." That's news, but certainly not significant to many readers. However, many might find significance in the human foibles promised by this statement: "Trying to outfit a team of ten-year-old disco roller skaters was the climax of my summer job."

When a piece of writing is produced on demand, the requirement itself leads to the core statment. It is built into the demand, and needs only refining. For example, if a supervisor says, "We need to know whether the modified transmission is better than the standard transmission," the writer of the report need go only one step further to decide "better on what grounds" and produce this core statement:

> In this investigation the modified transmission is compared with the standard item for durability and operating characteristics.

However, when a writer chooses the topic, he or she must determine what definite direction the topic will take.

Not all writers proceed in the same way. Some writers pick a subject, then read and take notes, determining their controlling idea —

the main point they want to make—somewhere during this prewriting process. Other writers pick a subject and decide immediately what their controlling idea will be. With the controlling idea determined in advance, writers can gather supporting material directly and more efficiently. This procedure, however, may shut off alternative paths that might emerge through the interplay of general reading and thinking.

What can happen, and often does, is that the processes overlap. You may, like other writers, establish a controlling idea in order to start, and then modify it, sometimes drastically, during your mental probing, reading, note taking, and writing. Writing is a discovery process just as scientific research is, with temporary hypotheses advanced for the purpose of discovering their validity. The information generated for this purpose often suggests another, more valid hypothesis. Everywhere along the spectrum of rhetoric, writers discover what they want to write in the writing of it. Often in the process you may consign painfully produced words to the wastebasket just as other writers do, but the effort is not wasted because it leads to a point worth making.

All effective core statements, then, have two fundamental characteristics: they present a narrowed subject, and they make a point about it that promises the reader some reward in reading. All core statements are written as declarative sentences.

In other ways, though, core statements differ from one another because they take different forms in differing situations. The core statement may present the controlling idea in a thesis, a theme statement, or a statement of purpose or problem.

Statement of Theme or Thesis

A statement of theme announces what the piece is about—what will be explained, analyzed, described, defined, or presented in a combination of ways. A thematic statement is information oriented. Readers are expected to absorb the material presented, not take issue with it. Thematic statements often appear in genres toward the factual end of the spectrum of rhetoric, where less effort at convincing an audience is necessary:

> I will now give a very brief account of three great classes of coral-reefs; namely, atolls, barrier, and fringing-reef, and will explain my views on their formation. . . .
>
> Charles Darwin, "Keeling Islands: Coral Formations"

> It is widely believed that every word has a correct meaning, that we learn these meanings principally from teachers and grammarians (except that most of the time we don't bother to, so that we ordinarily speak "sloppy English"), and that dictionaries and grammars are the supreme authority

in matters of meaning and usage. Few people ask by what authority the writers of dictionaries and grammars say what they say. . . .

Let us see how dictionaries are made and how the editors arrive at definition. . . .

S. I. Hayakawa, Language in
Thought and Action

Thematic statements also appear toward the other end of the spectrum, in, for example, personal essays, where the theme should appeal to feelings in the audience as well as to understanding, and thus will require greater effort at conviction, emotive as well as logical:

> During the time she was "working" with Papa Gassion, I didn't know very much about Edith. I knew she'd lived in a whorehouse, I knew what whores were — I saw them every day, I gabbed with them — but I didn't know what a "house" was. My mother said, "It's a hotel whores are shut up in." I decided they were numbskulls to shut themselves up like that when one's so free and happy in the street, but I didn't think any more about it; I didn't give a damn. At twelve I had other problems besides thinking about my fifteen-year-old sister.

Simone Perteaut Piaf, Piaf: A
Biography

The last line of this introductory paragraph to the second chapter of Edith Piaf's biography is the core statement. The chapter will delineate the twelve-year-old's problem in this situation.

In personal narratives, whether essay, autobiography, biography, or fiction, thematic statements are usually less explicit than Piaf's. The controlling idea — what the book is about — tends to lie just below the surface, inferred from the events of the narrative. The theme of John O'Hara's *Appointment in Samarra,* for instance, is the meeting of one's fate; the theme of Ibsen's *The Wild Duck* is the inability of humans to stand very much reality; and the theme of Frost's "Acquainted with the Night" is spiritual isolation in an unfathomable and nonethical universe.

Unlike a theme statement, a thesis statement is issue oriented. It takes a particular stance or viewpoint on a subject that will be proved or defended. "Bushes" is a general subject, "sturdy, evergreen bushes," a more limited subject. "Sturdy, evergreen holly bushes are a sensible choice for a privacy hedge" is a thesis. It is a proposition that requires a substantiating argument because readers can agree or disagree.

"Crime" is a general subject. Here are some possible thesis statements suggested by "crime":

> FBI tactics in Abscam, the year-long investigation of bribery and conflict of interest in Congress, irreparably damaged the reputations of public officials before they had been formally accused of a crime.

People turning back electric meters cause electric companies to lose millions of dollars a year.

Convicted prisoners who are released from prison still owing their fines should be sentenced to imprisonment if they do not adhere to strict repayment schedules.

Computers are vulnerable to fraud because of flaws in the security techniques devised, ironically, to help banks avoid fraud.

The first statement argues "irreparable" damage to reputations. The second asserts a cause for money loss. Both demand supporting evidence for their claims. In the third the burden is to show why prisoners should be punished again if they do not pay their fines. In the final example, the writer must prove that the suspected flaws actually exist and make the computers vulnerable. Because these arguments are clearly announced and can be pursued, these are all workable theses. In addition, they all promise something new and significant to readers.

These, on the other hand, are not usable theses:

People are more worried about crime now than twenty years ago.

Crime ought to be controlled.

Criminals are simply people who were brought up poorly.

Although the argument is clearly announced in each case, none can be pursued convincingly. Evidence for the first would be difficult or impossible to find; the second is a truism; the third is too general. Nor do any present a new or significant idea. They arouse yawns rather than curiosity. What is judged new and significant depends to a large extent upon the audience. What is novel and meaningful to one person may not be to another. As a rule of thumb, however, if a generalization sounds familiar to you, it will make a weak thesis statement.

This also is not a usable thesis, but for a different reason:

A review of the criminal justice system in the United States will reveal a hodgepodge of conflicting laws, regulations, and punishments.

It is significant and promises something new, and it can be argued convincingly. The problem with this thesis is the size of its promise. Unless you attempt several volumes, you cannot possibly handle all the material to be gathered and the arguments to be made.

A theme or thesis statement may occur at the beginning, middle, or end of an opening paragraph or may be delayed to a subsequent paragraph. Generally, the shorter the discourse, the earlier the core statement appears. When the theme or thesis statement begins the first paragraph, it introduces a deductive arrangement; at the end of the paragraph, it concludes an inductive arrangement. Those placed in the middle of the opening paragraph are both: the writer leading into the statement from particulars, inducing it, and then applying it with more particulars, deducing from it. A core statement placed in the middle of a paragraph loses the emphasis of a beginning or final paragraph position; the effect is more subtle.

Delayed theme or thesis statements often are preceded by necessary groundwork to prepare readers, to ease their understanding by first situating them in the background. Often the delay is intended to create suspense and arouse the reader's interest. One way is simple narration:

> Working a typewriter by touch, like riding a bicycle or strolling on a path, is best done by not giving it a glancing thought. Once you do, your fingers fumble and hit the wrong keys. To do things involving practiced skills, you need to turn loose the systems of muscles and nerves responsible for each maneuver, place them on their own, and stay out of it. There is no real loss of authority in this, since you get to decide whether to do the thing or not, and you can intervene and embellish the technique any time you like, if you want to ride a bicycle backward, or walk with an eccentric loping gait giving a little skip every fourth step, whistling at the same time, you can do that. But if you concentrate your attention on the details, keeping in touch with each muscle, thrusting yourself into a free fall with each step and catching yourself at the last moment by sticking out the other foot in time to break the fall, you will end up immobilized, vibrating with fatigue.
>
> Lewis Thomas, The Lives of a Cell

Another good way to build interest is to use an apt quotation:

> It is necessary to grasp the fundamental fact that women have had the power of naming stolen from us. We have not been free to use our own power to name ourselves, the world, or God. The old naming was not the product of dialogue — a fact inadvertently admitted in the Genesis story of Adam's naming the animals and the women. Women are now realizing that the universal imposing of names by men has been false because partial. That is, inadequate words have been taken as adequate. . . .
>
> To exist humanly is to name the self, the world, and God. . . .*

> In a society where men have controlled the conceptual arena and have determined social values and the structure of institutions, it is not surprising that women should have lost the power of *naming*, of explaining and defining for ourselves the realities of our own experience. In a patriarchal culture, men define (explain, analyze, describe, direct) the female as they define nearly everything else. The issue is not only that men perceive women from masculine perspectives, but that given the nature of social-

---

*Mary Daly, *Beyond God the Father* (Boston: Beacon Press, 1973), p. 8.

ization, all members of society, including women, perceive the female from the prevailing masculine perspective.

> Sheila Ruth, "The 'Naming' of
> Women," *Issues in Feminism*

Other interest builders are unexpected or startling observations:

> Yes, there was a real King Arthur and yes, he did lead the Britons.
> Romantic writers have mixed fact with fiction to give us the Arthur we know — lord of glittering Camelot, chairman of the Round Table, et al., but that rather tempting picture is none too accurate.
>
> Brian Antonson, "On the Trail of
> Arthur, the 'Once and Future
> King,' " *Los Angeles Times,* May
> 25, 1980

Or facts, figures, and statistics:

> It was, after all, only a harmless little New York City shopping spree — the kind every woman fantasizes about now and then. There was a charming silver service for $43,000, a selection of antique jewelry for $234,000, and a diamond-and-ruby necklace from Van Cleef & Arpels on Fifth Avenue for $100,000. That was just a sampling of one day's purchases. According to handwritten records of disbursements signed by her personal secretary and made public last week, First Lady Imelda Marcos spent almost $4.5 million in New York City from May to July 1983.
>
> "Picking Fifth Avenue Clean,"
> *Time,* March 31, 1986

Or predictions:

> If magic be defined as something "produced by secret forces in nature," and "secret" in turn defined as something "revealed to none or to few" (and these are legitimate definitions), then magic is not likely to be diminished by all the science we can muster. Research may provide us with answers, but these answers forever lead to new and more profound questions; and as our knowledge of the world grows more and more vast, most phenomena that can be said to be "revealed" will of necessity be revealed to fewer and fewer of us. . . .
>
> Howard Ensign Evans, "In Defense
> of Magic: The Story of Fireflies,"
> *Life on a Little Known Planet*

Or rhetorical questions:

> First of all, you know what a weasel is, right? It's a small, slimy animal that eats small birds and other animals, and is especially fond of devouring vermin. Now, consider for a moment the kind of winning personality he must have. I mean, what kind of guy would get his jollies eating rats and mice? Would you invite him to a party? Take him home to meet

your mother? This is one of the slyest and most cunning of all creatures: sneaky, slippery, and thoroughly obnoxious. And so it is with great and warm personal regard for these attributes that we humbly award this King of All Devious the honor of bestowing his name upon our golden sword: the weasel word.

> Paul Stevens, "Weasel Words: God's Little Helpers," *I Can Sell You Anything*

Or a firm statement of opinion to arouse reader's feelings:

> Any education that matters is *liberal*. All the saving truths and healing graces that distinguish a good education from a bad one or a full education from a half-empty one are contained in that word. . . .
>
> Alan Simpson, "The Marks of an Educated Man," *Context 1*, no. 1 (Spring 1961)

Often an interest builder is not necessary, and the writer can garner enough interest by beginning with the background itself:

> For the past two decades, Clyfford Still has enjoyed a reputation as the Coriolanus of American art. No other living artist has so vociferously loathed the art world as a system. None has managed to keep a closer control over the fate of his work. Since the 1940s, when he emerged as one of the founding fathers of abstract expressionism, Still has jealously guarded his output, releasing few paintings to collectors, rarely showing in private galleries, insisting on conditions of display that few museums were prepared to meet. Consequently, his farm outside Westminster, Md., houses most of his immense *oeuvre;* and though he is almost 75, his work has yet to be adequately studied. All these ingredients — the large talent, the inaccessibility, the crusty pride — have made Still a somewhat mythic figure in American painting and put him in a position to dictate terms to any museum in the U.S. So it is with his current retrospective at New York's Metropolitan Museum of Art, a panorama of 79 huge canvasses, Wagnerian in ambition and theme.
>
> Robert Hughes, "The Tempest in the Paint Pot," *Time*, November 26, 1979

If the background is extensive, the writer may use only some of it to lead toward the thesis statement, make the statement, and then apply the statement through the rest of the background material. Introductory chapters of books often have this form.

Beginning writers sometimes defeat themselves at the start with weak openings, such as apology: "I don't know very much about the Equal Rights Amendment, but I will discuss what will happen if it is passed." Or they unconsciously create mysteries by referring to something outside their discourse: "From the given list of words I have found seven different categories." Or the theme to be developed or thesis to be proved is too obvious at the start: "Utopian societies are ideal places to live." Such beginnings do not entice readers to continue.

It is wise to hold a beginning as temporary, as a working hypothesis and background necessary to propel you into the material. Usually it is best to write the beginning you want others to read after the paper is well along or even completed. Then you will find you have a choice of two or three types of beginning. You may then experiment to find the most suitable one for what you have already said or what you have carefully planned to say.

Statement of Purpose or Problem

The development and support of a core statement is the purpose of all discourse along the spectrum of rhetoric. Theses are most often used with forms occurring near the middle of the spectrum — the reasoning segments — and themes are often used with forms toward the emotive end. Explicit statements of purpose are used with forms near the factual end of the spectrum. They are rather simple formulations telling the reader precisely why the material is being presented, that is, why the writer is writing it and why the reader should read it. When the writing proposes to show the solution of a problem, the definition of that problem may substitute for the statement of purpose.

Theme and thesis statements always imply rhetorical purposes — to instruct, to convince, to explain, to entertain, to move. These purposes are the differing ways of bringing readers into agreement with writers along the spectrum of rhetoric. In essays, stories, and poems, the reader becomes aware of the purpose through indirection. Your purpose may be to convince an audience to vote for a candidate, but you are unlikely to announce it baldly. You might build an argument on this thesis: "Mark Sold is aggressive, intelligent, and an active participant in community affairs." The argument would follow the syllogistic pattern, of course: "We need aggressive, intelligent, and active people in office; Sold is aggressive, intelligent, and active; therefore, vote for Sold." In discourse toward the factual end of the spectrum, however, statements of purpose may combine with theme or thesis to form a special kind of core statement:

> The purpose of *Eight Modern Essayists* is to give students the opportunity to become familiar with the work of a few outstanding writers. In the belief that through such familiarity their own writing will greatly improve. . . .
>
> William Smart, Preface to *Eight Modern Essayists*

If this statement of purpose were rephrased as a thesis, "Students' writing improves through familiarity with the works of outstanding writers," then the author would have to argue to convince the reader of this assertion, but conviction is not his purpose.

Explicit statements of purpose are chiefly found in reports, especially functional reports, those offering some application of established information rather than presenting new information. The recording of events is often of this nature. Functional reports tend to be assigned, not the result of writing out of free choice. Statements of purpose may promise to instruct users of equipment, to direct an operation, to report the events of a meeting or field trip, to narrate a process, to describe the status of a project, or to announce a new product. In the example below, the purpose is to instruct. This statement of purpose promises to show users how to operate and maintain a tractor:

> This operator's manual presents the necessary information for operating and maintaining the tractor. Its primary purpose is to assist the operator in lubricating and adjusting the tractor for daily and seasonal operation.

Discourses reporting on investigations have at their core a statement or definition of a problem. Problems may range from determining the effectiveness of a new policy to assessing the applicability of a literary theory or judging how to apportion a personal budget for college. Unlike a functional report, the aim of an investigative report is always to establish new information. Investigative writing, however, usually contains a great many so-called facts, and thus it is referred to as a "report." Actually, the investigative report is charged with the discovery of meaning about facts; therefore, it is closer to the reasoning middle of the spectrum of rhetoric than the reportorial or factual end. Because it is considered reporting, the core statement, which is the definition of the problem, is often accompanied by a statement of purpose, although the purpose is quite obvious: to report the investigation. However, if the writer breaks this purpose statement into its component parts, the result will be valuable to the reader as a guide through the report. By giving an overview stating why the investigation was undertaken, how the results were obtained, what they mean, and what may be done in consequence, the writer states for the reader not only the report's purpose but the plan of the report as well.

A formal definition underlies the statement of a problem. As we saw in Chapter 7, a formal definition names a term, places it in a class of similar terms to which it belongs, and then distinguishes it from all other members of that class, as in this example:

> An oakleaf cluster [term] is a military decoration [class] made of bronze or silver clustered oak leaves and acorns, signifying a subsequent award to the basic decoration [differentiating features].

Statements of problem adapt this pattern. In defining the problem, the subject of the problem is taken as the term to be defined, placed in a class of similar problems, and then differentiated from all other members of the class, as in this example:

> The purpose of this test was to determine the effectiveness of the computer in receiving range input data and transmitting correct elevation data to the camera.

The problem here is the purpose of the test (not the purpose of the report). The subject of the problem is the computer. The class of the problem is determination of effectiveness. The rest of the statement isolates this particular problem from other determinations of effectiveness for this computer or any other. Here is another example (cited previously):

> In this investigation, the modified transmission is compared with the standard item for durability and operating characteristics.

The modified transmission is the subject of the problem. Comparison is the class of the problem. And the durability and operating characteristics are the differentiating features.

The definition of the problem is the core of the investigative report. As with other core statements, it may comprise the first sentence of the introduction, or it may follow inductively after the background of the problem has been rendered, creating a sense of development and even a touch of suspense.

Significance of the Core Statement

If readers are not given the significance of the core statement — the subject and what the author has to say about it — they can hardly be expected to read on. But the significance is not always stated. In personal essays, stories, plays, and poems, the author may not state the significance. It is, rather, part of the experience readers are supposed to absorb through the developing theme or thesis as represented in plot, characterization, mood, and scene. Because of such indirection, literary discourse may be more difficult to understand than other types of writing, but this difficulty is ameliorated by its high interest factor. It has built-in significance because it is about the human condition, an advantage not enjoyed by discourse ranging toward the factual end of the spectrum. It is, in other words, intrinsically appealing at the outset.

Writers of arguments, informative essays, and investigative and functional reports, on the other hand, must work harder to capture and sustain the reader's interest. They must tell the reader directly what their intentions are and why the piece should be read. In essays and articles the first paragraph or paragraphs usually lead up to the core statement and amplify the significance it promises. Sometimes these beginnings entertain as well as inform, by means of anecdote or narrative. They may also present the history of the idea to be discussed or of another author's thesis that will be disputed. In reports, the introductory section usually spells out the significance directly and flatly by means of background, scope, and plan.

Background

"This is an important problem." "Reading these instructions is vital." Why is the problem important? Why is careful reading of the instructions vital? The answers begin to provide the background material. In the background, writers can provide a basis for readers to understand new material or findings that will appear later and to decide whether or not the subject is important or vital. Without background materials, the writer is unconsciously employing totalitarian tactics: "It is important because I say so."

Backgrounds are usually generated by asking questions of the subject. What use will readers make of the facts presented? What should readers know before they can understand the implications of the core statement? How do the facts and findings of the report apply to a larger world? What could these facts and my attitude or viewpoint upon them mean in my reader's personal or professional life? Answers tell the reader the significance of the discourse. Commonly, background materials consist of history, need, and theoretical principles.

In the investigative or research report, background materials work to isolate the problem under study from all others. They render the situation in which the problem exists, its history, the need for a solution, and the theoretical principles upon which it rests. One of these elements will usually dominate the others, and not all of them are necessary in every background. The history of the problem tells how it evolved, what other investigations have revealed about the problem, and its current status and meaning. Need for a solution is expressed through an analysis of the situation. The theoretical principles upon which the problem rests give significance only if they isolate the problem and do not bury it. Only a review or abstract of theory is presented, not specific details, which are better presented at the point of use in the report.

Scope

The scope of a piece of writing is the extent of information the report will cover — the answers to the questions the report raises. Scope is limited by time and space; these limitations are imposed by the writing situation and may be indicated implicitly or explicitly.

At the reasoning and emotive portions of the spectrum of rhetoric, the scope is usually implicit as part of the core statement, as in this example:

> If one assumes that Arnold was destined to become a traitor, as virtually every American historian has done, then it is a simple matter to dismiss his military achievements as accidents, since no traitor could really be a good American general. Everything he did on behalf of the American cause can be written off as a prelude to his treason.
>
> But it is the purpose of this history to assume that we Americans are sufficiently mature to be able to understand the pressures that drove Benedict Arnold into the arms of the British. Remember, from King George's point of view, a view shared by many Americans loyal to the crown during the Revolution, men like Arnold were merely returning to their true allegiance.
>
> Brian Richard Boylan, *Benedict Arnold: The Dark Eagle*

Here, the scope is understood in the phrase, "pressures that drove Benedict Arnold into the arms of the British." Of all the things to be said about Benedict Arnold this book will confine itself to these pressures.

Discourses at the factual end of the spectrum of rhetoric tend to indicate their scope in a separate statement. Scope may be stated inclusively: "This report will analyze available alcoholic treatment programs, concentrating on the most promising option for the company in dealing with its employees' alcohol problems." Or the scope may state both what it will include and what it will exclude: "This report will analyze only the most popular alcoholic treatment programs that offer likely options for our employee alcohol problems. It does not consider any others." Or a scope statement may demonstrate the proportions or emphasis of what is included: "This report will analyze in depth the most popular alcohol treatment programs. Less popular programs will receive only cursory review."

Better writers attempt more personal and less machinelike statements of scope:

> For the past dozen years, my colleagues and I at the National Institute of Mental Health have been studying the brain's response to sensory inputs of all kinds. I have been particularly interested in how the brain reacts to variations in the intensity of different stimuli — pain, light, the size of objects.
>
> Monte S. Buchsbaum, "The Sensoristat in the Brain," *Psychology Today*, May 1978

This example illustrates another advantage of deft writing. It is economical. A closer examination will show that the writer has not only stated scope in terms of the whole project — his particular interest as opposed to his colleagues' — but at the same time has delivered his core statement.

Plan

All discourse needs to be planned, even when the technique used is a stream of consciousness. The plan may be altered as new ideas are discovered and new avenues explored during the thinking, writing, and revising processes, but unless the writer knows how the piece will proceed, it will tend to be incoherent. A separate plan statement at the beginning of the discourse may direct both writer and reader, but often a plan statement does not appear or is merged with the core statement.

The form of a discourse affects the plan. Fictions, for example, reveal their plan, their plot, as they proceed; they never state in advance where the story will go. Most essays and arguments — forms in the reasoning portion of the spectrum — also reveal their plan or structure as they develop the controlling ideas. If they have an explicit thesis, they subtly suggest the direction of development:

> More than three centuries ago a handful of pioneers crossed the ocean to Jamestown and Plymouth in search of freedoms they were unable to find in their own countries, the freedoms we still cherish today: freedom from want, freedom from fear, freedom of speech, freedom of religion. Today the descendants of the early settlers, and those who have joined them since, are fighting to protect these freedoms at home and throughout the world.
>   And yet there is a fifth freedom — basic to those four — that we are in danger of losing: *the freedom to be one's best.*
>
>> Seymour St. John, "The Fifth
>> Freedom," *Saturday Review,*
>> October 10, 1955

We do not know exactly what St. John's plan is, but we can predict that he will tell us why we are losing the fifth freedom and probably what to do about it. Sometimes, especially when classification is the means of development, the plan will appear more boldly as part of the core statement, as in this example:

> Eventually the whales, as though to divide the sea's food resources among them, became separated into three groups: the plankton-eaters, the fish-eaters, and the squid-eaters.
>
>> Rachel Carson, "Types of Whales,"
>> *The Sea Around Us*

We would be surprised if Carson talked about groups of whales that eat anything other than what she mentions.

Although reports are the form most likely to include a separate plan statement, no statement of plan is necessary in short reports with narrow scope. It can become form for form's sake rather than for the reader's sake. Nor is a separate statement necessary when the plan has been unfolded in stating the purpose or rendering the background. Usually, however, in a long report when the plan has not been made clear, a separate statement is necessary. Even here, though, the plan is not a table of contents and is not responsible for mentioning everything. The plan indicates the order in which the elements of the discourse will be treated. It may emphasize some elements over others, and it may even exclude some — for example: "This report describes the results of our search for gold deposits in the old mine at Cripple Creek." Certainly we can anticipate that the search itself will be described, but only the results are mentioned in the plan statement for emphasis. Some statements of plan are more complete:

> The report first discusses three proposed locations for a new bicycle path, then the effects on traffic patterns in the community observed, next the preferences of the path's potential users. Finally, it makes recommendations.

In an investigative or research report, the statement of plan indicates the general procedures used to attack the problem and obtain the data, what the data are and where they may be found, and whether or not conclusions and recommendations are included and where. Often, however, conclusions and recommendations are summarized in the beginning, before the reader arrives at the statement of plan.

In Chapter 19 you will find a model technical report illustrating the presentation of background, scope, and plan. The writer must judiciously establish significance through these elements. Usually, the less readers know about the subject or problem, the more background material they will require; that is, more will be required to bridge the connection between the information they already have and the information you wish to give them. On the other hand, if they are knowledgeable about the situation, they understand the what and the why and the how, then they will find background statements superfluous and even insulting. Yet, even in these circumstances, some background is needed, perhaps more to establish the writer's credibility than to impart meaningful information. Obviously, writers must carefully consider audiences in proportioning and emphasizing the elements of the introduction that show the significance of the controlling idea or core statement.

EXERCISES

1. Limit the following subjects and write theme and thesis statements for each, stating what the discourse will be about and then asserting something to be proved or defended.

telephones   friendship
computers   photography
nuclear energy   shoddy craftsmanship

2. Label each of the following a theme or thesis statement. Then be prepared to discuss their quality. Do they promise an interesting, significant piece of writing? Can they be supported convincingly or developed adequately? Are they manageable within a 500–750 word limitation?

The Japanese attack on Pearl Harbor on December 7, 1941, was precipitated more by the Japanese nation's desire to control the Pacific seaways than by its alliance with the Axis bloc.

My favorite vacation spot is in upper Michigan.

The Huntington Library in San Marino, California, has the largest single collection of Gainsborough paintings.

Marriage has become impermanent since the mid-point of the twentieth century because society in general is impermanent.

The social security system, originally designed to provide supplementary income to people over sixty-five, has become overburdened with other demands on its funds that it was never meant to sustain.

All college students should take more than one writing course to acquire basic writing skills or improve the ones they already have.

3. Take another look at our spectrum of rhetoric:

Reporting   Explaining   Evaluating   Arguing   Essaying   Fictionalizing   Lyricizing

Place each theme or thesis statement you have written in exercise 1 and those in exercise 2 on the spectrum of rhetoric.

4. What is the theme of this poem? State it in a declarative sentence.

Richard Cory

Whenever Richard Cory went down town,
We people on the pavement looked at him:
He was a gentleman from sole to crown,
Clean favored, and imperially slim.

And he was always quietly arrayed,
And he was always human when he talked;
But he still fluttered pulses when he said,
"Good-morning," and he glittered when he walked.

And he was rich—yes, richer than a king—
And admirably schooled in every grace:

In fine, we thought that he was everything
To make us wish that we were in his place.

So on we worked, and waited for the light,
And went without the meat, and cursed the bread;
And Richard Cory, one calm summer night,
Went home and put a bullet through his head.

Edwin Arlington Robinson

5. Analyze several magazine advertisements and write in a declarative
   sentence the implied thesis of each.
6. Find the theme or thesis statement in the following:

Watching television, you'd think we lived at bay, in total jeopardy, surrounded on all sides by human-seeking germs, shielded against infection
and death only by a chemical technology that enables us to keep killing
them off. We are instructed to spray disinfectants everywhere, into the air
of our bedrooms and kitchens and with special energy into bathrooms,
since it is our very own germs that seem the worst kind. We explode
clouds of aerosol, mixed for good luck with deodorants, into our noses,
mouths, underarms, privileged crannies — even into the intimate insides
of our telephones. We apply potent antibiotics to minor scratches and
seal them with plastic. Plastic is the new protector; we wrap the already
plastic tumblers of hotels in more plastic, and seal the toilet seats like
state secrets after irradiating them with ultraviolet light. We live in a
world where the microbes are always trying to get at us, to tear us cell
from cell, and we only stay alive and whole through diligence and fear.

Lewis Thomas, The Lives of a Cell

The Administration's Bakke brief is the most ominous document concerning race to issue from the federal government in this century. It says race
is "ordinarily" irrelevant to an individual's rights, and "generally" an
illegitimate basis for allocating opportunity. . . . But for the forseeable future America must cultivate "race-consciousness."

George F. Will, "The Bakke Brief:
A Call for Racial Bias," Los
Angeles Times, September 19, 1977

Once, in a Dry Season, I wrote in large letters across two pages of a
notebook that innocence ends when one is stripped of the delusion that
one likes oneself. Although now, some years later, I marvel that a mind
on the outs with itself should have nonetheless made painstaking record
of its every tremor, I recall with embarrassing clarity the flavor of those
particular ashes. It was a matter of misplaced self-respect.

I had not been elected to Phi Beta Kappa. This failure could scarcely
have been more predictable or less ambiguous (I simply did not have the
grades), but I was unnerved by it; I had somehow thought myself a kind
of academic Raskolnikov, curiously exempt from the cause-effect relationships which hampered others. Although even the humorless nineteen-

year-old that I was must have recognized that the situation lacked real tragic stature, the day that I did not make Phi Beta Kappa nonetheless marked the end of something, and innocence may well have been the word for it. I lost the conviction that lights would always turn green for me, the pleasant certainty that those rather passive virtues which had won me approval as a child automatically guaranteed me not only Phi Beta Kappa keys but happiness, honor, and the love of a good man; lost a certain touching faith in the totem power of good manners, clean hair, and proven competence on the Stanford-Binet scale. To such doubtful amulets had my self-respect been pinned, and I faced myself that day with the nonplused apprehension of someone who has come across a vampire and has no crucifix at hand.

Although to be driven back upon oneself is an uneasy affair at best, rather like trying to cross a border with borrowed credentials, it seems to me now the one condition necessary to the beginnings of real self-respect. . . .

Joan Didion, "On Self-Respect,"
Slouching Towards Bethlehem

There are some kinds of success, the painter Edgar Degas once remarked, that are indistinguishable from panic. So it seems with the present boom in the art market. For the past 15 years or so, collectors, dealers, auction houses and their willing accomplices, journalists, have been moved to pleasure, then wonder, and now to a sort of popeyed awe at the upward movement of art prices. If art was once expected to provoke *un nouveau frisson,* a new kind of shudder, its present function is to become a new type of bullion. Thus, we are told by art industry flacks, people now respect art. They flock to museums to see it; its spiritual value has been confirmed, for millions, by its wondrous convertibility into cash. You can't argue with it. It *means* something if somebody pays $2.5 million for a lummocking spread of icebergs by Frederic Church, a salon machine whose pedestrian invocations of the sublime are not worth one square foot of a good Turner.

Robert Hughes, "Confusing Art
with Bullion," *Time,* December 31,
1979

7. You are assigned to write a report on the factors involved in appraising a fire when an alarm sounds in the fire station. What process would the fire fighter in charge go through? Write a purpose statement for your report.

8. Some local businessmen are sponsoring a competitive float trip down the Potomac River. Winners will be in two categories: one award will go to the most unusual decorative raft, and another award will go to the raft which completes the journey first. You attended a meeting at which you and five other people discussed the project. You have been chosen to report on the meeting. Write a statement of purpose for your report.

9. Assume the same situation as in exercise 7. This time you must investigate a problem connected with the fire appraisal process. Write a statement of problem, and, if you wish, a separate statement of purpose.

10. Assume the same situation as in exercise 8. This time, though, you have been chosen to state the problem that a committee of six will investigate. Write a statement of problem, and, if you wish, a separate statement of purpose.

11. Take one of the theme or thesis statements you wrote in exercise 1. Invent some background material to accompany your statement. Experiment placing your thesis statement at the beginning, middle, and ending of an introductory paragraph.

12. Now rewrite your introductory paragraph using two or three different types of beginnings. Analyze the beginnings to discover which is the most suitable for your hypothetical discourse and which will be most likely to keep your reader reading.

13. Assume that you have applied for a job, been interviewed, and been rejected. You want to determine the factors that affected the employer's choice of employee so you can enhance your chance of being accepted when interviewed in the future. Mentally conduct your investigation. You might write a questionnaire and conduct interviews with the employer and others in the field, for example. Write the beginning of your investigative report. Show the significance of your subject; include background, and scope and plan statements. You may want to include a statement of purpose too.

14. Choose a subject, limit it, then write four core statements for it, one of each type.

15. Write an opening paragraph for each core statement, placing your core statement at the end of the paragraph. Generate background or use some other appropriate means to lead into your core statement. Then experiment with the position of each core statement, placing it first in the paragraph, then in the middle of the paragraph. Rewrite your paragraphs as necessary to accommodate these shifts.

Chapter 9

Ending

Every piece of writing must come to an end. To end is to reach the goal intended at the start, to give the reader a sense of a promise fulfilled.

In some types of discourse the sense of a promise fulfilled is reached without a formal ending. The proper way to finish then is simply to stop. Some functional reports, such as operating manuals, for example, have no formal ending. The last section, the completion of the instruction, functions as the ending. Descriptive-narrative discourse usually stops without formality, but with some sense of completion, as we can see in the ending of Thomas Hardy's *Tess of the d'Urbervilles*:

> Upon the cornice of the tower a tall staff was fixed. Their eyes were riveted on it. A few minutes after the hour had struck something moved slowly up the staff, and extended itself upon the breeze. It was a black flag.
> "Justice" was done, and the President of the Immortals, in Aeschylean phrase, had ended his sport with Tess. And the d'Urberville knights and dames slept on in their tombs unknowing. The two speechless gazers bent themselves down to the earth, as if in prayer, and remained thus a long time, absolutely motionless: the flag continued to wave silently. As soon as they had strength they arose, joined hands again, and went on.

For all the activity here, there is no really new action. It is a scene commemorating the book's theme and the author's attitude toward it. Even if you are unfamiliar with Hardy's novel, you can sense that all is winding up. " 'Justice' [is] done," and there will be no more sport with Tess. The novel's heroine is dead. The passage has words of finality (*done, ended*) and the tone and slow, stately movement of an elegy.

Often a short expository piece, say 500 words or less, stops with the last point under discussion. Brevity removes the need to recapitulate or make elaborate connections for the reader. A formal ending is not strictly needed. The sense of the ending is accomplished as the core statement is fulfilled in the discourse. The reader and writer have, after all, traveled the same informative road, and a formal ending seems excessive. In longer discourse, however, the reader must be reminded of points of interest along the road traveled. Simply stopping leaves the reader uneasy, the thrust of thought unresolved:

> But probably most student writers come to grief not with words that are colorful or those that are colored but with those that have no color at all. A pet example is *nice*, a word we would find it hard to dispense with in casual conversation but which is no longer capable of adding much to description. Colorless words are those of such general meaning that in a particular sentence they mean nothing. Slang adjectives like *cool* ("That's real cool") tend to explode all over the language. They are applied to everything, lose their original force, and quickly die.
>
> Beware also of nouns of very general meaning, like *circumstances, cases, instances, aspects, factors, relationships, attitudes, eventualities,* etc. In most circumstances you will find that those cases of writing which contain too many instances of words like these will in this and other aspects have factors leading to unsatisfactory relationships with the reader resulting in unfavorable attitudes on his part and perhaps other eventualities, like a grade of "D." Notice also what "etc." means. It means "I'd like to make this list longer, but I can't think of any more examples."
>
> Paul Roberts, *Understanding English*

These final paragraphs of the last section, "Colorless Words," of Paul Roberts' essay continue the structure and tone of preceding sections and so leave readers suspended, wanting some generalization for the specifics they have been accumulating as they read, some signal that Roberts has finished.

Formal endings show that the promise of the core statement has been fulfilled. They reinforce the agreement the writer has been drawing between the ideas presented and the reader. Another important dimension of a formal ending is aesthetic fulfillment. An ending completes the circle, replacing anticipation with resolution. Therefore, most discourse has some sort of formal close. The basic types are summary, conclusion, prediction, and recommendation. Although we distinguish these types for study, in practice endings usually combine them.

Summary

Summary endings gather together the main points of the discourse. The summary does not merely repeat the points advanced earlier but restates them in broader, newly focused terms and shows the relationships between them. Summaries typically end essays and articles that explain or inform, and they are the most common endings of functional reports.

Bertrand Russell uses a summary ending for his discussion of "Space-Time" in *The ABC of Relativity:*

We may now recapitulate the reasons which have made it necessary to substitute "space-time" for space and time. The old separation of space and time rested upon the belief that there was no ambiguity in saying that two events in distant places happened at the same time; consequently it was thought that we could describe the topography of the universe at a given instant in purely spatial terms. But now that simultaneity has become relative to a particular observer, this is no longer possible. What is, for one observer, a description of the state of the world at a given instant, is, for another observer, a series of events at various different times, whose relations are not merely spatial but also temporal. For the same reason, we are concerned with *events,* rather than with *bodies.* In the old theory, it was possible to consider a number of bodies all at the same instant, and since the time was the same for all of them it could be ignored. But now we cannot do that if we are to obtain an objective account of physical occurrences. We must mention the date at which a body is to be considered, and thus we arrive at an "event," that is to say, something which happens at a given time. When we know the time and place of an event in one observer's system of reckoning, we can calculate its time and place according to another observer. But we must know the time as well as the place, because we can no longer ask what is its place for the new observer at the "same" time for different observers, unless they are at rest relative to each other. We need four measurements to fix a position, and four measurements fix the position of an event in space-time, not merely of a body in space. Three measurements are not enough to fix any position. That is the essence of what is meant by the substitution of space-time for space and time.

Russell's summary ending is longer than usually justified by the length of the chapter (approximately 2,500 words), but the concepts are difficult. They bear copious, clarifying restatement. Most summaries, though, should not be long. A long summary is a contradiction in terms. A major pitfall to avoid in a summary ending is including too much information. As you reread your discourse to write the summary, re-viewing rather than re-saying your points should encourage brevity and discourage excessive repetition.

Final summaries sometimes extend themselves for another reason. As the discourse is reviewed in retrospect, it may reveal missing pieces, which the writer adds to the summary. If missing statements are uncovered, they need to be incorporated in the discourse itself before touching on them in a concluding summary. Readers may suffer long introductions because they anticipate what is to come, but there is no anticipation at the end. A final summary signals that your discourse is concluding; be brief.

Yet short summaries offer their own pitfall: a disconnected sequence of statements. One solution is to state only the most important points in carefully connected sentences, implying the rest. Willard Gaylin uses this strategy to summarize briefly at the end of "Being Touched, Being Hurt" (*Psychology Today,* December 1978):

> Being touched is the awareness of an unexpected sign of love from an unexpected source. It is a sign that someone who need not care does. But whether he cares or not is of minor relevance. We are not bound to him. There is no legitimate potential for real harm in the discontinuation of that affection.
>
> But we can be harmed by the withdrawal of love from members of that supporting network of friends and family on whom we all depend for our emotional survival. We can really be damaged by feelings of hurt, which signal the absence of such caring and identification from one who ought to be displaying them.

Another solution, one that is appropriate only for formal reports of a business or technical nature, is to restructure a short, choppy summary into a list. To retain the effect of expository style, however, the list needs an introduction that holds the items together, and, usually, a closing paragraph, as in the following example:

> We started out talking about the purpose of a company. This was considered to be important because a purpose sets the tone of operation for the entire company and in particular the engineering department. We then went on to discuss eight responsibilities that a chief engineer might have in our hypothetical, but nevertheless progressive and modern industrial concern. These eight were:
>
> 1. To advise top management on engineering policy.
>
> 2. To organize the department economically to provide the services required.
>
> 3. To supervise construction work.
>
> 4. To recommend contractors and consulting engineers.
>
> 5. To provide engineering services to operating departments.
>
> 6. To advise on product design and development and on process design and development.
>
> 7. To procure and develop competent engineers.
>
> 8. To devote an appropriate amount of time to constructive thinking.
>
> There are many versions of the responsibilities of the chief engineer or of an engineering department. However, if an engineering department fulfills these eight responsibilities, engineering has done its part in carrying out the purpose of the company.

Effective summaries are particularly important at the close of argumentative discourse. In fact, the old Greek term often used for the ending of an argument, *anakephalaiosis,* meant "recapitulation." We feel in argumentation a particularly keen desire to isolate the key points we have made earlier from their supporting details in order to hammer them home one by one and refresh the memory of our readers. Observe Clarence Darrow summarizing his argument for agnosticism:

> When every event was a miracle, when there was no order or system or law, there was no occasion for studying any subject, or being interested in anything excepting a religion which took care of the soul. As man doubted the primitive conceptions about religion, and no longer accepted the literal, miraculous teaching of ancient books, he set himself to understand nature. We no longer cure disease by casting out devils. Since that time, men have studied the human body, have built hospitals, and treated illness in a scientific way. Science is responsible for the building of railroads and bridges, of steamships, of telegraph lines, of cities, towns, large buildings and small, plumbing and sanitation, for the food supply, and countless thousands of useful things that we now deem necessary to life. Without skepticism and doubt, none of these things could have been given to the world.
>
> *Verdicts Out of Court,* edited by
> Arthur and Lila Weinberg

Summaries, of course, also occur elsewhere than at the end of discourse. Writers gather up threads in order to weave them anew more than once in a longer work, especially in histories and complex technical or scientific writing, but periodic summaries are useful for more familiar subjects too. They enhance readability by reviewing points that may have slipped the reader's mind or become hazy; they make necessary connections and provide bundles of thought for readers to carry as they plunge on to new material. (See also Chapter 17.)

Conclusion

Another type of ending draws general conclusions based on the various points made in the discourse or evaluates them. Conclusions are typically attached to discourse that attempts to reason or persuade, as well as to any type of investigative report. Like an overall summary of a discourse, conclusions should offer no totally new ideas. They should, however, offer a new perspective on the points that are being drawn together; they should offer some kind of illumination.

If the core statement has been clearly formulated and the development coherently rendered as it progresses, the reader should be fully prepared for the author's conclusions as they are presented. Conclusions serve the same aesthetic purpose as summaries. They complete the circle. They should shift the reader's activity from absorption of knowledge to recognition of that knowledge, and with recognition, the sense of an ending. When you start your conclusion, try to avoid "in conclusion" or any similar bald announcement. Try for a subtler, less conventional transition. Joyce Maynard achieves this in her essay "Looking Back: Virginity" (*Looking Back*) by picking up on two key words that have dominated the text:

> Privacy — and freedom — can be maintained only by disregarding the outside pressures. Freedom is choosing, and sometimes that may mean choosing not to be "free." For the embarrassed virgin, unsure now whether her mind is her own ("Do I really want to go to bed with him, or do I simply want to be like everybody else?") — for her, there's a built-in test. If she really wants to, on her own, she won't have to ask herself or be embarrassed. Her inexperience and clumsiness will have, for him, a kind of coltish grace. Our grandparents, after all, never read the *Kama-sutra,* and here we are today, proof that they managed fine without it.

Many writers find reiteration of a key word an appropriate way to lead into their conclusions. Other common transitions to conclusions are phrases on the order of these: "what we have been considering is"; "such evidence leads us to"; "our solution is"; or a reference to the core statement.

In longer pieces of expository discourse we may find tentative or partial conclusions along the way. The conclusions at the end, then, emerge from these miniconclusions and any material following the last miniconclusion, bringing everything into an overall generalization.

For certain kinds of discourse and subjects, the final commentary provides a chance to wax somewhat grandiloquent, to appeal more to the emotions than is appropriate elsewhere, although it is not wise to pull out all the emotional stops. Overindulgence breeds suspicion. How much emotional appeal you make depends upon your subject, readers, and occasion. For example, if a doctor were presenting a new medical technique in *The Journal of the American Medical Association,* any resort to emotional appeal would break the traditional tone of objectivity and hence alienate readers. However, if a doctor were arguing for or against a proposed government plan to nationalize the health care industry, we can easily imagine an impassioned conclusion. Arguments, especially those on highly controversial issues, often generate strong appeals to the emotions as they close. So do statements of personal belief or testimony:

> It takes a while, as I watch the surf blowing up in fountains at the end of the field, but the moment comes when the world falls away, and the self emerges again from the deep unconscious, bringing back all I have recently experienced to be explored and slowly understood, when I can converse again with my own hidden power, and so grow, and so be renewed, till death do us part.
>
> May Sarton, "The Rewards of Living a Solitary Life," *New York Times,* April 8, 1974

May Sarton appeals strongly to the emotions in this closing paragraph, raising the essay to almost lyrical heights.

Conclusions, like summaries, are best kept short. Once you have signaled to your reader that you are concluding, do not dawdle, especially to add extraneous thoughts not justified by the development of your discourse. Keep your commmentary in proportion to your beginning, certainly no longer and usually somewhat shorter.

Again, as with summaries, brevity may contribute to a series of disconnected short expository statements. In an essay or article, you will need to use transitions to smooth your conclusions into a unified, flowing whole. A report, however, offers the alternate choice of listing your conclusions:

1. The Johnson Motors VA–108–3 Engine successfully completed the 500-hour test outlined in Specification MI–E 13929.

2. Performance, durability, and wear compared favorably with similar characteristics of engines being used by Star Division.

3. Use of a porous chrome layer in cylinder barrels, positive valve rotators, and flanged heat-riser tubes should correct the deficiencies noticed in engine performance.

4. Available data are insufficient to assess the effects on cylinder life loss of the chrome overlay.

5. Endurance characteristics of the generator end of the spark plug are unsatisfactory.

6. Octane requirements of the engine under normal use conditions will be satisfied by Specification MI–G–3056A gasoline.

An introduction is not necessary when a list of conclusions is set off with a heading, but if one is included, a simple restatement of the overall problem can introduce the list rather than, "It is concluded that." Whether you list the conclusions or not, the most effective arrangement is to work from the most to the least significant, as in the list just quoted.

Formal reports and essays often join the summary and conclusion to bring the discourse to a close. The major points of the discourse are drawn together and related briefly to provide a springboard for relevant conclusions. For example, Willard Gaylin's summary of "Being Touched, Being Hurt," quoted earlier, leads to these conclusions:

We are extraordinarily sensitive in conditions central to our survival, and we survive in great part through our loving relations. Our "receptors" for feeling hurt are therefore finely tuned and low-threshold mechanisms. When such hurts occur too frequently, they demand an examination of ourselves and those with whom we share a common fate. Either we are getting less from our loved ones than we are entitled to, or expecting too much.

Predictions

Many reports and articles forecast future possibilities on the basis of conclusions reached. Although we cannot know the future and predictions frequently go awry, we are often compelled to polish our crystal balls. Educated guesses about the future proliferate in such writings as annual reports from companies, articles about political campaigns, financial outlooks, and reports of intensive investigations in science, technology, and medicine. Preliminary and periodic reports by their nature call for predicting the outcome of a project or investigation. Any studies calling for changes in laws must necessarily evaluate future impact. Predictions are common endings because they are effective, taking readers beyond the confines of the discourse itself and giving them food for thought:

> In the long run the most significant advances may come from learning how the cardiovascular system works on a cellular and chemical level. Says Goodman: "If we can understand more about the disease process, we can do more to retard or prevent it. Cholesterol's role in heart disease should become clearer in 1983 when the first results from a National Heart, Lung and Blood Institute–sponsored study begun in 1976 become available. Pharmacologist Philip Needleman of Washington University in St. Louis predicts that within five years doctors will begin testing drugs that limit the clogging of blood vessels initiated by platelets. Says he: "This is not a remote dream. This is a strategy that will have important applications quickly."
>
> Cardiologist Thomas James of the University of Alabama in Birmingham anticipates still other strides in basic knowledge. "In the next ten years," he says, "we will understand why artery walls degenerate and why hypertension happens, and develop the means for preventing both." Heredity's complex role in the cardiovascular illness will be better understood as well. Says Robert Brandenberg of the Mayo Clinic: "We're probably just on the edge of a whole new series of breakthroughs."
>
> He may be right if recent progress is any measure. Cardiovascular science has come a long way from 30 years ago, when all that could be done for a heart attack patient was to prescribe rest for four to six weeks. If innovations in diagnosis and treatment continue at the same impressive pace, cardiovascular disease may one day yield its claim to being the nation's No. 1 killer.
>
> Anastasia Toufexis, "Taming the
No. 1 Killer," Time, June 1, 1981

This writer could be sure her readers would be interested in future possibilities for saving lives after reading about the various advances in diagnosis and treatment of heart problems that were saving lives when the article was written.

Predictions may stand alone as an ending, growing out of implied conclusions, or they may follow explicitly stated conclusions or a summary plus conclusions.

Recommendations

Recommendations are most often actions to be taken or not taken. They grow out of conclusions and often take the form of a challenge:

> As teachers of the art of expression, we can have no greater goal than to teach students to think effectively, to make relevant judgments, to discriminate values, and to write with as much grace and precision as possible. We should pay more attention to the humanizing of ordinary language than we have in the past. We might take our cue from that first composition teacher, Shakespeare's Prospero, who successfully taught Caliban language. "I endow'd thy purposes with words," he tells Caliban, "that made them known." This also should be our aim — to endow student purposes with words that make them known.
>
> Frank D'Angelo, "Regaining Our Composure," *College Composition and Communication*, December 1980

When conclusions of an investigation indicate that some course of action should be taken, a separate section for recommendations can be added at the end of the report. If the conclusions are presented in paragraph form, the recommendations may be couched in the same form or listed. If the conclusions are listed, then the recommendations should be listed too. The order of presentation should match that of the conclusions even if each conclusion does not lead to a recommendation. The conclusion section of the report about the Johnson Motors Engine presented previously results in these recommendations:

1. The Johnson Motors AV–108–3 Engine should be considered qualified for use by Star Division.

2. Porous chrome cylinder overlays, positive exhaust valve rotators, and flanged heat-riser tubes should be used on production engines.

3. Further testing should be conducted to determine the effects of loss of the chrome layer or performance of the barrel of the cylinder.

4. Endurance characteristics of the generator and the spark plugs should be investigated.

5. A production version of the engine should be subject to a 500-hour test.

When separate conclusions and recommendations result in repetitive statements, they should be combined into one section headed "Conclusions and Recommendations," as in this example:

> Despite the initial high cost of word-processing equipment, decreased labor costs over the long term make buying word-processing equipment more economical than hiring extra secretaries. Daily costs are less too when automatic equipment is used because fewer documents require re-

typing when changes are necessary. In addition, quality is held consistently higher with automatic equipment.

The problem in converting to a word-processing system lies in the need to match the particular kind of work and quantity of documents produced to the appropriate word-processing equipment. Therefore, we recommend that XYZ Corporation authorize a study to determine the specific needs of its field offices and the particular word-processing systems that will satisfy those needs.

Essays and articles follow the natural sequence of events with summary, conclusions, predictions, or recommendations or a combination of two or more of these given in order at the end of the discourse. Formal reports, however, often change the sequence. A summary may precede the report for the convenience of readers who have a need to know only the gist of the report. The sense of completion comes with the filling out of the items summarized as the report is developed. If the conclusions are of paramount importance in a report, they will come first, and the sense of completion is achieved through the process of proof inside the report. When recommendations are the major point of the report and are thus inserted first, they may precede the conclusions. They also are substantiated for the reader in the development of the report. In many cases the entire order of presentation may be reversed.

Justification for such a reversal stems from concern for the audience. Although all readers are most interested in the outcome of a discourse, one particular audience — the one that is composed of executives and administrators — uses a report rather than reads it. Placing key information first accommodates the needs and desires of these readers.

Final Sentences

Short expository discourses or fictional pieces, which do not have fully developed endings, typically employ a sentence or two of finale to close smoothly. Even fully developed paragraph endings may add a sentence or two of finale. Some types of finales often encountered in either case are the following: an evaluation of the material presented, a restatement of the core statement (as in the Bertrand Russell selection quoted on p. 124), a reference to the title of a piece (as in the predictive ending of the *Time* article on cardiovascular disease, p. 129), an apt quotation or illustration, a telling question, a brief challenge, an ironic twist, a bit of humor or unexpected turn of thought, a return to a beginning image, or a statement of some larger truth.

A functional report, for example, could evaluate the information presented:

The techniques discussed are not, of course, the only approach to the problems presented in the manufacture of printed circuits. They do, however, present a method that is fast and efficient in layout, advanced in its component use, and flexible enough to permit as little or as much mechanical bracing as may be required.

An essay by Jill Aeschbacher exploring her problems as a writer, "It's Not Elves Exactly" (*College Composition and Communication*, October 1973), ends with a quotation:

> On the other hand, all that has kept me sane, if I am, in the hard moments of the wait is this:
>
> > There is here no measuring with time. No year matters and ten years are nothing. Being an artist means, not reckoning and counting, but ripening like the tree which does not force its sap but stands, confident in the storms of spring, without the fear that after them may come no summer. It does come, but only to the patient, who are there as though eternity lay before them, so unconcernedly still and wide. I learn it daily, learn it with pain to which I am grateful. *Patience* is everything.
>
> Rilke, Letters to a Young Poet

Robert Ardrey's "Light from an Ape's Jaw," from *African Genesis,* ends with a question:

> I had put the jaw on Dart's desk, just before me, and it jiggled. Dart stood at the window looking out at the storm while I contemplated the remnant of antique assassination. Evidence for murder lay clearly before me, but the mere question of murder shrank rapidly in significance. A specter far and away more grisly entered the dark periphery of my consciousness. Long before the time of man, had this creature surrendered his life to a weapon?

An essay on the disintegration of our cities might well end with a challenge (emphasized by repetition):

> The mess won't get swept away tomorrow. But we *can* change our cities, we *can* upgrade the quality of life in the ghettos, we *can* abolish the slums. We *can* make our cities the pride of our nation again.

An essay by Lewis Thomas, "The Attic of the Brain" in *Discover* (November 1980), ends with an unexpected humorous turn of thought:

> I have tried to think of a name for the new professional activity, but each time I think of a good one I forget it before I can get it written down. Psychorepression is the only one I've hung on to, but I can't guess at the fee schedule.

An article by Loren Eiseley, "The Star Thrower" in *The Unexpected Universe,* ends with a return to the beginning image:

I knew it from the man at the foot of the rainbow, the starfish thrower on the beach of Costabel.

And D. H. Lawrence ends "Why the Novel Matters," from *Phoenix: The Posthumous Papers of D. H. Lawrence,* with a larger truth:

> For out of the full play of all things emerges the only thing that is anything, the wholeness of a man, the wholeness of a woman, man alive, and live woman.

Suitable endings, however full or brief they are, depend upon the rhetorical situation, the combined interaction of writer, reader, subject, and occasion. The techniques for ending presented in this chapter can be applied to most writing situations you will encounter. With practice, you will be able to devise your own variations, because all ending techniques are actually variations of a single idea — conveying a final illumination that gives a sense of completion.

EXERCISES

1. Refer to the exercises at the end of Chapter 8 (p. 117).

   a. Assume that you have completed your investigative report on the factors determining an employer's choice of employee (exercise 13) and that you will share your information with other prospective applicants. Write an ending consisting of summary, conclusions, and recommendations.

   b. Take your four core statements for which you wrote introductory paragraphs (exercises 14 and 15). Write a closing paragraph for each assumed essay, experimenting with two different finales for each.

2. Read the following concluding paragraphs and be ready to comment on them. What type of endings do they have? How well do they achieve a sense of completeness?

   a. Watching with wonder — and no doubt a little envy — the whirling star named Sagan, some of his colleagues feel that he has stepped beyond the bounds of science. They complain that he is driven by ego. They also say he tends to overstate his case, often fails to give proper credit to other scientists for their work and blurs the line between fact and speculation. But they probably represent a minority view. Most scientists, increasingly sensitive to the need for public research, appreciate what Sagan has become: America's most effective salesman of science. His pitch in *Cosmos* — and indeed in all his popularizing — is classic Sagan. Says he: "Science is a joy. It is not just something for an isolated, remote elite. It is our birthright." What scientist could disagree?

   "The Showman of Science," *Time,*
   October 20, 1980

b. Marlow ceased, and sat apart, indistinct and silent, in the pose of a medieval Buddha. Nobody moved for a time. "We have lost the first of the ebb," said the director, suddenly. I raised my head. The offing was barred by a black bank of clouds, and the tranquil waterway leading to the uttermost ends of the earth flowed somber under an overcast sky — seemed to lead into the heart of an immense darkness.

Joseph Conrad, *Heart of Darkness*

c. In conclusion, excess risk for development of pneumococcal disease in diabetics has not been established. Once the disease is incurred, however, the presence of diabetes as a coexisting illness greatly increases the risk of mortality. Our results show that diabetics respond normally to immunization with pneumococcal polysaccharide vaccine. Whether protection is afforded remains to be proved.

Thomas R. Beam, Jr., M.D., and others, "Antibody Response to Polyvalent Pneumococcal Polysaccharide Vaccine in Diabetics," *Journal of the American Medical Association,* December 12, 1980

Chapter 10

Word Sense

Words are like individual beads, unimportant on their own but as critical to a complete discourse as beads are to a necklace. Like a jeweler stringing together beads, a writer stringing words into phrases, sentences, and paragraphs is hoping for a fine finished product. Effective writers carefully choose words that are exact, specific, concise, vivid, and appropriate, always keeping in mind their subject, audience, and purpose in their desire to represent the true image of their thought.

The English language has a hydralike quality, its words ever shifting, absorbing new meanings and discarding old, acquiring popularity and losing it, progressing from colloquial to informal to formal acceptance — or stopping along the way. English also has more words than any other language in the world, some 600,000, compared with, say, German, which has about 250,000. These characteristics make English flexible and creative, but they also make it a difficult medium to master. If you have not bemoaned your own limited vocabulary, you have undoubtedly heard college classmates or friends bemoan theirs. Such feelings of inadequacy stem from the knowledge that a rich vocabulary and a sensitivity to words are basic to effective expression.

When people lack these advantages, they give only vague indications of their meaning despite the resources at hand. Does this person's description of an event sound familiar to you?

> The shadow came right across as big as . . . came right across the sun.
> Boy, it was . . . well, something. I tell you, man, it was really *something*.

Only those in control of language, those who can put their ideas and feelings and images into words that convey clear meaning, can communicate fully with someone else. The best way to accumulate a wide vocabulary and use it effectively is to read widely in many fields and to write often on many subjects. You can enhance the process by jotting down unfamiliar words that you hear or read and checking their meanings in the dictionary. Also you might explore denotative and connotative meanings of both familiar and unfamiliar words in various dictionaries, thesauruses, and usage guides.

135

Dictionaries, Thesauruses, Usage Guides, and Other Sources

You know, of course, about standard desk dictionaries, such as *Webster's New Collegiate Dictionary* and *Webster's New World Dictionary*. Others that may not be as familiar are useful sources and are fascinating for the background information they offer. One of these is the *Oxford English Dictionary*. The *OED*, a historical dictionary published in England in 1928 and followed by four supplements, is immensely useful for tracing etymologies, that is, derivations of words and their changes in form and usage through hundreds of years, with illustrative quotations.

Have you ever wondered about the closeness of the words *guarantee* and *warranty*, their partial interchangeability, and why we have both? One reason is that speakers of English have always been ready borrowers, sometimes even borrowing the "same" word twice. Such words are called "doublets." *Guarantee* and *warranty* are a doublet. *Warranty* came from Norman French and later *guarantee* from Parisian French, a dialect in which the initial sound had changed from the Old French *w* to *g*. Since such doublets are uneconomical, through time these words have come to be used with slightly different senses. A warranty assures a product's integrity for a stated time period and the replacement of defective parts during that period. A guarantee generally assures the quality of a product, sometimes with a promise of reimbursement. *Warranty* is used more often as a noun, *guarantee* as a verb. The first sentence below is the one we would most likely hear, not the second:

Some U.S. automakers *guarantee* their cars with a one-year *warranty*.

Some U.S. automakers *warranty* their cars with a one-year *guarantee*.

Information of this sort is available for all the words you are likely to encounter in the *OED*, if the words were English in 1933 and were considered fit to print at the time. *A Dictionary of American English on Historical Principles*, a complement to the *OED*, gives histories of words as they have been used in the United States.

Both of these resources are worth browsing through. Even if you are among the few for whom the origins and histories of words hold no fascination now, you may find yourself engrossed once you trace a few words. Examine the origin and evolution of such words as *uh, huh, knight, lady, bonfire, shirt,* and *skirt* for starters. And take a look at all the pages devoted to *do* in the *OED*, more than for any other word.

Specialized dictionaries also exist — for example, those covering the vocabulary of law, education, medicine, psychology, and even computers. Some you may want to consult, depending on your needs and field of interest, are *Chambers Dictionary of Science and Technology,*

Dorland's Illustrated Medical Dictionary, the *McGraw-Hill Dictionary of the Life Sciences,* and the *Random House Dictionary of New Information Technology.*

A thesaurus — *Roget's International* is the best known — is another valuable word source to have on hand. Since a thesaurus categorizes words according to ideas rather than listing them alphabetically, you can go to it with an idea of what you are looking for, say, a word that means something like "high in stature," and search for the precise word. You could start with "high" in the index and select its nearest synonym to what you have in mind, say, *noble.* If *noble* is not exactly the word you want but is close, you can turn to the numbered section for *noble* and scan a series of associated words where you may find one that better suits your context. If no word is exactly what you are looking for, but one is closer than the original, you can in turn look that word up in the index and continue your search.

Teachers sometimes caution students to avoid a thesaurus because if they rely on it to supply "big" words, they may use unfamiliar words inaccurately. The trick is to choose only words that you recognize, that are in your reading (passive) vocabulary if not your writing (active) vocabulary, and begin to use them actively. Sometimes, even with this much familiarity, you will err in your choice. However, taking such risks at times and profiting from the criticism when you err increases your facility with words.

A thesaurus is also useful for ascertaining correct spelling. As some weak spellers have discovered to their sorrow, if they do not know the correct spelling of at least the first three letters of a word, they cannot find it in the dictionary. On the other hand, if the spelling of a word escapes you but you can remember a close synonym and its spelling, the thesaurus can come to your aid. As you look through associated words, your eyes will often alight on the correctly spelled word.

Although some people have been arguing for years that some of the niceties of English need not be observed because misuse is common even among writers published in the best journals and magazines, distinctions of certain kinds should be observed because your readers expect them. Dictionaries, of course, provide some indication of usage. But for detailed answers to complex questions of usage — such as when to use *because* instead of *since, comprise* instead of *compose, compared with* instead of *compared to,* or any of hundreds of other fine points of the language — usage guides are the place to go.

Wilson Follett's *Modern American Usage* is a standard, but two others of interest are Adrian Room's *Dictionary of Distinguishables and Confusibles* and Roy Copperud's *American Usage and Style: The Consensus.* Window-shop in these books and you will find it hard not to come away with a bargain insight or two.

Exactness

The precise use of language requires not only a wide vocabulary but the right word for the right situation and audience. "Do not write so that your words may be understood, but write so that your words *must* be understood" is a proverb attributed to many sources, including an unnamed Roman orator. It apparently represents widespread agreement that we need to select the exact word for each element in our thought, not a word that only approximates an element or gives a vague or wrong impression.

Denotation and Connotation

Accurate knowledge of the denotations and connotations of the words we use is critical to precise word choice. The denotation of a word is its essential, dictionary meaning. The connotations of a word are the senses that accrue to the word. Denotations express the generic meanings. They are objective, neutral. Connotations express attitudes connected with words and are subjective, emotional. For example, we might say, "He kept vigil over his property," or, "He kept watch over his property." *Watch* is comparatively neutral; *vigil* on the other hand, carries with it a sense of ceremony, religion, and intensity. *Watch* is more informal than *vigil* and less poetic. And so forth. Careful writers, who want to convey not only the accurate meaning but the accurate sense of a word, heed connotations when they choose a word. Consider, for example, these sets of words:

thin	citizen
svelte	patriot
slender	chauvinist
skinny	jingoist
lean	flag-waver
scrawny	
frail	
lanky	
gaunt	
underweight	

The words heading the lists, *thin* and *citizen,* are the most neutral. The other words carry stronger, differing connotations and allow or deny different applications that need to be kept in mind if we are to use them effectively in context. *Svelte,* for example, is inappropriate to describe a child or male of any age. *Lanky,* on the other hand, is more appropriate for a male stranger or young adult. On another level, *svelte* is more formal than *lanky, patriot* than *flag-waver. Frail* is more emotional than *underweight.* Furthermore, a consideration that goes beyond stylistic appropriateness is affective appropriateness. How will a reader respond to the word chosen? From the examples above, *patriot* might please, *chauvinist* offend.

Gauging reader response is never easy because individual experiences shape attitudes towards words. Some people recoil when they simply read the word *snake* or *blood.* How we react to *Republican, Democrat, liberal, conservative,* or *reactionary* depends upon our past experiences. Yet although we cannot precisely judge a particular reader's responses, we can take into account at least the generally known responses to certain connotations of words and avoid those words that will displease (unless our intent is to displease—then we would choose them deliberately).

Abstract/Concrete and General/Specific Words

Many problems with exact word choice, however, come not from choosing words with the undesirable connotations but from preferring abstract or general words to concrete or specific words.

Concrete words such as *crimson, screech, acrid, salty,* and *corrugated* appeal to our five senses—sight, hearing, taste, touch, and smell. Abstract words such as *justice, freedom, happiness,* and *sorrow* refer to qualities and ideas and appeal to our intellect. Unlike *concrete* and *abstract, general* and *specific* are relative terms rather than exclusionary terms. Generality and specificity are matters of degree. General words apply to many things, specific words to fewer things. When compared to *poodle, dog* is a general word, but when compared to *animal, dog* is a specific word. *General* and *abstract, concrete* and *specific* are often used in tandem, but *general* does not necessarily correspond to *abstract,* nor *specific* to *concrete. Dog, poodle,* and *animal* vary in generality (or specificity, depending on your starting point), but all are concrete words. *Creation* and *product,* on the other hand, are both abstractions, but *creation* is more general than *product.*

All things considered, writing that is more concrete and specific is easier to understand than writing that is general and abstract, but all four types of words are needed in writing. They simply are used with different purposes. Abstractions are needed, especially when we address serious issues and discuss complex ideas in religion, science, technology, philosophy, psychology, and so on. When William Faulkner accepted the Nobel Prize for literature in 1950, he spoke in abstract terms of the writer's obligation to concentrate on "the old verities and truths of the heart . . . love and honor and pity and pride and compassion and sacrifice."

When writers want to soften bad news, say, information about a loss or rejection of a request, generalities are more effective than specifically blunt statements. For example, if a personnel manager decided to turn down a job applicant, she would be much less likely to offend her reader by writing, "You were among many fine candidates who applied for the job; however, several of these candidates have qualifications and experience more in line with the requirements of our company," rather than, "We had many candidates with better than a 2.5 in accounting."

Specific and concrete words paint a more vivid picture; they are critical to narrations and descriptions. When Faulkner got down to fulfilling the writer's obligation he spoke of in Stockholm, he made concrete and specific those "old verities and truths" in his evocative stories and novels.

Abstractions and generalities usually tend to dull writing and even obscure meaning when used extensively. Many a muddy idea hides behind a curtain of generalities and abstractions. When abstract and general words must be used, they should be supported by specific and concrete words. For example, this general, abstract statement — "Attempts to identify the gifted and talented have a long, though somewhat unsuccessful, history" — needs to be supported by specifics:

> As early as 2200 B.C. the Chinese used formal examinations to find competent, talented people to fill powerful government positions. The examinations tested adults' proficiency in six "arts" — music, archery, horsemanship, writing, arithmetic, and the rites and ceremonies of public and private life.

It is always wise to look for abstract and general words as you revise your writing, keeping a particularly sharp eye for abstract words that are subjects of sentences. (The few specific, concrete words that hit the wrong note are, in general, immediately obvious.) Try to eliminate any you can, and make sure that the abstractions you decide to keep are clear and backed with specifics.

Nouns and Verbs

The basic sentence pattern in English is subject-verb-(object). The subject gives old information, arousing curiosity about what new will be said of it; the predicate gives the new information, satisfying that curiosity. Verbs move the sentence from beginning to end. An imprecise choice of verb can blight a whole sentence.

Because the same word can stand for different but similar things, writers with poor vocabularies, especially in professional writing where abstractions abound, can blunder into statements that they do not mean and never know the difference:

> The environmental testing describes an evaluation technique and program whereby smog control equipment on vehicles, cars, buses, and anything else are tested for their effect in an environmental situation.

The first problem we notice in this sentence is faulty use of *describe*. Testing cannot describe anything. The writer must have meant that environmental testing is a technique that can be used for evaluation. Reading on, we notice that the noun *vehicle* is misused. Because all the examples are vehicles, whatever *vehicle* stands for is vague. What is the writer trying to say? Probably this:

> The test program evaluates smog control equipment on vehicles, such as cars, buses, and trucks, for their effect on the environment.

But the writer should do this task for the reader, not vice versa.

Verbs need to be chosen not only for clarity, but also to give writing a dynamic quality. We cannot always express the action of the sentence in the verb, but when we can, the result will be clearer, more dynamic sentences. Precise, active verbs energize writing; vague or weak connecting verbs deaden it. Well-chosen verbs tend to eliminate the need for supporting adverbs or adjectives. If the natural power role of the verb is hidden in some other structure in the sentence, the sentence will stumble along ineffectively, as in this example:

> The construction of this building in ten months was made possible by the cooperation of our companies.

This sentence would read more forcefully and easily if natural, active verbs replaced the nominalizations:

> Because our companies cooperated, they constructed this building in ten months.

Nominalizations (nouns created from verbs or adjectives — such as *construction,* a noun created from the verb *construct*) are favorite abstractions of many professional writers, particularly the nominalizations that end with *-ion* or *-ment* following weak verbs such as *be, give, have, make,* or *take*. These are often the culprits in muzzling the power of verbs and creating lifeless, fuzzy prose. The following are some ready examples:

be in agreement	make an assumption
be in attendance	make a choice
be cognizant	make a comparison
be in possession	make provision for
be in receipt of	make an evaluation
be of the opinion	take appropriate measures
give authorization	take action
give consideration	take into consideration
give a description	take under advisement

give encouragement	arrive at a solution
give instruction	come into conflict
have a belief	effect an improvement
have a need	hold a discussion
have a requirement	extend an invitation

All it takes to release verb power is to change the nominalizations back to the verb forms and ignore the rest of the phrase. For example, *agree* can substitute for *be in agreement, decide* for *make a decision,* and so on. Some verbs are a little harder to detect, such as the *know* hidden in *be cognizant.* Can you make a single verb out of each of the rest of the phrases?

Some frequently occurring prepositional phrases that hamstring verbs are these:

before your departure
in accordance with your request
to the effect that
with the exception of
with the knowledge of

Before you leave energizes the first, *as you asked* the second. Can you figure out the others?

Clauses ending with verbs that mean "done" often signal more informative verbs swallowed by nominalization:

Destruction of the battery of guns has been effected. (The battery of guns has been destroyed.)

Reconstruction of the missing sentences was accomplished. (The missing sentences were reconstructed.)

The success of the project was achieved. (The project succeeded.)

Discovery of the missing link was realized. (The missing link was discovered.)

When verbs are not suppressed, they may be too vague. We use *walk* when *sauntered* or *strolled* or some other more specific verb would convey a clearer picture. "Came to a stop" could become "screeched to a stop" or "slammed to a stop" or "slid gently to a stop." We often encounter the same difficulties with nouns: We write "flowers" instead of "half a dozen burgundy roses" or "a smattering of daisies." On the other hand, too much screeching, hurtling, stumbling overpowers. A *bouquet* may be more immediate than a detailed account of the flowers composing it. Student writing, however, is seldom overburdened with specific nouns and energetic verbs. The error usually lies in too many slack verbs and general nouns.

Adjectives and Adverbs

Modifiers serve one purpose. They qualify a key sentence element to make it more exact. Adjectives qualify nouns and pronouns; adverbs qualify verbs, adjectives, and other adverbs. Unless precise modifiers are chosen and every one counts, they add no discriminations, nothing except words. How often do we hear that something is *awful* or *terrible* or, on the other hand, *nice, great,* or *terrific?* Or read about *appreciable* differences, *considerable* losses, machines that run with *comparatively* little trouble, or answers that are *definitively* known? Or read that something was *completely finished* or *totally revolutionized* — and know something twice that we are satisfied to know once?

Perhaps the most glaring instance of modifiers that work against clarity and exactness is a string of words — some adjectives, some nouns functioning as adjectives — that modify a single noun. The flexibility of the English language allows us to use nouns as modifiers and to create these economical structures called compound noun modifiers. They are very handy if the practice is not carried too far. *Stone wall* is more concise than *wall made of stone,* and equally clear. We get along very well with others such as *radio telescope, postage stamp,* and *daisy-wheel printer,* and reasonably well with *visitor reception building, blood pressure reduction, test ban treaty,* and *course evaluation committee.* But even at this level we can sometimes be left puzzled. Does *teacher evaluation* mean that someone will evaluate the teachers or that the teachers will do the evaluating?

Clarity has been sacrificed to brevity and, perhaps, habit. The very economy of compound noun modifiers makes them a favorite of people who write headlines and advertisements — "Johnson Space Center Management Announced Appointments," or "New Formula Beef Barley and Vegetable Cup-a-Soup Mix." Consequently, we read such phrases every day and accept them as the norm. Then everyone gets into the economy game, as in this string from Wall Street:

> By pooling the resources of many investors into a limited partnership, it is possible for individuals to benefit from *the multimillion dollar data management peripheral equipment leasing industry.*

The modifiers include one article, *the;* one borderline adjective-noun combination, *multimillion;* two "pure" nouns, *dollar* and *data;* two nouns derived from verbs, *management* and *equipment;* one verbal noun, *leasing;* and one adjective, *peripheral.* These eight modifiers pile a mountain of conceptual rubble on *industry.* Does the industry under discussion manage data or lease peripheral equipment? Or does it lease peripheral equipment that manages data? Or . . . ? Only those who wrote the sentence (may) know the meaning; readers certainly do not.

We would also guess that many are hard put to locate the meaning in this next string from NASA's Goddard Space Flight Center, which appeared in an advertisement for a colloquium: "Erasable Gigabyte Magneto-optic Data Storage Discs." Does Goddard have gigabyte magneto-optic data storage discs that are erasable? Or storage discs that have erasable gigabyte magneto-optic data? Or . . . ?

How about even this fairly simple string: "solar wind stream structure." Does this mean structure of the solar wind stream? Or stream structure of the solar wind? Or wind stream of the solar structure?

Whenever strings of modifiers, even short ones, appear in your writing, break apart the modifiers (as we did with *solar wind stream structure*) so that readers will absorb your exact meaning. Be especially alert for strings that are taken for granted by the "in" group. The strings may be completely grammatical, but they may also be completely incomprehensible by those beyond the "in" group.

Since nouns and verbs carry the main idea of a sentence (or should whenever possible), adverbs, adjectives, and other modifiers are important for the fine discriminations and qualifications they can make. Used sparingly and freshly, they add precision and color to writing:

> None of them knew the color of the sky. Their eyes glanced lower, and were fastened upon the waves that swept toward them. These waves were of the hue of slate, save for the tops, which were of foaming white, and all of the men knew the colors of the sea. The horizon narrowed and widened, and dipped and rose, and at all times its edge was jagged with waves that seemed thrust up in points like rocks.

Descriptive/narrative writing such as this in the opening passage of Stephen Crane's *The Open Boat* thrives on precise use of modifiers. Crane husbands his modifiers, but uses them tellingly: "the hue of slate," "jagged with waves"; "in points like rocks."

Notice, by comparison, how indiscriminate and stale modifiers echo emptily:

> The *green* palm trees swayed *gently* in the breeze as we arrived in *sunny* California, and we all smiled *happily* after our *long* drive from the *white* snows of Michigan, over the *high* Rocky Mountains, and through the *sandy* desert of Arizona.

Because the modifiers are either predictable ("swayed gently") or vacuous ("sandy desert"), they are not simply neutral; they detract from the piece. For this kind of writing the author needs to find more eloquent words. "Swayed sleepily" and "adhesive sand" would be a start. (But in this example elimination is best. Why?)

Modifiers in less evocative writing can also add to or detract from the impression of the whole. To see how they add, read this next passage, from a review in *Time* (May 21, 1984) of an exhibition of Pre-Raphaelite art at London's Tate Gallery:

The group [Pre-Raphaelite Brotherhood] was self-consciously "revolutionary": the year was 1848, and a secret society of dangerous young subversives had become one of the special phantoms of the English mind. The P.R.B. wanted to reform English art, to drag it from the swamp of maudlin genre and low-grade history painting. They believed, with the ardent simplicity of young minds, that this decay had set in three centuries before, with Raphael.

Wisely used modifiers — *self-consciously revolutionary, secret, dangerous, special, maudlin, low-grade history,* and *with . . . ardent simplicity,* coupled with *young,* which is repeated — combine to emphasize the group's naiveté and shaky position in the art world of Victorian England.

To see how unwisely used modifiers can detract, read the next sentences from a business memorandum and a technical report:

Fortunately, Mr. Smith apparently had this in mind when he recommended the modification.

The receiver was tuned for ultrasonic sound waves.

In the first sentence the two adverbs cancel each other. Perhaps the writer meant that Mr. Smith's recommendation turned out to be fortunate or that he had the modification in mind when he made the recommendation. In the second sentence, the precision of *ultrasonic* is destroyed when part of its meaning is repeated in the adjective *sound.*

When you revise your writing, ask whether you truly needed each modifier, whether you can combine its meaning with a noun or verb (like *torment* for *hell on earth* or *saunter* for *walk slowly*), and whether you can find a more precise, less shopworn adjective or adverb.

Wordiness

Sometimes we need to repeat words to emphasize a point:

There were twenty, yes twenty, errors on that first page.

Sometimes we repeat a word for clarity, especially to sustain a long sentence:

In his discussion of riddles Bryant argues that we have long since passed the golden age of conundrums when magazines were devoted to riddles and riddle contests absorbed kings and queens, an argument that in its length is both intriguing and obsessive.

And sometimes we repeat a word to ensure coherence:

A garish *poster* in the school lobby attracted the visitor's attention. The *poster* was intended to publicize senior work day.

These are examples of functional redundancy. Sometimes, though, we become so enamored of words that we spill out more than we need to express our thoughts. Like chocolate syrup on a chocolate-frosted chocolate cake, it is too much of a good thing.

Most of us know that *unique* needs no modification, but still we hear *most unique,* or *true facts, shared consensus, recent innovation, completely finish* (or *revolutionize*), *initially prepare, past memories* (or *experience, history, custom*), *future planning* (or *developments, prospects*), *sudden crisis, end result,* and so on. In each case the noun or verb repeats the meaning of the modifier.

Another source of redundancy is the matched pair. Matched pairs are composed of an Anglo-Saxon word matched with its more "learned," borrowed counterpart, usually from Latin or French. You are probably familiar with *each and every, wishes and desires, hope and trust, various and sundry.* At one time when foreign words were pouring into English, borrowed words were intended to enhance the user's status, but now matched pairs merely reveal the writer's lack of thought.

Periphrasis or circumlocution, the use of an unnecessarily large number of words to express an idea, is another form of wordiness. An example is the *not un-* construction: "The bowshock was a not unexpected result of the experiment" ("The bowshock was an expected result of the experiment"). Other round-about expressions are nominalizations ("to place increasing reliance" ["to rely more"]) and passive sentences: "Students are often seen by educators as achievers or nonachievers, advantaged or disadvantaged, but rarely as human beings" (Educators often see students as achievers or nonachievers, advantaged or disadvantaged, but rarely as human beings"). Other wordy constructions are modifiers accompanied by their categories: "red in color"; "rough in appearance"; "during this period of time"; "ten in number"; "large in size."

The way to eliminate such problems is not to remember the types of wordiness, but rather to recognize wordiness when you see it. The first drafts of papers will almost certainly contain unneeded words because writers must concentrate on invention, on what to say rather than the precision of form. As you revise, however, ask whether you can omit certain words. Searching for nominalizations, modifiers that hide verbs, and the other locutions mentioned will sharpen and tighten your writing. You can also keep an alphabetical list of commonly occurring redundancies to quickly check for the wordiness that often appears automatically. Or perhaps you have access to a computer program that can mark these for you, alerting you to avoid redundancies — again and again.

The following column by Andrew Zipser appeared in the *Phoenix Gazette* (July 21, 1982). It claims to include 41 of the 42 most frequently seen or heard redundancies as compiled by the Minnesota Newspaper Association. Can you find them?

Telling It Just Like (As) It Is: Please Pick One
Andrew Zipser

You think you have problems? Meet a friend of mine who is first and foremost the world's greatest defender of the English language — at least he thinks so.

Murray bounced into our office the other day, perspiring from the weight of all the exclamation marks hanging from his each and every sentence, and started waving a newspaper in close proximity to my face.

"Look at this!" he barked.

"What am I looking at?" I responded brightly.

"It's a newspaper!" he glared. "Enclosed you will find a piece of paper containing just a sampling of the various and sundry ways this rag has mutilated the English language!"

I examined the paper in question, finding it covered with Murray's crabbed handwriting, until he snatched it back impatiently.

"Newspaper journalism is an affront to clarity of thought!" he carried on. "It's patently obvious that reporters at the present time have no understanding of the rules and regulations of sentence construction! You writers seem to revel in writing prose replete with totally unnecessary verbiage!"

Looking at the paper again, I could see what he meant: it was filled with sentences containing words of exactly identical meaning. But Murray wasn't looking for understanding, only a soapbox.

"We have to cooperate together to root out all these redundancies!" he exclaimed, perspiration dripping from his brow. "The English language is too beautiful to be cluttered up with words gathered together for no purpose other than to make the speaker look erudite."

I nodded compassionately. "I know what you mean," I managed to interject. "Among my circle of friends the consensus of opinion is that we should write only what is absolutely necessary, sticking to the important essentials. That's the only reasonable and fair thing to do if you want to open up meaningful communication."

"You're different," Murray said, calming down a little. "You're the unusual writer who understands the necessary requirements of his craft, the right and proper approach to revealing true facts. But let me ask the question — how typical are you?"

I shrugged, basking in his compliment. "Well . . . Assuming you're right, though, how are we to prevail against the temporarily suspended use of incisive prose?"

"We must rise up!" Murray expostulated again. "We must show people the honest truth — that the fair and just thing to do is to cancel out all that excess dreck! And if no one will follow, then you and I must still remain true to our principles, refusing and declining to succumb to the other alternative."

"But how, Murray, how?" I asked.

"We must be vigilant," he responded. "Let us assemble together whatever egregious examples of language mutilation we can find, no matter how small in size they may be, and refer back to their sources. Send in those atrocities to their authors and demand they be redone again. Make a carbon copy of each error and save it for submission at a later day in case we don't get satisfaction on the first try. With a little advance planning, we could take the newspapers in the city of Phoenix by storm!"

Murray is right, of course—if we continue on as we have, the plain and simple truth is that the English language will be smothered under its own weight. That's why I decided not to postpone a column about Murray's thoughts until later; and that's why this column contains 41 of the 42 most frequently seen or heard redundancies, as compiled by the Minnesota Newspaper Association.

If you can find them all, consider yourself a guardian of the King's English. Only by refusing to fall down in our vigilance will we still remain a literate nation.

Honesty

Although the general purpose of writing emphasized in this book is to convey knowledge and understanding clearly and accurately, we know that not all writing has this intent. Some writing draws in "loaded" words, words that play upon the emotions instead of lighting up the understanding. Propaganda, for example, intentionally uses loaded words to manipulate readers unfairly: Hitler's words mesmerized his German audience and brought on the tragedy of World War II; Jim Jones' words made him a satanic pied piper who could lead 900 people into mass suicide in Guyana. Closer to home, advertisers use loaded words ("ring around the collar," "morning mouth") to transform trivial problems into momentous inadequacies and create needs we never knew we had ("transportation for people who are already there"—Riva by Yamaha) so we will buy the products that promise to obliterate those inadequacies or fulfill those needs.

Usually a mature sense of ethics prevents intentional use of words loaded with emotional freight, but we need to watch for unintentional use of loaded words, especially when we become emotionally involved with an issue. For example, two political candidates, Dee and Dum, enter a room. A reporter favoring Dee describes him as "striding into the room with a broad smile on his face" and Dum as "walking in protected by his retinue of followers," bestowing on the favorite an aura of strength and on the other an aura of weakness. These specific words are not loaded in and of themselves (as are *so-called, should, ought, hypocrite, scabs, sweetheart, blockhead, loyal*), but they are loaded in context and in comparison. Whether planned or unplanned, words that prejudice and conceal do not speak well of the writer and are sure to impede agreement for readers who detect the dishonesty.

Euphemisms are another deceitful use of words, "telling it like it isn't." Like loaded words, they also conceal and mislead. The difference is that euphemisms are "softer" expressions substituted for direct and forceful words, signifying taboo or unpleasant things. Many have to do with excrement, sex, and death. Few people die; they *pass away* or *go on to their reward* or *drop into eternal sleep*. A sociologist has even referred to death as *eternal living!* Euphemisms of this sort tend to be harmless, though at times inane.

Other euphemisms confuse. Mentally retarded children become *exceptional;* the poor become *disadvantaged,* as do the *handicapped,* who were once crippled; old people become *senior citizens,* enter the *golden age,* and live in *convalescent homes.* Illegal immigrants become *undocumented aliens.* Taxes become *revenue enhancement.*

Other euphemisms cover up things people would rather hide. Jews in Germany were sent for *special treatment,* meaning death, with identity papers marked *return unwanted,* meaning death, to *concentration camps,* a euphemism for prisons where they waited for death. (Later *detention camps* replaced *concentration camps* in the rather common process of euphemisms begetting new euphemisms as the unpleasant connotations of the old attach to the new.) Hitler labeled his killing of Jews the *final solution.*

Probably no society has outdone the Nazis in using neutral words to cover hideous actions, but in war all governments are adept. The Romans' *Pax Romana* meant war and devastation to the conquered. The Vietnam "War" (called a *peacekeeping action*) brought us *anticipatory retaliation* for bombing and the CIA's *terminate with extreme prejudice.* Even earlier the War Department became the *Defense Department* and the Korean War was never a war but a *police action.* Reagan calls the MX (experimental missile) the *Peacekeeper.* And the Soviets were *invited* into Afghanistan.

Sexism

English, unfortunately, has no neutral singular pronoun, as do French and some other languages. Tradition has decreed that a mistake is better made on the basis of sex than number; therefore, the male singular has been used for an indefinite antecedent. Recently, however, many people have become disturbed by this so-called generic male reference.

Current usage strongly favors avoiding sexism. It is wise, therefore, to seek alternatives to the generic *he* and adopt neutral job titles (*flight attendant* instead of *stewardess, police officer* instead of *policeman, letter carrier* instead of *mailman, fire fighter* instead of *fireman,* and so on), a shift which has been achieved with comparative ease in government and industry.

One option for the troublesome pronoun is to use *he/she* or *he or she.* If not used frequently, this alternative reference, though admittedly not graceful, is a satisfactory solution. When the alternative reference overwhelms a paragraph, however, the result annoys:

The typical factory worker belongs to a union and makes $15,000 a year. He or she dropped out of high school where he or she has worked ever since. He or she lives in a $30,000 home near the downtown section of a middle-sized city. His or her home has only one bathroom. He or she is always short of money.

There are better options. Compare, for example, the following paragraphs. The first is from the twelfth edition of *The Chicago Manual of Style*. It follows the traditional rule for the male singular pronoun:

The author most nearly approaches the ideal as indexer. Certainly, he knows better than anyone else both the scope and limitations of his work; and certainly, he knows the audience to which he has addressed himself. At the same time, he can be so subjective about his own work that he may be tempted to include in his index even references to milieu-establishing, peripheral statements. . . .

The next paragraph is from the thirteenth edition, published in 1982:

The author most nearly approaches the ideal as indexer. Certainly, the author knows better than anyone else both the scope and the limitations of the work, and the audience to which it is addressed. At the same time, authors are sometimes so subjective about their own work that they are tempted to include in an index even references to milieu-establishing, peripheral statements. . . .

The solutions this writer relied on are these:

1. Repetition of the noun: "The *author* most nearly approaches the ideal as an indexer. Certainly, the *author* . . ."
2. Shift from pronoun to article: "Certainly, the *author* knows better than anyone else both the scope and the limitations of *the* work. . . ."
3. Syntactic reconstruction: " . . . and the audience *to which it is addressed.*"
4. Shift to the plural: "At the same time, *authors* are sometimes so subjective about *their* own work. . . ."

All of these are highly recommended ways of handling the problem.

Another solution not illustrated in the paragraph is to use *he* on some occasions and *she* on others, especially when none of the above solutions works in a particular situation. Many books now being published use this solution when the reference is indefinite.

EXERCISES

1. Find a short passage in a newspaper, magazine, or book that contains five words that are new to your active vocabulary. Be prepared to discuss their meanings, origin, and effectiveness in context.

2. Make up sentences illustrating as accurately as possible the denotations and connotations of one of the following sets of words.

   a. abandon, forsake, desert, leave, defect, withdraw, jettison, depart

   b. pleasure, joy, ecstasy, elation, bliss, contentment, fun, kicks

   c. soft, lenient, tolerant, easygoing, lax, forgiving, indulgent, permissive

3. Discuss the connotations in the following proper names:

   a. Shelley, Denise, Mary, Lulu, Matilda, Edna; Jason, Mark, John, Edgar, Francis, Percy

   b. Josephine/Josie, Theodora/Teddy, Margaret/Maggie; Robert/Bob, Frederick/Fred, Anthony/Tony

4. Rewrite the following sentences, substituting specific, concrete details for the more general, abstract words.

   a. You may visit the California landing site for the next landing of a space vehicle.

   b. Troubles nearly always have some good come of them.

   c. The U.S. government has money problems.

   d. The cat ran for cover at the loud sound.

   e. The legal profession has tried to keep women out of partnerships by illegal means.

5. Read through a complete piece of your own writing—say a paragraph or two that add up to about 250 words. Underline the nouns once and the verbs twice; circle the adjectives and adverbs. Revise the passage, paying particular attention to these parts of speech, so that it is more precise, concrete, and forceful.

6. Give the following sentences verb power by revising the nominalizations:

   a. I had to put in an appearance in court because I was a witness.

   b. He will have to have an adjustment made on his next statement.

   c. Will someone please render assistance to this injured man?

   d. Fireworks have the capability of hurting people if handled carelessly.

   e. Why don't you try an experiment to see if an extra hour of study improves your grade.

7. Writers unfamiliar with language confuse words that sound alike or have similar meanings. Use the following sets of words in sentences that show you know the difference in meanings.

ability/capability	fewer/less
among/between	imply/infer
apt/liable/likely	mutual/common

balance/remainder   rare/scarce/unique
compose/comprise

8. Writers unfamiliar with the language are also apt to confuse words
that have similar sounds but different meanings. Use the following
sets of words in sentences that show you know the difference in
meanings.

accept/except   farther/further
affect/effect   fortunate/fortuitous
conscious/conscience   immigrate/emigrate
continual/continuous   linear/lineal
explicit/implicit   practical/practicable
precede/proceed   principal/principle
unsolvable/insoluble   valuable/valued

9. Underline the loaded words in the following advertisement for
Soloflex exercise equipment and be prepared to discuss how they
manipulate readers dishonestly:

We have been fascinated from the very beginning. By its beauty. The
sheer simplicity of line. As a machine, the human body remains the supreme invention. While able to perform the most intricate, the most
subtle of movements, it is, at the same time, capable of astonishing feats
of strength. Strangely enough, the more that we demand of this machine,
the more powerful, the more graceful it becomes.

To unlock your body's potential, we proudly offer Soloflex. Twenty-
four traditional iron pumping exercises, each correct in form and balance.
All on a simple machine that fits in a corner of your home.

10. Rewrite the ad substituting neutral words for the loaded words.
Compare the result with the original ad.
11. Revise the paragraph below twice to avoid sexist reference. Try
different strategies in the two versions. Be prepared to explain why
you prefer one revision over the other.

After a student is accepted at a college or university, he has to enroll
formally in a schedule of classes. This process is not easy for him for two
reasons. One is that if he hasn't decided on a major, he may have trouble
selecting courses that will eventually count toward the degree he chooses.
Another is that since enrollment goes by seniority, the courses he wants
may be closed by the time he tries to enroll in them.

Chapter 11

Sentence Sense

The sentence is a fundamental grammatical and rhetorical structure in discourse. It is the basic unit of meaning. Sentences that convey meaning in a style appropriate to the subject, audience, and purpose indicate a mature writer.

To achieve rhetorical effectiveness, sentences must first be grammatically correct. Otherwise, readers will pay less attention to the ideas themselves than to the mistakes, mentally correcting them or trying to figure out the sense (and perhaps failing). Important as correctness is, however, this chapter assumes that you know how to avoid sentence errors — faulty subject/verb agreement, incorrect pronoun reference, run-ons, fragments, and so on. (If your control is imperfect, you can refer to Chapter 21 before proceeding with the material in this chapter or as you work with it.)

Rhetorically effective sentences are unified, cohesive, appropriately emphatic and varied, and pleasingly rhythmic. Though treated separately, these features are inherently interdependent.

Unity

A sentence should present a unified statement. It should be of a piece, announcing a subject and predicating something about it without wandering off into a jumble of ideas. The sentence may be simple, like this one:

> The flying objects emitted an eerie glow and a strange noise like the beat of a heart heard through a stethoscope.

Or it may have several independent clauses:

> The subject of both is valor, and the manner is grand; there is much oration and little action, but the emotion is genuine.

Or it can have a combination of independent and dependent clauses:

> Although today the actual events of the Whiskey Rebellion would not be considered even first-rate rioting, in 1794 poor communication over the

153

mountains and the fearful imaginations of the frontiersmen combined to produce images of drunken wildmen raging through the countryside.

Or it may be laden with many modifiers:

He sat close, his tall, slim body arching forward with tightly coiled energy, arms akimbo on the table, one hand toying with a chopstick, the other absently fingering his beard, his light blue eyes intensely fixing her gaze.

To achieve unity, avoid introducing extraneous ideas into a sentence. Newspaper reporters occasionally write "freight-car sentences" that pull in minimally connected ideas in the interest of saving space:

During welcoming ceremonies at Hickam Air Force Base outside Honolulu on Oahu, an island steeped in the nation's history, on one of his stops on his 11,000 mile flight to China, the President told a crowd of about 2,000 base employees that he was beginning "a long journey for peace."

This sentence can be improved by dividing it into two unified sentences and rearranging parts:

One of the President's stops on his 11,000 mile flight to China was Hickam Air Force Base outside Honolulu on Oahu, an island steeped in the nation's history. During welcoming ceremonies, the President told a crowd of 2,000 base employees that he was beginning "a long journey for peace."

Lengthy compound sentences particularly risk disunity:

We could understand a foreigner or little child who said either sentence to us, but we would recognize that the speaker did not know English perfectly and that some rules or principles of English had not been followed, and we might correct the user of the sentences.

Sentences with relative clauses that modify relative clauses, that in turn modify other clauses, and so on, also risk disunity along with their uncontrollable sprawl:

Much recording of history has been done that has demonstrated scientific progress which is illustrated by improving technology resulting in improved computers which can be made to do work for us.

Can you break these last two sentences apart into separate unified sentences?

Cohesion

Even unified sentences, ones that contain related ideas, may not cohere. If elements are randomly ordered or connections are missing that show explicitly relationships between parts, a sentence may not lead the reader from point to point. In the following example, it is difficult to connect the idea of a close race with the information about some racers being forced out:

> Some of the race car drivers in the Indianapolis 500 are forced out of the race because of engine trouble or accidents, and when the winner finally shoots over the finish line, he is at least a half lap in front of the prime challenger, although occasionally a close race occurs.

By showing relationships and rearranging elements, the sentence coheres:

> Some of the race car drivers in the Indianapolis 500 are forced out of the race because of engine trouble or accidents, *so that, ordinarily,* close races do not occur, and when the winner finally shoots over the finish line, he is at least half a lap in front of the prime challenger.

Because students often fear piling too many ideas into a sentence or not making parts of sentences cohere, they write series of short sentences. Short sentences have their uses, of course, but too many make nervous reading. Reading good current prose from a variety of sources can give you the feel of longer sentences whose parts are effectively assembled. Analyze some sentences that seem particularly striking; with practice you can apply the same techniques to your sentences.

In preliminary drafts it is usually better to write sentences with little conscious attention (unlike the discourse as a whole, which benefits from our conscious plan and visualization of the general form), but as you work through later drafts, try consciously to revise sentences to help readers move logically through them, always keeping in mind that your choices depend on the rhetorical situation. Who is the audience? What is your purpose? How do the parts of a sentence fit together, and how does the sentence fit with those that come before and after? Here are some guidelines for writing more cohesive sentences:

1. Qualifying clauses such as those that state a condition, time, or place should precede rather than follow the main clause:

> If the respect given to athletic prowess and other extracurricular activities were given instead to academic achievement, we would see more students studying harder and striving for better grades.

Notice the next sentence in contrast:

> Television can be extraordinarily worthwhile, providing viewers with a vicarious window on the world when it finds the proper formula of time, talent, and imagination.

Readers would take the early part of the sentence as a positive generalization. Only at the end of the sentence would they realize the limitation of the conditional clause; then they would have to reconstruct the meaning of the whole.

When clauses beginning with *although* follow the independent clause, readers must recall what was said before and readjust to an unexpected contradiction.

> Our customer lines are open from 9:00 A.M. until noon and 1:00 P.M. until 4:00 P.M., although our working hours are between 6:00 A.M. and 6:00 P.M.

The subordinate clause appears tacked on, as an afterthought.

2. In order to sustain an elaborated sentence, repeat or rephrase a key idea or word:

> A broad education is desirable because of the wide variety of tasks public relations specialists are called upon to perform, *tasks* such as writing speeches and news releases, conducting tours and training sessions, organizing charity and recruiting drives, editing and producing company publications, and developing advertising and management policies.

Notice how readers would struggle with meaning if the writer had inserted *which include* in the place of the repeated *tasks:*

> A broad education is desirable because of the wide variety of tasks public relations specialists are called upon to perform, which include writing speeches. . . .

Or compare the confusion of the first sentence below with the clarity of the second:

> After many years of fund raising, the university finally built an aquatic center and sports arena that are the finest under one roof in the country, *which* feature separate pools for beginners, experienced swimmers, and divers and squash, tennis, and racquet ball courts.

> After many years of fund raising, the university finally built under one roof an aquatic center and sports arena that are the finest in the country, a *sports facility* that features separate pools for beginners, experienced swimmers, and divers and courts for squash, tennis, and racquet ball.

3. Keep modifiers as close as possible to what they modify:

> Researchers today believe that it may be possible to locate fixed areas in the brain that control motion, vision, and smelling, but that it is impossible to localize such a complex and coordinated function as language.

That revision locates the modifier more effectively than this original version of the sentence:

> Researchers today believe that for motion, vision, and smelling it may be possible to locate fixed areas of control in the brain, but that it is impossible to localize such a complex and coordinated function as language.

Modifiers such as *almost, even, hardly, merely, nearly,* and *only* require special attention. In speaking, we tend to place these modifiers carelessly next to the verb and depend on intonation (the variable stress we use when we talk) to clarify meaning. For instance, one might say, "I only have five dollars," and by emphasizing *only* indicate that no one else has five dollars or by deemphasizing it indicate that five dollars is the total the speaker possesses. Writing requires that the modifier be placed next to the word it modifies to make up for missing vocal cues and avoid ambiguity. *Only* preceding *I* limits the five dollars to the writer; *only* placed next to five dollars limits the amount of money.

4. A word on split infinitives is appropriate here. Purists demand that we avoid splitting an infinitive with a modifier: we should write, "to make a decision quickly," rather than, "to quickly make a decision." Nonpurists say that split infinitives occur commonly among even the best writers. Actually, the problem is not great. Examples of serious, expository prose will show that most infinitives are used without modifiers.

The best way to handle infinitives is to write them first as they naturally occur to you. Then in the revision process, check for those with modifiers and deliberately decide whether to move any modifiers that split infinitives. Do you want to create an air of informality or formality? (Efforts to avoid splitting infinitives call attention to careful editing.) Can the modifier be placed elsewhere and preserve clarity and the desired emphasis, yet avoid awkwardness?

5. Lengthy interruptions between grammatically connected units, such as subject and verb, are best avoided unless a particular effect such as suspense or hesitation is desired:

> The principle I have just mentioned as operating had been, with the most newly disembarked of the two men, wholly instinctive — the fruit of a sharp sense that, delightful as it would be to find himself looking, after so much separation, into his comrade's face, his business would be a trifle bungled should he simply arrange for this countenance to present itself to the nearing steamer as the first "note" of Europe.

This sentence from the opening paragraph of Henry James's *The Ambassadors* is designed to characterize the narrator's habit of mind — his agitation, his tendency to hesitate and qualify, to proceed by indirection. The suspended syntax helps to fulfill that intention. For most purposes, however, longer phrases and clauses that interrupt confuse and annoy:

> The purchase of microcomputers for faculty in the humanities, owing to the fact that university administrators on the occasion when they originally authorized the expenditure did not anticipate fully the demand that would result, has run into current attempts to institute organizational changes intended to reduce or eliminate some requests.

After the sentence has been revised, readers can complete the cause-and-effect link easily:

Because state legislators authorized the purchase of microcomputers for faculty in the humanities without fully anticipating the demand that resulted, we are forced now to make organizational changes that will reduce or eliminate some requests.

6. Place connectors such as *however, nevertheless, on the contrary* and *in contrast* close to the beginning of the sentence in which they appear, within approximately six words. Notice what happens when the connector moves away from the beginning of a sentence:

Most firms want workers with some "hands on" experience. These firms, *however*, have failed to explain where a graduating student is to get this experience.

Most firms want workers with some "hands on" experience. These firms have failed to explain where a graduating student is to get this experience, *however*.

In the second version we do not know that we are expected to keep the first sentence in mind in order to make sense of the second until we reach the *however* at the end. Readers need to anticipate the contradiction in some way to avoid backtracking.

7. Keep the pronoun reference clear:

The system of having a neighbor watch out for a child after school is most successful when *their* time is structured to some extent. If a child is given a schedule of things to do while mother is at work — finishing *their* homework, emptying the dishwasher, calling her at the office to report in — *they* will not feel abandoned.

Even though readers can figure out the writer's meaning, *their* and *they* have no true referent. Apparently the writer felt uncomfortable about a child being only a boy, so used the all-inclusive plural pronoun familiar to us in speech (*they, them, their*) rather than the traditionally correct male singular pronoun (*he, him, his*). Shifting to the male reference would bestow cohesion and correctness but not rhetorical effectiveness. The writer could gain all three by revising the sentence according to one strategy or a combination of strategies for avoiding sexism discussed in Chapter 10.

Which of the following possible revisions do you prefer? Why? Can you suggest any others?

The system of having a neighbor watch out for children after school is most successful when their time is structured to some extent. If children are given a schedule of things to do while their mothers are at work — finishing their homework, emptying the dishwasher, calling the office to report in — they will not feel abandoned.

The system of having a neighbor watch out for a child after school is most successful when time is structured to some extent. If children are given a schedule of things to do while their mothers are at work — finishing their homework, emptying the dishwasher, calling the office to report in — they will not feel abandoned.

Another change to enhance rhetorical effectiveness would be to substitute *parents* for *mother* to show joint or alternative responsibility.

8. Use parallel structure, the matching of grammatical forms, to link connected ideas of equal weight:

> Certain transition words signal a *contrast, qualification,* or *concession.* (nouns)
>
> But, in a larger sense, *we cannot dedicate — we cannot consecrate — we cannot hallow —* this ground. (clauses)
>
> . . . and that government *of the people, by the people, and for the people,* shall not perish from the earth. (prepositional phrases)

Parallel structure creates a powerful uniting force by quickly and firmly setting up a reader's expectations. Readers, therefore, are disagreeably surprised when parallel ideas continue but parallel structure stops:

> His proposal for a new writing program is practical, comprehensive, and conforms with the other courses offered by the department.

With parallelism continued, the sentence flows coherently:

> His proposal for a new writing program is practical, comprehensive, and consistent with other departmental offerings.

Notice that the last adjective, *consistent,* unlike the others, is followed by a prepositional phrase, but it is still parallel — in the same way that two beams of unequal dimensions may be parallel.

On the other hand, nonparallel ideas phrased in parallel structure will confuse the reader:

> A historian's research may be narrow in scope, fleeting in value, full of unanswered questions, and touched by excitement.
>
> The last step is turning the valve and releasing the pressure.

In the first sentence the reader expects the final parallel element to be another negative characteristic and has to readjust to the fact that it is not. The sentence lacks unity. The last idea should form a separate sentence. In the second sentence we may have two separate operations stated as one or one operation with its effect. Taking *last step* as a guide, we would assume the latter. Revised, the sentences would read:

> A historian's research may be narrow in scope, fleeting in value, and full of unanswered questions. But it may also be touched by excitement.
>
> The last step is turning the valve, which releases the pressure.

A special type of parallelism worth mastering is the balanced structure, which brings together parallel elements fairly equal in length and syntax. The matched parts are particularly effective for comparisons:

In view of Mary's known success in the sphere of personal contact, her steady aim to meet Elizabeth must be regarded *not as the caprice of an inquisitive woman, but as a sound piece of political reasoning.*

>   Antonia Fraser, *Mary Queen of Scots*

Ask not what your country can do for you—ask what you can do for your country.

>   John F. Kennedy, "Inaugural Address"

The pattern of children's typical behavior toward younger brothers and sisters when parents leave may reflect parental behavior: *boys model their father's casual caregiving,* while *girls imitate their mother's overindulgence.*

Pleasing as they appear, balanced structures should be used with caution. Even more than ordinary parallel structure, they can become monotonous and artificial. Even though an inaugural address is a set piece that traditionally calls for inspiring eloquence, President Kennedy used carefully balanced structures only three times in his speech, relying far more extensively on parallel structure. On the other hand, the eighteenth-century author Samuel Johnson used balanced structures to the point of annoying mannerism. There is another problem with balanced structures. If no true similarity or contrast is being made, they fall flat and may confuse readers.

Emphasis

Sentences may be unified and cohesive yet still be ineffective if emphasis is lacking. Writers need to consider not only how words flow and relate to each other, but also the relative significance of each word. Always there is a foreground and background of interest; the less important details are subordinated to the more important, and items of equal importance receive equal treatment.

Typographical Markers

The easiest, but not the finest, way to achieve emphasis is typographical or mechanical: the exclamation point, all capitals, italics (underlining on the typewriter or in writing), quotation marks to set off a word or phrase, dashes, lists, tabulations, different-colored inks, plenty of white space to set off a line or two of a paragraph, headings, and postscripts. Some of these markers are found in discourse from one end of the spectrum to the other—especially italics and dashes. Others, such as different-colored inks, all capitals, and postscripts, are more at home in business correspondence and advertisements. Still others, such as headings, lists, and tabulations, are typical of both business and technical documents.

Typographical means of emphasis are reliable and effective if they are not overused or incorrectly used. For example, a postscript at the end of a business letter can effectively set off an important, brief message; but a postscript is ineffective if it belatedly adds something omitted from the body of the letter. In reports, headings and subheadings signal content, arouse interest, and mark organizational breaks when used effectively. They become ineffective if they simply impose superficial signs of organization. Dashes in a piece of writing create an air of informality, which may be appropriate, but too many dashes, even in a very informal piece of writing, suggest a scatterbrained writer at work.

Overreliance on typographical or mechanical means of emphasis often indicates a distrust or failure of rhetorical emphasis. The exclamation point, for example, is rarely needed. The words in the sentence should do the exclaiming. Underlining words for emphasis is likewise usually unnecessary. If words are chosen and positioned wisely, the most effective emphasis will occur naturally.

Emphatic Positions

Beginnings and endings carry more emphasis in sentences or clauses than middles — beginnings because they are seen first, endings because they are seen most recently. Usually the end of a sentence is slightly more emphatic than the beginning because it is the last thing in our minds.

Prepositions. Most of us know the grammatical rule "Do not end a sentence with a preposition." But today, as in the eighteenth century when the rule was borrowed from Latin grammar, English sentences do end in prepositions. In fact, some sentences would be less effective if they did not. We could change the order of "Hope is what we live by" to "What we live by is hope," but the word order in the second version damages the emphatic balance of *hope* and *live by* as well as the rhythm of the sentence. The wise rhetorical choice would be the first version.

Most of the time, though, sentences are rhetorically improved by shifting a final preposition, or any other function word, to another position in the sentence and saving the last spot for content words (nouns, verbs, etc.). Often a one-word verb can substitute for a verb + particle: *left* for *went out*, *continue* for *carry on*, *treat* for *deal with*, and so on. Sentences read better with a strong finish, like the final push in a race. Notice the difference in this pair of sentences:

The fate of the energy bill was being argued about.

He was arguing about the energy bill.

Both sentences are "correct," but the second is more effective. *Energy bill* deserves emphasis far more than *about,* yet the first sentence buries it in the least emphatic middle.

Series. Arranging a series of items into a climactic pattern also takes advantage of natural emphasis. The most significant item in its context is held off until last:

> July and August are monsoon months in Arizona. Monsoon season seems mostly to mean high humidity, threatening evening skies, and a few dusty raindrops.

Such a delay is particularly effective if the series is meant to convey abundant emotion, whether serious or humorous, as is often the case with a series of four or five items. Notice this effect in the sentence below, a bit of Shelley's fervent pleading to his fellow poet Keats to come to Italy:

> I spare declamation about the statues, and the paintings, and the ruins, and in a greater piece of forbearance, about the mountain streams, fields, and colours of the sky, and the sky itself.

Periodic Sentences. A periodic sentence emphasizes the main clause by delaying it. The reader is suspended through one or more subordinate phrases or clauses before the grammatically independent clause introduces the main idea:

> When you die, when you divorce, when you buy a house, when you have an accident, not to mention a hundred or so other occasions in your lifetime when you have been cheated as a consumer by false promises and shoddy goods, a lawyer almost inevitably is involved.

In this sentence the series winds down from the most to the least serious in preparation for the main clause, which gains additional impact coming immediately after the most trivial item of the series. This arrangement may seem unquestionably the best for appropriate emphasis. But what about the arrangement of words in the independent clause? Would "a lawyer is involved almost inevitably" be a better arrangement? Why? Why not?

Many loose sentences are candidates for conversion to periodic sentences. The less significant details can be moved up front as subordinate phrases or clauses. This strategy, however, should not be overused. Most sentences should be loose, not only because they appear more "natural," but because you will paradoxically lose the emphasis you are trying to gain if you write many consecutive periodic sentences.

Adverbs and Adverbial Modifiers. Adverbs and adverbial modifiers have no fixed position. For cohesion, however, they usually follow the words they modify. Phrases and clauses used as adverbs are free to assume any appropriate position in a sentence. In placing them, therefore, seek the most emphatic position appropriate for the situation, or a position that will not deemphasize a more deserving sentence element. Always remember, however, to retain clarity.

Subject Postponers. Sentences that begin with *There is, There are,* or *It is* postpone the subject to the middle position and often weaken its emphasis. In these sentences the subject is buried:

> There is evidence pointing to the average age of students enrolled in college rising over the past five years.

> It was the case that the collecting buckets and jars were so overflowing with specimens that we had to change the water constantly to keep the animals alive.

By dropping *There is* in the first and *In the case that* in the second, both of which are hollow structures, the writer restores the natural emphasis to the subject:

> Evidence points to the average . . .

> The collecting buckets and jars so overflowed . . .

Notice too that the natural emphasis increases force by eliminating empty locutions.

Not all subject postponements can be cut to increase emphasis. Some cuts cause a loss of emphasis. The appropriate emphasis in these sentences would suffer if the subject postponers were omitted:

> It is the federal government, not the state and city governments, that is now struggling under a crushing debt load.

> There is a frown these days on the smiling cat of Cheshire Meow foods.

Postponing subjects in these sentences has actually increased their emphasis by making them phantom objects in phantom clauses: "It is the federal government," and "There is a frown." The greatest emphasis, we remember, is at the end of the simple sentence or clause, that is, the object or complement. Instead of saying "George did it," we gain the greater emphasis of the ending position by putting *George* there: "Who committed this deed? Why, it was George." Even more emphatic, "It was no one but George."

Emphatic Structures

Some grammatical forms carry more emphasis than others, and these should ordinarily contain the key ideas.

Independent Clause. An independent clause, no matter where it is placed, is more emphatic than a dependent clause. Look again at the periodic sentence about lawyers being inevitably involved in our lives. Even if the independent clause began the sentence, it would garner more attention than the subsequent details. Placed at the end of this periodic sentence, the independent clause captures extra emphasis because closure of the idea is suspended—meaning does not cohere until the end.

Compare the emphasis on the independent clauses in the following sentences:

> Because the vehicle completed the thousand-hour test without failure, *its condition was considered good.*
>
> *The vehicle's condition was considered good* because it completed the thousand-hour test without failure.

The same sentence could also have been written in parallel structure:

> The vehicle completed the thousand-hour test without failure, and its condition was considered good.

However, this last version with its two independent clauses loses the dependent relationship necessary to the precise meaning.

Parallelism. Parallel structures, especially balanced structures, give equal emphasis to equal ideas, and the repeated structures themselves capture a reader's attention:

> Let us never negotiate out of fear. But let us never fear to negotiate.
> > John F. Kennedy
>
> When I sell liquor, it's called bootlegging; when my patrons serve it on Lake Shore Drive, it's called hospitality.
> > Al Capone
>
> You see an awful lot of smart guys with dumb women, but you hardly ever see a smart woman with a dumb guy.
> > Erica Jong
>
> Amateurs hope. Professionals work.
> > Garson Kanin

Because balance fosters memory, it underlies the formation of proverbs:

> A stitch in time saves nine.
>
> When the cat's away, the mice will play.

Inversions. Occasional inversion of a sentence's normal word order (Subject-Verb-[Object]) is another means of emphasis. Inversion sharply emphasizes one part of the sentence in the same way a rock singer wearing iridescent nail polish emphasizes hands. To say "I won't do that," places far less emphasis on *that* than to say, "That I won't do."

Adverbs or structures used adverbially are prime candidates for inversion because they can be moved with relative ease. The first sentence below is in normal order. The other versions shift sentence elements to create different emphases. Which sentence do you prefer? Why?

> The shadow of a huge man crept menacingly through the half-open door.
>
> Menacingly, the shadow of a huge man crept through the half-open door.
>
> Menacingly, through the half-open door crept the shadow of a huge man.
>
> Menacingly, through the half-open door the shadow of a huge man crept.

Like balanced structures, inversion becomes a mannerism and loses its emphasis when overdone. Some years ago when *Time* magazine writers were prone to use inversions ("Singular was the U.S. attitude"; "Imminent seemed disaster"), the style was parodied unmercifully by *The New Yorker:* "Backward run the sentences until reels the mind." Inversions no longer occur frequently enough in *Time* to draw attention. At one time the inversion "Came the dawn" was an effective subtitle in silent films.

Awkward inversions can so startle that they destroy the effect desired. In the following inverted sentences, readers may question whether the increased emphasis on the names justifies rearranging the sentence parts:

> By the writer Tom Wolfe and by the social critic Christopher Lasch the phenomenon of self-absorption has been ridiculed as the "me" decade and the "culture of narcissism."

Since adjectives normally precede the nouns they modify, emphasis can be gained by placing adjectives after the noun:

> The airplane, huge and full, lumbered along the runway for its takeoff.

Adjectives receive even greater emphasis when they are placed in the object position as predicates:

> General Electric's J–47 was a single-stage gas turbine.
>
> The gas turbine of General Electric's J–47 was single stage.

Repetition. Occasionally, to make sure our readers fully absorb a key point, we rephrase it. And we often signal our intention with transitional phrases such as "in other words" or "to put it another way." The repetition puts the idea into simpler, more concrete terms, clarifying it as it is rephrased. Henry David Thoreau's "Civil Disobedience" provides an example:

> But when the friction comes to have its machine, and oppression and robbery are organized, I say, let us not have such a machine any longer.

In other words, when a sixth of the population of a nation which has undertaken to be the refuge of liberty are slaves, and a whole country is unjustly overrun and conquered by a foreign army, and subjected to military law, I think that it is not too soon for honest men to rebel and revolutionize.

Sometimes, particularly in an argument when we want to reinforce a point like the pounding of a fist on the table, we may choose to repeat phrases like Martin Luther King, Jr., does in his "Letter from Birmingham Jail":

I had hoped that the white moderate would understand that law and order exist . . . I had hoped that the white moderate would understand that the present tension in the South . . .

Here is one other instance from the same piece:

Isn't this like condemning a robbed man because . . . ? Isn't this like condemning Socrates because . . . ? Isn't this like condemning Jesus because . . . ?

Emphasis, like other special effects in sentences, needs to be tested during revision, especially when it involves the placement of mobile adverbials. The writer should step back and take the role of a challenging reader.

Variety

Some writers are inclined, consciously or not, toward shorter sentences that isolate details in simple patterns; others toward longer sentences that combine details into more complex patterns. But no one pattern or length is ideal for all situations. For example, shorter, simpler sentences characterize advertisements, letters, and most discourse appearing in narrow columns. Longer, more complex sentences characterize articles and essays presenting serious ideas, as well as newspaper leads where an attempt is made to summarize the who, what, where, when, and why of a news item in the first sentence or two. Nonetheless, no matter what the conventions or your natural inclinations, too many similar sentences in a row, whether similar in form or length or both, work against achieving needed emphasis and pacing the flow of ideas. Such a series of sentences is also monotonous and sure to bore readers.

Variety of Length

Varying the length of sentences, though not as important as varying form, is one way to enliven prose style. Notice the monotony and the childlike sound of the following:

Captain John J. Janeway has a libel suit against the *Springfield Star*. It is not scheduled to come to trial until this fall. But both sides keep trying to settle the case before the public. Time and again, each camp has claimed to have found the "smoking gun." Each side says it would demonstrate the other's guilt.

The sentence lengths are 12, 11, 12, 13, and 9 words, compared with the 54-word original sentence:

Although Captain John J. Janeway's libel suit against the *Springfield Star* is not scheduled to come to trial until this fall, both sides keep trying to settle the case in the court of public opinion, each camp claiming time and again to have found a "smoking gun" that would demonstrate the other's guilt.

Many sentences of this length in a row not only would be as monotonous as the series of short sentences, but also would strain the reader. This one was surrounded by a 14-word sentence and a 26-word sentence. If most of your sentences are short, look for ways to combine them, especially by using subordination. If most ramble on, look for ways to break them up. Sentence length itself can serve emphasis. A short sentence in the midst of long ones captures emphasis, as does a long one in the midst of short sentences.

Variety of Form

You are undoubtedly familiar with the use of questions and exclamations to vary the sentence type naturally used the most, the declarative sentence, even though you probably also know that interrogatives should be used only occasionally and exclamations only rarely. And you probably try to break away from simple sentences with some compound, complex, and compound-complex sentences for variety.

Inversions can also create variety, as can a periodic sentence in the midst of loose ones, or a fragment in the midst of complete sentences. Parallelism and balanced sentences can break the flow of a series of more casually constructed sentences.

The Cumulative Sentence. Still another option for creating sentence variability is one you may be unfamiliar with: the cumulative sentence. A cumulative sentence consists of a base plus bound modifiers (such as articles, adjectives that precede nouns, and some prepositional phrases — modifiers that are not set off by commas and cannot be freely moved about in a sentence) and free modifiers (phrases and clauses, normally set off by commas from the rest of the sentence, that can usually be moved about in the sentence without destroying meaning). For example, in "A cloud of gloom hung over the decaying castle," the modifiers *of gloom* and *decaying* are bound. In "He plodded along slowly and hesitantly down the dark street, with big wet snowflakes falling on the shoulders of his cashmere coat and clinging to the hair over his ears," the modifying phrase "with big wet snowflakes . . . his ears," can be freely shifted:

> With big wet snowflakes falling on the shoulders of his cashmere coat and clinging to the hair over his ears, he plodded along slowly and hesitantly down the dark street.

> He plodded along, with big wet snowflakes falling on the shoulders of his cashmere coat and clinging to the hair over his ears, slowly and hesitantly down the dark street.

These free modifiers that qualify or add details to the base may precede the base, interrupt it, or follow it. In the following sentences the base appears in italics:

> Half-rooted to the rocky shore, one leg sinking firmly into the sand for balance, the other leg raised, a delicate sliver of sinew, *the last heron marked the end of summer.*

> *The dress,* a red rustle of silk for the holidays, *stroked her slender body.*

> *He sat close,* leaning forward intensely, one hand toying with a chopstick, the other absently touching his beard, his light blue eyes fixing her gaze.

An advantage of modifiers preceding the base is that some suspense is created because the base being modified is delayed. In the sentence above about the heron, the modifiers accumulate an image of the heron before we know what to attach the bits of description to. A disadvantage of modifiers preceding the base is that they must be fewer and expanded less, or else the sentence becomes front-heavy; readers' short-term memories become overtaxed. The sentence about the heron, with its four modifiers preceding the base, would collapse of its own weight if the base were held off much longer.

Some suspense also results when modifiers interrupt the base. The effect is an accelerated motion toward anticipated details about the announced subject and then a reflection back to the subject, which brings the entire idea into focus. Free modifiers that interrupt the base suggest that the writer has foresightedly organized a sentence before beginning it. Like modifiers that precede the base, however, too many modifiers embedded in midsentence can confuse readers. The sentence above about the dress does not, of course, have this problem.

Modifiers spun out after the base follow the natural flow of thought, the naming of a topic followed by comments on it. More modifiers and more detailed modifiers can be added following the base than in the other two positions because such an arrangement is fundamentally easier to read, moving from a completed generalization to amplification of it. The danger of this arrangement of free modifiers is that a sentence may ramble loosely, carelessly.

No matter what the arrangement of modifiers, the writer's task is to stay controlled and artful while sounding perfectly natural and devoid of artifice. Part of the art lies in creating a more dense, textured style that will appeal to readers. One of the problems with student writing is low-density prose, that is, ideas presented in a spare manner, insufficiently combined, subordinated, or expanded as if all the ideas were equal. Free modifiers that expand, limit, or illustrate the general point of the base and each other at ever more specific levels of modification help create a denser, more textured, more mature style, as the following sentences, with their various levels marked diagrammatically (level 1 is the sentence base), illustrate:

```
    2   Peddling swiftly along the bikeway,
        3   muscles taut with the effort,
    2   glancing occasionally at the river to her left,
        3   as the wind whipped her hair across her face,
1   she was the picture of grace in motion.

1   The contract negotiator stood firm,
    2   her values intact,
    2   serene in her confidence that all problems would be solved.

1   Jeffrey, ↟ , controls the F-111's ground-hugging midnight flight.
    2   a young man whose terror threshold rises with each new adventure

1   The time is long past when hard-core modernists, ↟ ,
    2   secure in their belief that nearly everything England produced be-
        tween the death of Turner and the arrival of Roger Fry was either
        hopelessly sentimental or irredeemably quaint
    assigned the Pre-Raphaelite Brotherhood to the dustbin of history.

1   Corporate leaders, ↟ ,
    2   who last week were attending the spring meeting of the Business
        Council
        3   the organization of the top U.S. executives,
    did not fault the Federal Reserve,
    2   even though they expect rates to continue to climb.

1   There was a completeness in it,
    2   something solid like a principle,
    2   and masterful like an instinct —
        3   a disclosure of something secret —
            4   of that hidden something,
                5   that gift of good or evil that makes racial difference,
                5   that shapes the fate of nations.
```
Joseph Conrad, Youth: A Narrative

Sentences with accumulated free modifiers, such as the first, picturing a girl riding a bicycle, are particularly effective in discourse at the affective end of the spectrum of rhetoric because they zoom in like a camera to reveal sharper and sharper details and create a dynamic sense of movement. But as the sentence above about corporate leaders illustrates, cumulative sentences also function usefully, though less dramatically, in discourse toward the factual end of the spectrum, where they vary form and rhythm and expand base clauses gracefully.

Active and Passive Voice. If you write most of your sentences in active voice, you will be effective most of the time. Active voice is dynamic and creates smooth, flowing sentences:

> The presidential candidate debated the issue of a mandatory balanced budget.

Passive voice is static because its main verb draws in the *be* verb, which states mere existence and is wordy. Nevertheless, writers in scientific, technical, and academic fields often choose it because it allows writers to deemphasize the doer in favor of what was done and gives the appearance of objectivity:

> The oil-viscosity balance method can also be used in either a two- or three-dimensional steady flow.

It is also the choice of writers for any kind of writing if the agent is far less important than the object of the action:

> John was lifted into the ambulance and rushed to the emergency room of the hospital.

When passive voice is used sparingly, it can be a technique for gaining emphasis (John certainly is more worthy of emphasis than the anonymous lifter). It can also help achieve coherence:

> The San Joaquin Valley is an elongated basin or trough oriented on a northwest-southeast axis dropping slightly in elevation in a northwest direction toward San Francisco Bay. Most of the study area is drained by the Fresno Slough, which flows in the center of the valley, approximately dividing the study area.

When overused, however, as it often is in serious, formal prose, it creates a leaden style. Look through your final drafts for passive constructions to see if you can enliven your prose by rephrasing passive constructions into active ones.

Sound and Rhythm

We often lose sight of the importance of sound and rhythm in writing because we think of them as critical only to oral interpretations. But compare these two phrases as you say them aloud: "world enough and time" and "time and world enough." The words are the same, but their different ordering changes the rhythm. You will realize why Robert Penn Warren chose the former, not the latter, as the title of one of his books. To put the importance of sound and rhythm to a greater test, read aloud an average news story, government document, or technical report. Because they are planned for the eye only, reciting them will be like riding a carpet over cobblestones. Even though prose intended to be read silently is not expected to appeal conspicuously to the ear like fiction, poetry, or speeches, it nonetheless affects readers positively or negatively depending on its sounds and rhythm. Pleasant sound and rhythm alone will not bring readers into agreement, but they can smooth the way.

Qualities of Sound

Most vowels by their nature are pleasant sounds; they carry the "music" of language. A number of consonants, on the other hand, are harsh (*g, k,* and *d,* for example). They can even influence the unpleasantness of a vowel like the short *u* in such words as *mud, slug,* and *cud.* Unpleasant sounds explain why names such as *Waukegan, Muskogee, Pismo,* and *Cucamonga* grate on our ears while *San Marino, New Orleans, Louisiana,* and *Hawaii* do not. Avoiding harsh consonants, especially in close repetition, makes even discourse intended to be read silently more pleasant. Groups of consonants that are hard to pronounce have an effect similar to that of harsh consonants. Keep in mind the trouble some people have pronouncing such words as *chrysanthemum* and *aluminum* and revise sentences like this: "The seething mass of shiny sea shells shifted in the sunlight."

Other awkward, annoying sounds are series of unstressed syllables ("seemingly needlessly she checked each slat on the blind for dust"), rhyme ("The Life Sciences staff at Ames aims to . . ."), and alliteration, repetition of the same sound at the beginning of words or the beginning of stressed syllables within words ("the scratchy screen door"). Alliteration is a poetic device and abounds in advertising (Tony the Tiger, the Jolly Green Giant); it is best avoided in other kinds of writing unless the attention it draws to the particular words is justified.

The best way to catch unpleasant sounds and sound sequences is to read your prose aloud, listening for problems as you go. Any sentence that is difficult to enunciate needs reworking. With all the choices of words and word orders we have in English, finding substitute words or alternate arrangements is fairly easy.

Qualities of Rhythm

The rhythm of sentences, as well as their sound, conditions the reader to receive the ideas presented. Although there are methods available to scan prose (Marjorie Boulton presents a detailed study in *The Anatomy of Prose*), for most purposes our ears can adequately detect obvious awkwardness of phrasing. Most of us can sense when prose has a varied, smooth rhythm, with pleasantly varied stress. Our ears can easily distinguish the casual rhythm of ordinary conversation from the more elaborate rhythm of formal prose, with its balanced structures and antithesis.

The rhythm of a piece should, of course, be appropriate to its formality or informality. The examples below move from the most to the least formal:

At first cats would not seem to offer a likely clue to human history. Yet when one considers that the writing of adequate histories of human populations began scarcely 200 years ago, that writing itself dates back only about 6,000 years and that for many populations historical, linguistic and cultural records are inadequate or nonexistent, cats appear in a different light. They have been associated with human beings for a long time, but they have never had any economic significance and only rarely have they had much social significance. Genetically they, unlike other domesticated animals, have been left largely to themselves. The study of the population genetics of cats is therefore rewarding not only for what it reveals about the evolution of cats but also for what it suggests about the movements of human populations.

Neil B. Todd, "Cats and
Commerce," Scientific American

Although to be driven back upon oneself is an uneasy affair at best, rather like trying to cross a border with borrowed credentials, it seems to me now the one condition necessary to the beginnings of real self-respect. Most of our platitudes notwithstanding, self-deception remains the most difficult deception. The tricks that work on others count for nothing in that very well-lit back-alley where one keeps assignations with oneself: no winning smiles will do here, no prettily drawn lists of good intentions. One shuffles flashily but in vain through one's marked cards — the kindness done for the wrong reason, the apparent triumph which involved no real effort, the seemingly heroic act into which one has been shamed. The dismal fact is that self-respect has nothing to do with the approval of others — who are, after all, deceived easily enough; it has nothing to do with reputation, which, as Rhett Butler told Scarlett O'Hara, is something people with courage can do without.

Joan Didion, "On Self-Respect"

The most miserable and lonesome half day I ever spent in my life was one morning in Madrid. I got up at 8:30 and went out on the street. Well, from then to noon I had Madrid entirely to myself. They commenced piling out for coffee about eleven. That don't mean the working people don't work; they do. You will see them going to it at night in the fields and in the city up to and after nine o'clock.

Will Rogers, Letters of a Self-Made
Diplomat to His President

Notice that the paragraph from *Scientific American* begins with a direct, minimally modified, fairly short sentence, followed by a stately periodic sentence, a compound sentence with some understated parallelism, a sentence with a parenthetical interruption, and finally a logical conclusion (explicitly marked by *therefore*) with a balanced structure ending the paragraph on a strong note.

On the other hand, Didion puts her sentences together in a more conversational, apparently less considered manner. The alternation between tension and relaxation in the paragraph as a whole, however, indicates that Didion was fully conscious of the effects she was trying to create. Notice the slow movement of "in that very well-lit back-alley where one keeps assignations with oneself" followed by the rushed finality of the two negations. Notice too the effect of the dashes on what follows, for example, the piece-by-piece parallelism of "the kindness done . . . ," as if Didion is, indeed, flipping through cards, picking and choosing what she will mention.

Despite its conversational quality, however, the balanced structures, the bunching of strongly accented syllables, and other devices keep the Didion passage from the colloquial rhythms of the Will Rogers paragraph. Rogers's sentences are short, direct, and simple, except the last, which is slowed by its sound sequences, "going to it at night" and "in the city up to and after" to match the slow start of the workers. "Well" demands a pause and marks a turn. The paragraph is, on the whole, very close to a report on the Madrid morning that Rogers might have given orally to a friend or written in a personal letter.

A Case in Point

The aesthetic dimension of writing provided by sound and rhythm is necessary in all kinds of writing, even technical, scientific, or academic discourse. Unfortunately, in these professional areas, gracefulness is often sacrificed to degrees of accuracy that are pursued by habit, beyond necessity. Typical is this excerpt from *Administrative Attribution Theory* by James and Romana Frasher:

> It has been observed that life outcomes are distributed in an asymmetrical manner. Most outcomes are judged to be positive, but extremely negative outcomes occur more frequently and are judged to be even more pervasive in effect than extremely positive events.

The air of scientific objectivity and machinelike rhythm of the sentences contrast sharply with the gracefulness of natural speech. Although the following revision is not an outstanding aesthetic gem, it does move with a more human rhythm, with its simpler word choices, parallel structure, and active instead of passive voice:

> Although in life more good naturally occurs to people than bad, extremely bad events loom larger than extremely good ones and affect people more deeply.

The revision sacrifices only the conventions of professional discourse, not meaning.

We could present hundreds of examples of writing that echo stylistic crystallizations from other professional discourse, but let us settle for one more, the linguist Charles Osgood's (ironical) definition of style as

> an individual's deviation from norms for the situation in which he is encoding, these deviations being in the statistical properties of those structural features for which there exists some degree of choice in his code.

Is such convolution necessary? Does it say any more or is it any more accurate than the following more graceful and concise translation?

> Style is the choice of words that writers make in particular situations.

Much writing for college and after will be in the professional genres, but it need not imitate bad examples of professional style. No matter what the subject or genre, all writing should incorporate the gracefulness of one human making something for another.

Sentences as a Whole

From the detailed discussion in this chapter, constructing effective sentences may seem much more difficult than it is. With practice and experience, the general texture and flow of your sentences will begin to improve intuitively. As you experiment with unfamiliar structures and revise haphazardly written sentences, you will more rapidly and easily arrive at sentences that say gracefully what you intend them to say so that someone else will be glad to read them.

EXERCISES

1. Make one unified sentence from the following series of choppy, disconnected sentences:

   The casket was closed. It was light gray trimmed with brass. A simple wreath lay on its top. It was made up of red and white roses intertwined with baby's breath and ferns. The casket held what was left of Fayne's body. The murderer had shot her. He had put her body in the trunk of the Cadillac. The body had been in the trunk several days before it was found.

2. Break apart the following into separate, unified sentences, or rewrite each to form one unified sentence:

a. The factory makes cars, and the robots installed on the assembly line to attach bumpers are increasing productivity.

b. Silicon Valley consists of a narrow corridor of land stretching from San Jose north along the west side of San Francisco Bay up to San Francisco, and it is the home of many high-tech companies.

c. Some organizations use a format for investigative reports in which the introduction is a summary in which the introductory questions are fully answered, and the developing sections are briefly mentioned only as a means to reach the conclusions, which receive major emphasis.

This next one (from Gore Vidal's introduction of Seward in his book *Lincoln*) is for the brave:

d. Once red-haired, now white-haired, large-nosed, pale-eyed long-time master of the state of New York not to mention of the youthful Republican Party, as well as President-that-might-have-been had Lincoln's managers not outmaneuvered his managers at the Chicago convention, William H. Seward was seven years older than his rival the new President, whose hand he now shook, saying in a husky voice, richly seasoned by a lifetime's addiction to cigar smoke and snuff, "You're every bit as tall as I thought you'd be, Mr. Lincoln."

3. Recast the following sentences to achieve better coherence:

a. Margaret would much rather make an attempt, no matter how weak, at swimming in Senior Masters' competition herself, than watching an Olympic race.

b. To become a good swimmer, a person must learn to coordinate arm and leg movements and correct breathing must be mastered.

c. The AFL has advocated expansionism since the days of the union's first president, Samuel Gompers.

d. The right of the states to call a constitutional convention exists, but perhaps it should not be tested, for an amendment requiring a balanced budget might hamstring Congress in emergencies, yet something needs to be done to bring spending in line with taxes.

e. Submit time cards each Monday following the close of a week's work prior to ten o'clock.

f. In 1967 in Michigan, a suit was denied for recovery of emotional damages for a mother who watched petrified from a park bench as her son was killed by a negligently driven automobile. In California in 1968, the Supreme Court, then probably the most progressive in the country, allowed recovery for mental suffering for a mother who had witnessed her child's death by a negligently driven automobile, however.

g. Often before a person decides to major in a particular discipline, they take introductory courses in the subject in which they discover an intense interest.

h. Stocks, in relation to the extremely attractive returns available in money market funds, remain at a disadvantage, meanwhile, despite the excellent records and promising prospects of many top-quality issues.

4. Take the sentence "Jeffrey wants a 1933 classic MG." Rewrite it with *only* placed to indicate the following meanings:

    a. Jeffrey, no one else.

    b. Jeffrey wants but won't buy.

    c. Jeffrey doesn't want any other kind of car.

5. Assume you have these three clauses: "the process was modified"; "the problem was solved"; and "the photograph was obtained." Why does the combination of the clauses cohere in sentence a but not in sentence b?

    a. After the photograph was obtained and the problem solved, the process was modified.

    b. After the photograph was obtained, the process was modified, though the problem was solved.

6. Recast the following sentences to achieve more effective emphasis:

    a. Conflicting data was all the tests resulted in.

    b. There is the crucial factor of public opinion to consider, however.

    c. This game would determine the championship. Would that starting gun never go off! My heart was racing. My hands were clammy. My cheeks burned.

    d. The reason people do not listen to alternative views is because they feel threatened, Carl Rogers says.

    e. It was evident to the mayor that the strike against Bonanza Copper Company would create never-ending animosity between the strikers and the nonunion workers who had taken their place.

7. Read each of the following sentences carefully. All are written in passive voice. Determine which carry appropriate emphasis. Recast in active voice those that would achieve more effective emphasis in that form.

    a. John Hinkley was found not guilty by reason of insanity after a lengthy trial.

    b. A lost leg, or a lifetime of pain, or scarred beauty cannot be repaid by money.

    c. Knowledge is acquired when we succeed in fitting a new experience into the pattern of our past experiences.

    d. The momentous decision to divorce was made by them in the midst of a casual conversation.

8. Combine these short sentences into a periodic sentence that holds off the main thought until the end. Keep the original meaning as you subtract unneeded words and add connectors and other needed words during the rearrangement.

The city world is so alien to the world of open fields, woods, and streams. It seems impossible that people choose the former over the latter. There are throngs of people. There are buses, darting taxis, honking horns. Gaudy billboards proclaim their wares. Glass and brick, asphalt and cement, stone and steel bisect the area.

9. Combine the following to take advantage of parallel structure and climactic order for emphasis:

Music Center audiences are captivated by the ballerinas. The ballerinas perform accurate tiptoe spins. They twirl effortlessly and execute endless leaps and pliés. They are also able to float like light down.

10. Invert the order in the following sentences to gain emphasis:

   a. The pilot proceeded bravely, but not fearlessly, to land the plane on the bomb-pitted, litter-strewn runway.

   b. That evening the flood crested with dramatic force.

   c. The solitary, crumbling gray shack on the cliff loomed ominously over the beach.

11. The sentences in the following passages have been deliberately broken into small units from the original (Isaac Asimov's "The Case Against Man" from *Science Past–Science Future*). Recast the passage to provide sentences of varied structure and length.

The average density of population of the earth's land surface is about 73 people per square mile. That is at the present moment. Increase that density ten thousandfold. Then the average density will become 730,000 people per square mile. That will be more than seven times the density of the workday population of Manhattan. We might assume that mankind will somehow spread itself into vast cities floating on the ocean surface (or resting on the ocean floor). The average density of human life at the time when the last nonhuman animal must be killed would be 310,000 people per square mile over all the world. The world would include land and sea alike. That would be little better than three times the density of modern Manhattan at noon.

We have the vision, then, of high-rise apartments. They would be higher and more thickly spaced than in Manhattan at present. They would spread all over the world. They would spread all across the mountains. They would spread across the Sahara Desert, across Antarctica, across all the oceans. The apartments would all have their load of humanity. There would be no other form of animal life beside. And on the roof of all those buildings are the algae farms. The little plant cells would be exposed to the Sun so that they might grow rapidly. They would form protein for all the mighty population of 35 trillion human beings. They would do this without waste.

12. All the sentences in the next paragraph are cast in the passive voice. For the sake of variety, cohesion, emphasis, or all three, recast all the sentences except one in the active voice. Be prepared to justify your choice. Create agents for the actions as needed for subjects that fit in with the topic.

During the course of the project, several training workshops and a demonstration were held to introduce XYZ personnel to the application of Landsat data in the planning and routing of electric transmission lines. The Landsat demonstration was held at the XYZ general offices in Sacramento. The various workshops were conducted throughout the project to train two XYZ employees in greater depth on Landsat image processing techniques and procedures. Two field trips were made to the Fresno area for ground data collection at the study site.

13. Compose ten cumulative sentences using the following base clauses. Try to add at least three free modifiers at different levels of specificity.

   a. The rain peppered the roof.

   b. Gregory spent several hours on the beach at Malibu.

   c. The young man edged around the crowd.

   d. The black smoke filtered through the window.

   e. There she stood.

14. Collect several samples of your writing with different subjects, audiences, and purposes. Then find well-written professional samples with similar subjects and purposes. Read your writing aloud, and then read the professional writing to realize the potentialities of rhythm related closely to subject matter, audience, and purpose. Look for strategies you can adopt in your own writing.

Chapter 12

Paragraph Sense

As we think, organize, and phrase, then rethink, reorganize, and rephrase, we clarify and validate our ideas, not only to draw others into agreement with them but also to achieve agreement with ourselves. Ordering the continuous flow of ideas in our minds, we sort and shape and finally make chunks of meaning — paragraphs. Paragraph indentations and surrounding white space represent on paper what we sense as thought units. Such signals guide readers through the progress and development of our ideas.

A paragraph can be seen as a microcosm of the whole discourse. It often starts by announcing something general about a topic, then proceeds to elaborate and support this generality. If it is the entire discourse, the paragraph ends with a sense of resolution. If not, it ends with a partial sense of resolution that leads into the next paragraph, and so on until the resolution of the final paragraph is reached. This basic building block can also be seen as a macrocosm of a sentence, stating a topic and, through its details, predicating something about it. Like the whole discourse and its individual sentences, effective paragraphs depend upon unity, coherence, emphasis, and variety. They also rely on rhythm, which accrues from the sentences that compose them. But paragraphs enclose something beyond individual sentences. As Gertrude Stein said, "A sentence is not emotional; a paragraph is."

Unity

We might record ideas floating in our minds:

I admire Chicago's beaches. Surfing the big waves at Malibu demands superb balance and uncommon daring. Many people in Eastern Oklahoma enjoy float trips down the Illinois River.

We can write them down so that they form the shape of a paragraph, but they do not produce a paragraph. Some vague connection — water — exists, but the sentences are not obviously related. They are a random list in need of added ideas and connectives to unify them.

179

To produce a unified paragraph, we seek a unifying idea, a topic sentence that operates much like the core statement of an entire discourse except that it draws together a smaller unit of detail. For example, the first sentence in this paragraph is a generalization for all the details that follow:

> The oddest thing about the twentieth-century chimera of security is that it was forged in the age of greatest threat. No disaster so imminent and so uncontrollable as total war was ever dreamt of before the atomic age. It seems as if men have only to defuse one kind of threat before another takes its place. Disease grows more complicated; the possibilities of aggression and destruction exceed Pope Gregory's wildest dreams. An international agreement proscribes the use of gas and so germ warfare must be developed. And so forth. Insecurity in human life is a constant factor, and I suppose efforts to eliminate it are just about as constant.
>
> Germaine Greer, "Security," *The Female Eunuch*

Greer's paragraph leans on description. Expository and argumentative paragraphs usually contain more explicit topic sentences:

> This grief, shame, and guilt are not very far from feelings of anger and rage. The process of grief always includes some qualities of anger. Since none of us likes to admit anger at a deceased person, these emotions are often disguised or repressed and prolong the period of grief or show up in other ways. It is well to remember that it is not up to us to judge such feelings as bad or shameful but to understand their true meaning and origin as something very human. In order to illustrate this I will again use the example of the child — and the child in us. The five-year-old who loses his mother is both blaming himself for her disappearance and being angry at her for having deserted him and for no longer gratifying his needs. The dead person then turns into something the child loves and wants very much but also hates with equal intensity for the severe deprivation.
>
> Elisabeth Kübler-Ross, "On the Fear of Death," *On Death and Dying*

In both paragraphs, a topic sentence guides the development, ensuring against digressions, against the inclusion of extraneous matter. Notice, by contrast, this next paragraph:

> The Democrats sent two basic kinds of delegates to their 1984 convention. Under the 1984 rules, however, pledged delegates were not forced to vote for their candidates. Some delegates wondered before they went to the convention if there might be an alternative candidate to Mondale, Hart, or Jackson. But the party pros doubted that a viable fourth candidate could emerge.

The first sentence leads readers to expect development of two categories of delegates. The second sentence appears to establish one category, that of pledged delegates, which would imply a second category of unpledged delegates, but the second category never appears. The paragraph moves associationally throughout: 1984 and delegates in the first sentence lead to 1984 rules and pledged delegates in the second sentence, all of which leads to some delegates (presumably pledged ones) wondering about a fourth candidate, which in turn leads to a statement about the party pros' opinion on a fourth candidate.

Although associational organization might be workable in some writing at the affective end of our spectrum (think, for example, of the long, purposefully meandering paragraphs in Faulkner's novels or some of Tom Wolfe's semijournalistic pieces), for most writing, paragraphs need logical development.

A topic sentence at the beginning of a paragraph tells both writer and reader where the details will be heading. Sometimes, however, topic sentences belong in the middle of a paragraph, forming a bridge between the material coming before and after. At other times, especially when readers need to be seduced into the generalization being presented because they might not agree with it on the spot, an inductive order is more appropriate, with the topic sentence held off until the specifics have been presented.

Not all paragraphs have topic sentences. Professional writers frequently imply rather than state them. Writers in early stages of development, however, find the topic sentence indispensable as a guide for the paragraph and as a device to check the development of the core statement. Just as the sentences of a paragraph should develop the idea of the topic sentence, topic sentences should develop the ideas of the core statement.

Coherence

No definite rules assure order and connection in all discourses. Let us take a piece of writing about an accident for an example. A police report would start with the activity closest to the accident itself and proceed through subsequent events, avoiding colorful comments or descriptions peripheral to the matter at hand. Transitional devices would be in evidence, but the chronological progression of events, the narrative, would provide coherence. Placement of words and phrases would emphasize the "actor" in the accident:

> A medium blue 1969 Mercedes 230 four-door sedan crossed the intersection of Yale and McClintock. . . . It swerved sharply. . . .

A reasoned argument for the innocence of the driver, on the other hand, would offer more choices in ordering ideas. A writer might begin with the driver, or perhaps the scene, and would shift perhaps to the driver's psychological state or other information not suitable for a report. A poem inspired by the accident would be filled with strong appeals to the senses, with colorful and noisy imagery, emphasizing the sounds and sights of violent activity. Transitions might be omitted altogether, and ideas would be arranged in a way that would convey an overall impression of the disorder of the scene. In fact, the poet might even jumble images incoherently to exaggerate the chaos.

In most prose you will write, however, coherence within paragraphs is achieved by assembling related ideas that develop one main idea and by weaving the sentences together through logical bridges and connectives. Coherence between paragraphs is achieved the same way.

The following paragraph appears to have a clear topic sentence and a series of sentences that bear on the topic sentence:

> Some important advances in computer technology came in the 1940s. The first digital computer was the Mark I. Howard Aiken completed the first digital computer in 1944. Aiken was a Harvard University professor. He called his computer Mark I. John von Neumann was an American mathematician. He developed the process for storing a computer program in computer memory. The process was a significant discovery. Both mechanical and electrical devices were used to control the operations of Mark I. The first digital computer controlled by vacuum tubes was ENIAC. University of Pennsylvania engineers built ENIAC in 1946. ENIAC is an acronym for Electronic Numerical Integrator and Computer.

Although the sentences individually relate to advances in computer technology or are subordinate to sentences that do so, the reader is unable to construct meaningful relationships because the sentences are incoherently assembled. Compare this revision:

> Some important advances in computer technology came in the 1940s. John von Neumann, an American mathematician, made the most significant discovery of the decade. He developed the process for storing a computer program in the computer's memory. And in 1944 Howard Aiken, a Harvard University professor, completed the first digital computer, which he called Mark I. Both mechanical and electrical devices were used to control the operations of the Mark I. Then in 1946 some University of Pennsylvania engineers built the first digital computer controlled by vacuum tubes. They called it the Electronic Numerical Integrator and Computer, but it quickly became known by its acronym ENIAC.

Now instead of stumbling, readers can glide through the paragraph without having to figure out relationships between ideas. The topic sentence provides the unifying core; example and chronology provide the means of organization. Each sentence not only foreshadows the content but also echoes and amplifies the idea that has preceded. The technological advances march steadily forward, each one followed by a detail or two, a pattern that emphasizes each advance in turn. The coherence is assisted by connectives, for example, pronoun reference (*von Neumann/he*) and transitional words (*then*) to join sentences.

The appropriate rhetorical operations, details, and connectives for achieving coherence will appear almost automatically as you write, but other possibilities will elude you because you are so close to the writing. In general, first drafts should be as full of details as possible. It is much easier to cross out details that do not fit when you revise than to reopen paragraphs and put in more detail. It is also easier to pay attention to connective devices during revision, both those between sentences and those between paragraphs.

Downshifting

Structure is usually imposed by one or more of the rhetorical operations. The computer paragraph above, for example, was structured with exemplification and chronology, which are the operations of definition and narrative. A way to examine the structure of a paragraph, regardless of what operations are employed, is to look at whether and how a paragraph "downshifts," that is, how the paragraph accumulates sentences that support the topic sentence and each other. Some supporting sentences serve as minor topic sentences, having a lower level of generality and generating still more specific supporting statements:

> Some important advances in computer technology came in the 1940s.
> > John von Neumann, an American mathematician, made the most significant discovery of the decade.
> > > He developed the process for storing a computer program in the computer's memory.
> > And in 1944 Howard Aiken, a Harvard University professor, completed the first digital computer, which he called Mark I.
> > > Both mechanical and electrical devices were used to control the operations of the Mark I.
> > Then in 1946 some University of Pennsylvania engineers built the first digital computer controlled by vacuum tubes.
> > > They called it the Electronic Numerical Integrator and Computer, but it quickly became known by its acronym ENIAC.

Notice that the first sentence, the topic sentence, is set off on one level, with all the other sentences subordinate to it, and that along the way sentences are subsubordinate to the subordinate sentences. Notice, too, that with each lower gear, the material becomes more specific, provides a detail for the more general sentence it supports.

Try to use downshifting consciously as you write and revise.

Transitional Words and Phrases

Transitional words and phrases establish relationships between connecting statements. They signal or mark the meaning between consecutive ideas. The most common words and phrases are these:

Addition
again
also
and
besides
equally important
finally
first, second, etc.
further
furthermore
in addition
last
likewise
moreover
next
nor
or
similarly

Contrast
after all
although
at the same time
but
conversely
for all that
however
in contrast
in spite of (that)
nevertheless
nonetheless
notwithstanding
on the contrary
on the other hand
still
yet

Comparison
in the same way
likewise
similarly

Result
accordingly
as a result
consequently
for this reason
hence
in short
so
then
therefore
thus
truly

Purpose
for this reason
to this end
with this purpose

Emphasis
in any event
in fact
in particular
indeed
more important
most important
particularly
specifically

Example/Illustration
for example
for instance
in particular
in this manner
namely
that is
to illustrate

Reiteration
in other words
that is
to put it another
    way

Concession
after all
although this may be true
at the same time
I admit
naturally
of course

Conclusion/Summary
finally
in brief
in conclusion
in short
in summary
last
lastly
thus
to conclude
to sum up
to summarize
on the whole

Passage of Time
after a while
afterward(s)
at lag
at length
immediately
in the meantime
lately
later
meanwhile
presently
shortly
since
soon
temporarily
then
thereafter
thereupon
until
while

In guiding readers through a discourse, transitions enhance coherence, but they do not make it. A superficial sprinkling of *consequently*s, *moreovers*, *howevers*, and *on the other hands* is too weak a glue to hold together illogically assembled ideas. Even if the ideas are logically assembled, the sprinkling of transitions becomes an annoying mannerism. But how often and where shall we use them?

Fortunately, research in memory and comprehension can give writers some guidelines. This research shows that we process negative statements more slowly than positive ones. (It is a good reason to rewrite negatives as positives whenever possible: "Limit your driving speed to fifty-five" rather than "Don't drive above fifty-five.") Furthermore, we process reversal statements more slowly than continuing statements. Sentences apparently raise expectations of "something similar to follow." As long as something similar does follow, we can automatically supply the connection. Conversely, when a sentence discontinues the pattern of the preceding one, we are much more in need of a stated connection, a transition.

As an example of a paragraph that raises and fulfills the expectation of more of the same to follow, look again at the piece about advances in computers. Because the arrangement is straight chronology, transitions between sentences are often omitted and those that are included (*and* and *then*) could be omitted without loss of coherence. We can supply the connectives easily:

> Some important advances in computer technology came in the 1940s. [For example] John von Neumann, an American mathematician, made the most significant discovery of the decade. [That is] he developed the process for storing a computer program in the computer's memory.

On the other hand, notice what happens to coherence if a connective that points to something opposite is omitted:

> If such changes include a reduction in size and cost and an increase in operating capability, it is easy to assume that the user will be encouraged to communicate more frequently than he does at present. The major influence of the telephone on his life might come from an interaction between communications technology and other factors which have nothing to do with technology.
>
> James Burke, *Connections*

Burke assured coherence by starting the second sentence with *but*. Insert it and notice how much easier the sequence reads.

In general, transitions mark the more continuous relationships that are not obvious. Since simple addition is the most easily perceived relationship, the *ands* and *alsos* between sentences and paragraphs are least needed. On the other hand, if you want to call attention to accumulated details, you might use "not only . . . but also."

Type of relationships and emphasis, then, to a large extent determine how often to use transitions.

Transition Sentences and Paragraphs

Within and between paragraphs of shorter pieces, transitional words and phrases usually suffice to maintain coherence, provided, of course, that all paragraphs bear some organic relation to each other. Longer pieces, however, may require larger elements — sentences and even transitional paragraphs. These may be summaries of the preceding material followed by foreshadowing. They are ways of reinforcing the reader's memory and forecasting what is to come. Notice how the opening sentence of the second paragraph below accumulates the material of the preceding paragraph and applies it to the material that follows:

> From the beginning, the new state was built on four interrelated means of control: centralized and absolute authority, bureaucracy, terror and militarism. Lenin's Commissar of War, Leon Trotsky, once declared, "The dictatorship of the Communist Party is maintained by recourse to every form of violence." Violence was institutionalized in two forms, the secret police for dealing with the internal threats to Soviet rule and the Red army for dealing with external ones. From the birth of the Soviet Union, both institutions enjoyed special powers and privileges.
>
> *Autocracy, bureaucracy, terror and militarism all reached their culminations under Joseph Stalin.* He converted the party into a reflection of his personal will, made the secret police a state within a state, and during World War II became the first political leader to award himself the rank of Marshal of the Soviet Union. Carrying the logic of Marxist-Leninist vigilance and militancy to grotesque extremes . . .
>
> "The Specter and the Struggle,"
> *Time,* January 4, 1982

Sometimes a transitional paragraph presents a climactic statement about the preceding discussion and then announces the subject of the upcoming discussion. In the following excerpt the first sentence comes on the heels of a compressed history of school lunch programs dating back to 1970. The second signals the subject of the next half dozen paragraphs.

> Enter Richard Nixon, attuned to the public mood. In language that could have been taken from any liberal Democratic manifesto, Nixon proclaimed: "Something very like the honor of American democracy is at issue. America has come to the aid of one starving people after another. But the moment is at hand to put an end to hunger in America itself for all time." At his behest, Congress in 1970 passed amendments to the National School Lunch Act that gave the program its current structure.
>
> "Backing Down on Benefits," *Time,*
> October 12, 1981

Even lengthy discourses, however, may rely on transitions consisting of only a single word or a short phrase to map connections between paragraphs. More critical than the length of the whole discourse is the complexity of the subject matter and its familiarity to the audience. The more complex the subject and the less knowledgeable the audience, the more need for fuller transitions that review and forecast as well as point out relationships, especially turns in another direction.

Equivalence Chains

Equivalence chains are another device to mark connections between logically related sentences. They may be either exact repetitions of a key word or synonyms for a key word. Although repetition can be ungainly, it is often necessary. Unnecessary repetitions typically say again what was easily understood the first time. Necessary repetitions insure that the reader understands some complex idea, or in the case of equivalence chains, bind the sentences of a paragraph into a unit. Note how the repetition of *rule(s)* functions in this excerpt:

> [In a newly formed psychotherapy group] certain behaviors become *rules* merely as a result of their occurrence and uncontested acceptance (or uncontested modification) by the other group members. In communications research, this phenomenon is called limitation and refers to the fact that every exchange of messages, however given, inevitably narrows the number of possible next moves. In other words, even though a given event may never be officially mentioned, let alone officially approved, the mere fact that it happened and was tacitly accepted sets a precedent and thereby creates a *rule*. The breaking of such a *rule* then becomes intolerable, or at least wrong behavior. This is just as true for animals defining their territory as for interpersonal or international relations.
>
> Paul Watzlawick, "The Emergence of Rules," *How Real Is Real?*

Sometimes, when variations on a term can be easily understood, a writer chooses a chain of synonyms to achieve coherence:

> *Oppressed people* cannot remain oppressed forever. The yearning for freedom eventually manifests itself, and that is what has happened to the *American Negro*. Something within has reminded him of his birthright of freedom, and something without has reminded him that it can be gained. Consciously or unconsciously, he has been caught up by the *Zeitgeist*, and with his *black brothers* of Africa and his *brown and yellow brothers* of Asia, South America and the Caribbean, the *United States Negro* is moving with a sense of great urgency toward the promised land of racial justice. If one recognized this vital urge that has engulfed the *Negro community*, one should readily understand why public demonstrations are taking place. The *Negro* has many pent-up resentments and latent frustrations, and he must release them. . . .
>
> Martin Luther King, Jr., "Letter from Birmingham Jail"

Synonyms, however, might confuse readers. For instance, if a writer were discussing surveillance of the enemy, the writer would choose *electronic surveillance* and *surveillance plane* rather than *electronic eavesdropping* and *patrol plane* because readers might know too little about defense strategies. If the synonym might bewilder readers, repeat the key word instead.

Pronoun Reference

One of the most obvious devices to achieve coherence, so obvious we might overlook it, is pronoun reference. Used too often, pronouns bore; used without a clear reference, they confuse; but used appropriately, personal pronouns directly and simply indicate to the reader that "these sentences belong together."

> As the 10-year plan took shape and the capability grew, there were many other gaps to be filled. NASA was going to be markedly different from NACA in two important ways. First, *it* was going to be operational as well as do research. So, *it* would not only design and build launch vehicles and satellites, but *it* would launch *them*, operate *them*, acquire data from *them*, and interpret the data. Second, *it* would do the greater part of *its* work by contract, rather than in-house as NACA had done.
>
>   Frank W. Anderson, Jr., *Orders of*
>   *Magnitude: A History of NACA*
>   *and NASA, 1915–1980*

Equally useful as linking devices are demonstrative pronouns and adjectives: *this, these, those, that,* and *such,* provided they are used clearly. We call these words demonstrative pronouns when they point back to something near the end of the preceding sentence or paragraph: "*This* was what I wanted." We call them demonstrative adjectives when they are accompanied by a noun and point both backward and forward to the noun that follows: "*This result* was what I wanted." Demonstratives can refer to extensive material, an entire, detailed sentence, or even a paragraph:

> At midnight Luknitsky awakened his friend Ludmila Fedorovna. They sat down to a New Year's feast — a bottle of champagne he had saved from the war, 200 grams of almonds he had gotten at the Writer's Union and three pieces of dog meat which he had saved especially for the occasion. *This kind of scene* was enacted all over Leningrad on New Year's Eve.
>
>   Harrison E. Salisbury, "The Sleds of
>   the Children" *The 900 Days: The*
>   *Siege of Leningrad*

Notice how *this kind of scene* summarizes and clarifies the preceding sentence for readers. Compare the ambiguity of the demonstrative pronoun in the following:

> Kathleen's report on student activities on campus was outstanding, and her grades have improved. *This* should help her when she looks for a job.

One of the following revisions, depending on the meaning intended, would clarify matters for the reader:

> Kathleen's report on student activities on campus was outstanding, and her grades have improved. *This writing skill* should help her when she applies for a job.

> Kathleen's report on student activities on campus was outstanding, and her grades have improved. *This academic record* should help her when she applies for a job.

With complex material, careful reference becomes even more important for readers:

> The major difficulty associated with any attempt to determine shock normals from observations at a single spacecraft is the problem of obtaining the proper values for the pre- and post-shock plasma parameters. In the case of a fast quasi-perpendicular shock, the plasma parameters upstream and downstream of the shock generally remain fairly constant, and *this* is easy. But for slow shocks . . .

The demonstrative pronoun needs to become a demonstrative adjective, followed by a clarifying noun. *Task* following *this* would help, especially if the sentence parts were reversed:

> This task is easy in the case of a fast quasi-perpendicular shock because the plasma parameters . . . But for slow shocks . . .

As you revise your writing, be alert for demonstrative pronouns (especially the ubiquitous *this*) to see if their reference is perfectly clear; if not, change them to demonstrative adjectives and add a clarifying noun or noun phrase to sum up for your readers the gist of what you are referring to before they move on.

Parallel Structure

We have already mentioned the advantages of parallel structure within sentences. As you will remember, structures are parallel when their grammatical patterns match:

NOUNS:	Certain transitional words signal a *contrast, qualification,* or *concession.*
PREPOSITIONAL PHRASES:	Government *of the people, by the people, and for the people.*
NOUN CLAUSE:	The report shows *how the film is exposed and developed* and *why the process should be modified to enhance finer distinctions.*

Such structural repetition links the ideas that are expressed in the repeated structures; it gives prose continuity and, if used often, a certain distinctive rhythm.

These advantages hold for paragraphs as well as sentences. In "Letter from Birmingham Jail," Martin Luther King, Jr., uses parallelism to connect ideas not merely within individual sentences, as in this example:

> So *let him march: let him make prayer pilgrimages to the city hall: let him go on freedom rides*—and try to understand why he must do so.

He also uses parallels to connect sentences within paragraphs:

> *I have traveled* . . . On sweltering summer days and crisp autumn mornings *I have looked* . . . *I have beheld* . . . Over and over *I have* found *myself asking* . . .

E. B. White ties together an entire essay, "Khrushchev and I: A Study in Similarities" in *The New Yorker* (September 26, 1959), by using parallel structure in topic sentences of paragraphs, as with tongue in cheek he compares himself to Nikita Khrushchev:

> Khrushchev, the story says, is a "devoted family man." . . . Khrushchev, the article says, "enjoys walking in the woods with his five grandchildren." . . . The newspaper story says Khrushchev leads a "very busy life." . . . Khrushchev's wife, it says here, is a "teacher." . . . Khrushchev, it turns out, has a daughter who is a "biologist." . . . Khrushchev's son is an "engineer." . . . During vacations and on Sundays, it says, Khrushchev "goes hunting." . . . Khrushchev has been an "avid reader since childhood." . . . "Mr. Khrushchev is the friend of scientists, writers, and artists." . . . Mr. Khrushchev, according to the news story, "devotes a great deal of his attention to American-Soviet relations." . . . "he always finds time to meet Americans and converse with them frankly on contemporary world problems." . . . Mr. Khrushchev, the story goes on, "has a thorough knowledge of agriculture and a concern for the individual worker."

White finds, as you will too, that parallelism serves ideally to balance thoughts when comparing and contrasting objects, people, or ideas. He relies on it heavily in this essay, notably in his last paragraph, where his irony turns darkly serious at the end:

> Well, that about winds up the list of points of similarity. It is perhaps worth noting that Khrushchev and I are not *wholly* alike—we have our points of difference, too. He weighs 195; I weigh 132. He has lost more hair than I have. I have never struck the moon, even in anger. I have never jammed the air. I have never advocated peace and friendship; my hopes are pinned on law and order, the gradual extension of representative government, the eventual federation of the free, and the end of political chaos caused by the rigidity of sovereignty. I have never said I would

bury America, or received a twenty-one gun salute for having said it. I feel, in fact, that America should not be buried. (I like the *Times* in the morning and the moon at night.) But these are minor differences, easily reconciled by revolution, war, death, or a change of climate. The big thing is that both Khrushchev and I like to walk in the woods with our grandchildren. I wonder if he has noticed how dark the woods have grown lately, the shadows deeper and deeper, the jay silent. I wish the woods were more the way they used to be. I wish they were the way they could be.

Reports or scientific and technical articles depend on parallelism less dramatically and frequently, but to no less effect. Albert Einstein maintains flow and cohesion with a series of questions:

> But what is the origin of such ethical axioms? Are they arbitrary? Are they based on mere authority? Do they stem from experiences of men and are they conditioned indirectly by such experience?
>
> Albert Einstein, "The Laws of
Science and the Laws of Ethics,"
My Later Years

It is important to remember that all these methods of creating coherence from sentence to sentence, paragraph to paragraph, and section to section can succeed only if the materials are unified. Relationships can be shown, that is, only if they exist.

Emphasis

The primary means of achieving paragraph emphasis are position and length. Like emphasis within sentences, the naturally emphatic positions for sentences within a paragraph and for paragraphs within a discourse are first and last. Uniqueness of length is also a means of achieving emphasis; that is, a short sentence or paragraph may be placed in the midst of long ones, or a long one in the midst of short ones.

We have already pointed out the importance of the beginning and ending paragraphs of a discourse, the beginning paragraph (or two in a longer piece) because in it the writer makes a commitment to the reader and the last paragraph or two because they reinforce the readers' understanding of what they have read and their attitude toward it.

Topic sentences, as mentioned earlier, may occur elsewhere than as the first sentence in a paragraph, but for reasons of both coherence and emphasis, they usually are the opening sentence. Occasionally, however, suspense may be appropriate to the subject matter and the author's aim, and holding off the topic sentence until the end of the paragraph may enhance its force:

It can start in just one of the body's billions of cells, triggered by a stray bit of radiation, a trace of toxic chemical, perhaps a virus or a random error in the transcription of the cell's genetic message. It can lie dormant for decades before striking, or it can suddenly attack. Once on the move, it divides to form other abnormal cells, outlaws that violate normal genetic restraints. The body's immune system, normally alert to the presence of alien cells, fails to respond properly; its usually formidable defense units refrain from moving in and destroying the intruders. Unlike healthy cells, which stop reproducing after repairing damage or contributing to normal growth, the aberrant cells respect few limits or boundaries. They continue to proliferate wildly, forming a growing mass or tumor that expands into healthy tissue and competes with normal cells for nutrition. Not content with wreaking local damage, the burgeoning tumor sends out groups of malevolent cells, like amphibious invasion forces, into the blood stream, which carries them all over the body. Some perish on their mission. But here and there, many of these mobile cells establish beachheads on healthy tissue and begin dividing, forming new tumors. Eventually the marauding cells infiltrate, starve and destroy vital organs, incapaciting and usually bringing death to their unwilling host. Cancer has claimed another victim.

> "The Big IF in Cancer," *Time,*
> March 31, 1980

The last two sentences jointly form the topic sentence. Notice the impact of the very last sentence, which is not only short and emphatic but also solves the "mystery" of the subject under discussion.

Just as all paragraphs do not have topic sentences, all paragraphs do not have concluding statements. Some simply end with a final detail. Often, the concluding statement is delayed for several paragraphs until the topic has been sufficiently developed. But when it does appear, whether summing up one paragraph or several, it shows how the preceding material, the topic, and details fit the overall subject.

Positioning old before new information also creates emphasis. If a writer gives readers something familiar, the new information naturally captures the most attention as readers relate it to the preceding information:

With the booming economy of the 1960s and most of the 1970s, many Americans discarded their old belief that hard work, self-denial, and moral rectitude brought their own rewards. These traditional notions were replaced by a new belief, held fervently and misguidedly by some, that more *important was the realization of one's own full potential.*

The first phrase of this paragraph sums up the economic and social conditions of the 1960s and 1970s discussed in the previous paragraph; then the rest of the sentence goes on to list discarded old beliefs. The subject of the second sentence sums up the now old information of the first; the predicate of the second sentence adds a new dimension to the subject. The last idea stated is the most important of the whole paragraph. The key point of the paragraph, emphatically arranged to make sure readers remember it, is tied to the information at the start.

Try this pattern of moving from old to new information. Or, if your ideas need several paragraphs for development, hold your most significant ideas for the end of the last paragraph to achieve climactic force.

A short paragraph in the midst of longer paragraphs also draws the reader's attention. It is an excellent way to summarize a series of key points before moving on or to highlight a main point or change direction in the midst of a presentation:

> Berkeley personnel did their best to supply all of the data HEW requested. The review culminated in a demand that the university adopt an affirmative action hiring program, although the university was never specifically charged with having discriminatory hiring practices. Nor was the university told what it had to do. The frustration of the university was best expressed by Robert Kerley, the vice chancellor for administration, who said: "It was a bit like being in a ballgame against a team that was making up the rules as it went along."
>
> The university never really had the benefit of a clear-cut Government position. There was never any explicit charge or specific demand.
>
> The responsibility for developing an "acceptable" — to HEW — affirmative action program was on the university. What the university was required to overcome was not a charge of discrimination, but of "underutilization" of minorities, a determination that was in part based on the population composition of the bay area. What that had to do with Berkeley's hiring practices is unclear, but it was part of the utilization formula against which the university was judged by bureaucrats having the discretionary power to withhold substantial Federal funding.
>
> James L. Buckley, *Congressional Record*, March 2, 1976

In this sequence Buckley uses the short paragraph to highlight a key point. Elsewhere in his statement, Buckley uses a long sentence to create emphasis:

> Discriminatory hiring practices have no place in our country. America should pride itself upon guaranteeing each of its citizens an equal opportunity to earn a decent living. To benefit one man at the expense of another, for reasons no more relevant than sex, or race, or national origin, is a perversion of civil rights.

As is often the case, this emphatic long sentence occurs in a pattern of sentences that successively increase in length; the accumulating length reinforces the emphasis of the final statement.

Variety

When the discourse has achieved coherence and unity, all parts add up to the intended meaning. It coheres into a unified whole; ideally the seams do not show. Yet the discourse may not be effective if its paragraphs lack variety.

The means of achieving variety in paragraphs are primarily mode of development, length, and scale.

Mode of development is varied by thoughtful application of rhetorical operations. For example, if the discourse or part of it proposes to analyze and compare two objects, the analysis may procede to define, exemplify, classify, describe, narrate. An argument may need to define a term in one paragraph, give reasons in another, illustrate in a third, and so on.

Although paragraph length is often determined by accepted practice in a genre (newspapers require short paragraphs for their narrow columns and so do books for young minds), aspects of the subject can justify varied length in most prose. Serious and complex subjects call for longer paragraphs than light and simple subjects. Accepted convention also provides reasons for variation. Narrative episodes dealing with rapid action typically appear in a series of short paragraphs, while descriptive paragraphs are longer. Accepted practice also calls for a separate paragraph when the narrative shifts to dialogue, as well as a new paragraph for each shift to another speaker. Paragraphs for emphasis, as we have seen, are shorter or longer than their neighbors.

The scale of paragraphs refers to their depth and breadth. These are relative terms. A paragraph of depth might develop in detail one sentence in a paragraph of breadth, usually a subtopic of that paragraph. Here is an example of a paragraph of depth:

> During normal operations, the air passes directly through the filters and drier beds into the tunnel. After the bauxite has become saturated with water, it is put on a reactivating cycle. During this cycle air is drawn in through the filters by the fan, through the burners (the coolers are inactive in this cycle), the beds, and out through the valve. The burners heat the air to approximately 400°F so that the moisture can be driven off. The beds are then cooled by running the fans in the reverse direction.

If the scale of the subject of the discourse as a whole is broad, then rather than using paragraphs to elaborate details about a single topic, the writer assembles the topics into broader units. Summaries and abstracts are always paragraphs of breadth. In paragraphs of breadth, individual topics take the place of details, and all the topics relate to one larger topic, or subject. The preceding example is reduced to a single sentence, or less, in the paragraph of breadth, which may serve to introduce the paragraph of depth we have just read and others like it:

The tunnel can be operated either as a propulsion wind tunnel (open circuit) or as an aerodynamic wind tunnel (closed circuit), depending upon the position of the 24-foot diversion valve which is downstream of the compressor. With the valve in proper position, the tunnel operates as a propulsion wind tunnel. *Air is drawn from the atmosphere through the drier and cooler.*

However, even with allowances made for convention and particular rhetorical situation, it is true that writers in professions generally write longer paragraphs, intersperse paragraphs of breadth with paragraphs of depth, and also vary the lengths of their paragraphs more than student writers. Short paragraphs, especially in the serious kinds of writing done in college and the professions, often indicate a phase of the subject that has been insufficiently developed. Except for transition paragraphs or those intended to emphasize a point, a rule of thumb is that a paragraph with less than three sentences is probably insufficiently developed. Too many paragraphs of breadth often signal too much generality. The lack of such paragraphs, on the other hand, may inhibit the reader's view of the whole.

A Final Paragraph

When revising paragraphs, the key to remember is accountability. Writers are accountable for what they say. And they are accountable to the reader for saying it in a logical, coherent, and emphatic way, for providing paragraphs that have variety and interest. Nothing is sacred about paragraphs as written in first drafts. Work with them until they show a progression of thought, one after another, and each is a forceful structure in itself.

EXERCISES

1. The following excerpt is from the World section of *Time* (May 21, 1984), a weekly magazine, which uses three columns on a page for its news reports:

   By traveling to the frontiers of the Christian faith [referring to the Pope's May 1984 trip to New Guinea], John Paul wanted to dramatize his conviction that the future of Roman Catholicism lies in the developing world. About one-third of Papua New Guinea's 3.4 million people are Catholics, but the church leaders have had to struggle to adapt their faith to a culture in which cannibalism is still a living memory. A tongue-in-cheek column in a local newspaper assured the Pope, "Don't be scared, sir. We won't eat you." After the tight security that surrounded John Paul's visit to South Korea, the Pope seemed to revel in the enthusiastic reception that greeted him in Port Moresby, the capital of Papua New

Guinea. The Pontiff won many hearts when, at a Mass, he said the Lord's Prayer in pidgin English, the most common local patois. "Papa bilong mipela, yu stap long heven . . ." At the local sports field he watched benignly as bare-breasted women in grass skirts chanted hymns and drummers sporting feathered headdresses pounded out an accompaniment on hollow logs covered with animal skins. When the Pope gave his blessings to the crowd, the shouts of "Mi laikim Jon Pol!" were deafening. Warring tribesmen had called a temporary truce in honor of the Pontiff's visit. At Mount Hagen, from an altar covered with a thatched roof and lavishly decorated with hibiscus, orchids, bougainvillea and battle shields, the Pope made a plea for permanent peace to the crowd of almost 130,000. Then he gave Communion to warriors who glistened with pig fat and wore headdresses of black hawk feathers and crimson and golden plumes from the bird of paradise.

Out of the river of words and sentences, mark off meaningful segments into paragraphs. Be prepared to justify your choice of paragraph demarcations on the basis of paragraph unity.

2. Read the following paragraph. Decide which sentence is the topic sentence. What effect would be created if the sentence were moved to other places in the paragraph?

The thematic approach attempts to divide the past into subjects such as Transport, Communications, Sail, Steam, Warfare, Metallurgy, and others, but this implies a degree of foreknowledge where none exists. Thus Bouchon's use of perforated paper in 1725 to automate the Lyons silk looms had nothing to do with the development of calculation or data transmission, and yet it was an integral part of the development of the computer. The Venturi principle, basic to the structure and operation of the jet engine or the carburetor, was originally produced in an attempt to measure the flow of water through the pumps. Gutenberg's movable typeface belonged as much to metallurgy or textiles as it did to the development of literacy.

James Burke, "Inventing the Future," *Connections*

3. Take the following jottings for a paper. Arrange them into groups that could become unified paragraphs in a paper arguing for or against students working their way through college. Then write one paragraph:

summer jobs
the working student
getting into graduate school
getting a career job
choice of occupation
choice of college
grades

social life
college costs
independence
developing responsibility
time management
money management

4. Reorder the following sentences into a coherent paragraph. Be prepared to explain the elements in the sentences that determined your decisions.

The other planets (except Mercury) rotate quickly on their axes.

But Venus is not only rotating slowly; it is also rotating in the "wrong" direction.

Astronomers do not know why Venus rotates so slowly.

Mercury has been slowed by tidal friction because of its closeness to the Sun.

One possibility, proposed some years ago, is that Venus once had a big satellite that revolved around it in the retrograde direction.

The Sun could not have caused this.

This satellite crashed into Venus and stopped the planet's rotation, or perhaps even pushed it a little into rotating the opposite way.

5. In the following paragraphs from Justice Harry Blackmun's observations on the Bakke decision (*Petitioner* v. *Allan Bakke,* June 28, 1978), the transitional words and phrases have been replaced by blanks. Using the list of transitional words and phrases on page 184 as a guide, supplemented by transitional words that come to mind which are not on the list, fill in the blanks. Be prepared to explain your choices.

I yield to no one in my earnest hope that the time will come when an "affirmative action" program is unnecessary and is, _____, only a relic of the past. I would hope that we could reach this stage within a decade at the most. _____ the story of Brown v. Board of Education, 347 U.S. 483 (1954), decided almost a quarter of a century ago, suggests that hope is a slim one. At some time, _____, beyond any period of what some would claim is only transitional inequality, the United States must and will reach a stage of maturity where action along this line is no longer necessary. _____ persons will be regarded as persons, _____ discrimination of the type we address today will be an ugly feature of history that is instructive, _____ that is behind us.

   The number of qualified, _____ highly qualified, applicants for admission to existing medical schools far exceeds the number of places available. Wholly apart from racial and ethnic considerations, _____, the selection process inevitably results in a denial of admission to many qualified persons, _____, to far more than the number of those who are granted admission. _____, it is a denial to the deserving. This inescapable fact is brought into sharp focus here because Allan Bakke is not himself charged with discrimination and yet is the one who is disadvantaged, _____ because the Medical School of the University of California at Davis itself is not charged with historical discrimination.

6. Take a paragraph from a composition you have written, one of at least five sentences. Cut the sentences into separate pieces of paper,

and clip the pieces together. Trade paragraph pieces with a class-mate. Try various orders for the sentences. When you achieve the most logical, coherent arrangement, draw circles around the words or phrases used to connect the sentences. Underline examples of parallel structure. Add any needed devices to achieve coherence; bracket any of your additions. Discuss with your trading partner the results of your work.

7. Find several advertisements from magazines or sales letters (the "junk" mail you often throw out). Analyze the means used to achieve emphasis. Pay particular attention to the last paragraph.

8. Take a composition you have written and experiment by combining two short paragraphs into one longer paragraph for emphasis and isolating a sentence or two into a short paragraph, again to create emphasis. Or add material to accomplish emphasis. Clip the old and new versions together and exchange with a classmate. Critique the attempt to achieve emphasis.

9. Choose a topic from a field that particularly interests you and develop it into two paragraphs, one a detailed paragraph of depth and the other a general paragraph of breadth.

10. Read the following material, which represents part of a news report by Amy McKay in the June 21, 1984, issue of *The Astrogram,* an in-house publication for the employees of NASA at Ames Research Center, Mountain View, California. Paragraph it first for a newspaper column, then for a textbook page. Add topic sentences as needed for your textbook paragraphs. Try to deliberately vary the length of your paragraphs within the constraints of the genres specified.

Comet Encke, now traveling between Earth and Venus, is losing water at a rate approximately three times greater than expected for its distance from the Sun. This surprising finding, scientists say, could be due to the particular arrangement of ice and dust that the comet is made of, or to crumbling of "mesas and hills" that may cover the surface of the 2 kilometer (1.2 mile) diameter comet nucleus. The Pioneer spacecraft in orbit around Venus made the Comet Encke observations. On April 13, mission controllers at Ames turned the long-lived Orbiter upward from observing the cloud-shrouded planet to look across the solar system at the passing comet. The Pioneer Venus Orbiter was launched in 1978 to make a detailed scientific study of Venus, and the spacecraft continues to study atmospheric circulation and other Venus phenomena. However, the recent comet observation was only the second time since Venus's arrival that the Orbiter has been used to examine another object. Since Comet Encke is closer to the sun than the last time measurements were made (in 1980), astronomers expected the rate of water evaporation to be higher, but only a third as high as the Pioneer observations indicate. Comets are thought to be made mostly of dust, rocky material, and water ice — cosmic dirty snowballs hurtling through space. However, the distribution of cometary ingredients may vary, which would explain why the rate of water evaporation varies. Astronomers theorize that the ice and dust could be distributed unevenly, so that as the comet rotates, at the rate of once every six and one-half hours, it exposes different materials to the Sun. Particularly icy portions would vaporize faster. Since comets probably aren't smooth round balls, surface irregularities like steep-sloped hills and mesas may also cause variations in water evaporation rates. However, the exact makeup of comets — whether the ice and dust are layered, mixed together in chunks, or form hills and valleys — remains a mystery.

SECTION THREE

Rhetorical Forms

As we go from one end of the spectrum to the other, our uses of rhetorical structures and operations become more or less formal, that is, more or less complete and logically precise.

Approaching the affective or poetic pole, language grows more metaphorical; instead of merely explaining or exemplifying abstract ideas, we represent them with concrete images. We render them with personal experience. Instead of stating our purpose and following operational forms rigidly at this end of the spectrum, we accumulate a dominant impression or mood. We seek concrete words to embody experience directly rather than abstract words that discuss or analyze experience. More importantly, the tone of voice of our discourse becomes more pronounced at the affective end of the spectrum. Tone tells the reader how to accept the words: satirically, ironically, lyrically, sentimentally, joyously, sadly, wistfully. At the poetic pole of the spectrum, the logical precision of words as they relate to the external world of things becomes less important than the emotive precision of words as they relate to the private, internal world of the writer.

In the other direction along the spectrum, through the argumentative and factual portions, the rendering of dominant mood or impression is replaced with the statement of purpose or problem, with the logical processes of thought, and with more formal structures that accompany these processes: classificatory, analytic, comparative, descriptive, definitive. Emphasis lies more on the subject itself than on the writer's attitude. The writer's individual voice, however, can never be eliminated to achieve the ideal of complete objectivity, often identified as scientific tone.

In general, essays, reports, letters, and other forms can be categorized for study and practice according to some position along the spectrum of rhetoric. We can envision the essay at the emotive or affective end of the spectrum growing more formal as it becomes more argumentative and factual, its voice fading and its images of reconstructed experience yielding to the abstractions and facts of research papers and reports.

It has been common to speak of personal or informal as opposed to formal essays, but, actually, the idea of formality contradicts the original idea of the essay. Its inventor, Michel de Montaigne, described the essay in 1580 as a personal effort "without straining or artifice." As for subject, "It is myself I portray." Thus the essay was originally an effort to present self. It was personal or, we might say, familiar. And it is still essentially informal, as distinct from reports and treatises. In popular and professional periodicals, the term *article* usually replaces the term *essay*, regardless of degrees of formality or familiarity. The term *article* is also applied to reports, where it is assumed that information is transferred from writer to reader without the writer's personal voice.

Frequently, however, reports are arguments that reach conclusions and make recommendations. Some reports that merely pass on information are called informal and seem closer to the expository article. To add to the confusion of terms for the various forms of discourse, a writer may choose to report information in a letter or memo, or write an essay as a report as in the new journalism. One way of distinguishing professional reports or research papers from articles and essays, whether argumentative or merely descriptive, is by way of formal apparatus. Professional reports and research papers are written for specific, usually captive, audiences — readers who must read. They are often organized according to formats that have distinct parts and subparts with appropriate headings and documentation. Letters also have formats, but these are conversational, beginning with a salutation ("Dear Stan:") and ending with a complimentary close ("Sincerely,") which are extensions of personality, however formal. Letters always retain voice, as essays or articles do. They have tone, which carries the writer's attitude. In even the most informative of essays and explanatory of letters, as distinct from research papers and reports, the reader is influenced by the writer's voice and tone.

Chapter 13

The Letter

In the Middle Ages, letter writing displaced the messenger or envoy who could adjust the sender's message. If the envoy's news was particularly unwanted and the receiver unduly emotional, the bringer of the news could be killed. And perhaps with some justice. Because the message was shaped by the messenger's tone, given in his voice, he was partially responsible for the meaning. Perhaps the tradition for cordiality in modern letters originated in the necessity for survival among ancient messengers.

Although the first rhetoricians had many things to say about oral discourse, they provided no instruction or theory on written rhetoric. Not until the fourth century did writing instruction appear in the work of a rhetorician, and then it was introduced as *epistola,* letters. Like sermons, the medieval epistle was clear and brief, an oration. From the beginning then, we have the closeness of sender and receiver and the goals of clarity and brevity. However, the letter was not yet seen as a written conversation. It was mostly for exchanges between people on affairs of state, court, and business; it followed, therefore, certain procedures of formal decorum. The written equivalent of a boisterous laugh or drunken garrulity was offensive to the reader. Openings were elaborate and closings even more so.

Two types of letters were soon distinguished — official letters (*negotiales*) and familiar letters (*familiares*). Letters of negotiation argued serious matters of government, commerce, and church and explained matters in history, the sciences and arts, and philosophy, all less formally than tracts or treatises. Familiar letters offered advice and exchanged social niceties with their own decorum. Writing to a person of superior social status, the sender avoided jocular tones. Writing to a social equal, the sender avoided discourtesies. Writing to a social inferior, the writer avoided condescension. All letters, official or familiar, had to use language appropriate to the purpose, whether to praise, blame, request, congratulate, inform, console, claim, or convince. The salutations and signatures showed relative station or status and degree of friendship.

With the epistles of Augustine and Jerome, letter writing in the fourth century became literature, but then with the failing of the Roman Empire in the following centuries, men of high station became less literate and required servants to write and read for them. Professional letter writers emerged. Soon they devised formulas for recurring situations, and by the eleventh century, letters were forms having three distinct parts: an exordium or introduction that prepared readers for what was to follow and created goodwill; a narration that explained the matter or purpose of the letter; and a conclusion that summarized, attitudinized, or requested the action the writer desired and again sought the reader's goodwill. Essentially we have here the concerns of form and tone we practice in letter writing today.

Familiar Letters

The familiar letter is the means of "declaring the mind of him who sends to the mind of the one to whom it is sent," wrote the twelfth-century master of letters, Bernard de Meung. At least since the twelfth century the familiar letter has simulated intimate conversation, but suggests, nevertheless, a larger audience with several others reading over the addressee's shoulder, even when the letter is specifically marked "Private." It also retains some flavor of a literary piece written for the entertainment of the receiver or an official record written for posterity, especially when produced by persons aware of their public importance. It is because of this extra dimension that we learn from and enjoy still the letters exchanged between John Adams and Thomas Jefferson.

The familiar letter directly expresses our thoughts and how we think them, whether to close friends or acquaintances. It is the offering of personality, a matter of style. Here is George Bernard Shaw responding to an aspiring writer:

Private   29 Fitzroy Square W.
                                                     2nd December 1894

Dear Sir

The best service I can do you is to take your notice and jot down on it without ceremony the comments which occur to me. You will find first certain alterations in black ink. In them I have tried to say, as well as I can off hand, what you are trying to say: that is, since it was evident you were dodging round some point or other, I have considered the only point there was to make, and have made it. It came quite easy when I had altered your statement about Frenchmen at large to what you really meant — the conventional stage Frenchman. Always find out rigidly and exactly what you mean, and never strike an attitude, whether national or moral or critical or anything else. You struck a national attitude when you wrote that about the Frenchman and Englishman; and you struck a

moral attitude when you wrote "She has sunk low enough in all con-
science." Get your facts right first: that is the foundation of all style,
because style is the expression of yourself; and you cannot express yourself genuinely except on a basis of precise reality. . . .

Although Shaw's letter was marked "Private," it found publication,
perhaps as intended. We may also notice that it is essentially a reply to
a request, which is a standard occasion for the writing of a business
letter. Shaw's personality, however, his dramatic sensibility, will not
allow him to write one. He is style above all, as his content insists. And
the style certainly reveals Shaw's personality, primarily in the contradiction between his advice against striking attitudes and the attitude he so
staunchly strikes, that style, the "expression of yourself," is based on
"precise reality."

The reality expressed in personal letters is perhaps more internal
than external. Writers who use imitative and ornamental language can
seldom express their internal selves or reach their readers. Instead of
being simple and direct like Shaw, they sound remote and pompous in
their letters, like this:

> Dear Jonathan,
>
> I most heartily acknowledge your recent commentary on my work and
> desire to express my gratitude. Were we any less than veteran comrades
> in arms, which is not to imply a closeness that permits more than society
> sanctions, that is, as Achilles and Patroclus, I could have been hard put
> to conclude that your missive contains not a small degree askance. If
> I may be so bold as to . . . .

This is false and fatty prose that suggests an artificial personality. "A
writer who appreciates the seriousness of writing so little," Hemingway
said, "that he is anxious to make people see he is formally educated,
cultured, or well bred is merely a popinjay."

In letters to close friends or relatives, however, senders rarely take
writing so seriously. Form matters little although writers usually preserve at least the salutation and signature: "Dear June," or simply "Hi
John," with a disregard for conventional punctuation. Unless motivated
to request something (a student writing home for money), we tend to
ignore design—beginning, middle, ending—or carefully developed
paragraphs. We proceed rather spontaneously, as things occur to us.
Private letters reveal a sense of style as an innate expression of self.
Perhaps more than in any other form of writing, our style in familiar
letters directly reflects the quality of our thought and feeling. When a
close friend circles a meaning and then says, "Well, Jimmy, you know
what I mean," it may very well be that the reader does know. But it also
may be that he can't know because the writer herself may not know
until she says it, until she has clarified it for herself in sentences. Usually
unclear sentences reflect unclear thought.

Style, like personality, is far more than clarity. To give even to the closest friend an account of one's experience or attitudes or to advise or gossip, the writer needs flavor, color, and grace — all inexact qualities that yield pleasure, that attract beyond reason or direct utterance, and thus arouse goodwill. The means for achieving these qualities of style are the same as those in all other writing.

Aspects of Style

In the Middle Ages, there were elaborate efforts to define style in letter writing. Texts on the subject concentrated on classical figures of speech called *colores* because they gave color. Prose rhythms were also emphasized. To find and develop a personal voice, students for centuries after the Middle Ages were set to imitating various rhythms, sentence structures, and metaphorical forms. They imitated the ribaldness and copiousness of the Renaissance writers and the balance of Samuel Johnson, whose regular sentence rhythms and exactness implied the very essence of the Age of Reason, a thorough belief in human perfectibility. In our era, students have imitated the lean reportorial style of Hemingway. Enduring aspects of all these styles are found in all good writers.

Conscious efforts to write poetically, however, mostly result in overwrought prose that is likely to cause laughter:

> Dear Elaine,
>
> The sky on this quiet Hawaiian eve is purple and blue with white striations, and I am thinking of that moment at the picnic last year when all the mystery of existence leaped into my heart; it was before the cruel sorrow of your rejection on the moonless night that followed, so dark and bleak.

Elaine will have to fight the urge to laugh at the artificial sentiment of such poetic prose. The voice is certainly personal, but it is not one that can be heard for very long. Perhaps some genuine feeling can be transmitted by means of the imagination. The writer may realize, for instance, that everything suggests Elaine's rejection.

> Even this Hawaiian evening — purple and black — reminds me that I no longer have you.

Or perhaps the writer can suggest his meaning symbolically by seeing some import in the sky:

> The evening was bewildering in its deep silence, as if something had happened in the world; as if the soul of it had been turned upside down.

Familiar letters, like familiar essays, pass on experience, information, or gossip with attitudes about them. To breach the solemnity of straightforward statements of attitudes, letter writers employ humor as most people do in day-to-day conversation. Here is Robert Frost, for example, in *Letters to Louis Untermeyer*, acknowledging a request for information from a friend:

> Department of English
> Amherst College
> Amherst, Massachusetts
> December 1, 1917

Dear Louis:

  I seize this department stationery to give you a new sense of what a merely important person I am become in my decline from greatness. Will you please by return boastage make us knowing to any humors or emollients you have been unable to understand from under?

  I notice that there are a number of poems by various people in the magazines for last month and this month — or rather I assume there are: I haven't looked to see.

  Answers in full to all your recent questions by telegram are going forward to you by slow fright.

> Always and forever yours,
>
> Robert

Frost's playful tone carries him to the extreme of Joycean punning, "boastage" for postage and "fright" for freight, which in itself would be a joke at the expense of the swiftness assumed in telegraphy. Such humor has roots in the Rabelaisian prose styles of the Renaissance, practiced most notably in English by William Shakespeare.

Another source of humor in familiar letters is the use of balanced sentences for antithesis, which stress contrast rather than similarity:

We are preserving peace by preparing for war.

It is a sin to believe evil of others, but it is seldom a mistake.
  H. L. Mencken

She was not curious but wise.

He started the fight; she finished it.

Irony — meaning the opposite of what you say — also brings humor, sometimes very serious humor:

He rose, ferocious, but she calmed him with a club.

"Shut up," he explained.

We abolished them utterly, leaving not a baby alive to cry for its dead mother. This is incomparably the greatest victory that was ever achieved by the Christian soldiers of the United States.
  Mark Twain

We had to destroy the village to save it.
U.S. soldier in Vietnam

One aspect of style popular in modern fiction — stream of consciousness — comes directly from familiar letters. In fiction the flow of thought without syntax or punctuation is intended to imitate the rush of sensations, fantasy, and reflections as they occur:

> I'll see if he has that French letter still in his pocketbook I suppose he thinks I don't know deceitful men all their 20 pockets aren't enough for their lies then why should we tell them even if its the truth they don't believe you.
>
> James Joyce, *Ulysses*

Coherence among these fragments usually emerges by their juxtaposition and by their association within the stream. Writers of familiar letters have always used the stream of consciousness, not as imitation of thought, but as an actual representation of it. The stream of consciousness in letters may actually be more telegraphic than associational, especially when the sender and receiver are close. Each shares much of the other's experience and so can complete the thought:

> Dear Stan,
>
> Funny, I got the money this week. The first day was frightening without it. But classes are possible. . . .

Stan may translate:

> I got the money this week, although I needed it for tuition last week. I feared they wouldn't let me begin without it, but they did. I'm finding the classes are not as difficult as I thought.

Business Letters

Some elements of the medieval formulaic letter, as we have noted, continue in the familiar letter, at least the salutation and close. In the same way, the conversational tone of the familiar letter carries over to the business letter, especially in its indications of goodwill. Since friendship with the reader is not assumed, the writer must be more aware of the reader's perspective, which letter-writing texts call the "you" attitude. Consider this example:

> I assume your office will understand, for obvious reasons, that I am in no position at this time to honor your request for payment.

Instead of making the reader guess, a writer aware of the reader's perspective might offer the reasons why payment cannot be made and request forbearance:

May I have a brief extension without causing you any great inconvenience? I will appreciate your patience at this difficult time for me.

Misunderstanding the "you" attitude as the use of the *you* can lead to ruffled feeling:

You didn't send your check.

The preceding statement is less aware of the reader's perspective than this one:

We didn't receive your check.

Tone

The writer's tone carries his or her attitude toward the reader, the respect for feelings, desires, and states of knowledge. We must remember that carelessness in grammar, usage, and spelling indicates a lack of manners, and therefore a lack of respect. So do excessive abstractions, stinginess in giving the reader sufficient information, or garrulity in giving too much. We also affront readers when we shower them with jargon, the slang of a profession, or clichés taken from the stockroom of letter writing in previous times. These habitual ways of writing destroy the conversational element that all letters retain. The sensitive receiver of this message would probably infer that a dehumanized machine is addressing him:

Pursuant to your notice of October 10, I regret to advise you that this organization is not cognizant of the fact that we have agreed to conform as per our contract. Presently we are hopeful of an alteration in our circumstances, and in that event, we shall correspond with you again. Be informed, however, that we do not hold ourselves liable under existing agreements. Enclosed you will find, for your edification, a copy of contractual agreements between our organizations. We remain,

Sincerely yours,

But even this chilling tone is not as damaging to relations as direct assaults:

No, I don't want any repairs or replacements. I demand that your lousy company immediately send this office a refund for that worthless piece of junk you call a word processor.

An assumed pomposity to express indignation is equally insulting:

Be informed that we are appalled at the lack of workmanship in the recently purchased equipment and find it inoperative. Neither repair nor replacement will sufficiently restore our confidence. Only full restitution will be satisfactory.

Courtesy and respect for the reader have a better chance of getting the response the writer seeks. The writer might state the failure of the equipment, and the reasons why only one solution — a refund — is acceptable, then request it:

> Unfortunately, the word processor has not performed as well as you promised, and since we have lost all confidence in it, we call upon your other promise — the stated guarantee — for a full refund.

Here are some of the more commonly used clichés writers of business letters take from the stockroom:

cognizant of	(knowing that)
inoperative	(not working)
institute	(make or begin)
commence	(begin, start)
prior to	(before)
anterior	(front)
posterior	(back)
subsequent to	(after)
facilitate	(help)
encounter difficulty	(find difficulty)
presently	(soon [does not mean "at present"])
at the present time	(now, at present)
at this point in time	(now)
in this time frame	(during this time)
in the event that	(if)
in view of the fact that	(because, since)
due to	(caused by, because of)
with regard to, with reference to	(about)
the case in question, the subject in question	(the case, the subject)
enclosed please find	(enclosed)
advise	(tell)
numerous and sundry	(many)
permit me to say, please be advised	[say nothing]
it has come to my attention	(I have been told, informed)
in accordance with your request	(as you requested)

The Writer's Ethos and the Reader's Desires

To achieve an effective tone writers must observe more than mere manners. They must be aware of their readers' expectations, as in conversation, and attend to the standard questions all readers raise on all rhetorical occasions:

1. Is the writer credible? Qualified to address me on this subject?
2. Is the writer honest with me? Open-minded with the subject or partial to one view of it? Is information being withheld or distorted?

Answering these questions as her own reader, the writer assumes an acceptable *ethos,* a character that attracts the reader. An acceptable — that is, good — character encourages the reader to agree on the material presented. Another related appeal is the quality of the writer's logic, whether or not she presents the material sensibly. If readers notice non sequiturs or illogical chains of cause or effect, their serious attention often turns to laughter.

Another appeal is to the reader's pathos or desires. The writer may not appeal directly to a reader's desires but must know enough about the reader so that he does not contradict or frustrate them. If the writer does not know the reader's moral, religious, or political attitudes, all implications and all possibilities of inferences should be avoided. Writers, however, can freely appeal to common desires for contentment, wealth, love, beauty, belonging. According to Abraham Maslow (in *Motivation and Personality*), the most successful emotional appeals are first physical — food, sleep, drink, and sex. Once these have been satisfied, people respond next to security — safe home, safe income, safe family, and fortune. Next, they respond to their need for belonging, for affection, family love, and social recognition. Once these needs have been fulfilled, however, they seek status, esteem among others by means of position, material consumption, pride of ownership, and power. Last they seek fulfillment of the self personally. Writers can use Maslow's scale to analyze exactly where their readers are. Of course, there are other desires: a sense of individuality, exclusiveness, the return of a lost one, convenience, holiness, even an innate need for conflict or the overcoming of it.

The brevity and completeness of a letter also bear on the writer's ethos and the reader's desires. In general, readers of business letters desire both brevity and completeness. If the writer rambles on without giving new information or gives irrelevent information, the reader will tend to lose respect. As ethos diminishes, so does credibility and the probability of influencing the reader. Too much brevity, on the other hand, may violate the conversational atmosphere of a letter and be taken as too curt or brusque. A writer can appear too curt when the task of a letter is to give information and the writer merely mentions where the information can be found. Again ethos is diminished. Of course, the writer has to set limits to the amount of detail, judging what to put in and what to leave out, but decisions should be made from the reader's point of view. The problem is usually resolved with appropriate generalizations and examples of important points.

Organization

The introductory paragraphs of a letter, as in all discourse, imply or state the purpose, whether it is to request or impart information, to reveal an attitude or a policy, to give advice, to suggest or require action, or to move the reader's mind. If the reader's interest in the writer's purpose is not apparent, then the writer establishes a mutual interest. In addition, writers who are not known to the reader must identify themselves. The statement of purpose may be delayed until a background statement allows the purpose to be fully appreciated:

> We are always concerned when a customer is less than satisfied, and we make every reasonable effort to assist with any problems of service. But this office is not authorized to provide the service we think is necessary. For that reason I am sending your letter to our headquarters in New York, along with my own comment favoring the action you requested.
> As I see the problem . . .

The second general part of the business letter is elaboration, which begins in the previous example with, "As I see the problem . . . " In this part the writer gives reasons for an attitude or policy held, for action taken or not taken. In the case of giving information or instruction, the elaboration is the detailed information itself, whether a description, narration, analysis, chain of causes and effects, or comparison. The elaboration may even incorporate history to explain how the effects came about if such detail relates to the purpose of the letter.

A third general part of business letters limits the material given in the second part, if limitations exist. This part is equivalent to a refutation in an argument or the statement of probable error in an investigation. To what extent can the reader rely on the information just given? How accurate or complete is it? What are the negative effects of the attitude or policy just explained? Why should they be acceptable? And how can one find ways to live with them? Why is this position the best one to take under the circumstances? Good writers always try to justify limitations:

> Unfortunately, we cannot give you all the information you need because of proprietary requirements, and some is classified by the U.S. government as secret. But I think my summary does present the general idea without violating any regulations. If I can further clarify the information, please call on me again.

The last part of the business letter is directed to the reader's reception of the content, to the question of the reader's benefit and goodwill.

Has the reader gained what the writer wished him to gain? Has the letter helped the reader make a decision? Become more knowledgeable? Rest more easily? The writer can summarize the benefit as he or she sees it. Here the writer strives for the same politeness and degree of friendliness that close conversations, extending good wishes and a desire to be more helpful if possible.

Through all parts of the organization, the writer should be aware of the following factors:

> *the purpose to be achieved* — whether arguing for or against a policy or attitude or stance, requiring or granting information, asking or granting a favor, sharing good or bad news, getting a job interview;
>
> *the reader* — whether colleague, business or professional associate, satisfied or dissatisfied customer, supervisor, employee, expert, policymaker, politician, professor, stranger;
>
> *the information the reader needs* — names, descriptions, locations, specifications, definitions, reasons, other details; and
>
> *the reader's impression* — Will the reader be persuaded? Satisfied? Pleased? Confused? Angered? Will the reader imagine the writer friendly, articulate, pretentious, unctuous, servile, obnoxious, illiterate?

The writer's courtesy generates goodwill through all parts of the letter. Notice that the letter on page 214 begins with a courteous statement and that, although the subject is technical, *you* and *I* appear frequently as they do in personal conversation. The letter's brevity and completeness extend the courtesy. There are no frills and no long-winded statements that might irritate by either confounding the reader or repeating what is already known. Although there are technical terms, there is no professional jargon or vague expression that might be misinterpreted.

Courteously using the reader's point of view, although the first person *I* and *we* occur whenever natural, also generates goodwill. Less mechanical but more important is the writer's awareness of the reader's reaction as he reads. The writer anticipates the questions his statements raise in the reader's mind (particularly in the third paragraph) and clearly answers them. For contrast, here is the opening of a letter that ignores the questions it raises:

Dear Mr. Hench:

This letter proposes the development of a pilot project to determine whether a minimum of 60 percent of the estimated oil in the Jinx field can be recovered by steam flooding in six years.

The questions that arise immediately are why the writer thinks oil recovery can be increased in this field by steam flooding and on what basis he sets the figure at 60 percent for six years? What has been the

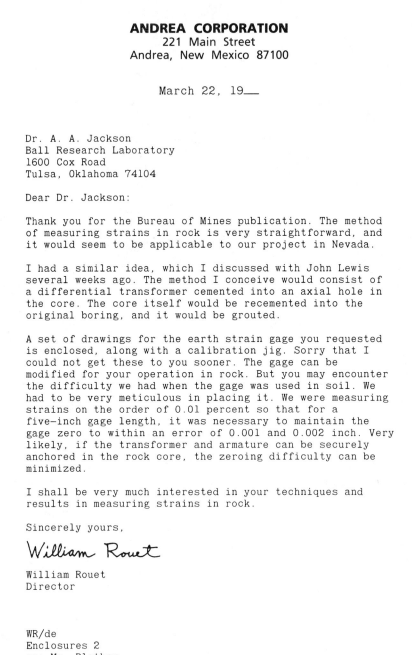

ANDREA CORPORATION
221 Main Street
Andrea, New Mexico 87100

March 22, 19___

Dr. A. A. Jackson
Ball Research Laboratory
1600 Cox Road
Tulsa, Oklahoma 74104

Dear Dr. Jackson:

Thank you for the Bureau of Mines publication. The method
of measuring strains in rock is very straightforward, and
it would seem to be applicable to our project in Nevada.

I had a similar idea, which I discussed with John Lewis
several weeks ago. The method I conceive would consist of
a differential transformer cemented into an axial hole in
the core. The core itself would be recemented into the
original boring, and it would be grouted.

A set of drawings for the earth strain gage you requested
is enclosed, along with a calibration jig. Sorry that I
could not get these to you sooner. The gage can be
modified for your operation in rock. But you may encounter
the difficulty we had when the gage was used in soil. We
had to be very meticulous in placing it. We were measuring
strains on the order of 0.01 percent so that for a
five-inch gage length, it was necessary to maintain the
gage zero to within an error of 0.001 and 0.002 inch. Very
likely, if the transformer and armature can be securely
anchored in the rock core, the zeroing difficulty can be
minimized.

I shall be very much interested in your techniques and
results in measuring strains in rock.

Sincerely yours,

William Rouet

William Rouet
Director

WR/de
Enclosures 2
cc: Mr. Blather

production history? What sort of rock and soil compose the field? What is the significance of six years? Why not ten? But rather than the answers to any of these questions, we get instead this detail:

> The proposed 65-acre section of the field is located by a connecting line drawn between wells 136, 119, 151, 262, 213, 251, 381, then back to well 131.

The reader is not ready to know the specific where and how of this proposed project without first knowing what and why.

Format

A final aspect of courtesy is the letter format itself. The format consists of a heading or return address, the inside address, the salutation, the text, the close, and the signature.

The *heading* includes the address of the sender and the date. If a printed letterhead is used, the date is placed two spaces below it, to the right, or to the left, flush with the margin. If there is no letterhead, the date appears below the sender's address, which may be placed left, flush with the margin, or just to the right of the center of the page. The date should be the day of mailing.

```
                                    411 West Fifth Street
                                    Tulsa, Oklahoma 74102
                                    December 8, 1984
```

The *inside address* appears next, four spaces down, flush with the left margin. It includes the name and address of the reader. Mr., Mrs., Ms., and Dr. are exceptions to the rule against abbreviations in letters. Do not write Capt. for Captain or Supt. for Superintendent. Titles precede the name unless they are names of offices. These follow, either on the same line or a separate line:

```
Dr. Henry Hench, President
Hench Industries
1111 First Street
New York, New York 10005

Ms. Henrietta Hench
Director of Industrial Relations
Ace Research Laboratories
101 Second Avenue
New York, New York 10005
```

It is discourteous to misspell or to write the name of the addressee any way other than the way the addressee writes it. Whenever possible, address the letter to a specific person. If the name is not known, address the letter to an office or position: Manager, Dean, President, Director. If the letter is addressed to an organization and the writer wishes a particular person to receive it, an attention line is used. It is indented and placed two spaces below the inside address:

```
Attention: Ms. Falls, Chief Engineer
```

Reference lines may also be included. In writing to some organizations, such as the Internal Revenue Service or a court, they are necessary:

```
Reference: File 102345

Reference: JC—7604
```

The *salutation* greets the reader. Unless the writer knows the reader rather well, the salutation is formal:

```
Dear Ms. Alwell:
Dear Professor Readall:
Dear Dr. Getwell:
Dear Senator Fogal:
```

Again, use the person's position if you do not know the name or sex:

```
Dear Customer:
Dear Credit Manager:
Dear Director:
```

Dear Sir can be taken as an affront if the reader turns out to be female. The same problem arises with *Gentlemen. Dear Sir or Madam* appears to be a solution, but it is awkward at best. A better solution when you do not know the name or title of the recipient is to use an attention or subject line in place of a salutation:

```
Attention:   Credit Department Manager
Subject:     Incorrect Billing on Account 408396
```

Notice that in business letters, the full colon replaces the comma of the familiar letter. Semicolons are never appropriate. Artificial openings, whether excessively formal ("My Dear Sir") or informal ("Howdy, Ms. Jackson"), are also avoided.

The *text* of the letter begins two spaces or so below the salutation. Paragraphs are single-spaced and may be indented or flush with the margin. They are separated by double-spacing. The text contains all of the discourse, including the conclusion and final assertion of goodwill.

The *complimentary close* is placed two spaces below the last line of the text, usually to the right. If the paragraphs have not been indented, the close is placed flush with the margin to give a block effect. Letter closings are conventional signs of politeness. They are forms that indicate a sense of familiarity with the reader. The most enduring are *Sincerely yours, Sincerely, Yours truly,* or *Truly yours.* To show particular respect, the writer may use *Respectfully* or *Respectfully yours,* and to show an extra degree of friendliness, *Cordially* or *Cordially yours.* On occasion, greater familiarity can be expressed with *Best wishes, Best,* or *Warmest regards.* Only the first letter of the phrase is capitalized, and a comma always follows.

The signature is aligned with the closing. It consists of the writer's name in script directly above the name in type and the writer's position title. Four spaces should be left between the close and the typed name to make room for the actual signing:

Yours truly,

Ann Peton

Ann Peton
Public Relations Assistant

If you are writing in the name of an organization that bears legal responsibility for the letter's contents, the name of the organization typed in capital letters should precede the writer's signature:

Yours truly,
MONTAGE MOVIES INCORPORATED

Ann Peton

Ann Peton
Public Relations Assistant

In addition to these major parts of the format, the typist's initials appear with the writer's (unless the writer also typed the letter, in which case no initials appear), together with a notice that enclosures are included and that copies have been distributed if either is the case. All these additions are exemplified in the letter on page 214. Postscripts may be added to indicate material that was left out either intentionally or unintentionally. A postscript follows all other notations and is placed flush with the margin.

EXERCISES

Exercises for this chapter, "The Letter," are combined with those for Chapter 20, "Kinds of Business Letters." These exercises are found on page 413.

Chapter 14

The Familiar Essay

Instead of a systematized progression of ideas, the familiar essay is a casual rendition of them. It is a conversational voice talking. The familiar essay conveys qualities of a writer's mind and emotions as it renders a subject, and it does so directly, as opposed to fiction, in which the writer's traits are distributed through characters and his or her personality masked by the requirements of dramatic form. Familiar essays present directly what writers think and feel about themselves and others or about societal conditions, events, situations, and manners. The familiar essay speculates and philosophizes about ideas and things — the past or future of mankind, the first typewriter, computers. But always the writer's attitude is prominent. The overall statement is personal rather than public: "What I believe," Montaigne said, "not what is to be believed." Rather than learn lessons, the reader experiences the writer's mind and feelings.

Quality of Voice

The style of a familiar essay, therefore, is not stuffed with "oratorical flourishes," as William Hazlett, a famous nineteenth-century essayist, called the pretentiousness of his day. The major requirement of style in the familiar essay is to convey a sense of honesty or candor, an honesty not to be achieved in the application of rhetorical operations or stylistic devices, although technique is essential in the expression of experience and thought. Honesty results from the desire and deliberate effort to tear through masks of appearances and postures. It comes from a willingness to penetrate observations both inside the mind and out, to seek the naked state of things, the "unvarnished truth" as Herman Melville called it. All Henry David Thoreau's writing was familiar essay, a simple, sincere account of his own life, not merely what he heard of other men's lives. E. B. White, a famous twentieth-century essayist who was influenced by Thoreau, found the charm of the familiar essay in its "gifts of natural candor," the avoidance of "deceit or concealment." To achieve candor, he urged writers to go to the "scene of the accident without galoshes on." Here is an example of E. B. White's candor:

> When I was in my teens, I lived in Mount Vernon, in the same block with J. Parnell Thomas, who grew up to become chairman of the House Committee on Un-American Activities. I lived on the corner of Summit and East Sidney, at No. 101 Summit Avenue, and Parnell lived four or five doors north of us on the same side of the avenue, in the house the Diefendorfs used to live in.
>
> Parnell was not a playmate of mine, as he was a few years older, but I used to greet him as he walked by our house on his way to and from the depot. He was a good-looking man, rather quiet and shy. Seeing him, I would call "Hello, Parnell!" and he would smile and say "Hello, Elwyn!" and walk on. Once I remember dashing out of our yard on roller skates and executing a rink turn in front of Parnell, to show off, and he said, "Well! Quite an artist, aren't you?" I remember the words. I was delighted at praise from an older man and sped away along the flagstone sidewalk, dodging the cracks I knew so well.
>
> The thing that made Parnell a special man in my eyes in those days was not his handsome appearance and friendly manner but his sister. Her name was Eileen. She was my age and she was a quiet, nice-looking girl. She never came over to my yard to play, and I never went over there, and considering that we lived so near each other, we were remarkably uncommunicative; nevertheless, she was the girl I singled out, at one point, to be of special interest to me. Being of special interest to me involved practically nothing on a girl's part — it simply meant that she was under constant surveillance. On my own part, it meant that I suffered an astonishing disintegration when I walked by her house, from embarrassment, fright, and the knowledge that I was in enchanted territory.
>
> E. B. White, "Afternoon of an American Boy," *The Second Tree from the Corner*

White's effort to examine his experience honestly is most apparent in his confessions: "to show off," "I was delighted at praise," and his real concern, Parnell Thomas's sister, "of special interest to me." More penetrating, however, is the ego-destroying recognition that the "special interest" was on his part only and that he "suffered an astonishing disintegration" when he merely walked by her house. We are also struck with the irony of his innocence, his reaction to Parnell's condescending "Well! Quite an artist aren't you?" He is so thrilled he remembers the very words. The sense of honesty is abetted, as it always is, by White's effort to share the scene, to render it rather than tell it, by assuming familiarity.

White begins to share his experience from the very start, with the exact details of where he lived — as if it made a difference whether he lived at No. 101 Summit Avenue on the corner of Summit and East Sidney, or just off the corner at No. 103. Still, the detail yields immediacy that gives the reader a feeling of familiarity. The house of the Diefendorfs is mentioned for the same purpose; it could have been the Wolfs' house or the Lambs'.

Candor, of course, does not require the writer to tell us everything. The details are highly selected for White's purposes, the impression he wishes to render. It is not just any sidewalk he skates on, but a flagstone one, and we feel his delight as he dodges the cracks that he knows so well. Of course there were other details in the scene that he could not use: trees, fences, other houses, perhaps other people on the flagstone sidewalk. We should also notice the importance of the writing voice. Although the focus of the essay at first glance seems to be on Parnell Thomas and then his sister, they are described minimally, two details each. The focus of the piece turns quickly to White's feelings of himself as a boy. The dominant mood is the nostalgic irony of the grown-up boy looking back. His voice is the primary experience of the essay.

Although candor is an essential quality of voice, it is not sufficient. The voice, however honest, must also have a tone. As we see in White's essay, the man looking back writes nostalgically, and this approach establishes the mood of the piece. Tone is established by the writer's choice of words and arrangement, that is, by the writer's style. Many of the words may be abstract and arranged in complicated sentences, as in this example:

> Theories of rhetoric conceived as stylistics, or as the psychology of language and symbolic behavior, or as propaganda, do not require a conception of the public. Such theories do need a notion of audience — a class of persons whose cognitive and affective states and whose habits of thought and language must be understood by a communicator who would inform or persuade effectively.

This style may be suitable for an expository article that appeals to the intellect, but not for the familiar essay, where it strikes us as pretentious. Abstractions remove the breath of life, the personality. At worst such a style invites ridicule by way of contrast with the anticipated candor:

> My respiration increased and I found myself retreating with alacrity from the hitherto ubiquitous feature so suddenly waxing abnormally in my garden.

A more familiar version might read like this:

> I began to breathe heavily and quickly stepped back from the familiar vegetable that suddenly was growing out of control in my garden.

But the use of metaphorical and imaginative language brings the experience to life:

> I gulped the air and recoiled as the cabbage in my garden ballooned before my eyes.

The tone is also influenced by allusions or references to others, to history and literature, to scientific and social theories. Allusions and references engender the learned, authoritative voice of a writer who has done her homework, who has earned the right to be heard. Of course, excessive references and allusions again approach the danger of pretentiousness. The danger, however, can be "toned down" with Montaigne's own idea of the essayist's proper attitude, one of uncertain inquiry, which gives to the writer's voice a tone of humility. Virginia Woolf admired Montaigne mainly for this tone, which "qualified the rash assumptions of human ignorance." For her, "his uncertainty translated into tolerance for human frailty and fallibility." Considering where we are—on a speck of rock in the immense universe—some tentativeness seems a requirement for the struggle with honesty, with finding the appropriate words and arrangements for representing what is felt and meant. Notice in this excerpt from Woolf's "Modern Letters," how gracefully and functionally she inserts and uses her references to English writers:

> There, of course, lie some of the chief distinctions between the old letters and the new; more care, more time went to their composition. But need we take it for granted that care and time are wholly to the good? A letter then was written to be read and not by one person only. It was a composition that did its best to deserve the expense it cost. The arrival of the post was an occasion. The sheets were not for the wastepaper basket in five minutes, but for hanging around, and reading aloud and then for deposit in some family casket as a record. These undoubtedly were inducements to careful composition, to the finishing of sentences, the artful disposition of trifles, the polish of phrases, the elaboration of arguments and the arts of the writing master. But whether Sir William Temple, who wished to know if Dorothy was well and happy and to be assured that she loved him, enjoyed her letters as much as we enjoy them is perhaps doubtful. Sir Horace Mann or West or Gray did not, one guesses, break the seals of Walpole's thick packets in a hurry. One can imagine that they waited for a good fire, and bottle of wine, and a group of friends and then read the witty and delightful pages aloud, in a perfect confidence that nothing was going to be said that was too private for another ear—indeed, the very opposite was the case—such wit, such polish, such a budget of news was too good for a single person and demanded to be shared with others. . . . Indisputably they practiced to perfection a peculiar art, born of special circumstances; but to go on, as we in our rash condemnatory mood so often do, to say that their art was the art of letter writing and that we have lost it, and that our art, because it differs from theirs, is not art at all, seems an unnecessary act of pessimism and self-deprecation.

Woolf's humble tone is preserved by the invitation to share her questions, "But need we take it for granted that care and time are wholly to the good?" and also to share her imagination, "One can imagine that they waited for a good fire, and bottle of wine. . . ." Woolf's humble tone is essential because her point is to uphold modern letters against the charge that they are not as artistic as those of previous ages. (Note the unified structure, beginning and ending on the point.) We may also observe that she characterizes the letters of previous times in terms of tone; that is, the wit is so engrained in them that we know them by their witty tones.

The personal voice, however, may carry into excessive familiarity, that is, when the tone is more familiar than the occasion:

> Lawyers, looking for a way to give themselves the honorific clout that doctors had with *Dr.* and *M.D.*, adopted *Esq.* It was and is purely affectation. Many women who are lawyers like it because it shares the pomposity equally. "Now *esquire* has general acceptance," says Irene Redstone, president-elect of the National Association of Women Lawyers. (I would say "female lawyers," but prefer to avoid litigation.) "The idea is to represent the individual as an attorney regardless of gender. The sooner we all accept *Esq.* as a term without gender, the better." (I would say "sex," rather than gender, because I don't mind dirty words.)
>
> William Safire, "On Language,"
> *New York Times Magazine* 15
> (September 15, 1985)

Both of Safire's parenthetical sentences are out of keeping with the subject of and occasion for his discussion. Less experienced writers also find it difficult to restrain themselves when they have personal experience with the subject:

> . . . the banking business, and I know it well, having put in years at the First National of Canton . . .
>
> Charles Heston, whom I met on more than one occasion, says that . . .
>
> One night Ronnie Reagan told me outright . . .

The possible variety of tones seems endless. Tones are as varied as the attitudes they convey. Besides the quality of humility or pride, tone contains a yea or nay dimension. Do we appreciate the tax we are discussing, or find it disturbing? Do we hate the new development in biology, the ability to duplicate forms of life? Or do we admire it? Are the military extravaganzas of little countries with gold-braided generals ridiculous or pathetic?

The tone tells the reader how the writer feels toward the subject. Sad? Humorous? Indifferent? Is the writer angry? Joyous? Loving? Hating? Arrogant? Indignant? Bitter? Amused? Unless writers are extremely experienced, they are wise to use language that maintains a consistent tone. Two tones for one essay confuse readers. They do not know whether to laugh or cry, whether the writer approves or disapproves, or whether he or she hates, loves, or is merely indifferent to the subject.

Whatever the specific tone of a particular essay, the fact that it is a familiar essay imparts certain general qualities of tone. The tone of a familiar essay is casual; we find in the style a strong use of personal pronouns, colloquial expressions, humorous exaggerations, and ironical understatements and inversions. The language tends to metaphor. The words build images rather than propositions and proofs. And they are concrete more than abstract. Concepts are familiar; therefore, few definitions are required (unless the essay is an effort at informal definitions). The tone of the familiar essay verges on the tone of friendly conversation, but for that reason, the writer must be cautious that the tone keeps some distance, does not become cloying or suffocating like a friend who holds her head too close or constantly touches or hugs. The assumption of too much familiarity becomes offensive. A casual tone is quite distinct from an intensely personal tone.

Use of Rhetorical Operations

Description and narration are the major operations used to develop familiar essays, but all the other operations provide strong assistance. In describing, we want the reader to perceive and sense things — to think, hear, smell, and feel — as we do. To impart such experience we have first to absorb it, and to absorb it we must observe the world both outside and inside at once, that is, how we experience the world. Then we have the task of rendering the experience, not in abstractions (it must be stressed once more), but in imagistic and metaphorical language. Description shows rather than tells. It shows what things look like, what scenes feel like, what people seem like: "a thin man of middle years, his arms dangling to his knees." Description characterizes others by what they say and how ("Cuff that young-un, Sister") or by what they own and wear or how they create the scene:

> She brought with her two uncompromising hard black boxes, with her initials on the lids in hard brass nails. When she paid the coachman, she took her money out of a hard steel purse, and she kept the purse in a very jail of a bag which hung upon her arm by a heavy chain, and shut up like a bite.

In this introduction to Miss Murdstone in *David Copperfield*, Charles Dickens employs almost as much metaphorical language as objective. He concludes by naming the dominant impression the description was intended to create. "I had never, at that time, seen such a metallic lady altogether as Miss Murdstone was." Even the adjective that names the dominant impression, "metallic," is a metaphor.

In creating a dominant impression writers concentrate on details that contribute; that is, they use them in relation to each other to build up a commonality, to create "a metallic lady," and omit details that do not contribute. For example, it would destroy the focus, the force of the impression, if Dickens had told us what the coachman wore, how the coach was painted, and whether one or two horses drew it. In Mark Twain's famous river scene that opens *Old Times on the Mississippi,* notice how each detail contributes to the dominant impression of drowsiness, which he names in an offhand way:

> I can picture that old time to myself now, just as it was then: the white town drowsing in the sunshine of a summer's morning; the streets empty or pretty nearly so; one or two clerks sitting in front of the Water Street stores, with their splint-bottomed chairs tilted back against the walls, chins on breasts, hats slouched over their faces, asleep — with shingle-shavings enough around to show what broke them down; a sow and a litter of pigs loafing along the sidewalk, doing a good business in watermelon rinds and seeds; two or three lonely freight piles scattered about the "levee"; a pile of "skids" on the slope of the stone-paved wharf, and the fragrant town drunkard asleep in the shadow of them; two or three wood flats at the head of the wharf but nobody to listen to the peaceful lapping of the wavelets against them; the great Mississippi, the majestic, the magnificent Mississippi, rolling its mile-wide tide along, shining in the sun. . . .

Twain's point of view clearly moves down the street to the wharf and finally to the river. It provides the structure for the description, while his way of seeing, the drowsiness, provides the unity for that structure. Because the scene does not offer movement or action, the writer must. Movement is essential in all description, even of a scene showing inaction. But the mood changes:

> . . . instantly . . . a drayman, famous for his quick eye and prestigious voice, lifts up the cry, "S-t-e-a-m-b-o-a-t a-comin!" and the scene changes! The town drunkard stirs, the clerks awake, a furious clatter of drays follows, every house and store pours out a human contribution, and all in a twinkling the dead town is alive and moving. Drays, carts, men, boys, all go hurrying from many quarters to a common center, the wharf. Assembled there, the people fasten their eyes upon the coming boat as upon a wonder they are seeing for the first time. And the boat *is* a rather handsome sight too.

From the moment the drayman announces the steamboat, the scene is all action; people stir from their drowsing, run to the river, and focus all attention on the glory of the Mississippi, the steamboat itself. And now, with the town's attention fully absorbed by the spectacle of the boat, the writer suspends the action and resumes the operation of description to render what they see, first the physical boat itself, overview followed by selected details, and then the people on it — again the general view, the crowd on deck, followed by the particular, the captain. Then the action is resumed, steam screams, the bell rings, wheels stop, passengers scramble ashore and on board, freight is discharged and loaded, the steamer gets under way once more, and soon the town goes back to sleep, where the description began, completing a full circle:

> . . . the pent steam is screaming through the gauge-cock; the captain lifts his hand, a bell rings, the wheels stop; then they turn back, churning the water to foam, and the steamer is at rest. Then such a scramble as there is to get aboard and to get ashore, and to take in freight and to discharge freight, all at one and the same time; and such a yelling and cursing as the mates facilitate it all with! Ten minutes later the steamer is under way again, with no flag on the jack-staff and no black smoke issuing from the chimneys. After ten more minutes the town is dead again and the town drunkard asleep by the skids once more.

The only digressive details would seem to be the flag at jack staff and the black smoke, which are prominent when the steamer comes to town but absent when it leaves. Twain stresses the character of steamboat life by highlighting these details. They represent the showmanship of the Mississippi captains, who put on a performance for the grand arrival but not for the mundane departure.

Experience of the Familiar Essay

Approximating but not imitating casual conversation, the familiar essay avoids invective, excessive sentimentality, rote feelings, and other superficialities. Although Montaigne conceived of the familiar essay as a trial or test (*essai,* that is, a trial run of an observation from life), it was still an argument, an argument with himself, to bring himself into agreement with himself and, if offered to a reader, to bring the reader also into that agreement. What makes a familiar essay agreeable to the reader?

1. It should mesh with the reader's experience and make the reader recognize the material.
2. It should entice and satisfy the reader; the language and arrangement of thought should be interesting and attractive.
3. It should provide new experience, emotional and intellectual. All writing of value involves this element of learning.

Largely then, the familiar essay shapes and transfers experience, and this process is largely a matter of communicating one's perceptions of existence or reality.

The problem of bringing others to agree with us resides in the ambiguous nature of things. In a courtroom, the truth of what happened cannot be observed. Truth is decided, or rather composed, from a variety of differing accounts. But what is reality outside of a person's experience of it? Each one encounters reality differently, and the way an individual encounters reality is the personal experience of the essay, the perceptions to be communicated, to be agreed upon. In the world out-side ourselves, we are aware of a totality of events occurring within a frame of a moment—fish eating other fish, fresh vegetables being stacked in the supermarket, ants building hills, cars crowding a high-way, a child playing with a dog, a wife and husband arguing, a young couple marrying. Many of these things could be going on, say, within five blocks of our home. Meanwhile, on the other side of the continent, and then across the sea, and within us, and in the skies above . . . and so on. Obviously we cannot order that reality. When we try, we get overwhelmed with a sense of chaos. Thus we must shape our percep-tions, our experiences, design and re-create experiences by selection and arrangement. To communicate them, we use patterns familiar to the reader, that is, our rhetorical operations and conventions.

These patterns stimulate our imaginations; they suggest associa-tions with experiences stored in our memories, and new connections, ideas, and visions surge forth. Sometimes these processes of the imagi-nation work unconsciously, as we find after deciding to "sleep on it," and lo, come the morning, our ideas are shaped, ready for the type-writer. Such uses of the unconscious are the uses of our experience. Grasping these processes we may consciously learn what we really think and feel. However, we cannot rely on the inspirations of the unconscious: they are sporadic at best. Even when we do, we must remember that shaping a composition, an essay, is a rational process, although it is imagination, emotive and intellectual, that is shaped. The shaping, we must remember, is not only to discover what we think and feel but also to bring our readers into agreement with what we have found. Success depends on the amount of sameness or agree-ment already present in our social, cultural, and psychological back-grounds. These are patterns in the reader's mind that must be touched by the essay. Actually, each reader, having distinct experiences, will receive them differently, but ideally each reader should also experience the writer's meaning as intended. It is the experience of that common meaning that we consider communication, or rhetorical agreement.

EXERCISES

1. This excerpt illustrates the importance of tone in the discussion of affairs of the nation. Politics and diplomacy, as you may know, are more matters of tone, which conveys attitude, than information. In fact, we may say that often tone *is* the information, to mimic McLuhan's "the medium is the message."

   The White House of Teddy Roosevelt was quiet but gave the nation and the world an impression of extreme toughness, little talk, and much ac-tion. Through promotion of himself as a roughrider storming San Juan

Hill, as a big game hunter slaying African lions, and so on, the president of the United States set the tone of American imperialism in his time. America would say what it meant, and any challenges would be met by force. It would brook no nonsense. "Speak softly," said Teddy Roosevelt, "and carry a big stick." And that was the tone in which affairs of state were to be conducted in the embassies and consulates abroad and in the agencies at home.

Less than thirty years later, Teddy's cousin spoke to a depressed and fearful nation in another tone, one that aimed at lifting shattered spirits. "My friends," President Franklin Delano Roosevelt began his intimate fireside chats on radio, "we have nothing to fear but fear itself." He talked much and talked well, not in the same accents and tones of the farmer and mechanic and merchant, but in a distant Harvard accent and vocabulary. On the newsreels he was seen in flowing cape, clutching in his smiling teeth a long, elegant cigarette holder with a lit cigarette, jauntily tilted into the air, a stance that illustrated to the world the unquestioned confidence of a blasé character out of *The New Yorker* magazine.

Instead of cudgeling the world into obedience as his cousin's tone suggested, Franklin Roosevelt's tone exhuded belief that the nation could regain the affluence that the depression had all but destroyed.

Determine the tones in this piece and how they are achieved. Go through the editorials in your newspaper, select an appropriate one, and write an analysis of tone, paying particular attention to the way it is achieved and how it colors the information. Is the writer's attitude, carried by the tone, as important as the content?

2. Here is one famous friend's eulogy for another. It is a selection of memories, anecdotes, that fuse into a characterization:

Marshall McLuhan, RIP
Hugh Kenner

The media sage of the Sixties was created, he surely knew, by the media. The Marshall McLuhan I began to know in the mid-Forties was a tall, trim pipe smoker ("Cigarette smokers are not interested in tobacco") whose passion was aiding people such as me to knit up what he considered unexamined lives.

Our trouble — yours and mine — was insufficient attention to what we were doing. We smoked, but weren't interested in tobacco. We flipped through magazines, but didn't adequately ponder half their content, which was ads. We drove cars — he didn't — but failed to reflect that our cars were driving us. Twenty years later his famous slogan, "The Medium is the Message," simply generalized that order of preoccupation. What you're taking for granted, it says, is always more important than whatever you have your mind fixed on. On that principle, Marshall would undertake benign regulation of any life that came near.

Precisely because my mind was fixed on teaching, I had but to reflect that it was not what I was doing. Like it or not, I was embarked on a survival game, for which to begin with I needed a PhD. Most of my Toronto instructors had been content with the Oxford MA. For my part I had a Toronto MA. Did that not suffice? I had been told it did. No, said Marshall, your mentors inhabit a backwater. The fields of force no longer emanate from Oxford. A PhD; and it had better be from Yale, where his friend Cleanth Brooks had just been installed as doyen of the New Criticism.

Twenty-four hours later we were headed south from Toronto in my car. In New York we paused to ascertain what anyone less rash would have checked before starting out, whether in that particular June week Cleanth Brooks was even to be found at Yale. He was not. We had five days to put in. Just time for a side trip to Washington where (a passer-through had indicated) the allegedly mad Ezra Pound was accessible to visitors. (Half of my subsequent life was derived from *that* visit.) Then to New Haven where the bemused but unfailingly courteous Cleanth Brooks undertook to see what could be done about getting Marshall's new protégé admitted *now*. Three months later I was in New Haven again, a doctoral candidate.

Having since been a director of graduate admissions, I am in a better position than most to be awestruck at the prodigies Cleanth must have accomplished: one more gauge of Marshall's imperious persuasiveness.

And all those dozens of hours on the road—before freeways, remember; we putter New York–Washington and return on U.S. #1, poking block by block through every obstacle, even Baltimore—he saw tirelessly to my education, which my profs had (of course) neglected shamefully. They had not even told me, for example, about T. S. Eliot, his sanity, his centrality.

Eliot was Marshall's talisman in those years. We started to collaborate on an Eliot book and read through the canon together, Marshall pontificating, I annotating. As to why that book never got written: its plan got lost, because as you can see (back to principle) if you are thinking Eliot is important, why, he can't be.

That was a problem with the McLuhan system: its emphases were by definition self-destructive. Eliot, he came to think, was fencing insights stolen from Mallarmé. If you objected that Eliot barely mentioned Mallarmé, that merely proved what an old shyboots he was.

Later he had decided that Mallarmé in turn was retailing Buddhism, and later still everybody you can think of was feeding the world hidden Buddhism at the prompting of a fraternity of Freemasons. That was dangerous knowledge, and he even came to think the Freemasons had a contract out on him. By that time we were out of touch.

A few years later he discovered media, and became famous, rightly. I don't know of anyone else who has sucked himself down into a conspiracy theory and come triumphantly out of it. Conspiracy theories are normally terminal. But Marshall was unique.

What always saved him was his ability to get interested in something else. Nothing was too trivial. "Let us check on this," he would say, and steer the two of us into a movie house, where we stayed for twenty minutes. "Enough." Out in the light he extemporized an hour of analysis.

I think he did get a television, finally. I know he read books and books and books. (MARSHALL McLUHAN READS BOOKS ran a bumper sticker in the Sixties.) He read them especially on Sunday afternoon: long demanding books like Lancelot Andrews's *Sermons*. He would nap at two, wake up at three, and start reading, pausing to pencil numerous tiny notes on the flyleaves.

A last glimpse. Marshall's unappeasable mother, in the back seat of the car, is sampling the Pisan Cantos. She is baffled, and means her bafflement to be a reproach. "What you have to understand, Mother," he improvises, "is that in the poetry you are used to things happen one after another. Whereas in that poetry everything happens at once." It served to quell her. As it stands it's not a good formula, but you can think how to go on from it, if you don't get flypapered. I've been going on from extemporization of Marshall's for thirty years.

National Review, January 23, 1981

What is the dominant impression Kenner gives of Marshall McLuhan? Point out the expressions that contribute to this impression.

3. The major rhetorical operation is narration; we get events but not a series of events in sequence. Trace out Kenner's way of using narration. What other operations does he employ?
4. Determine the tone and the elements that contribute to it. How do the references affect tone?
5. Describe Kenner's use of metaphor and image. When is it emotive? When is it definitive?
6. Write an essay in which you appraise another person who has contributed to your life.
7. In the following essay from *The Autobiography of Bertrand Russell: 1872–1914,* determine what rhetorical operation is used for development, and whether metaphor and imagistic language have been employed effectively:

Three passions, simple but overwhelmingly strong, have governed my life: the longing for love, the search for knowledge, and unbearable pity for the suffering of mankind. These passions, like great winds, have blown me hither and thither, in a wayward course, over a deep ocean of anguish, reaching to the very verge of despair.

I have sought love, first, because it brings ecstasy — ecstasy so great that I would often have sacrificed all the rest of life for a few hours of this joy. I have sought it, next, because it relieves loneliness — that terrible loneliness in which one shivering consciousness looks over the rim of the world into the cold unfathomable lifeless abyss. I have sought it, finally, because in the union of love, I have seen, in a mystic miniature, the prefiguring vision of the heaven that saints and poets have imagined. This is what I sought, and though it might seem too good for human life, this is what — at last — I have found.

With equal passion I have sought knowledge. I have wished to understand the hearts of men. I have wished to know why the stars shine. And

I have tried to apprehend the Pythagorean power by which number holds sway above the flux. A little of this, but not much, I have achieved.

Love and knowledge, so far as they were possible, led upward toward the heavens. But always pity brought me back to earth. Echoes of cries of pain reverberate in my heart. Children in famine, victims tortured by oppressors, helpless old people a hated burden to their sons, and the whole world of loneliness, poverty, and pain make a mockery of what human life should be. I long to alleviate the evil, but I cannot, and I too suffer.

This has been my life. I have found it worth living, and would gladly live it again if the chance were offered me.

8. What is the principal operation that develops the second paragraph? The third and fourth paragraphs?
9. Note the concluding sentences of the middle three paragraphs and explain why the writer places them in the sequence he does. How are the conclusions of these paragraphs related? How do they accumulate into Russell's attitude about his life's experiences?
10. Do you find Russell's tone persuasive? Is the passion of his language justified? What of his candor? Describe his tone.
11. Notice that Russell exemplifies but does so only in a general way. He offers no detailed personal narrative as example. Write an essay on the topic of love, knowledge, or human sympathy in which you exemplify Russell's attitude (if you cannot do so in candor, then exemplify your own) with a detailed narrative of your personal experience.

Chapter 15

The Argumentative Essay or Article

The excerpt from Virginia Woolf's "Modern Letters" (which appears in the preceding chapter) is a familiar essay, but it is also an argument setting forth a proposition. It moves the reader to agreement mainly by logical appeal to reason, while the familiar essay by E. B. White (also in Chapter 14) moves the reader to agreement through its experiential or emotive appeal. White's "argument," we may say, is by way of empathy or sympathetic association. As writers attempt to neutralize the influence of personality, to minimize voice, their arguments approach the ideal of rational objectivity. Appeals to the reader's psychological patterns and emotions are eliminated as much as possible.

In the argumentative article, notions of reality are confined to logical constructs of reality, and disputes are ideally approached with systematic thought. Such thought is the ideal to which most people in Western civilization adhere and is the tool of industrial, technological, and academic approaches to physical, biological, social, and psychological sciences, to anthropological and historical researches, and to studies of language and literature.

Structuring the Argument

All reasoning is argument, either with oneself or with another. We aim first to convince ourselves that a proposition is true and then to convince others. If we are not convinced and try anyway to convince another, the argument is spurious, even deceitful. Ideally, in the Platonic sense, the aim of an argument is not to win but to find the truth and bring others to see it, as Plato's Socratic dialogues are intended to show. Actually, however, in the dialogues Socrates argues with loaded dice, manipulating his students toward realization of his own preconceived conclusions. All of us argue with loaded dice, of course, with our preconceptions and conviction of the way things are, were, and ought to be. We cling most tightly to our notions that are least amenable to observation and reason—our notions of liberty, beauty, love, morality, loyalty, religion. Where our emotions and values are deeply touched, we feel threatened as if our very lives were at stake. We tend to defend our vital beliefs in arguments with charged language, even name calling, with fallacious logic, and with slanted vision which excludes disturbing evidence or questions. We present only our side of the case.

Advocates in law courts are set on winning, but judges and juries are interested in the truth of the case. An attorney seeking the truth in a court of law would have few clients. However, attorneys cannot win unless they bring judges and juries into agreement. They must discover their arguments, therefore, by testing them against possible opposing arguments before they enter the court or write their briefs, and often they change the argument so it will appeal to judge and jury as a more probable approximation of truth. Scientists follow much the same process in testing hypotheses. They test their ideas of the way things are to see if they can disprove what observations have led them to believe. If they cannot disprove a hypothesis, it gains credibility, and eventually, with more testing, it may become theory, or even law.

This means of discovering probable truth and bringing others into agreement with it has been used throughout the history of Western civilization. The rhetorical structure of argument was already well established in ancient Rome when Cicero outlined it in his rhetoric. After introductory statements in which the background is presented and the issue defined, described, and delineated, Cicero's outline proceeds to the argument itself, consisting of the *confirmatio,* the reasons for agreeing with the advocate's point of view on the issue, and of the *refutatio,* the reasons for disagreeing with this point of view. Successful advocates are in the habit of presenting their opponent's best case and then refuting it, thereby enhancing their own point of view.

Cicero's structure for argument has a modern counterpart in the rhetorical approaches based on the work of the psychotherapist Carl Rogers. In *On Becoming a Person,* Rogers finds each position in a classical argument to be concerned less with understanding the other's point of view, the why and how of it, than in justifying one's own. The values of each arguer are threatened by the values of the other, and so each defends what is his or hers. Agreement in this situation is impossible. But if each person in the argument would try to divorce his or her attitude from the issue in order to define it, and then try to see the other's reasoning and attitude, cool rationality could prevail. The issue might then be argued with a view toward synthesis or compromise. Obviously the tone of voice in such argument could not be overbearing, unduly authoritative, or derogatory:

> We must use nuclear energy in large quantities. Our would-be street experts who have no responsibility to the public, who do not understand the technical and economic aspects of power generation, tell you that everyone else in the world is wrong. Let me show you briefly just how wrong these anti-nuclear activists can be.

Rather, the voice would have to allow for at least some uncertainty, which suggests the ideal argumentative tone of neutrality. The image desired is of a person thinking. Here, for example, is Martin Luther King, Jr., in a public letter that has the same effect and purpose as an article, incorporating and synthesizing an opposing view:

> You may well ask: "Why direct action? Why sit-ins, marches, and so forth? Isn't negotiation a better path?" You are quite right in calling for negotiation. Indeed, this is the very purpose of direct action. Nonviolent direct action seeks to create such a crisis and foster such tension that a community which has constantly refused to negotiate is forced to confront the issue. It seeks to dramatize the issue that it can no longer ignore. My citing the creation of tension as part of the work of the nonviolent-resister may sound rather shocking. But I must confess that I am not afraid of the word "tension."
>
> I have earnestly opposed violent tension, but there is a type of constructive, nonviolent tension which is necessary for growth. Just as Socrates felt that it was necessary to create a tension in the mind so that individuals could rise from the bondage of myths and half-truths to the unfettered realm of creative analysis and objective appraisal, so must we see the need for nonviolent gadflies to create the kind of tension in society that will help men rise from the dark depths of prejudice and racism to the majestic heights of understanding and brotherhood.
>
> The purpose of our direct action program is to create a situation so crisis-packed that it will inevitably open the door to negotiation. I therefore concur with you in your call for negotiation. Too long has our beloved Southland been bogged down in a tragic effort to live in a monologue rather than dialogue.
>
> One of the basic points in your statement is that the action that I and my associates have taken in Birmingham is untimely. Some have asked . . .
>
> Martin Luther King, Jr., "Letter
> from Birmingham Jail"

King's refutation synthesizes opposing views; both seek the same end, negotiation. He argues for agreement with this synthesis, point for point, beginning with the assertion that his action has been "untimely." Notice the control of almost all connotations. King refrains from coloring his words except those that offer images held in common and not at issue: "bondage of myth"; "dark depths of prejudice"; "majestic heights of understanding." Nevertheless, he also allows negative connotation in the words that support his own position, the need for "nonviolent gadflies." His use of Socrates is also connotative, providing support by association with authority. The issue itself is defined clearly, with uncharged language.

King begins with background, leading to the statement of the issue or thesis:

> While confined here in the Birmingham city jail, I came across your re-
> cent statement calling my present activities "unwise and untimely." Sel-
> dom do I pause to answer criticism of my work and ideas. If I sought to
> answer all the criticisms that cross my desk, . . . I would have no time for
> constructive work. But since I feel that you are men of genuine good will
> and that your criticisms are sincerely set forth, I want to try to answer
> your statement in what I hope will be patient and reasonable terms.
>
>   I think I should indicate why I am here in Birmingham, since you have
> been influenced by the view which argues against outsiders coming in. I
> have the honor of serving as president of the Southern Christian Leader-
> ship Conference, an organization . . .

These introductory elements establish not only the issue, "why I am
here," but at the same time set a tone that is humble, candid, respectful,
and not absolute: "since . . . your criticisms are sincerely set forth, I
want to try to answer your statement in what I hope will be patient and
reasonable terms."

The Refutation Argument

If King's purpose were only to deny the statement that his activities
were "unwise and untimely," and if he did not seek synthesis in explaining "why I am here," his argument would be solely refutation. The
argument of refutation states the falseness found in the opponent's
thesis or main argument. To make such a statement, the writer must
first examine the opponent's whole argument, seeking faulty premises,
faulty definitions, faulty logic, faulty uses of evidence and authority, or
undesirable applications of the argument, and then make a general
statement of the opposing view:

> Many language critics deplore euphemism, pointing out that "revenue
> enhancement" is still a tax increase, and a "police action" is still a war.
> Indeed, euphemisms do not change facts. . . .

The writer goes on to give reasons why euphemism should not be
deplored:

> To deal with highly emotional subjects, to get by the knee-jerk reaction
> that certain words produce, we must change the word. And sometimes
> that is good. No one of us likes to deal with drunks, but we can under-
> stand a problem drinker. Public assistance is not nearly as demeaning to
> the receiver or to the taxpayer as welfare. . . .

If possible, the writer should soften the refutation argument by admitting the opponent's strong points before stating the flaws. In presenting
the case of those who deplore euphemisms, the writer might have mentioned the political uses of euphemism, Hitler's "final solution" to ex-
terminate Jews, for example, or the bombing of defenseless villages that

has been called "pacification." Such a presentation of the other point of view might lead the writer to arrive at a less simplistic conclusion about euphemisms.

Fact, Opinion, and Action Arguments

An argument that proposes to refute is obviously a negative argument, without a thesis of its own. Positive arguments, whether one argues to establish fact or opinion or to propose action, begin with theses. A thesis of fact or opinion states the belief that something is so or was so:

> The most serious hazard in the women's liberation movement is the temptation to make men enemies.
>
> The supreme tragic event of modern times is the murder of 6 million European Jews.
>
> The struggle of our time is with feelings of homelessness.
>
> The universe is expanding from a single "big bang" explosion of infinitely condensed matter, or it's expanding and contracting eternally.

The thesis of action states that a change should be made. It is essentially a proposal or recommendation:

> We must abandon the confusion of our current tax system and adopt a simple flat rate.
>
> Nuclear weapons should be banned in all countries.
>
> Since the profit picture is bleak as far as we can see in the future, I believe we should close the shop.

Both types of theses are argued with evidence, which must be established and related for significance. The facts substantiate the opinion and demonstrate the need for change. In arguing for an opinion, the writer abets the evidence or facts with the opinions of established authorities, but a writer cannot substantiate opinion with the use of authority alone. With the thesis of action, the writer provides, in addition to evidence and considerations of authority, the reasons why the action would be practical and beneficial. In both theses, of opinion and action, opposing arguments are presented and refuted.

Using Rhetorical Operations

The means of all arguments are the rhetorical operations, induction and deduction above all. Whether we argue by means of evidence, definition, analysis, comparison, cause and effect, or most likely a combination of these operations, we are using induction and deduction. We move from particulars to generalizations, or from generalizations to particulars (cautiously, of course, avoiding logical faults and fallacies). We substantiate our propositions with evidence — facts, data, authoritative testimony, and reports. And we reason syllogistically from major premise to minor premise to conclusion. Definitions, for example, are used syllogistically to prove that one thing is really the same or very much alike or unlike something else as claimed:

> Israel justified the invasion of Lebanon by declaring that its only intention was to wipe out the Palestinian camps whose inhabitants had for years been terrorizing Israeli settlements. But Israel was charged with committing genocide, ironical for a state established as a result of that very abomination. The Genocide Convention of 1948 defined genocide as acts committed with the goal of full or partial destruction of an ethnic, religious, racial, or national group. Specifically, acts of genocide are killing, maiming, injuring, or mentally harming members of a group. They also include measures taken to prevent births in a group and abolishing conditions necessary for a group to exist.
>
> The Israelis would be guilty of genocide according to this definition if they had rounded up and killed any group of people whether or not they were Palestinians. But no one has presented evidence or testimony of such an event. The Israelis are reported, rather, to have committed acts of war upon the Palestinian terrorists. War is not genocide. The charge should be dismissed from any fair mind as a concocted piece of propaganda.

The falsity of the proposition "Israel committed genocide" is shown by syllogistically comparing the definition of genocide with the Israeli troops' actions. The definition of genocide supplies the meaning of the major thesis, the application to the actual events supplies the minor thesis, and the conclusion is drawn appropriately. The validity of this syllogistic argument depends upon the validity of the definition.

In written arguments, an inductive approach is actually a rearrangement because the writer has already arrived at a generalization or proposition in the thinking and prewriting stage of composition. Writing inductively, you state the topic but not the proposition, then develop the evidence and reasons that lead to the proposition as a conclusion. You might start, for example, by presenting the issue and opposing views, then show faults according to some desired, agreed-upon standard, and follow with reasons, causes, or evidence that shows how one view fulfills the desired goal. Comparison of the two with the stated standard would lead directly to acceptance of the one that is stated as a concluding proposition:

> Rarely do the left and right agree on matters of taxation, but the recent spate of new bills in Congress indicates a bipartisan convergence toward replacing the existing income tax-structure with a flat-rate tax.
>
> The current tax code is highly progressive and riddled with deductions

and exemptions. The result is that some income is highly taxed and other income is not taxed at all. In fact, a large industry that is expert in shifting income from high-taxed to low-taxed areas has developed.

Even worse, under the current tax code it often pays for people in high brackets not to make profitable and productive investments that would increase both their taxable income and, through higher employment that would result, the incomes of others. Instead it pays for them to purchase tax shelters that lower the taxes on their existing income. There is something wrong with a tax system that lets people do better by minimizing their taxes than by maximizing their earnings. The rising rate of unemployment over the last decade is one of the costs of a system that encourages capital to move out of productive investments and into tax shelters.

A flat-rate tax would eliminate all deductions and exemptions, taxing all income at the same rate. And, because the tax base would be much larger, the tax rate would be much lower. A 13 percent flat-rate tax should raise the same revenues as the existing progressive income tax. Such a reasonable tax rate would encourage people to use their talents to maximize their taxable incomes rather than to avoid taxes.

Is a flat tax fair?

First, it treats all income the same, whereas the current tax system discriminates in favor of, and against, different sources of income. For example, there is nothing fair about taxing income from private pensions, but not from Social Security pensions, or taxing income from savings accounts and investments at a higher rate than income from wages and salaries. These are just a few of the ways in which a progressive tax system discriminates.

Second, a flat-rate tax would treat all individuals and households the same, whereas the current tax system discriminates against individuals and households on the basis of marital status and size of income.

For most people, the gains and losses of the transition from the current system to a flat rate system would balance out, leaving their average tax rate the same. For example, home-owners would lose their mortgage interest deduction but would be paying a comparable amount less in income taxes.

For the poor, who are already paying less than 13 percent, an income exclusion could be instituted.

A low flat-rate tax would make shelters unprofitable, encourage productivity in all aspects of the economy, and greatly improve the fairness of the tax system for everyone.

The argument begins with cause and effect (first four paragraphs) and proceeds by comparison according to the standards of productivity (or earnings) and fairness. In citing examples, however, the writer is not entirely fair, suppressing the reason, for instance, why the government taxes different kinds of income at different rates. The principle that work is more productive than the investment of cash is ignored rather than presented and refuted. The argument merely asserts, "There is nothing fair about . . . taxing income from savings accounts and investment at a higher rate than income from wages and salaries," and does so wrongly. The statement is untrue according to IRS regulations.

When we use analogy in comparative arguments, we must proceed with extreme caution. Analogical arguments suggest that things alike in some respects are alike in all respects: "A university is a corporation as any other business is and should act more businesslike in dealings with its students, its customers." Obviously there are essential ways in which a university ought to cater to its students, to give value for money and time received, but the analogy is not entirely valid, since a business is not charged with the intellectual discipline of a mind, requiring evaluations, nor can all receive the same value for their money. At best, the argument from analogy enlightens or clarifies; analogy serves definition and almost always needs further qualification.

A *fortiori* arguments are kinds of comparisons in which one fact or probability logically implies another.

> Old enough to vote, old enough to drink.
>
> She ought to win the congressional seat; she was so popular and bright in the movies.
>
> It was easy to make ten thousand in those stocks, and I've only begun. I ought to make millions. Invest with me.

The assumption in all these applied comparisons is the same as in the analogy: if things are alike one way, they are alike in all ways. If something is true on a small scale, it must therefore be true on the larger scale. A fortiori arguments ignore the differences that make the compared things dissimilar.

When we argue from causes or from effects, we must remember to examine the circumstances and to show immediate connection. The conviction actually resides in these qualities. "We lost the Vietnam War because we weren't committed to it." How can we show the connections between the loss and the commitment? And what of the circumstances, what of other communist powers that might also have become committed if our commitment had been greater? "The President is responsible for the recession." Perhaps he made no effective moves to alleviate it, but the circumstances of a recession occur over a period of time, not suddenly when a candidate wins a presidential election. If we argued this proposition by showing the progressive steps of how the recession came about, we might find ourselves changing the proposition in the process, concluding, perhaps, not that the President caused the recession, but caused a deepening of it, or that he was ineffective in alleviating it, or on the other hand, that his actions would in time alleviate it.

In human affairs, where causes can never be pinpointed precisely, circumstances themselves are taken as cause, or motive. A shabby, poverty-stricken environment may be taken as the cause for criminal behavior; on the other hand, it may be taken as the motive for ambition that leads to wealth. Circumstance is the basis for psychological propositions and for character in literature: "He was attached to older women because there were only his aunts to care for him after his father died." When we argue the case of inevitability, that we have "no other choice than to join the establishment," we are also arguing from circumstance. Because the circumstances are so overwhelming in such instances, we argue that we either submit or perish (symbolically if not actually). Argument from circumstance is obviously weak, and often used to justify personal belief and action. We strengthen these arguments by means of analysis, by description and definition, and by appropriate use of evidence.

To argue convincingly that we lost the Vietnam War because we weren't committed to it, the writer would have to define first the meanings of "lost" and "commitment" and then analyze point for point, the chain of causes, the immediate connections between commitment and loss, and finally each of the causes in the chain of connections. In presenting evidence, the writer could cite extant reports, statistics, personal testimony, and authorities, with due caution to show the reader that the evidence is valid, that the report is unbiased, the statistics not skewed, the testimony not merely hearsay, and the authorities actually qualified to address the subject. In the following passage, the writer argues that computer theft of information and money will increase rapidly. The argument is from the circumstances of steeply rising computer use:

> At peak operating times, the wires of the Federal Reserve System process $100 million per second. Imagine tapping that line and siphoning just a few seconds of work into your own bank account.
>
> This is the dream of the most modern of criminals — the kind armed with computer terminals instead of guns. There are more than 500,000 personal computers in the United States, as well as 10,000 large government installations and perhaps 100,000 more installations in private industry. More than three million remote terminals hook up to these systems. Leonard Krauss, vice president of Data Systems Development Review at Chase Manhattan Bank and the author, with Aileen McGahan, of the book *Computer Fraud and Countermeasures,* estimates that very soon one out of ten will work directly with a computer, and, according to FBI crime statistics, one out of every ten who does will attempt to commit a computer crime.
>
> "Computer crime" is the generic term for various categories of theft, fraud, embezzlement, sabotage, and industrial espionage in which a computer system is milieu, accomplice, or victim. A rapidly developing branch of white collar crime, computer crime is so clean, so aseptic, so anonymous and so devastating that no one is willing to say for sure how much of it is really going on. Experts will tell you that the annual loss

from computer crime may be as high as $3 billion, that 85 to 95 percent of computer crimes go undetected or unreported, that the average take from a computer heist is 20 to 40 times that of an old style bank fraud or robbery. But the numbers are meaningless, according to Don Parker, a leading computer-crime consultant and scholar: "There has never been an accurate mechanism for getting figures on white-collar crime and there certainly isn't for computer crime," says Parker. "We do know that crime by computer is growing, by the very fact that the number of computers in our society is growing."

Roberta Grant, "Systematic Crime,"
TWA Ambassador, May 1982

The thesis argued is presented at the beginning of this excerpt and iterated at the end through the mouth of an authority. We may notice how the first authority used for circumstantial evidence is introduced with his credentials, his exact position, and authorship. The elaboration of this introduction allows the writer enough credibility to merely introduce his second authority with generic description, "leading computer-crime consultant." The circumstances for the argument are described by means of statistics, which are presented with enough uncertainty of tone — "There are more than 500,000" and "perhaps 100,000 more installations" — that the reader feels confidence in the writer's concern for validity. In addition to the testimony of the authority, we notice, the second paragraph develops by means of definition and description.

Inductive and Deductive Arguments

As you will recall from Chapter 6, reasoning may proceed either inductively or deductively, that is, from particular instances to a general conclusion or from a general statement to a particular instance and a conclusion about it. In either case the reasoning proceeds logically in order to draw conclusions from observations, facts, or hypotheses. However, no matter which kind of reasoning we have followed to come to a conclusion, in the writing we can arrange the argument deductively, supporting a direct statement of the proposition with evidence, or inductively, moving from pieces of evidence to a proposition as a conclusion.

Inductive arguments depend on incomplete, limited evidence to draw a conclusion, evidence that usually appears as examples, cause and effect, analogy, and testimony. Because we rarely can examine all the facts in a case, we must make an inductive leap from the evidence available to a conclusion that can only be probable. The only way for us to be certain of a conclusion would be to examine every member of the class being dealt with — for example, to examine every apple in a box to say they are all large ones rather than looking at only a half dozen.

Because inductive arguments proceed incrementally to a final position, they have the subtlety that risks losing less sophisticated readers. Readers are uncertain until the end about exactly what they are asked to believe and do. On the other hand, when we want to argue a proposition on an emotionally charged issue that will not readily gain the reader's assent, inductive arguments have the advantage of drawing readers in bit by bit on minor points they can assent to before announcing the proposition. Also, because the inductive approach involves readers more intently in the process of discovery, inductive arguments are inherently more interesting.

Before going on to discuss deductive argument, let us take a look at an example of an inductive argument, one that is not only interesting, but highly entertaining.

Economics and Corned Beef
Art Buchwald

The president keeps saying that inflation is way down, and he has government statistics to prove it. But if it is, President Reagan doesn't buy his corned beef sandwiches from the same delicatessen I do.

In 1980 a corned beef sandwich on rye at Ben's cost me $1.50, including a nice large slice of dill pickle. The same sandwich today costs $3, although I've noticed the rye bread slices are smaller and the pickle is much thinner.

"How come," I asked Ben, "if Reagan says he's cut down inflation to five percent, your corned beef sandwich costs twice as much as it did when he took office?"

Ben was steaming. "If you think I'm making more money on a $3 sandwich than I was when it was $1.50, then you're crazy."

"According to the Department of Agriculture, food prices have been holding steady."

"I don't know from food prices," Ben said. "But there is more that goes into a corned beef sandwich than bread, beef and Russian dressing."

"What's that?"

"City taxes, Social Security and health benefits for my employees. My electric bill looks like monthly rent, and my telephone bill now looks like my electric bill. How come these hot shot statisticians in the government don't take those things into account before they publish their statistics?"

"Don't get mad at me, Ben. I was curious as to why your prices had doubled in a period of single-digit inflation."

I apparently opened a can of beans. Ben said, "You see that pipe up there that is leaking? In 1980 the plumber charged me $30 to walk in the door. Now he wants $60. So what does a government computer know about plumbers?"

I tried to change the subject. "How's your wife?"

"She just got out of the hospital. Her room cost $400 a day. The same room three years ago cost $190. They threw in a television set free then. Now they charge $5 a day for it. The doctor used to charge $25 a visit. Now you have to pay $50 up front, and wait twice as long to see him. That all goes into the price of a corned beef sandwich.

"You want to know about my kid? In 1980 his tuition was $6,000. This year it's up to $9,000. It's a bargain compared to how much more I'm paying for his automobile insurance. The president says interest rates are down to 11.5 percent. Maybe for Ed Meese. But own a delicatessen and see if you can get a loan for less than 14.5 percent. Put that in your corned beef sandwich and eat it."

"I'm sure everything you say is true, Ben," I told him, "but government statistics don't lie. Reagan has cooled inflation and he has the print-outs to prove it."

"Then why has my laundry bill for aprons risen 15 percent?"

"Probably because aprons aren't included in the price index."

"Nothing that goes up seems to be included in the price index. If you want to make a big deal about what I'm charging now compared to 1980, why has the price of the Sunday paper you write for gone up 25 percent?"

"That's simple. We had to raise it or no one on our staff could afford your corned beef sandwiches."

Washington Post, May 8, 1984

Buchwald's way of arguing humorously about serious matters is, of course, a talent that cannot be taught, but if you have the germ of such talent, develop it. Effective argument need not always be serious. Readers who categorically refuse to accept humor in serious matters will not be moved by such arguments, but it may be that they are unmovable.

The argument is a piece of analysis, taking major consumer expenditures such as food and medical care and showing with each how prices have increased in spite of the statistics mentioned at the start that "prove" inflation is down. At the end, the writer, acting in his role as government spokesman, ironically concedes, "nothing that goes up seems to be included in the price index." He has not charged that the index for measuring inflation is altogether wrong, but it certainly fails to reflect the consumer's actuality, which effectively restates the observation. Only at the end are we moved to accept this observation as substantiated proposition.

Deductive arguments sometimes take the form of a syllogism or, more often, an enthymeme, a shortened form of a syllogism. They start with a direct statement of the proposition, then apply it to a particular instance with substantiating evidence and reasons. Evidence and reasons opposing the propositions may be presented and then shown to be false before the writer draws the conclusion.

When the proposition is stated at the outset, readers can be certain of the writer's stance. They know what is being argued and what they are asked to believe or do. Because the syllogistic form is so persuasive simply as form, a tightly organized deductive argument can capture assent even if its premises are untrue.

Arguments on Public Issues

Although Buchwald's inductive argument is about a public issue, the usual pattern for arguing about such issues is deductive and the usual tone is serious. Often they begin with sober statements that sound more like fact than proposition:

> Thirty years after the U.S. Supreme Court outlawed officially sanctioned racial segregation in public schools, the challenge of that historic event remains unfulfilled.

In this example, the writer follows the proposition with the history of the issue, a narrative of events leading up to his factually stated proposition (not really a fallacy of argument, but misleading nevertheless):

> On May 17, 1954, the high court shattered the complacency of the Eisenhower era by ruling in a landmark case — *Brown* v. *Board of Education* — that school segregation deprives blacks of "equal protection under the law."
>
> In the landmark case, Oliver Brown, a black minister, sued the Topeka school board seeking the rights to have his daughter Linda . . .

The history traces the subsequent events of the thirty years since that moment, showing how the Supreme Court has continued to attack segregation, up to the moment in 1971, when

> the high court . . . turned down the objections of the Nixon administration and endorsed busing as a major tool of high school desegregation. Shifting its attention to the north for the first time in 1973, the high court held that the entire Denver, Colorado, system could be subject to desegregation.

The evidence to substantiate the proposition that the Supreme Court's challenge "remains unfulfilled" is introduced with this assertion:

> And yet for all its commitment to the *Brown* decision, the Supreme Court has shed the unanimity it displayed during the 1950s and 1960s.

A reasonable reader will first look for statements of fact substantiating the word "unanimity," because the history presents not the voting record among the court members but only the outcome, the majority decisions. (This unwarranted assumption is a fallacy of argument.) Whether or not the court was previously unanimous, the argument goes on to show that it is not now so:

> This was apparent in 1974 when the high court sharply divided over how to desegregate the Detroit schools.

Statistics follow to show that northern schools remain segregated:

> Statistics provided by the Joint Center for Political Studies show that Illinois has the most segregated classrooms, where 65 percent of the black students attend schools with a 90 to 100 percent minority enrollment. In four other states . . .

To abet the statistics, authority is invoked:

> "Our progress has been enormous," said David Tatel, a Washington lawyer and former director of the U.S. Office for Civil Rights. "But the country still has a long way to go."

Other authorities follow, emphasizing the "long way to go," which supports the proposition that the challenge "remains unfulfilled." In the end, this proposition is repeated in terms of a then very recent case — the St. Louis plan for desegregation — which the state of Missouri fails to support. And the state, the argument concludes, is upheld by the Justice Department. Such a conclusion effectively implies, rather than restates, the proposition. Although we have pointed out a logical fallacy here and a misdirection there, this deductive argument is stronger than most that we find on issues in the forums of our media.

Arguments of Science and Sales

Scientific papers are inductive arguments in essence, although in the final form of the paper a summary of conclusions may precede the introduction or be included within it. The arguments themselves are about the procedures and the data that result from the procedures. These are interpreted for and against the problem or hypothesis. The outcome of the interpretation is an answer or solution to the problem, or support or lack of it for the hypothesis. Such conclusions are induced propositions, with their evidence preceding them:

> All evidence shows that our company would increase efficiency and compete with advantage if we installed a central computing system.

> The data in this investigation do not sufficiently support the recent theories of corrosion put forth by Hines and Katch.

Arguments that induce the reader to buy goods and services or vote for candidates and issues, on the other hand, often appear inductive but are invariably deductive. They appear inductive for the greater strength of involvement, but actually their propositions are known at the outset: "Buy what I sell"; "Vote for me or my issue." The approach, of course, gives the appearance of induction, offering to fulfill the reader's desires.

Sales appeals employ all available means of bringing audiences into agreement. They differ only in motive from arguments seeking to convince readers of the truth or validity of things religious, scientific, or philosophical. Perhaps seasoned salesmen and politicians are the most adept at creating bonds or bridges with targeted audiences. Like poets and storytellers, they avoid direct statements, that is, speaking their minds directly without awareness of audience reaction. Rather, they render arguments by engaging the reader's experience, knowledge, attitudes, values, and authorities.

Audience Appeal

To engage the reader's experience and knowledge, writers make abstractions concrete and clarify unknown terms or circumstances. They employ the techniques of definition: example, description, metaphor, analogy, direct comparison, derivation, history. If complexities require excessive explanation, the seasoned arguer deletes them. Here is an example of a writer, arguing in a letter to the editor for a modern interpretation of a renowned source. The language is of common experience. Notice the use of example (sentence 2), description (sentences 3 and 4), comparison (sentence 5), and especially the effect of the metaphor, "trapped housewife," in the last phrase:

[1] Those who take the time to read beyond the first few pages of Genesis will find additional material that increases the understanding of male/female relationships. [2] For example, the description of the ideal wife in Prov. 31:10–31 may surprise those people who think the Scriptures outdated. [3] This proverb describes a wife who is gainfully employed, confident, talented, dignified, powerful, praiseworthy, and God-fearing. [4] She makes real-estate investments, manages her business, teaches loyalty and wisdom, and is honored in their community. [5] This is obviously a "model" for a full partner, not a subordinate doomed to suffer the "trapped housewife" syndrome.

> D. Alan Eastwood, Poughkeepsie,
> N.Y., Letter to the Editor, *Omni*,
> February 1984

In appealing to audience values and attitudes, writers have traditionally tapped the great common motives and interests of the human race — love, security, community, religion, money, pleasure, and so on. These are not held equally of course, but in some hierarchy, one more important than the other. In general, middle-class American readers are more apt to change attitudes about money and pleasure, for instance, than religion or loyalty. (At least, that assertion would seem to hold true for public consumption, and the writings discussed here are public acts.) The hierarchy is usually discerned by students long before they enter college. Of course, a hierarchy of values and attitudes in one society is not always applicable to another. It is wise, therefore, when writing for an unfamiliar audience, to learn something of their social history and mores, and in writing, to favor those values and attitudes that have the highest priority.

Most difficulties are encountered at the lower levels of the value hierarchy — political, economic, and ethical. Obviously the Democrat appealing to the Republican, the advantaged to the disadvantaged, or the unwashed to the sterile will have to find common ground. Usually it will be in values and attitudes at the top of the hierarchy, shared by all in society. To argue effectively, then, writers must identify their propositions with these values. To eliminate nuclear waste, a writer must convince those who produce it that they risk destroying the race. Those who must produce nuclear waste in order to run their businesses will offer countering arguments that show the risks are not existent or are so negligible that they are worth taking for the gains (social gains, of course). Again, seasoned salesmen are best at such arguments. A quite common example is health. Everyone wants it. Florida sunshine and juices foster your health. So fly there — on our airline.

Public issues are more complex — welfare, for instance. Most people uphold charity more or less, but how much milk of human kindness can we spill without going dry? Or consider defense. How much do we need? And at what expense to welfare? In this conflict, the rational approach would be to recognize the values held on all sides and work out the best course of action for all, admitting that no one could be completely satisfied, a solution that would be equitable and charitable and at the same time provide security. To forestall the natural opposition of greed and self-interest, the writer might emphasize compromise as a virtue and invoke an authority that all might accept — for example, say, of the Founding Fathers at the Constitutional Convention.

Fallacious Arguments

In the world of advertising and sales, authority is the most recognizable technique to bring the audience into agreement, to make people buy or accept what is offered. If a star of stage or sports endorses Pepsi-Cola, it must be worth buying. To unthinking people, the medium itself is an authority; what is heard, read, or seen must be so. Taken as authority, such voices may reason fallaciously with rewarding effect. If it is desirable to be thin, and fewer calories abet thinness, and Diet-Pepsi contains only one calorie per glass, why, drink it! Buy it! In such fallacious seas reasonable people do not swim.

Fallacies of Authority

The fallacious use of authority to endorse products is obvious, but authority also dominates arguments in college texts, pulpit literature, and corporate and government papers. Confucius say. So do Will Shakespeare, Ben Franklin, and Henry Kissinger. The Scriptures say also, and the boss, and the law.

Authority may supplement evidence in an argument; but whenever authority supplants evidence, the argument is fallacious.

Authority, we should be reminded, is a force. All of us are familiar with stories of soldiers who are forced by authority to act against their own values, sometimes to destroy and kill. At this point, of course, we are beyond argument. Nonetheless, this is the point approached when argument leans on authority.

In addition to the testimony of individuals who have achieved authoritative status, there is the testimony of the people, the great unwashed or just plain folks. A most obvious example is the television advertisement of a person at the washing machine endorsing soap. The rehearsed hesitations and groping for the simplest words are intended to convince by identification with the common folk, who must struggle for the slightest of thought.

Fallacies of Generalization

In Chapter 6 we investigated valid and invalid generalizations. Invalid generalization, however innocent in the making, is fallacious. In deductive or syllogistic reasoning, we should recall, writers err when they reason from premises that are not valid, their assumptions untrue. Three basic areas of invalid generalizations were delineated: hasty, a priori, and analogical generalizations.

Hasty or Sweeping Generalization. When the writer has too few examples and too little evidence or data for generalizing, the result is a hasty or sweeping generalization. "My car broke down. It's a Chevy. They're lousy." Such hasty generalization may be called unqualified and can be corrected by using qualifiers: "Some Chevys are lousy," or even, "A lot are . . . " Qualifiers also correct a sweeping generalization. Instead of writing, "People who drink get drunk," the writer might say, "Some people should not drink." The writer who makes hasty or sweeping generalizations jumps to conclusions.

A Priori Generalization. When the writer concludes before examining evidence, the fallacy is called a priori generalization. This fallacious reasoning is often motivated by prejudice. Because a single member of a group, nation, race, religion, union, profession, or business acts atrociously once or twice or even habitually, the entire group is condemned: "They're all like that." A prejudiced person has difficulty saying, "Some are, some aren't." *Slanting* is a subtler form of a priori generalization. The writer slants by emphasizing strengths over weaknesses in supposedly objective comparison or by omitting weak elements in an analysis. If one omits description of the service on an airline because it was poor while displaying all the other elements, as in objective analysis, then the reasoning is slanted.

Analogical Generalization. Assuming that things similar in one way are similar in all ways is analogical generalization: "I can't understand how he could have done it; he was gentle as a lamb." Perhaps under certain conditions he was. Analogies are also invalid when they falsely compare one thing with another: "The United States is run like a lottery, with longer odds and bigger payoffs." In a sense any decision made for the future is a gamble; therefore, we could say our politicians gamble with long odds when they enact certain laws, but that doesn't make the running of the government like the running of a lottery.

Fallacies of Relevance

Logicians have compiled long lists in Latin terms that define fallacies of relevance, where the evidence and the conclusions do not directly bear on the question. We have simplified and grouped the essential fallacies as follows:

Begging the Question. Writers who assume the truth of a premise that actually needs to be demonstrated beg the question: "Welfare payments only encourage the unemployed to stay that way." If the writer argues from this premise that the payments be discontinued rather than proving that they encourage unemployment, he or she begs the question. Sometimes a writer begs the question by *reasoning in circles,* like a dog chasing its tail, and applies a premise as its own validation: "The USA is the best country in the world because the best people live there." The Salem Puritans relied on circular reasoning to identify witches: "She will not confess her sins because she is possessed."

Ignoring the Question. By shifting to another issue or proposition when we confront a contradiction or when we cannot carry the chain of reasoning any further, we ignore the question. This evasion is sometimes called "dragging a red herring across the trail." An applicant who is fully qualified for a position is told someone less qualified was hired, because "John is a generous and kindly man who has lived through many experiences." The question could be addressed at least to some extent by adding, "even though he lacks the appropriate experience."

Other forms of ignoring the question are *name-calling* and *argumentum ad hominem.* Rather than examining the issue, the writer ignores it by calling the proponent a fascist, a Red, or a pig of one sort or another. Actions against the writer's interest are perpetrated by the "extreme right" or the "longhairs" or the "communist inspired." A most effective bit of name-calling is "troublemaker" applied to anyone who resists unfair treatment, real or imagined. *Argumentum ad hominem* is an argument against the person rather than the issue. "We have discovered Jane is an unwed mother; therefore she is no longer qualified to be our typist."

In the fallacy of *argumentum ad populum,* which is similar to name-calling, we ignore the question by association. We associate the issue with something sacred or despised: God, country, home, mother, apple pie, devil, income tax, atheist, President Nixon. Politicians, labor and business leaders, ministers, and educators use such appeals to win over the audience, pretending to be "one of us," the neighbor next door. They claim unwarranted sympathy or disapprobation for an issue not by reason but sentiment.

The *bandwagon* is a variation of *argumentum ad populum.* This device urges the reader to follow the crowd. "Everybody's switching to Zany cigarettes." Appeals are often directed to common ties of nationality, race, religion, sex, or vocation. The issue should be supported in the interest of all farmers or auto workers, Jews or Arabs, or schoolteachers. Flattery is often used to enlist residual prejudices.

Hiding the Question. When a single answer is demanded of a complex question, the real nature of the question is hidden: "Okay, tell me, then, the real reason we are at war?" or, "Why should we let the munitions makers drive us into war for their profits?" Is there only one reason for war? Is it a fact that munitions makers drive us into wars? And all by themselves? The *either/or fallacy* is a way of hiding the question. Here the writer hides all possible choices except two. The two "horns of a dilemma" may eliminate some possible choices. "At college I'm going to waste my time either way, being a grind or having fun." Surely the student can find a way to study, play, and do more — for example, reflect on life alone or with another, explore the nature of others, plan the future, or deepen the experience of life through music, art, and relationships. Often the either/or fallacy is subtle, and the reader has to be acute:

> In El Salvador, the army and the right-wing "death squads" work together to target suspected "subversives." A "subversive" by government definition, does not have to be a guerrilla, a communist, or even a leftist. Victims of government terror have included clergy, teachers, students, health care workers, and people who chose not to vote in the recent compulsory "elections."

The subtlety of definition decides who is included and who is not, that is, whether you're for us or against us, either/or.

Given the subject of the excerpt on El Salvador, the writer can be excused perhaps for *slanting*. He does so by calling the government action "terror" and the objects of the action "victims," and also by casting aspersions with the adverb "compulsory" and the quotation marks surrounding "elections." As in fallacious analysis and comparison, slanting is a way of hiding the question by emphasizing details that are more favorable to our view and subordinating or even eliminating details that are not. It generally uses biased language and phrasing:

> Tom is firm.
>
> Worse, he's inflexible.
>
> Baloney, he's just plain pigheaded.

Such slanting is hardly distinguishable from name-calling. The difference matters little.

Failing to Follow. The Latin phrase for this fallacy, *non sequitur,* means "not in sequence." "June Albright is surely the most popular young woman in our class. Her English prof is bound to give her an A." Only in the most remote way would June's popularity be related to her academic acumen. The conclusion is not warranted by the evidence. Other examples of the non sequitur are irrelevant arguments, where the writer starts to prove one thing and then cites evidence proving another. A legislator, for example, may substantiate her argument for a particular foreign aid bill with evidence showing the poorly housed and fed people of the beneficiary nation, even though the bill contains more provisions for arms than food or shelter. And in a court of law, it would be a foolish prosecutor who attempted to prove guilt by delineating the viciousness of the crime itself.

An argument beginning with the assertion,

> In theory, under the Constitution, the people's representatives could abolish frauds such as Social Security tomorrow.

incurs the responsibility to follow the claim of "fraud" with an argument that shows it to be so. If it does not, we have a most dangerously fallacious argument, a compounding of fallacies, the non sequitur as well as name-calling and the failure to examine the assumptions of the premise.

Assigning False Cause. The most primitive of fallacies remains the most persistent. "The tree hit me," thought the savage who had walked into a tree on his way out of the forest after the eclipse. He had just finished beating his drum, thereby causing the sun to reappear. If assigning cause is no problem for the primitive, it is for us. It is the essential problem in most scientific and historical enterprise. The problem, of course, is to assign the proper cause to the observed effect. It is often confused by the occurrence of one event before another, as in Charles Lamb's famous essay "A Dissertation upon Roast Pig," in which the method for roasting pig is burning the house down, since the first pork roast was the outcome of such an accident. For centuries physicians continued to bleed patients because most of them managed to recover in spite of such treatment. The treatment caused the result of recovery, repeatedly, just as the beating of the drum repeatedly brought back the sun after an eclipse. Although modern physicists are finding causation itself an unprofitable way to examine the universe, it remains our singular means for explaining why and how things happen. To avoid assigning false causes, the writer must analyze the situation, determining all possible causes, and then select the one most likely, with appropriate qualification. Usually an effect has several causes, but people enjoy the drama of singularity, pointing out this or that as the cause, as if it were villain or hero: "The cause for low test scores of high school students is television." It is also the cause for high test scores, depending upon what the test requires.

Appealing to Pity or Circumstance. The Latin name for this fallacy is *argumentum ad misericordiam,* and it can be understood as another way of ignoring the question. It is also a non sequitur or *argumentum ad hominem.* It fails to follow because it addresses itself to the condition of the arguer (*hominem*) or reader rather than the argument. Essentially the arguer ignores the job of proving the question and instead appeals on the basis of his circumstances or those of the readers. Devout Christians may be led to accept or refute a proposition because the Scriptures sanction or forbid it. (Here again is the authoritative argument.) Arguments on the basis of mercy and charity often replace those of reason. Pity is the argument promoted by lawyers in defending juveniles accused of brutal crimes. We may remember the case of the young man who admitted murdering his mother and father. The court, he argued, should be lenient. Was he not an orphan?

In the following excerpt, a humorist touches upon most of the fallacies we have examined.

Love Is a Fallacy
Max Shulman

"Holy Toledo!" said Petey reverently. He plunged his hands into the raccoon coat. . . . "Holy Toledo!" he repeated fifteen or twenty times.

"Would you like it?" I asked.

"Oh, yes!" he cried, clutching the greasy pelt to him. Then a canny look came into his eyes. "What do you want for it?"

"Your girl," I said, mincing no words. . . .

I went about it, as in all things, systematically. I gave her a course in logic. It happened that I, as a law student, was taking a course in logic myself, so I had all the facts at my finger tips. "Polly," I said to her when I picked her up on our next date, "tonight we are going over to the Knoll and talk."

"Oo, terrif," she replied. One thing I will say for this girl: you would go far to find another so agreeable.

We went to the Knoll, the campus trysting place, and we sat down under an old oak, and she looked at me expectantly. "What are we going to talk about?" she asked.

"Logic."

She thought this over for a minute and decided she liked it. "Magnif," she said.

"Logic," I said, clearing my throat, "is the science of thinking. Before we can think correctly, we must first learn to recognize the common fallacies of logic. These we will take up tonight."

"Wow-dow!" she cried, clapping her hands delightedly.

I winced, but went bravely on. "First let us examine the fallacy called Dicto Simpliciter."

"By all means," she urged, batting her eyelashes eagerly.

"Dicto Simpliciter means an argument based on an unqualified generalization. For example: Exercise is good. Therefore everybody should exercise."

"I agree," said Polly earnestly. "I mean exercise is wonderful. I mean it builds the body and everything."

"Polly," I said gently, "the argument is a fallacy. *Exercise is good* is an unqualified generalization. For instance, if you have heart disease, exercise is bad, not good. Many people are ordered by their doctors *not* to exercise. You must *qualify* the generalization. You must say exercise is *usually* good, or exercise is good *for most people*. Otherwise you have committed a Dicto Simpliciter. Do you see?"

"No," she confessed. "But this is marvy. Do more! Do more!"

"It will be better if you stop tugging at my sleeve," I told her, and when she desisted, I continued. "Next we take up a fallacy called Hasty Generalization. Listen carefully. You can't speak French. I can't speak French. Petey Burch can't speak French. I must therefore conclude that nobody at the University of Minnesota can speak French."

"Really?" said Polly, amazed. "*Nobody?*"

I hid my exasperation. "Polly, it's a fallacy. The generalization is reached too hastily. There are too few instances to support such a conclusion."

"Know any more fallacies?" she asked breathlessly. "This is more fun than dancing even."

I fought off a wave of despair. I was getting nowhere with this girl, absolutely nowhere. Still, I am nothing if not persistent. I continued. "Next comes Post Hoc. Listen to this: Let's not take Bill on our picnic. Every time we take him out with us, it rains."

"I know somebody just like that," she exclaimed. "A girl back home—Eula Becker, her name is. It never fails. Every single time we take her on a picnic—"

"Polly," I said sharply, "it's a fallacy. Eula Becker doesn't *cause* the rain. She has no connection with the rain. You are guilty of Post Hoc if you blame Eula Becker."

"I'll never do it again," she promised contritely. "Are you mad at me?"

I sighed deeply. "No, Polly, I'm not mad."

"Then tell me some more fallacies."

"All right. Let's try Contradictory Premises."

"Yes, let's," she chirped, blinking her eyes happily.

I frowned, but plunged ahead. "Here is an example of Contradictory Premises: If God can do anything, can He make a stone so heavy that He won't be able to lift it?"

"Of course," she replied promptly.

"But if He can do anything, He can lift the stone," I pointed out.

"Yeah," she said thoughtfully. "Well, then I guess He can't make the stone."

"But He can do anything," I reminded her.

She scratched her pretty, empty head. "I'm all confused," she admitted.

"Of course you are. Because when the premises of an argument contradict each other, there can be no argument. If there is an irresistable force, there can be no immovable object. If there is an immovable object, there can be no irresistable force. Get it?"

"Tell me some more of this keen stuff," she said eagerly.

I consulted my watch. "I think we better call it a night. I'll take you home now, and you go over all the things you've learned. We'll have another session tomorrow night."

I deposited her at the girls' dormitory, where she assured me that she had had a perfectly terrif evening, and I went glumly home to my room. Petey lay snoring in his bed, the raccoon coat huddled like a great hairy beast at his feet. For a moment I considered waking him and telling him that he could have his girl back. It seemed clear that my project was doomed to failure. The girl simply had a logic-proof head.

But then I reconsidered. I had wasted one evening; I might as well waste another. Who knew? Maybe somewhere in the extinct crater of her mind, a few embers still smoldered. Maybe somehow I could fan them into flame. Admittedly it was not a prospect fraught with hope, but I decided to give it one more try.

Seated under the oak the next evening I said, "Our first fallacy tonight is called Ad Misericordiam."

She quivered with delight.

"Listen closely," I said. "A man applies for a job. When the boss asks him what his qualifications are, he replies that he has a wife and six children at home, the wife is a helpless cripple, the children have nothing to eat, no clothes to wear, no shoes on their feet, there are no beds in the house, no coal in the cellar, and winter is coming."

A tear rolled down Polly's pink cheeks. "Oh, this is awful, awful," she sobbed.

"Yes, it's awful," I agreed, "but it's no argument. The man never answered the boss's question about his qualifications. Instead he appealed to the boss's sympathy. He committed the fallacy of Ad Misericordiam. Do you understand?"

"Do you have a handkerchief?" she blubbered.

I handed her a handkerchief and tried to keep from screaming while she wiped her eyes. "Next," I said in a carefully controlled tone, "we will discuss False Analogy. Here is an example: Students should be allowed to look at their textbooks during examinations. After all, surgeons have X-rays to guide them during an operation, lawyers have briefs to guide them during a trial, carpenters have blueprints to guide them when they are building a house. Why, then, shouldn't students be allowed to look at their textbooks during an examination?"

"There now," she said enthusiastically, "is the most marvy idea I've heard in years."

"Polly," I said testily, "the argument is all wrong. Doctors, lawyers, and carpenters aren't taking a test to see how much they have learned, but students are. The situations are altogether different, and you can't make an analogy between them."

"I still think it's a good idea," said Polly.

"Nuts," I muttered. Doggedly I pressed on. "Next we'll try Hypothesis Contrary to Fact."

"Sounds yummy," was Polly's reaction.

"Listen: If Madame Curie had not happened to leave a photographic plate in a drawer with a hunk of pitchblende, the world today would not know about radium."

"True, true," said Polly, nodding her head. "Did you see the movie? Oh, it just knocked me out. That Walter Pidgeon is so dreamy. I mean he fractures me."

"If you can forget Mr. Pidgeon for a moment," I said coldly, "I would like to point out that the statement is a fallacy. Maybe Madame Curie would have discovered radium at some later date. Maybe somebody else would have discovered it. Maybe any number of things would have happened. You can't start with a hypothesis that is not true and then draw any supportable conclusions from it."

"They ought to put Walter Pidgeon in more pictures," said Polly. "I hardly ever see him any more."

One more chance, I decided. But just one more. There is a limit to what flesh and blood can bear. "The next fallacy is called Poisoning the Well."

"How cute!" she gurgled.

"Two men are having a debate. The first one gets up and says, 'My opponent is a notorious liar. You can't believe a word that he is going to say.' Now, Polly, think. Think hard. What's wrong?"

I watched her closely as she knit her creamy brow in concentration. Suddenly a glimmer of intelligence — the first I had seen — came into her eyes. "It's not fair," she said with indignation. "It's not a bit fair. What chance has the second man got if the first man calls him a liar before he even begins talking?"

"Right!" I cried exultantly. "One hundred percent right. It's not fair. The first man has *poisoned the well* before anybody could drink from it. He has hamstrung his opponent before he could even start. . . . Polly, I'm proud of you."

"Pshaw," she murmured, blushing with pleasure.

"You see, my dear, these things aren't so bad. All you have to do is concentrate. Think — evaluate — examine. Come now, let's review everything we've learned."

"Fire away," she said with an airy wave of her hand.

Heartened by the knowledge that Polly was not altogether a cretin, I began a long, patient review of all I had told her. Over and over again I cited instances, pointed out flaws, kept hammering away without let up. It was like digging a tunnel. At first everything was work, sweat, and darkness. I had no idea when I would reach the light, or even *if* I would. But I persisted. I pounded and clawed and scraped, and finally I was rewarded. I saw a chunk of light. And then the chunk of light got bigger and the sun came pouring in and all was bright.

Five grueling nights this took, but it was worth it. I had made a logician out of Polly; I had taught her to think. My job was done. She was worthy of me at last. She was a fit wife for me, a proper hostess for my many mansions, a suitable mother for my well-heeled children.

It must not be thought that I was without love for this girl. Quite the contrary. Just as Pygmalion loved the perfect woman he had fashioned, so I loved mine. I determined to acquaint her with my feelings at our very next meeting. The time had come to change our relationship from academic to romantic.

"Polly," I said when next we sat beneath our oak, "tonight we will not discuss fallacies."

"Aw, gee," she said, disappointed.

"My dear," I said, favoring her with a smile, "we have now spent five evenings together. We have gotten along splendidly. It is clear that we are well matched."

"Hasty Generalization," said Polly brightly.

"I beg your pardon," said I.

"Hasty Generalization," she repeated. "How can you say that we are well matched on the basis of only five dates?"

I chuckled with amusement. The dear child had learned her lessons well. "My dear," I said, patting her hand in a tolerant manner, "five dates is plenty. After all, you don't have to eat the whole cake to know that it's good."

"False Analogy," said Polly promptly. "I'm not a cake. I'm a girl."

I chuckled with somewhat less amusement. The dear child had learned her lessons perhaps too well. I decided to change tactics. Obviously the best approach was a simple, strong, direct declaration of love. I paused for a moment while my massive brain chose the right words. Then I began:

"Polly, I love you. You are the whole world to me, and the moon and the stars and the constellations of outer space. Please my darling, say that you will go steady with me, for if you will not, life will be meaningless. I will languish. I will refuse my meals. I will wander the face of the earth, a shambling, a hollow-eyed hulk."

There, I thought, folding my arms, that ought to do it.

"Ad Misericordiam," said Polly.

I ground my teeth. I was not Pygmalion. I was Frankenstein, and my monster had me by the throat. Frantically I fought back the tide of panic surging through me. At all costs I had to keep cool.

"Well, Polly," I said, forcing a smile, "you certainly have learned your fallacies."

"You're darn right," she said with a vigorous nod.

"And who taught them to you, Polly?"

"You did."

"That's right. So you do owe me something, don't you, my dear? If I hadn't come along you never would have learned about fallacies."

"Hypothesis Contrary to Fact," she said instantly.

I dashed perspiration from my brow. "Polly," I croaked, "you mustn't take all those things so literally. I mean this is just classroom stuff. You know that the things you learn in school don't have anything to do with life."

"Dicto Simpliciter," she said, wagging her finger at me playfully.

That did it. I leaped to my feet, bellowing like a bull. "Will you or will you not go steady with me?"

"I will not," she replied.

"Why not?" I demanded.

"Because this afternoon I promised Petey Burch that I would go steady with him."

I reeled back, overcome with the infamy of it. After he promised, after he made a deal, after he shook my hand! "The rat!" I shrieked, kicking up great chunks of turf. "You can't go with him, Polly. He's a liar. He's a cheat. He's a rat."

"Poisoning the Well," said Polly, "and stop shouting. I think shouting must be a fallacy too."

With an immense effort of will, I modulated my voice. "All right," I said. "You're a logician. Let's look at this thing logically. How could you choose Petey Burch over me? Look at me—a brilliant student, a tremendous intellectual, a man with an assured fortune. Look at Petey—a knothead, a jitterbug, a guy who'll never know where his next meal is coming from. Can you give me one logical reason why you should go steady with Petey Burch?"

"I certainly can," declared Polly. "He's got a raccoon coat."

We have used the term *essay* in discussing discourse at the affective end of the spectrum. As we have proceeded through the logical portions, the material has become less personal, the discourse more openly logical in order to convince others of our reasoning, and the term *article* has replaced the term *essay*. In the next chapter we will turn to the expository article near the factual end of the spectrum.

EXERCISES

1. The following essay by Edwin Diamond contains both personal experience and opinion as well as other information. Is it essen-

tially a familiar essay, argument, or expository article? Where would you place it along the spectrum of rhetoric?

I suppose there are still some intellectuals who denounce television as the boob tube or idiot box. Perhaps some blinkered critics still believe in "audience flow theory"—that is, viewers sit video-tranquilized in front of the television, tuned to one channel through the evening.

The intellectuals and critics, of course, are as behind the times as a black-and-white television set with no remote control or videocassette attachment. Television and the television viewer have changed while the theorists weren't looking. We no longer watch television qua television: we now watch specific programs, and for specific purposes. Television has become a lively part of our social transactions, much like the out-of-town visitor whom we invite our friends to meet, or the late-arriving guest who picks up the party just before it sags.

Not all television, obviously, has grown up to be literate and adult; but enough has changed to warrant a systematic look at the social role of television. The contemporary role of television as social instrument recalls the earliest days of the medium: When a family on the block was the first to buy a television set, the rest of us flocked over to marvel at the new technological wonder. No matter that the wonder brought Uncle Miltie's old burlesque routines or primitive two-camera coverage of sports; television viewing was a social occasion. . . .
. . . .
As might be expected, television has become a focus of social life for younger men and women, the under-thirty-five year olds who have grown up with the medium. A twenty-seven-year-old friend of mine recently threw a big Saturday night party with plenty of food, wine, and disco music. At 11:30 everyone sat down to watch "Saturday Night Live." The party didn't die; it shifted into a different gear, and the hostess didn't complain.

Some of my older, more sophisticated friends find television much more of a social experience than, say, going to a Broadway play or to the movies. While no talking is allowed in the theater, social television encourages interaction between audience and set, and among the audience. The viewers can guess at the dialogue and plot of dramas, editorialize on the news, predict the Oscar winners, or single out from the semifinalists the next Miss America. It can be much more fun to talk back to the set than to sit silently in a darkened theater (the product on the screen being equal, naturally).

I am not claiming that social television has brought back the wit and brilliance of the salon to American homes. Social television can't replace real conversation or tête-à-têtes or a good book or a blazing fireplace or solitary thought.

Television has proved, on the whole, to be a good guest in the house, especially when it is not invited to perform too often. Most of our work and much of our play forces us, as individuals, into specialized roles. Even our reading materials have become like private languages—father is down at the *Wall Street Journal* or looking into his *Fortune;* mother can be found, or may be lost, in *The Women's Room;* the college kids are like a *Rolling Stone.*

Television can be a national tongue. At its best, television can provide a common basis for experience, maybe a few laughs, some information and insight, perhaps the chance to engage one's intelligence and imagination. In these days of runaway prices, inflated mediocrities, and deflated hopes in our public lives, that's not a bad record. Television has a standing invitation to come to my place.

Edwin Diamond, "The Social Set,"
American Film, February 1979

2. Do you find the title appropriate? How does it suggest the theme or thesis? What is the theme or thesis and where is it stated?
3. How does the author substantiate his theme or thesis? And where does he state limitations?
4. How does the author personalize the essay? What is the tone? Do you believe the tone is appropriate or excessive? Why?
5. Can you find any instances of charged language? If you do, what effect does the charged language produce?
6. How would you refute the author's assertions?
7. Rewrite, adding possible refutations and, if appropriate, further information from your own experience of television.
8. The title of the following article strongly indicates that it will concentrate on refutation. By showing the invalidity of the opposing argument, the writer hopes to strengthen the validity of his own. Does he succeed?

Where the Anti-Nuclear Argument Fails
Dr. John C. Zink

Nuclear power is here now. Right now there are 70 nuclear power plants operating in the United States generating approximately 1/8 of all the electricity in this country. Last year nuclear energy generated more electricity than hydroelectric dams, and next year nuclear energy will probably surpass even natural gas in the generation of electricity. The Chicago area gets over 1/3 of its energy from nuclear energy. Parts of New England receive 3/4th of their electricity from nuclear energy.

These plants operate safely and reliably and perform a great service to the communities in which they are located. You might recall that during last year's coal strike, during a very bitter cold winter, some 20 people froze to death one weekend alone in New England. How many more would that have been if nuclear power hadn't been there generating 75% of the electricity? One weekend in Dallas this summer, 22 people died of heat prostration. How many more would it have been without adequate electricity to power labor saving devices and to provide cooling? Adequate energy supplies are essential for all — rich and poor.

I believe nuclear power to be the most economical, safest, most environmentally sound means available for generating electricity from now until well into the 21st century. All of our experience with power confirms this belief. Last year nuclear powered electricity cost 25% less than that generated using coal and 69% less than that using oil. The trend seems likely to continue.

Although nuclear plants are expensive, their construction costs are going up less rapidly than those of coal plants. And the fuel cost for nuclear plants has been going up at a rate less than half that of the price of coal. Ironically, one day last spring there were two letters to the editor of our local newspapers opposing our proposed Black Fox station: one because it is too expensive and will make our electric bills go up, the other because it is too cheap and will draw undesirable heavy industry into the area. The fact remains that nuclear power is more economical than any other source of electricity available to us for the rest of this century.

That nuclear power is safe has been demonstrated by its flawless operating history. In spite of many claims to the contrary by individuals ideologically opposed to nuclear energy, the perfect record speaks for itself. A recent study by the American Medical Association shows that nuclear power is 400 times less hazardous than the generation of electricity from coal. A study by the Canadian government shows that nuclear power is even less hazardous than the use of solar energy, which seems to be the favorite of our anti-nuclear activists. You will find that nearly all of the reputable researchers in the area of solar energy are, in fact, in favor of nuclear energy because they understand and work daily with the limitations of solar energy.

That nuclear energy is environmentally sound is demonstrated over again in every environmental impact statement reviewed and approved by the Environmental Protection Agency for new power plants. In spite of claims to the contrary, the proven facts are that nuclear power is environmentally better than the alternatives.

Perhaps the most telling argument in favor of nuclear power is the fact that, throughout the world, all different types of governments, all different types of electric companies, be they private, public, large or small, municipal, state, federally owned or membership owned, are turning to nuclear power. These people who are responsible for meeting their obligations to serve the public in the most reliable, safe and economical way possible have all reached the same conclusion. That is, we must use nuclear energy in large quantities. Yet our would-be street corner experts, who have no responsibility to the public, who do not understand the technical and economic aspects of power generation, tell you that everyone else in the world is wrong and they are right.

Public Service of Oklahoma pamphlet

9. The writer has analyzed the opposing argument and finds three points to refute. What are they?

10. The writer chiefly aims to show faults in the opposing argument. What are the faults in his? They are especially prominent in the second paragraph. You might notice also that the third paragraph begins, "I *believe* nuclear power to be most economical," and the fourth paragraph ends, "The *fact* remains that nuclear power is more economical. . . ."

11. Trace the pattern of induction and deduction in his argument.
12. Comment on the tone. What changes would you make to approach a tone that Carl Rogers might appreciate?
13. Rewrite the argument or write an argument of your own response.
14. The following argument, "The Anachronism of Marriage" (*New York Times,* June 1, 1972), seems to begin with the thesis, "Marriage is the hell of false expectations," and so we anticipate a deductive development. Trace the steps that the author uses to validate the opening statement. Is our expectation justified? Is the opening statement the thesis, or is it actually reflected in the title? Notice that the phrase of the title is repeated in the first statement of the fifth paragraph. If this is the thesis, has the author proceeded inductively? Trace the movement.

The Anachronism of Marriage
Kathrin Perutz

Marriage is the hell of false expectations, where both partners, expecting to be loved, defined and supported, abdicate responsibility for themselves and accuse the other of taking away freedom.

Our modern legend has it that one man and one woman choose each other over all others and enter into love like an enclosed garden from which there is no retreat. Here they are in their own place; each day they will feast on and with the beloved, for they are blessed with happiness, their natural inheritance. Here legend ends; here Briar Rose is kissed by the king's son and whispers, "Is it you, Prince? I've waited so long." Her long sleep is over, and so is the fairy tale.

All husbands and wives know that moment: the sudden clarity when the honeymoon or partying has to stop, when the two who are brought together by God or judge resume their separate selves and wonder whatever made them do it.

The state of wedlock produces a kind of lockjaw which prevents the victim from talking about his plight. Not to have a "healthy relationship" is to admit invalidism, and most people would rather manipulate the symptoms than diagnose the malady. They babble about "meaning" and "communication" instead of finding something worth saying. A conspiracy is maintained against the unmarried, because marriage or the family is a perfect working mechanism of intake and output, a consuming function necessary for the economy of America. The image of marriage is held out like a national carrot, always in front of us, never seized, and we follow behind like beasts of burden.

For marriage as we insist on seeing it is an anachronism based on old roles, functions, and imperatives. We say that marriage is "natural" and to that end develop anthropomorphic tautologies to show that animals "marry." But human behavior is purely human, and to call marriage as practiced today in America and Europe "natural" is to invoke sympathetic magic. Our marriage is neither a natural outcome of our standards and beliefs, nor is it an institution we can characterize as human because of its prevalence in history.

Only in Victorian times did marriage achieve its present sanctimony. Industrialization and the concept of modern democracy brought the idea of equals, the household lost eminence as the center of work and education, and romantic love was appropriated from the illicit to compensate husbands and wives whose relation to each other and their work were no longer obvious. Marriage, like other institutions, was to be the same for all classes and so was both rigidified and sentimentalized.

We all suffer from it. A wife is still legally the property of, or at least answerable to, her husband. Social custom still requires that husbands are breadwinners. We marry for children despite overpopulation, and though our view of sex has altered in the last twenty years, marriage for sex remains as a quaint monument to a society that existed before birth control, penicillin and the discovery of female orgasm. In Victorian times, marriage provided containment. Now marriage is supposed to provide sexuality, and we expect sex to redeem us, though we are not closer to our bodies than we ever were. . . .

If we continue practicing this dangerous anachronism, we will lose not only ourselves and our mates, but also our children. Banalities about marriage suit us as well as the Emperor's new clothes. What we need is recognition that each person is himself, married or not; that the journey into oneself is more important than the ego trip; that we belong to each other only by willing it and making a conscious commitment. We can't make promises to an impossible idea, or take the name of someone else because we live with him, or vow to live forever with someone we have never lived with at all. The only true words of a wedding ceremony are: "I know you and I love you and I commit myself to you. I'll try to do you no harm." Children of such a union would have parents who know themselves, and would have something to grow up to.

15. The fifth paragraph implies this syllogism:

> Marriage results from human standards and beliefs. These standards and beliefs are not "natural." Marriage, therefore, is not "natural."

Find and delineate other syllogisms in the article. Also show the writer's reliance on cause and effect and on metaphorical language.

16. Is the conclusion justified? If so, how? And how about the recommendation that one needs to take "a journey into oneself"? Is there any prior concern with this "journey"?

17. Write a full critique of this article.

18. Write an argumentative essay or article. Formulate a thesis with a valid point before you begin your draft and jot down means of substantiating and refuting the point. Write your first draft; then examine it for fallacies. Revise to eliminate the fallacies and then rewrite.

Chapter 16

The Expository Article

Exposition is explanation, the exposing of information or ideas. Unlike argumentation, the expository article does not rely on inductive and deductive reasoning. Instead of reasoning, it relies on authority, or *ethos,* the credibility of the writer. The writer's credibility is established and sustained through appropriate and effective use of language and the rhetorical operations and conventions. Along the spectrum of rhetoric discourse becomes more expository as it approaches more factual material, that is, material that may be taken as obvious, axiomatic, or easily provable in external reality. The facts of history, dates of wars, and the principal actors of history, for example, are expository material, but with the move toward relating facts, such as calling events preceding a war the causes of war, the writer enters the range of argument.

Since we can hardly have discourse without relationship, argument resides even in the most factual of expositions. Indeed, the most factual discourses are about objects and processes external to the human being, but we know that these change in time, and so even a statement about a mechanism may be true only momentarily. We know that the instrument we use to measure things changes the dimensions as we measure them. But for the sake of societal existence, we agree in general about external things to the extent we can, even though we know our facts are actually approximations. After all, Gibraltar is still there, however changed from year by year. When we write expositions about human beings and their societies, factuality becomes less certain. In economics or business, it is possible to list the facts about production and consumption, although statistics, we know, are generalized and manipulated and thus are open to argument. If we take statistics for facts, however, we certainly cannot take the statements built upon them as factual — say, the "fact" that production of wheat will increase next year because it has been increasing every year for the past decade. Nor can the social worker really say anything factual about the family she has analyzed without speaking of relationships, which of course are not factual and thus open to various interpretations. The same situation applies to the psychoanalyst seeking causes for a patient's behavior. Nevertheless, for the sake of societal existence, we take as factual some generalizations that have been made about the relationships in human and social affairs, and we use them without explicit argument in expository articles as though they were factual. Whenever possible, the writer ought to attribute such generalizations to the source, making a factual statement out of it — for example, "according to Freudian theory" — and then what is said, either quoted or paraphrased, is factual to the extent that it is accurately restated.

Structuring the Exposition

Instead of a thesis or proposition to be argued for or against, the expository article has a topic, which it explains and elaborates through rhetorical operations. The writer of such an article must gather information and shape and scale it to appeal to the audience's understanding and interest. If the writer has too much information and renders it too densely, in terms too abstruse for the audience, he may lose ethos because he has been rhetorically unwise, going over the heads of readers. If the subject is simpler than the language in which it is rendered, the audience may laugh at the incongruity. If the writer has not gathered enough material, oversimplifies what is more complicated, or fails to shape the information into some understandable form, the audience may find the discourse incompetent and the writer unacceptable or not authoritative. Errors in grammar, spelling, and punctuation will almost automatically detract from the writer's ethos, his or her credibility as an authority.

Although the topic is freely chosen, the information that the topic promises is not. The writer may be selective but must represent major facts of the topic or points of information. If the topic were "Hindu strains in the Beat literature of the 1950s in America," the writer could hardly exclude Allen Ginsberg or Jack Kerouac, two of the major writers, although he might not mention all the works in which Hindu strains appear. Or the writer promising to relate the history of baseball could hardly ignore the Chicago Black Sox scandal in 1919.

There are, of course, wide areas for selectivity. In introducing the topic, the writer might show its significance with a background of need, starting with a startling statistic:

> One of the more challenging problems in heart medicine is sudden cardiac death. Most of the 400,000 such deaths each year in America can be traced to a malfunction of the electrical control system of the heart. Though many arrhythmias can now be treated with pacemakers and medicines, others can result in heart stoppage and sudden death. These cardiac arrests can often be reversed by a massive electric shock applied to the chest, using a defibrilla-

tor. But until now only large hospital-building defibrillating machines have been able to do the job, and only when applied within minutes of the arrest.

HELP Newsletter, Tulsa,
Oklahoma, July 1984

The paragraph introduces the need for the "mini-defibrillator," which is the topic of the following exposition. (Notice how neatly context is used to define "arrhythmias.")

Or the topic may be introduced against a background that is conjectural, where "the facts" lead to significant possibilities:

> By the end of the century, according to a study that has just been published, a large part of the labor force will be working out of the home rather than commuting to the office, thanks to the wonders of something called "videotex." What effect this will have on the human race can only be conjectured, but it is expected to be profound.

The facts of this background are the study itself, which contains the conjecture. Here the writer is presenting the fact that the study conjectures. He or she may argue the effects conjectured, or merely present current information about the videotex along with the predictions made in the study. This writer chose to write an expository article.

> Actually, videotex simply pulls together a lot of existing communications technology, including the TV screen and the typewriter, and builds upon them. But like the wheel, one thing then leads to another. . . .

Although the facts of the topic must be taken up, we notice the writer has a free choice in the way they will be presented.

History is perhaps the most common way of introducing a topic:

> During the past decade, biologists who have given up dissecting frogs for more exotic pursuits have learned to slice genes as easily as links of sausage. These brave new experiments have created bacteria that produce insulin, interferon, and human hormones the way most other bacteria produce disease. Now, the biologists are probing the mysteries of cancer, with some startling results.

HELP Newsletter, Tulsa,
Oklahoma, July 1984

In all introductions of expository articles, the writer tries to enliven the information, attracting the reader at the outset by appealing to some basic human desire or sense of wonder. The writer also enlivens the language through descriptive imagery and metaphor, "to slice genes as easily as links of sausage."

The information developed through the exposition fulfills the promise of the topic. If the exposition has been developed well through appropriate uses of the rhetorical operations, the reader should feel a sense of a circle completed. The ending completes the circle by prodding the reader into the full recognition that the writer has fulfilled the promise of the topic. A comparison of ending and beginning shows whether or not the author completed the job. The reader's mental process ideally changes from the absorption of information to the realization that it has been received, that is, from information to knowledge. In fulfilling the promise, the ending replaces the sense of anticipation with the sense of completion.

Like the beginning, the ending again emphasizes the significance of the information and the ideas it suggests. The generalizations should cover all the reader's questions raised in the process of absorbing the information. In one way or another, the generalizations of the ending summarize the exposition. In long papers, the ending should reflect the development of the basic points in the exposition. If one or two points have been emphasized over others, then the summary concentrates on these.

Because summary is review, writers tend to include too much information; and because reviews encompass the whole structure, they tend to show what is missing. If writers discover missing materials as they summarize, they should revise the exposition by opening it up at an appropriate place and adding new information. They should not add the new information in the summary at the end. The longer the ending in relation to the report, the less it summarizes and the more it repeats. A long summary ending is actually a contradiction in terms.

Short summaries for relatively long papers are equally inappropriate. Such summaries tend to become a sequence of disconnected statements. Transitions that relate statements to one another usually smooth the summary into an expository paragraph or two that flow from idea to idea:

> Psychological tests have paid good dividends. If properly instituted and if administered by qualified personnel, they will benefit most organizations. But testing is of value only as part of the selection program. In case after case, evidence has shown that it is a grievous mistake to select solely or even primarily on the basis of test scores. Tests, therefore, should not supplant other means of selection, but should be used to implement them, and, in fact, to encourage the consideration of other factors. Administrative officers cannot make psychological tests either the instrument or scapegoat. They retain the responsibility for selection and must accept the consequences of their choices.

Shorter papers may end with a sentence or two. These endings may serve as summaries by implication rather than statement. They imply the most important points developed and leave the reader with a sense of significance, often looking ahead:

> The future of the fission process must, of course, await further work, but this tantalizing goal is like many prizes sought in research — the jury is still out, and the final verdict will depend upon the results of future investigations.

The metaphor of a courtroom trial may be somewhat hackneyed, but it is intended to brighten this ending. Actually what the writer is saying, most readers know. The sentence functions as an aesthetic close; it does not summarize points, but it does emphasize the major point of the exposition — the tantalizing goal of the fusion process, its enormous utility.

Using Rhetorical Operations

We often think of the expository article as the transcription of facts, but of course the facts have to be conceived and related in the writer's mind before they can be transmitted to the reader. In this process, the facts often seem less factual, and the exposition may fade into argument. Nonetheless, if the aim remains expository, the writer concentrates on his or her conception of the material, not on establishing validity, nor on judging or evaluating:

> Eskimos living along the western shores of Greenland have a remarkably low incidence of heart attacks and strokes. Their secret, according to a report at a recent meeting in Charleston, SC, seems to be fish oil.

Rather than argue the proposition, this writer instead assigns an authority, the report, and then concentrates on exposing the information, which only "seems" to be so.

Because the rhetorical operation of definition tends to assimilate all the others, as we have seen in Chapter 10, it is sometimes taken as the essence of exposition itself. All exposition attempts to answer the question of definition, "What is it?" although it usually answers other questions along the way. The following article, for example, employs a good deal of exemplification, narration, and comparison to render the topic, which is a definition of a computer system for recording dance, given explicitly in the third paragraph:

> Few art forms are as ephemeral as dance. Choreographers themselves speak of it as the illiterate art; there is no score, no permanent written record for most of the world's repertoires. Last year, for example, the American Ballet Theatre decided to revive George Balanchine's 1949 creation, *Bourrée Fantastique*. Presented with this suggestion, Balanchine was not optimistic. "Oh no, dears, it's too old fashioned," he said, "and besides, no one remembers the steps." Former Balanchine dancers were gathered together to reconstruct the pattern of assemblées, jetés, and other movements. And ABT researchers also discovered a written record of *Bourrée Fantastique* in the oblique, symbolic language of choreographic notation.
>
> But this was a rare and lucky chance. Notation is not widely used. Few ballets and almost no modern dances are protected from oblivion in this way. Many attempts have been made to provide dance with a formal

notation system like that used for music, but none has provided a true equivalent—a medium in which choreographers can compose to produce a score dancers can use. The latest attempts, however, are different, for they make use of the memory, manipulative powers, and perhaps most important, the graphic abilities of computers.

The new computer graphic systems, now in their early stages, are designed to record dance by analyzing movement and translating the information into an animated human figure displayed on the screen. Like written notations for dance, the resulting computerized "score" can provide a permanent record, a library of dance.

It is not difficult to spot the writer's use of example, in the very first paragraph, nor to see that the example is itself narrative. Nor are the comparisons difficult to spot, mainly of a dance record and a musical score. After details developing the point that the world lacks a universal system for notation, the writer employs informal classification to show what does exist:

Despite the need for language and preservation, there is still no universal system of notation. In fact, three systems compete in the Western world. In the United States the most widespread and comprehensive is Labanotation.

He then uses analysis as the means of exposing the inadequacies of the most dominant existing system:

... the geometric staves and legions of tiny rectangles, triangles, and diamonds which make up the Labanotation representations are intimidating. ... many dancers see symbolic notations as inadequate. Although Labanotation is the most thorough system, it is still primarily concerned with positional information and is weak in describing stylistic qualities or relative force of movement. Modern dancer Merce Cunningham says, "Symbol-based notation doesn't work because of translating the steps. Notators translate steps into symbols. The dancer later looks at the symbol and translates back. This is not the way dancers work." Ordinarily dance steps and combinations are taught by demonstration. Furthermore, even a short ballet can take weeks to record. A notator must view at least four full productions to capture all the movement and nuances.

Joseph Menosky, "Video Graphics and Grand Jetés," *Science 82* (May)

As we have seen, analysis is a useful aid to expository definition, for example, in the first section of the article on video graphics above:

The latest attempts, however, are different, for they make use of the memory, manipulative powers, and perhaps most important, the graphic abilities of computers.

Analysis also provides the skeleton for expository description and narration. In the following paragraph, the concept "growth of industry" at the beginning is the same as "new kind of world" at the end. The parts of this conceived structure are the working man, motorcars, aircraft, wireless communication, moving pictures, and electricity:

> The Edwardian era could perhaps be called the naive period in twentieth century living. It was a transitional period that saw the growth of industry into a gigantic institution. Social reform began to improve the plight of the working man. Motorcars, experimented with and refined during the Edwardian decade, changed many aspects of life. Aircraft were developed in the period. Wireless communication was refined. Moving pictures became a popular diversion for people in all walks of life. Electricity came into its own as the best means of lighting and powering homes and industries. Edward was not only a new King in a new century, we were seeing a new kind of world emerge.
>
> Philip May, 20 Silver Ghosts: The
> Incomparable Pre–World War I
> Motorcar, 1907–1914

The writer could elaborate on each of the parts named, devoting a paragraph or so to each, and produce an article on the growth of industry in the Edwardian era. Actually, this writer enclosed the conceptual structure being analyzed within a larger one, the Edwardian era in general; the growth of industry is only one part. Other major parts are entertainment, art, family life, politics, societal life, and so on. The following paragraphs describe life in terms of the "country jaunt":

> Most of the wealthy set were content to live the high life that seemed to consist mainly of weekend visits to country estates of "friends." The King was an active participant in these elaborate country jaunts. Complicated was certainly one of the words that apply to these visits since it usually meant that about fifty people invaded someone's estate beginning Friday afternoon and ending Monday afternoon. Keeping up with the social whirl could be a financial disaster for those within the circle whose means were not what they looked to be. Most visitors would arrive by train and be met with a mixed assortment of carriages and motorcars to convey them to the house of the victim. Along with the people came mounds of baggage and servants to help the ladies dress. The men brought along their cased shotguns, riding clothes, and billiard cues.
>
> Once the guests were ensconced in their apartments, the first order of the day was to change clothes. Men usually changed their complete attire four times a day. The women often changed more than that, and indeed, on looking back, some of the ladies admitted that a great deal of their time in the Edwardian era was spent getting in and out of clothes.
>
> During these visits, men usually went off by themselves to take part in some sport or another. Ladies would take tea and sew, chatting all the while. Afternoons were often taken with games of croquet, one of the King's favorite social pastimes.
>
> Philip May, 20 Silver Ghosts: The
> Incomparable Pre–World War I
> Motorcar, 1907–1914

Within these descriptive paragraphs, the writer employs narration on a very general level to render a social procedure. The steps are arrival of visitors, changing of clothes, and pursuit of activities. These steps are general and more or less sequential; that is, we do not follow one person through specific steps. In the third step, for example, a visitor has a choice of any number of activities. The narration of a specific process, on the other hand, guides the reader through a definite set of operations.

> If the boat [is under sail] then, at the moment of fastening, the mast and sail are lowered and quickly stowed to project over one quarter: meanwhile the line is leaping around the loggerhead and down the boat as the whale starts to run. As soon as he slackens, the line is checked at the loggerhead, but the boat does not tow long before the whale is taking out more line. Thereafter, the time before the whale is killed may be long or short, the object being to close with the whale, sometimes by hauling on the line and sometimes by rowing, until the harpooner can stand up and pitch his lance into the whale's side, preferably behind the flipper, seeking the lungs. The boat must get right up to the whale, often wood to black skin. If the harpooner gets a chance, he may "churn" his lance, plunging it up and down in the wound. A whale may be lanced several times before he goes into the grim and impressive death struggle called the flurry.
>
> *The Whale*, produced by The
> Trychare, 1968

In both generalized and specific narrations, we notice that description provides the details. For example, the first step in the Edwardian era article — arrival of visitors — is rendered with these details:

> Hosts' servants with assortment of carriages and motorcars.
>
> Mounds of visitors' baggage and servants.
>
> Cased shotguns, riding clothes, billiard cues.

The last sentence of the whaling article is mostly descriptive. Perhaps you can find other descriptive detail in the paragraph.

Narratives of processes or events are not strictly sequential, we notice, nor are descriptions of historical moments, mechanisms, or objects strictly spatial. Description is almost always used to develop the steps of narrations, and narration is almost always used to show how a described object moves or works. Narration always enlivens description, as in this paragraph:

> The harpoon used in the Azores today is the toggle iron invented by a Negro blacksmith called James Temple at New Bedford in 1848. The steelhead is so pivoted on the wrought-iron shaft that when the iron takes strain after entering the whale, the head swings out at right angles and toggles against the inside of the blubber or, after a skillful and lucky

dart, between two of the whale's ribs. The harpoon, mounted on a six-foot pole, makes a heavy weapon nearly nine feet in length.

> *The Whale,* produced by The
> Trychare, 1968

The enlivening touches of narration are "the iron takes strain after entering the whale, and the head swings out . . . toggles against . . ."

Tone of Voice

Enlivening elements like active verbs obviously contribute to the tone of the expository article. The voice in the exposition, as in all other discourse, influences readers. The voice is more prominent in some expositions than in others, but all exposition should avoid a tone that unduly colors the information; that is, the author's attitude or bias should not become integral with the information. On the other hand, if the tone is made totally neutral, as most instruction in report writing recommends, we create dullness that leads the reader's attention to wander. Ideally, the tone of expository articles should enhance clarity and understanding and should not be too brief or long-winded, nor too dense or too simple, but caring of the readers, their motives and capabilities in reading. A proper tone for exposition results almost automatically when the writer's motive is to communicate with the reader, rather than to express himself without special regard to communication.

Writers who write down to readers, who condescend to impart information, who assume readers know the sources of their remote references, the meanings of their abstract terms, and the history of their concepts, cannot avoid a tone of arrogance, although they imagine that their work is objectively toneless. This attitude leads to a common failing in communications among professionals: the author plays a distant role, pretending that the perceptions and conceptions exist in an abstract region of divine kings of the profession, divorced from human considerations of understanding. Too often the tone that actually emerges is supercilious, whether unconsciously or self-consciously so. Frequently, the reader's effort to absorb the material is hampered by the writer's irksome tone.

Pomposity is not a tone peculiar to our contemporary overorganized professions and bureaucracies. It has been with us at least since the medieval cabal of priests and the magical power of words. In "A Letter to a Young Gentleman," in 1719, Swift warned that affectation is

> one of the most general defects among scholars . . . who run on in a flat kind of phraseology, often mingled with barbarous terms and expressions. . . . Professors in most arts and sciences are generally the worst qualified to explain their meanings to those who are not of their tribe: a

common farmer shall make you understand in three words, *that his foot is out of joint, or his collarbone broken;* wherein a surgeon, after a hundred terms of art, if you are not a scholar, shall leave you to seek. It is frequently the case in law, physics, and even many of the meaner arts. . . . The faults are nine in ten owing to affectation, and not to the want of understanding.

Although the voice in an expository article is restrained, it should indicate the writer's desire to have the reader understand, to take the extra step for that purpose. Abstractions are necessary but are frequently pinned down with concrete applications, examples, metaphors, analogies, or direct comparisons. Personal pronouns are introduced to put an actor into the sentence so that an excess of passive constructions can be replaced with active voice. Above all, the barbarities of bureaucratic language are avoided, especially nouns made into verbs and verbs made into nouns:

The files are now *accessed* by *hybridization* of *electronized* programs.

The maintenance of the human voice throughout the expository article enhances readers' ability to see the material as the writer sees it, as though they were looking at a landscape through a clear window.

EXERCISES

1. The passages below are expository. Concentrate on the differences in tone and explain how you would order them along the expository portion of the spectrum of rhetoric:

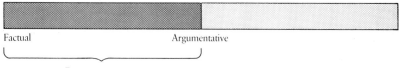

Factual   Argumentative

Expository portion

   a. Along with Mike Fink and Simon Girty, Judge Hugh Henry Brackenridge is one of the eccentrics in the legend of the early frontier west of the Alleghenies. There is the abiding image of the circuit rider charging the jury, beard unshaven and hair disheveled, tie askew, shirt sprung open and soiled almost to the color of his rusty black waistcoat, and his bare feet propped on the bar of justice. It was said he owned no stockings. Caught riding naked through the rain, he pointed to his only suit under the saddle, "The storm, you know, would spoil the clothes, but it couldn't spoil me." In the East he had become notorious as the "worst of the Whiskey Rebels," and in the West the elected representative of the backwoodsmen who sold them out "for a dinner of some stockholder's fat beef."

Appointed a Justice of the Supreme Court of Pennsylvania for his role in Jefferson's victory (1799), he was congratulated with a summary account of his career, beginning with an exposé of the new "Supreme judge and sapient philosopher too . . . seen 'stark naked' and nearly 'stark mad' from too much tipple in the face of open day." The description touched upon his role in the Whiskey Rebellion, his advocacy of the French Revolution and of the Federal Constitution, his sermons to correct his countrymen's morals, and his reputation as a writer: "President of the Jacobin Society . . . Biographer of the Insurgents . . . Auctioneer of Divinity . . . Haberdasher of Pronouns." And because he had hired a Jewish editor for his Jeffersonian newspaper, *Tree of Liberty,* "Brackenridge of late seems to have a hankering after the Jews . . . like his friend Jefferson the philosopher and the Rogues of France . . . that he should turn Jew in his old days and build him a synagogue in his own ground surprises nobody. . . . If in one of his crack-brained magazines Hugh has submitted to the Knife of the High Priest, is it expected that every man, woman, and child will do the same? Are we all to be circumcised without benefit of clergy?"

Daniel Marder, "Introduction," *A Hugh Henry Brackenridge Reader, 1770–1815*

b. The origin of Scotland's annual Highland games goes back so far into the mists of time that no one knows exactly when they began to wrestle, throw weights, toss sabers, and dance and play music.

The only clue we have is an ancient document that states that Malcolm Canmore, King of Scotland in the 11th century, was responsible for organizing the first games to be held in Braemar, but whether or not this was the first of all games was never established.

The document tells us that when the King was staying at the royal hunting lodge — the remains of which can still be seen — he became very dissatisfied with the speed of his messengers and ordered that the young men should gather to hold contests of speed and endurance so that he could choose the best among them for his service.

The pioneers of those early games little thought that centuries hence these displays of strength and skill would delight and thrill countless thousands of folk from countries far beyond the shores of Scotland every year. Maybe the glorious settings . . . maybe it is the stirring sight of the arenas filled with brawny men in colorful kilts competing in the heavy field events; or the dancers and members of the pipe bands, resplendent in their traditional attire . . .

Trevor Hollaway, *Christian Science Monitor (Tulsa Tribune,* July 28, 1982)

c. Ten years ago, when *The Population Bomb* was written, the United States population explosion was alive and well — and projected to get even healthier. Virtually all demographers thought that the early

1970s would be a time of rising birth rates in the United States and that it would take decades, at the very least, for fertility to decline to replacement reproduction (an average family size at which each generation just replaces itself). We agreed with them; their reasoning made sense.

But we were all dead wrong. In the early 1970s the women who had been born in the postwar baby boom were in their early 20s, their prime productive years. Because a high proportion of the population were young people at an age when they would be having families, demographers had predicted a surge in the birth rate (conventionally expressed as number of babies born per 1,000 people in the population per year). But contrary to all expectations, the birth rate plunged dramatically from 18.4 in 1970 to around 15 by 1973, and it has remained there ever since.

Correspondingly, the net reproductive rate in the United States has fallen to just below one and has stayed there. The net reproduction rate is a measure of the relative reproduction of generations. A rate of one is replacement reproduction — technically, each female baby born alive in one generation is replaced by exactly one female baby born alive in the next. A rate of two theoretically indicates a population that roughly doubles each generation; a rate of .5, a population that halves each generation. In the mid 1970s the net reproductive rate in the United States was about .9, a little below replacement. If this level continued and if there were no immigration, population would decline.

> Paul R. Ehrlich and Anne H. Ehrlich, "What Happened to the Population Bomb?" *Human Nature,* January 1979

2. Analyze each passage above for elements of tone, and on the basis of your analysis describe and name the tone of each.
3. What sort of background does the author of each passage above employ to introduce the topic?
4. State the topic of each passage. Is it explicit or implied?
5. Compare the passages for the uses of metaphor for definitive or imaginative effect. Write a brief analysis that renders your findings.
6. Write a description of the way each passage employs rhetorical operations.
7. Study the two versions of the same article below, noting in the first the effect of omitted details, comparisons, images. Write a critique estimating the effects of these omissions. Be sure to contrast tones.
8. Indicate in the second version where context is used rather than formal or informal definition to render meanings of unfamiliar terms.
9. Write an analysis of the second version that shows how the writer structures the material. Be sure to comment on beginning, middle,

and ending, and on the use of rhetorical operations. Where, for instance, does narration come to the aid of description? You might exemplify by noting one or two processes within the article, step by step.

Version I

The earliest known fossil dragonflies are from the Carboniferous Period. The wingspan of the largest was as much as 27 inches. They are the largest known insects which ever existed on earth. Dragonflies lived 150 million years ago during the age of the giant dinosaurs.

The dragonfly of today have characteristics that show they are primitive insects and have changed very little in millions of years except in size. Their wings are able to move only up and down, having no coupling device joining the front and back wings as in higher insects, and have a network of "veins" supporting the membrane. The four wings are usually transparent and colorless, but may be tinted or patterned, and the bodies are often brightly colored.

The estimated speed of dragonflies varies from 35 to 60 miles an hour. Dragonflies extend their wings on each side.

Dragonflies are found most often near water where they breed, but it is not unusual to see them far away from their breeding territory. The males patrol and defend their breeding and hunting territories against other males of their species. The sense used most is sight. The antennae are minute and the eyes are enormous. They can detect movement 40 feet away. Dragonflies may bite, but do not sting.

The male dragonflies mate with any female of their own species which flies into their breeding territory. The eggs of the female are almost always laid in water. Some females insert their eggs in stems of water plants; some force the eggs into sand or gravel at the edge of shallow streams; and others fly close to the surface of the water and dip the tip of their bodies. The eggs are washed off and sink to the bottom. When fully grown, the larva crawls up the stem of a plant and undergoes its final moult above the surface of the water, becoming an adult dragonfly.

Adults and their young are predatory. The adults catch insects on the wing with their front legs and chew them with powerful jaws. Their larvae catch prey with their labium, which is armed with two hooks. When not hunting and at rest, the labium is folded under the head. They breathe by drawing water into their rectum and then expelling it again — propelling themselves forward in a simple form of jet propulsion.

Some species of dragonfly are migratory and fly great distances over land and water.

Dragonflies and their larvae are beneficial to man. They feed on mosquitoes, midges, and other small insects and help keep them under control. The dragonfly larvae are probably an important food source for freshwater fish.

Destruction of their habitat by pollution, drainage, dredging, and fillings are serious threats to these primitive insects.

Version II

In the summer, dragonflies visit the low-growing shrubs across the front of our house — no blossoms there, but lots of flying insects! We watch these strange, gossamer-winged insects and marvel at their fragile beauty.

The earliest known fossil dragonflies are from the Carboniferous Period, between 220 million and 275 million years ago. Impressions of their wings show that the wingspan of the largest was as much as 27 inches, about the size of the wings of a crow! They are the largest known insects which ever existed on the Earth. Dragonflies similar to those that visit our shrubs lived 150 million years ago during the age of the giant dinosaurs.

The dragonflies of today have characteristics that show they are primitive insects and have changed very little in millions of years except in size. Their wings are able to move only up and down, having no coupling device joining the front and back wings as in higher insects such as butterflies, and have a network of "veins" supporting the membrane. The four wings are usually transparent and colorless, but may be tinted or patterned, and the bodies are often brightly colored.

Very swift and powerful fliers, the estimated speed of dragonflies varies from 35 to 60 miles an hour. Unlike damselflies, small relatives which hold their wings over the back when at rest, dragonflies extend their wings on each side.

Dragonflies are found most often near water where they breed, but it is not unusual to see them far away from their breeding territory, resting on trees and bushes. The males patrol and defend their breeding and hunting territories against other males of their species, and before summer is over many dragonflies appear with torn wings and injured legs. The sense used most is sight. The antennae are minute and the eyes are enormous. They can detect movement 40 feet away. Dragonflies may bite, but do not sting.

The male dragonflies mate with any female of their own species which flies into the breeding territory. The eggs of the female are almost always laid in water. Some females insert their eggs in stems of water plants; some force the eggs into sand or gravel at the edge of shallow streams; and others fly close to the surface of the water and dip the tip of their bodies. The eggs are washed off and sink to the bottom. When fully grown, the larva crawls up the stem of a plant and undergoes its final moult above the surface of the water, becoming an adult dragonfly.

Adults and their young are predatory. The adults catch insects on the wing with their front legs and chew them with powerful jaws. Their larvae catch prey with a "mask" which is their enlarged extendible lower lip, or labium, which is armed with two hooks. When not hunting and at rest, the labium is folded under the head. The larvae catch tadpoles, small fish and a great number of mosquito larvae. They breathe by drawing water into their rectum and then expelling it again — propelling themselves forward in a simple form of jet propulsion.

Some species of dragonflies are migratory and fly great distances over land and water. In mid-September several years ago, hundreds of chimney swifts, traveling from the north and northeast toward the south and southwest, passed slowly overhead for hours.

Dragonflies and their larvae are beneficial to man. They feed on mosquitoes, midges, and other small insects and help keep them under control. The dragonfly larvae are probably an important food source for freshwater fish.

Destruction of their habitat by pollution, drainage, dredging, and fillings are serious threats to these primitive insects.

Fleeca C. Dunaway, "Dragonflies
Spring from Dinosaur Age, Are
Helpful to Man," *World of Nature*
(Tulsa World, July 25, 1982)

10. Write an expository article. After conceiving your topic and limiting it, gather information that is appropriate, then examine your topic and its limitation again to make sure it fits the scale of your information. Determine, before you begin to write, what means of introduction you may use and what rhetorical operations you may employ and how.

Chapter 17

Summaries, Abstracts, and Reviews

The ability to produce effective summaries, abstracts, and reviews is an indispensable skill, vital not only for practical performance in the college classroom and on the job but also for intellectual development. These brief reports of longer original discourses focus on the points that express the essence of the original. Summaries and abstracts are neutral in tone and intent, hewing close to the original in their entirety. Reviews add critique and recommendation.

Summaries and Abstracts

A familiar, everyday process for most of us is to condense information for ourselves and others and read or hear others' condensations. You take notes of a college lecture, writing down the key ideas only, not every word. Or a friend informally runs over the main points and purpose of a class lecture you missed. (Both of you know that the best students usually are those who zero in on essential information to study for exams.) You survey your accomplishments over the semester so far and select the outstanding ones as a prelude to asking your parents for some money. When you call collect and start to give all the details, your parents ask you for the gist of your problem.

Information is condensed more formally too — put into writing for the record. The owners of a small retail furniture chain want to increase their profits. They hire a consultant to summarize what similar chains have done to increase business, then summarize the findings and make recommendations. A law professor reads the opinions submitted for a recent Supreme Court decision, extracts the main points, presents them in an article, and discusses their implications. A résumé summarizes the qualifications of a job applicant. An employee is asked to record the minutes of a meeting or to summarize progress on a project. You summarize portions of books, articles, and reports as you research a topic for a paper. In the process, you are grateful for a succinct, informative abstract in a key journal that puts the article into perspective. You are equally grateful for chapter summaries in textbooks when the reading load becomes heavy.

Except for the résumé, these condensations are essays in miniature, a microcosm of the macrocosm; they should be able to stand alone without reference to the original. They retain the meaning, emphasis, and organization of the original. Condensations of technical discourse are usually presented in simpler terms than the original. Although some readers may be well informed on the subject, others may not be. Therefore, the safe course is to use common terms whenever possible (*painful menstruation* instead of *dysmenorrhea*) and explain at the risk of using extra words rather than create confusion or ambiguity with too few words. We are all high school readers in most fields other than our own. Brevity is important, but clarity and readability are paramount.

The terms *abstract* and *summary* are often used interchangeably, but they are not quite synonymous. Although everyone doesn't agree on terminology, *summary* is usually applied to a condensation of nontechnical material (the plot of a novel, for example, or an article or book written for a general audience). The term is also used to head a section within a report that recapitulates the most important information in the report, say, toward the end before the conclusions and recommendations are presented. *Abstract,* on the other hand, often is applied to condensations of technical material (reports and articles in engineering, medicine, computers, and the like) that are attached to the original and precede it, rather than occur as part of it. Abstracts are shorter than summaries, typically running 150 words or less no matter how long the original, whereas summaries are usually one-tenth to one-fifth as long as the original. Summaries are always informative, which means they present the principal points and conclusions of the original. Abstracts may be informative or descriptive. Descriptive abstracts are essentially a table of contents in prose form, simply indicating the main topics discussed. They tell what the discourse is about; informative abstracts tell what is *in* the discourse. Summaries and informative abstracts can be substituted for the original discourse. Descriptive abstracts can only help the reader decide whether to read the original.

The following abstracts of the same original report illustrate the difference between descriptive and informative abstracts:

Descriptive abstract:

This report discusses a study made of suggested locations for a new bridge to supplement the existing Church Street bridge connecting the city of Leigh and the village of Worseley. The study examines three possible locations in terms of the stated aim: to provide maximum traffic relief with minimum cost and destruction of property. Recommendations are included.

Informative abstract:

This study of three suggested locations for a new bridge to supplement the existing Church Street bridge connecting the city of Leigh and the village of Worseley shows that the bridges at Marsland Green Lane or Pennington Road would be more economical to construct than a Turl Street bridge because approaches to the Turl Street bridge would require demolition of two buildings. The Turl Street bridge, however, would provide maximum traffic relief and a more direct connection to Route 11. Building a new bridge at the Turl Street site would better serve the two communities.

It is often helpful to write a descriptive abstract of a piece before writing an informative abstract. Descriptive abstracts are relatively easy to write, and they can serve as a clarifying perspective from which to write an informative abstract. To write a descriptive abstract:

1. Read the original through for overall meaning and emphasis.
2. Read the original more slowly, outlining the major sections as for a table of contents.
3. Convert the outline to a prose paragraph, avoiding the use of "I" statements even if you are the author of the original.
4. Check the abstract against the original, making sure points of equal weight all appear and that no information not in the original has been added.

Summaries and informative abstracts are more difficult to write. The following list suggests techniques to make writing them easier, followed by an illustration of their application.

1. Read fairly rapidly the entire original, or entire sections of the original if it is very long, to get a complete sense (unless you wrote the original) of the author's style, tone, and central idea before condensing the information. When reading, do not overlook the title; if it is straightforward, it frequently forecasts the central idea. Avoid reading a few sentences, condensing them, and then repeating the process with the next few lines to the end of the original; the result will be disconnected bits and pieces.
2. Reread the original, marking in some way (underlining, bracketing, etc.) only the important points or making notes about them. Include only essential information, such as the following:
   a. The core statement, often found or implied at or near the beginning of a discourse.
   b. Major points supporting the core statement, often set forth in explicit topic sentences. Discourse of approximately five paragraphs or more presents at least two main points but rarely more than six. Don't mistake the forest for the trees. If in doubt

about a few items of borderline importance, include them at least the first time around. It is easier to write a more detailed condensation and pare it to a minimum coherent statement than to write a short, coherent, accurate representation immediately.

    c. Important names, dates, and statistics.

    d. Major conclusions or recommendations.

Exclude insignificant elements, such as these:

    a. Introductory material.

    b. Illustrative anecdotes, signaled by a switch to narrative in the midst of exposition.

    c. Restatements of points made, often indicated by markers such as "that is" and "in other words."

    d. Digressions, rhetorical questions, and details.

    e. Metadiscourse, that is, directions to readers on how to take the ideas presented ("The last point I would like to make"; "as everyone knows"; "In this next section of the report"; etc.).

    f. Most examples and definitions.

In a tightly organized paragraph, the topic sentence and concluding sentence often provide the gist of the paragraph. In a tightly organized piece, parallel structure is often used for main points so that once the first main point is found, the others are easily spotted.

3. Edit the underlined words, phrases, and sentences, cutting needless words.

4. Write a rough draft from the underlined portions or notes, combining the words, phrases, and sentences into your own sentences and paragraphs that follow the order of the original as much as possible. Avoid judgmental comments and your own metadiscourse ("This is an interesting finding"; "The author says"; "I believe"; etc.). Even when summarizing your own original, state information impersonally as though the original had another author. As a rough guide, in a longer summary a paragraph may be devoted to each major point; in a shorter summary or abstract, one sentence to each major point; for a book, maybe one paragraph per chapter.

5. Reread the summary or abstract, making sure that sentences make sense in sequence, that the entire abstract or summary forms a coherent, unified whole, and that style and tone conform to the original. Even though subordinate clauses and modifiers provide a key way to cut words, keep the syntax from becoming so complex and abstract that readability suffers. Make sure you have a logical plan of development — a core statement, supporting points, important details.

6. Polish your own abstract or summary, cutting unnecessary words but adding transition words for cohesion. Use nontechnical style as much as possible, even for technical material. Try to achieve grace

in the summary or abstract, but sacrifice it to brevity if you must for a result that is precise, clear, and readable.

7. Compare the original with the abstract or summary, making sure nothing in the original is distorted in meaning, emphasis, or tone. The implications from the summary or abstract should be the same as readers would receive reading the entire report.

8. Document the source immediately following the abstract or summary unless it is of your own material.

Let us apply these techniques now to summarize the following extended definition of an abstract.

Core statement (formal definition)	An [abstract] is a [brief summary of the content and purpose of an article.] In APA journals the abstract is
Nonessential details	used in place of a concluding summary and appears directly under the by-line. All APA journals except *Contemporary Psychology* require an abstract.
Important descriptive details	The abstract [allows readers to survey the contents] of an article [quickly.] Because, like the title,
Nonessential dependent clause	it is used by *Psychological Abstracts* for indexing and information retrieval, the abstract should be [self-contained and fully intelligible without reference to
Nonessential detail (suitability implied in what precedes)	the body] of the paper and suitable for publication by abstracting services without rewriting. [Information or conclusions that do not appear] in the main body of the paper [should not appear in the abstract.] Be-
Helpful advice but nonessential	cause so much information must be compressed into a small space, authors sometimes find the abstract difficult to write. Leaving it until the article is finished enables you to abstract or paraphrase your own words.
Main point in topic sentence	An [abstract of a *research* paper] should [contain statements of the problem, method, results, and con-
Nonessential supporting details (note parentheses)	clusions.] Specify the subject population (number, type, age, sex, etc.) and describe the research design, test instruments, research apparatus, or data gathering procedures as specifically as necessary to reflect their importance in the experiment. Include full test names and generic names of drugs used. Summarize the data or findings, including statistical significance levels, if any, as appropriate. Report inferences made or comparisons drawn from the results.
Main point in topic sentence (structurally signaled by parallelism)	An [abstract of a *review* or *theoretical* article] should [state the topics covered, the central thesis, the sources used] (e.g., personal observation, pub-
Parenthetical material is nonessential.	lished literature, or previous research bearing on the topic), and the [conclusions drawn.] It should be
Nonessential examples	short but informative. For example, "The problem

was further discussed in terms of Skinner's theory" is not an informative statement. The abstract should tell the reader the *nature* or *content* of the theoretical discussion: "The discussion of the problem centered on Skinner's theory and the apparent fallacy of determinism."

Main points (the first signaled by parallel structure)

An [abstract for a research paper] should be [100–175 words;] one for a [review or theoretical article, 75–100 words.] General style should be the same as that of the article. Remember, to the degree that an abstract is succinct, accurate, quickly comprehended, and informative, it increases your audience.

Publication Manual of the American Psychological Association, 2nd ed.

The first draft of the abstract might look like this:

An abstract briefly summarizes the content and purpose of an article. It allows readers a quick survey. It should not require reference to the article or contain information not in the original. Abstracts of research papers should state the problem, method, results, and conclusions. Abstracts of reviews or theoretical articles should state the topics covered, central thesis, sources used, and conclusions drawn. Abstracts for research papers run 100–175 words, for reviews or theoretical articles 75–100 words. Style should match that of the article. Accurate, concise, readable information increases the audience.

Notice that the draft primarily orders the ideas, with only minor attempts at subordination and cutting words. One method that is used, though, to condense the information is to convert nominalizations into verbs. (For example, "An abstract is a brief summary" becomes "An abstract briefly summarizes"; and "Abstracts of research papers should contain statements" becomes "Abstracts of research papers should state.") This syntactic change is an excellent way not only to cut words but also to achieve a more direct style. Changing the singular "an abstract" to the plural "abstracts" is another simple way to reduce words.

The abstract would probably pass through several stages to reduce it to a more suitable length, approximately 40 words (the first draft reduces the original's 367 words to 81). Related ideas can be combined and details of less importance omitted while still ensuring that the abstract preserves representative meaning and emphasis. The result might look something like this:

Abstracts briefly summarize an article's content and purpose, keeping the same style. In 100–175 words abstracts of research papers state the problem, method, results, and conclusions. In 75–100 words abstracts of reviews or theoretical articles state the topics, thesis, sources, and conclusions.

Notice that whole sentences become modifiers as related ideas are combined and less important details are omitted; yet the abstract still accurately represents the essential nature of the original extended definition.

EXERCISES

1. Go to the library and find and photocopy five abstracts from a variety of journals and magazines, say, one each from the social sciences, the humanities, the sciences, engineering, and art. Bring them to class, and be prepared to compare their characteristics.
2. Summarize the following paragraph in one sentence, first descriptively, then informatively:

   The Hollow Men ends with a nursery rhyme again adopting its repetitive round, suggesting "This is the way we go to church" — with half-articulated prayers in a make-believe religion. In this context the hollow men are overwhelmed by the Shadow, and their world ends neither with the bang of Guy Fawkes Day nor of the "lost violent souls" but in whimpers of fear, aimlessness, and despair. On the other hand, the hollow men have *begun* to pray, even if only in fragments. In this context the whimper suggests the cry of a new-born baby leaving one world of emptiness and alienation for a new world of harmony with God through faith and repentance. In either case, though the whole of the poem is dominated by the horror of an earthly hell, it does reveal, if only fleetingly, that a way to salvation has been perceived. Ultimately, in the poems following The Hollow Men, it is the slight signs of affirmation in the The Hollow Men that bear fruit.

3. Write a one-paragraph descriptive abstract of a chapter in this text. Then write a summary one-fifth the length of the chapter. Then write a one-paragraph informative abstract of the chapter. Follow the guidelines spelled out in this chapter.
4. First write a brief, one-paragraph descriptive abstract of the article below. Then write a three-paragraph informative abstract, then a two-paragraph one, and finally a one-paragraph, 150-word informative abstract. Follow the guidelines spelled out in the chapter.

Communication: Its Blocking and Its Facilitation
Carl R. Rogers

It may seem curious that a person whose whole professional effort is devoted to psychotherapy should be interested in problems of communication. What relationship is there between providing therapeutic help to individuals with emotional maladjustments and the concern of this conference with obstacles to communication? Actually the relationship is very close indeed. The whole task of psychotherapy is the task of dealing with a failure in communication. The emotionally maladjusted person, the "neurotic," is in difficulty first because communication within himself has broken down, and second because as a result of this his communication with others has been damaged. If this sounds somewhat strange, then let me put it in other terms. In the "neurotic" individual, parts of himself which have been termed unconscious, or repressed, or denied to awareness, become blocked off so that they no longer communicate themselves to the conscious or managing part of himself. As long as this is true, there are distortions in the way he communicates himself to others, and so he suffers both within himself, and in his interpersonal relations. The task of psychotherapy is to help the person achieve, through a special relationship with a therapist, good communication within himself. Once this is achieved he can communicate more freely and more effectively with others. We may say then that psychotherapy is good communication, within and between men. We may also turn that statement around and it will still be true. Good communication, free communication, within or between men, is always therapeutic.

It is, then, from a background of experience with communication in counseling and psychotherapy that I want to present here two ideas. I wish to state what I believe is one of the major factors in blocking or impeding communication, and then I wish to present what in our experience has proven to be a very important way of improving or facilitating communication.

I would like to propose, as an hypothesis for consideration, that the major barrier to mutual interpersonal communication is our very natural tendency to judge, to evaluate, to approve or disapprove, the statement of the other person, or the other group. Let me illustrate my meaning with some very simple examples. As you leave the meeting tonight, one of the statements you are likely to hear is, "I didn't like that man's talk." Now what do you respond? Almost invariably your reply will be either approval or disapproval of the attitude expressed. Either you respond, "I didn't either. I thought it was terrible," or else you tend to reply, "Oh, I thought it was really good." In other words, your primary reaction is to evaluate what has been said to you, to evaluate it from *your* point of view, your own frame of reference.

Or take another example. Suppose I say with some feeling, "I think the Republicans are behaving in ways that show a lot of good sound sense these days," what is the response that arises in your mind as you listen? The overwhelming likelihood is that it will be evaluative. You will find yourself agreeing, or disagreeing, or making some judgment about me such as "He must be a conservative," or "He seems solid in his thinking." Or let us take an illustration from the international scene. Russia says vehemently, "The treaty with Japan is a war plot on the part of the United States." We rise as one person to say "That's a lie!"

This last illustration brings in another element connected with my hypothesis. Although the tendency to make evaluations is common in almost all interchange of language, it is very much heightened in those situations where feelings and emotions are deeply involved. So the stronger our feelings, the more likely it is that there will be no mutual element in the communication. There will be just two ideas, two feelings, two judgments, missing each other in psychological space. I'm sure you recognize this from your own experience. When you have not been emotionally involved yourself, and have listened to a heated discussion, you often go away thinking, "Well, they actually weren't talking about the same thing." And they were not. Each was making a judgment, an evaluation, from his own frame of reference. There was really nothing which could be called communication in any genuine sense. This tendency to react to any emotionally meaningful statement by forming an evaluation of it from our own point of view, is, I repeat, the major barrier to interpersonal communication.

But is there any way of solving this problem, of avoiding this barrier? I feel that we are making exciting progress toward this goal and I would like to present it as simply as I can. Real communication occurs, and this evaluative tendency is avoided, when we listen with understanding. What does that mean? It means *to see the expressed idea and attitude from the other person's point of view, to sense how it feels to him, to achieve his frame of reference in regard to the thing he is talking about.*

Stated so briefly, this may sound absurdly simple, but it is not. It is an approach which we have found extremely potent in the field of psychotherapy. It is the most effective agent we know for altering the basic personality structure of an individual, and improving his relationships and his communications with others. If I can listen to what he can tell me, if I can understand how it seems to him, if I can see its personal meaning for him, if I can sense the emotional flavor which it has for him, then I will be releasing potent forces of change in him. If I can really understand how he hates his father, or hates the university, or hates communists — if I can catch the flavor of his fear of insanity, or his fear of atom bombs, or of Russia — it will be of the greatest help to him in altering those very hatreds and fears, and in establishing realistic and harmonious relationships with the very people and situations toward which he has felt hatred and fear. We know from our research that such empathic understanding — understanding *with* a person, not *about* him — is such an effective approach that it can bring about major changes in personality.

Some of you may be feeling that you listen well to people, and that you have never seen such results. The chances are very great indeed that your listening has not been of the type I have described. Fortunately I can suggest a little laboratory experiment which you can try to test the quality of your understanding. The next time you get into an argument with your wife, or your friend, or with a small group of friends, just stop the discussion for a moment and for an experiment, institute this rule: "Each person can speak up for himself, only *after* he has first restated the ideas and feelings of the previous speaker accurately, and to that speaker's satisfaction." You see what this would mean. It would simply mean that before presenting your own point of view, it would be necessary for you to really achieve the other speaker's frame of reference — to understand his thoughts and feelings so well that you could summarize them for him. Sounds simple doesn't it? But if you try it you will discover it is one of the most difficult things you have ever tried to do. However, once you have been able to see the other's point of view, your own comments will have to be drastically revised. You will also find the emotion going out of discussion, the differences being reduced, and those differences which remain being of a rational and understandable sort.

Can you imagine what this type of approach would mean if it were projected into larger areas? What would happen to a labor-management dispute if it was conducted in such a way that labor, without necessarily agreeing, could accurately state management's point of view in a way that management could accept; and management, without approving labor's stand, could state labor's case in a way that labor agreed was accurate? It would mean that real communication was established, and one could practically guarantee that some reasonable solution would be reached.

If, then, this way of approach is an effective avenue to good communication and good relationships, as I am quite sure you will agree if you try the experiment I have mentioned, why is it not more widely tried and used? I will try to list the difficulties which keep it from being utilized.

In the first place it takes courage, a quality which is not too widespread. I am indebted to Dr. S. I. Hayakawa, the semanticist, for pointing out that to carry on psychotherapy in this fashion is to take a very real risk, and that courage is required. If you really understand another person in this way, if you are willing to enter his private world and see the way life appears to him, without any attempt to make evaluative judgments, you run the risk of being changed yourself. You might see it his way, you might find yourself influenced in your attitudes or your personality. This risk of being changed is one of the most frightening prospects most of us can face. If I enter, as fully as I am able, into the private world of a neurotic or psychotic individual, isn't there a risk that I might become lost in that world? Most of us are afraid to take that risk. Or if we had a Russian communist speaker here tonight, or Senator Joe McCarthy, how many of us would dare to try to see the world from each of these points of view? The great majority of us could not *listen:* we would find ourselves compelled to *evaluate,* because listening would seem too dangerous. So the first requirement is courage, and we do not always have it.

But there is a second obstacle. It is just when emotions are strongest that it is most difficult to achieve the frame of reference of the other person or group. Yet it is the time the attitude is most needed, if communication is to be established. We have not found this to be an insuperable obstacle in our experience in psychotherapy. A third party, who is able to lay aside his own feelings and evaluations, can assist greatly by listening with understanding to each person or group and clarifying the views and attitudes each holds. We have found this very effective in small groups in which contradictory or antagonistic attitudes exist. When the parties to a dispute realize that they are being understood, that someone sees how the situation seems to them, the statements grow less exaggerated and less defensive, and it is no longer necessary to maintain the attitude, "I am 100% right and you are 100% wrong." The influence of such an understanding catalyst in the group permits the members to come closer and closer to the objective truth involved in the relationship. In this way mutual communication is established and some type of agreement becomes much more possible. So we may say that though heightened emotions make it much more difficult to understand *with* an opponent, our experience makes it clear that a neutral, understanding, catalyst type of leader or therapist can overcome this obstacle in a small group.

This last phrase, however, suggests another obstacle to utilizing the approach I have described. Thus far all our experience has been with small face-to-face groups — groups exhibiting industrial tensions, religious tensions, racial tensions, and therapy groups in which many personal tensions are present. In these small groups our experience, confirmed by a limited amount of research, shows that this basic approach leads to improved communication, to greater acceptance of others and by others, and to attitudes which are more positive and more problem-solving in nature. There is a decrease in defensiveness, in exaggerated statements, in evaluative and critical behavior. But these findings are from small groups. What about trying to achieve understanding between larger groups that are geographically remote? Or between face-to-face groups who are not speaking for themselves, but simply as representatives of others, like the delegates at Kaesong? Frankly we do not know the answers to these questions. I believe the situation might be put this way. As social scientists we have a tentative test-tube solution of the problem of breakdown in communication. But to confirm the validity of this test-tube solution, and to adapt it to the enormous problems of communication-breakdown between classes, groups, and nations, would involve additional funds, much more research, and creative thinking of a high order.

Even with our present limited knowledge we can see some steps which might be taken, even in large groups, to increase the amount of listening *with,* and to decrease the amount of evaluation *about.* To be imaginative for a moment, let us suppose that a therapeutically oriented international group went to the Russian leaders and said, "We want to achieve a genuine understanding of your views and even more important, of your attitudes and feelings, toward the United States. We will summarize and re-summarize these views and feelings if necessary, until you agree that our description represents the situation as it seems to you." Then suppose they did the same thing with the leaders in our own country. If they then gave the widest possible distribution to these two views, with the feelings clearly described but not expressed in name-calling, might not the effect be very great? It would not guarantee the type of understanding I have been describing, but it would make it much more possible. We can understand the feelings of a person who hates us much more readily when his attitudes are accurately described to us by a neutral third party, than we can when he is shaking his fist at us.

But even to describe such a first step is to suggest another obstacle to this approach of understanding. Our civilization does not yet have enough faith in the social sciences to utilize their findings. The opposite is true of the physical sciences. During the war when a test-tube solution was found to the problem of synthetic rubber, millions of dollars and an army of talent was turned loose on the problem of using that finding. If synthetic rubber could be made in milligrams, it could and would be made in the thousands of tons. And it was. But in the social science realm, if a way is found of facilitating communication and mutual understanding in small groups, there is no guarantee that the finding will be utilized. It may be a generation or more before the money and the brains will be turned loose to exploit the finding.

In closing, I would like to summarize this small-scale solution to the problem of barriers in communication, and to point out certain of its characteristics.

I have said that our research and experience to date would make it appear that breakdowns in communication, and the evaluative tendency which is the major barrier to communication, can be avoided. The solution is provided by creating a situation in which each of the different parties come to understand the other from the *other's* point of view. This has been achieved, in practice, even when feelings run high, by the influence of a person who is willing to understand each point of view empathically, and who thus acts as a catalyst to precipitate further understanding.

This procedure has important characteristics. It can be initiated by one party, without waiting for the other to be ready. It can even be initiated by a neutral third person, providing he can gain a minimum of cooperation from one of the parties.

This procedure can deal with the insincerities, the defensive exaggerations, the lies, the "false fronts" which characterize almost every failure in communication. These defensive distortions drop away with astonishing speed as people find that the only intent is to understand, not judge.

This approach leads steadily and rapidly toward the discovery of the truth, toward a realistic appraisal of the objective barriers to communication. The dropping of some defensiveness by one party leads to further dropping of defensiveness by the other party, and truth is thus approached.

This procedure gradually achieves mutual communication. Mutual communication tends to be pointed toward solving a problem rather than toward attacking a person or group. It leads to a situation in which I see how the problem appears to you, as well as to me, and you see how it appears to me, as well as to you. Thus accurately and realistically defined, the problem is almost certain to yield to intelligent attack, or if it is in part insoluble, it will be comfortably accepted as such.

This then appears to be a test-tube solution to the breakdown of communication as it occurs in small groups. Can we take this small-scale answer, investigate it further, refine it, develop it and apply it to the tragic and well-nigh fatal failures of communication which threaten the very existence of our modern world? It seems to me that this is a possibility and a challenge we should explore.

Presented on October 11, 1951, at
Northwestern University's
Centennial Conference on
Communications

Reviews

One of the chief components of a review is a summary, but a review adds another dimension, that of critiquing what is summarized. A review is a narrowly focused, critical report whose main purpose is to tell about a book, a play, a film, a television program, or something similar and judge the author's or creator's presentation of the subject.

A review is an inappropriate vehicle for making general statements about a subject or an area, but it must provide enough context so that readers will be able to understand and come to agreement with the recommendations of the reviewer. An effective review, therefore, contains all the information needed to help readers decide if they want to read the book or see the play, film, or television show, or buy a record-album (although, it must be noted, some people read reviews for pleasure or instead of reading the book or viewing the film). In addition to summarizing, the review explains such things as the writer's or actor's background and qualifications, the setting, how a book or film fits into a context. A review may also report the reviewer's feelings about the object of the review, but this part is not crucial. The aim of a review is not self-expression, nor, even though it may end with a recommendation, is its aim primarily persuasive. Its aims are expository, to discuss the object under review for its own sake, and evaluative. To do so, like other pieces of discourse, a review can tap any or all of the rhetorical operations.

Instructors often assign reviews in college, especially book reviews. Since college instructors are typically familiar with the object being reviewed, they are not themselves seeking a recommendation. Their intent is to encourage students to read a book or view a show carefully and select major points, see relationships, and judge and consolidate their understanding of the ideas presented. Nonetheless, in the writing of reviews for a college class, students are expected to address hypothetical readers in order to help them make a decision, thus gaining the experience of reviewing in the everyday world. In the process, students gain a fuller appreciation of the reviewer's task and become better critics of critics.

The best reviews reveal broad, sound knowledge of the field; in fact, the reviewer often knows the subject almost as well as the author, director, or creator. You as a student are unlikely to be so knowledgeable, but you can still write a valid review if it is based on thorough reading, observing, and studying.

The following are some strategies that will help you produce a good review:

1. If your instructor assigns the object for review, it generally will be significant in the field. If you choose the object for review, your choice should stem from substantive reasons too, not, say, in the

case of a book, its being short or required reading for another class.

2. With the object assigned or chosen, first read the book; see the play, film, television program, or art show; or listen to the concert. Take notes as you watch, read, or listen.

3. Search out as much information as you can on the author, director, actors, artist, composer, or others who produced the work to discover their qualifications and background.

4. Keep this information in mind as you reread your notes to determine the author's, director's, or artist's perspective and purpose. Even a documentary or scientific treatise is shaped by the director's or author's view of objective reality and underlying purpose. Your research plus careful reading of a representative chapter of a book or observation of a scene or painting will often help you determine the point of view and purpose.

5. Reread the book or return to see the play, film, television program, or art show, selecting and noting points and examples to support your analysis and evaluation. Determine the organizational pattern. Books are organized into chapters, plays into acts and scenes, symphonies into movements, paintings into groups. But within these overall architectural frameworks other fundamental patterns occur. The material may be organized chronologically, inductively, deductively, thematically, and so forth. Certain rhetorical operations may dominate, such as comparison, classification, or definition. You will want to take these matters into account as you write your review.

6. Summarize the whole.

7. Determine the relationship of the parts to the whole. How does characterization in a film or events in a history contribute to the outcome? How does each painting in an artist's retrospective contribute to the theme or themes? How does the style of a piece affect its appeal? Select examples that illustrate the major points, overall viewpoint, and purpose.

8. With the information you have accumulated, evaluate the object you are reviewing. Decide whether your review will be favorable, unfavorable, or neutral. Avoid simply saying, "I like it," or, "It is good," or, "I don't like it," or, "It is bad." These are statements of taste, not judgment. You may, in fact, not particularly like the object you are reviewing, yet see its strengths and value. Or like the object, yet see its failings. Whatever your judgment, it needs to be justified in the review. Since what is assigned or chosen for review for a class tends to be important in its field, it is more than likely that a review written for class will be favorable. If you plan to write a negative review, your review needs to be particularly well thought out and your case presented quite convincingly.

9. Determine your audience for the review. Decide what your readers need to know or might want to hear and the diction, style, and arrangement for the review that will appeal to them, always, of course, presenting the material fairly and accurately.

The book review that follows was written in line with the strategies discussed above. Our marginal notes mark the typical features that any review includes, although the order of the items may vary.

Review of *Mary Queen of Scots* by Antonia Fraser. New York: Delacorte Press, 1970.

Summary

Much of her life was the stuff of fiction. In fact, its events were almost too improbable for the most imaginative romancer. Adored and protected in the French court in her childhood, she married the sickly dauphin at fifteen, became queen of France at sixteen, and was widowed — possibly still a virgin — at seventeen. When she reentered her native Protestant Scotland as its Catholic ruler, she was greeted with bitterness and hatred. Her life became a rush of brief, tragic marriages, intrigues, murders, captures, and daring escapes from forbidding castles. The one sexual passion of her life was her second husband, a vain, traitorous young coxcomb, whose murder before his twenty-first birthday was plotted by the man who became her third husband after, in quick succession, he abducted and raped her, only to leave her abandoned and temporarily deranged a month later. After spending most of her last twenty years in captivity, she was condemned as a traitor. On a cold February morning in 1587, her life ended at age forty-four with a histrionic stripping to a bodice and petticoat of a martyr's liturgical crimson as she laid her head on the executioner's block and a sudden dramatic lurching to the floor of her severed, graying head from the flowing auburn wig that had covered it, then the executioner raising her skull on high.

Author's treatment of the subject combined with summary

Category the book fits into

Author's viewpoint

Yet despite their air of unreality, these events are a sampling of the actual history of Mary Queen of Scots, one of history's most controversial and fascinating figures. Lady Antonia Fraser responds to such soap opera theatricality in her biography by viewing the events through the eyes of Mary and her contemporaries — human, fallible eyes unable to see into the future. With such compassionate handling, Mary emerges — despite the fact that most decisions in her life were unwise — as more sinned against than sinning. The fact that during her seven years of active rule she achieved nothing notable in either foreign or domestic policy is set against the religious revolt and political opposition in her native Scotland, at that time a small, backward nation. Her ill-fated marriages with Lord Henry Darnley and the Earl of Bothwell become humanly understandable; the gradual yielding of her power to a horde of fiercely contending noblemen is seen as inevitable. Even her last decision, to seek refuge in England after she escaped from Lochleven, a decision that proved not only foolish but fatal, is cast as an eventual triumph over Queen Elizabeth I, because it was Mary Stuart who captured the greater imagination of posterity and it was her son James who ascended the throne after Elizabeth.

Author's purpose and style

Fraser's graceful, unobtrusive narrative style recreates Mary's life in a way that demonstrates that biography not only is history but can be as absorbing as a piece of literature as well. Here, for example, is a brief moment from Mary's last hours.

> The traveller was now ready for her last journey on earth. The queen lay down on her bed without undressing. She did not try to sleep. Her women gathered round her already wearing their black garments of mourning, and Mary asked Jane Kennedy to read aloud the life of some great sinner. The life of the good thief was chosen, and as the story reached its climax on the cross, Mary observed aloud: "In truth he was a great sinner, but not so great as I have been." She then closed her eyes, and said nothing further. Throughout the night the sound of hammering came from the great hall where the scaffold was being erected. The boots of the soldiers could be heard ceaselessly tramping up and down outside the queen's room, for Paulet had ordered them to watch with special vigilance in these final hours, lest their victim escape her captors at the last. The queen lay on her bed without sleeping, eyes closed and a half smile on her face. (p. 534)

The one noticeable flaw in Fraser's biography is her persistently harsh portrait of Elizabeth, who in her critical hands falls short in every comparison with Mary except caution. To her credit, though, Fraser marshals her evidence eloquently and convincingly and is generous enough to allow for interpretations that differ with her own. Her Mary emerges as neither devil nor saint, but as a high-spirited, romantic woman, given by heredity to physical and mental collapse under great stress, brave but not very bright.

Author's background
and qualifications

Antonia Fraser was to the typewriter born. Her father, the Earl of Longford, once leader of the House of Lords, produced six books on such topics as banking, politics, and philosophy. Her mother, writing under the name of Elizabeth Longford (the family name is Pakenham), authored two biographies, one on Queen Victoria, another on the Duke of Wellington. Her brother Thomas has written on the Irish Rebellion of 1798, her sister Judith produces textbooks, her sister Rachel novels. Fraser herself previously authored some children's books and A *History of Toys*.

Her enthusiasm for history and biography began in childhood, as did her identification with Mary Queen of Scots. She play-acted Mary's execution scene with her brothers and sisters, and when she married at twenty-three, she wore a replica of Mary Stuart's first bridal headdress. Fraser's major interest at Oxford was history, and in 1965 she began three years of intensive and extensive research on Mary's life in libraries and at key sites in England, Scotland, and France.

Recommendations

Because many people have been fascinated with Mary Queen of Scots since she died, we have detailed accounts of the more fascinating episodes in her life. Most notable are the murder of her second husband, Darnley, at Kirk o'Field; the almost certainly forged Casket Letters alluding to an adulterous liaison between Mary and Bothwell; and the Babington Plot, actually two conspiracies, one a bogus attempt to assassinate Queen Elizabeth, the other a real plan to free Mary. The same fascination has also produced a psychological study of Mary by Stefan Zweig in the 1930s and a biography by T. F. Henderson in 1905. Nevertheless, Fraser's account is a much-needed clarification of the often inaccurate and conflicting legends surrounding her name. Fraser's new historical insight into Mary Queen of Scots as a person would be richly rewarding reading to any history buff—or lover of a resounding tale.

EXERCISES

1. Write a review of a film based on a book, and include a comparison with the book. Even though the conventions are different for the two media, you can often still judge which is the more successful effort considering the limitations in the medium.
2. Choose a book. Find three reviews of the book in the library. Make photocopies of the reviews. Analyze the similarities and differences

in the reviews and bring them to class prepared to point out the similarities and differences to your classmates.

3. Assume that your best friend, whose tastes are similar to yours but not identical, has asked your opinion of a book you recently read or a film you recently saw. Your friend is attending college in another state. Write a letter to your friend reviewing the book or film, including at least five items specifically supporting your recommendation.

4. Write a full length review of a nonfiction book.

5. Attend a concert, a play, or an art show and write a review of it.

Chapter 18

Research Reports

College courses often require the writing of research reports based on extensive investigations of various sorts. Performing such investigations and writing about them require all the rhetorical operations you have been practicing—description, narration, comparison, classification, analysis, induction and deduction, and definition. Writing research reports also develops other skills: finding, selecting, and weighing evidence, making inferences, reaching decisions, and logically arguing and supporting a substantive thesis with proven facts and authoritative testimony. These skills will serve you well not only in college but also in business, industry, and the professions after you graduate.

Reports are important in all fields; progress is made possible with the objective interchange of information in reports. Research reports may present information of new discoveries gained first hand through experiments, observations, interviews, and questionnaires. Or they may shed new light on what is already known, presenting previously unrecognized but significant facts and relationships that are based on secondary information, information discovered and published by other authors. Scientists and engineers often write investigative reports presenting new information; historians and literary critics often write reports based on secondary or preestablished information. Depending upon the field they are written in, and, therefore, the preponderance of original or secondary research they contain, research reports carry different names. In the humanities, they are often called research or library papers. In technical and scientific fields and business, they are called investigative or functional reports, depending upon the activities to be reported (the solution to a problem or an explanation of how something fulfills its intended function), or the all-encompassing term *technical report* is used. We will use the term *library paper* for the reports written in the humanities, and *technical report* for those written in technical and scientific fields and business.

Library papers and technical reports are alike in many ways—voice, style, and need for documentation. They are also similar in the steps we follow in putting them together, except for methods of obtaining information. They differ from each other sharply in topics covered, of course, but they also differ in the system of documentation used and the format.

Characteristics of Research Reports

Research reports are characterized by neutral voice, formal style, and careful documentation of information sources.

Voice

Authorial voice in writing at the reportorial end of the spectrum tends to be neutral and objective. Writers use unemotional, unbiased language because their principal aim is to gain intellectual agreement from listeners or readers. We may narrate an accident we have witnessed in emotional or biased terms to family or friends when we seek their sympathy or empathy, but our ethos, our credibility, suffers if we use the same terms to report the accident to the police, to a court, or to an insurance agency. Typically, in these situations, even when we are highly wrought up, we try to choose neutral terms to speak dispassionately. With friends and family, our primary aim is to express our strong feelings; with outsiders, our primary aim is to inform or convince, and an unbiased or neutral voice is most convincing.

Writers declare findings from empirical research to be "new," not "revolutionary." Instead of saying that professionals in a certain academic discipline "are at each other's throats over basic theoretical concepts," a writer would say, "There is a general lack of agreement about explanatory and theoretical models."

Neutral, objective voice does not occur only in reports, of course. It occurs at appropriate points in all writing, even, occasionally, in highly expressive, literary pieces. Nevertheless, in what are commonly labeled reports, it dominates; emotional voice is seldom appropriate.

Style

Another common characteristic of all research reports is formal style. The features of formal style are presented in the following subsections.

An Appropriate Level of Diction. Reports demand words that are most likely to express to readers the exact meaning intended. However, more than precision is needed. The words must also be appropriate. Colloquialisms and slang, for example, may verge close to the mark but are too casual for formal reports. The results of an experiment may be *super,* but *significant* would be the appropriate word choice. Report writers need to look out for casual kinds of phrasing like "It was an OK thing to do," or words like "a lot" and "just" used routinely in place of more precise and formal synonyms, and so forth.

On the other hand, bureaucratic pomposity should be avoided. Words like *approval, use,* and *publish* are as accurate as and more forceful and readable than their pompous counterparts: *approbation, utilize,* and *promulgate. Notwithstanding the fact, concerning the matter of,* and *has the capacity for* can be replaced by the simpler *although, about,* and *can.*

The use of jargon presents a problem all its own. It is easy to say "get rid of it all," especially when we run across such monstrosities as the following:

> The alleged murderer effectuated ingress into the Smith family domicile by application of an attenuated instrument to the external locking mechanism of a rear aperture.

The sentence is so overburdened with pomposity and jargon that it is virtually unreadable. Some jargon, however, is appropriate and necessary, that is, when the jargon consists of acceptable technical terms. Compare, for example, the two statements below. The first, from an advanced linguistic text, demands technical knowledge. The second, from an introductory text, demands little more than ordinary intelligence.

> According to Bloomfield a sentence is "an independent linguistic form, not included by virtue of any grammatical construction in any large linguistic form." . . . The point of Bloomfield's definition can be stated more concisely as follows: *the sentence is the largest unit of grammatical description.*

> All theories of grammar recognize that English sentences have two basic parts. These are called subject and predicate in traditional grammar, and noun phrase and verb phrase in transformational grammar.

The linguist would find the second condescending; the general reader would find the first impenetrable. The trick is to keep the audience in mind all the time, and to err, if at all, on the side of simplicity. Overuse of jargon tires even those within the profession. The audience for the second statement has all the jargon it can cope with.

Concise, Clear, Moderately Complex Sentences. Wordy, tangled sentences are unwelcome in any sort of writing. Yet research reports are particularly prone to summon from a writer's stylistic repertoire all the turgid, excessively leaden sentences absorbed from reading other research reports. Nevertheless, complex ideas often demand complex structures. Writers often need the subordination that comes with complex sentences to show relationships and establish appropriate emphasis. Sentences in formal reports are usually longer than those in other writing, and more of them contain nominalizations ("There were expectations that the application would receive a review," versus, "The committee expected the application to be reviewed") and passives ("Records were kept daily of the alcohol in stock," versus, "The clerk kept daily records of the alcohol in stock"). Any excessive use of these features will make the writing incomprehensible. Use occasional short sentences to compensate for the tendency to write long ones, and seek opportunities to use active voice by putting agents in the subjects and actions in verbs ("We expected that" is preferable to "Expectations are that").

Standard English Grammar, Spelling, Punctuation, and Usage. Following the conventions of standard English in a report is a negative virtue; rarely are writers praised for fulfilling a reader's expectations for correctness, but readers do criticize writers who take liberties with standard English. Whether their response is valid or not, readers often believe writers do not know their subject if they so much as misspell a few words.

Third Person Singular. Most research reports avoid first person pronouns as much as possible and all instances of the indefinite *you*.

For example, in "Horror movies are not good ones for children because *you* do not know if they will be frightened," *you* is inappropriate because a reader may not take children to movies. When first person is used, as often as possible it should be the plural *we*, which is certainly preferable to excessive use of passive voice, from which agents so often disappear ("We broke the contract," rather than "The contract was broken").

Full Forms of Words. Formal reports avoid all contractions (except in quoted material) and most abbreviations. For example, the ampersand (&) is never acceptable except in standard abbreviations of company names (AT&T). Abbreviations which are acceptable in formal writing are for titles (Mr., Ms.), time (A.M., B.C.), lineage (Jr.), academic degrees (M.A., Ph.D.), certain common Latin expressions (i.e., e.g., cf., etc.), and names of organizations and agencies in acronym form, chiefly, but not always, without periods (IRS, NASA, USC, U.S.).

Aesthetically Pleasing Appearance. A research report represents the writer. The value a reader places on the idea and the author depend not only upon clear expression but on neat appearance as well. Do not let the manner of presentation divert the reader's attention away from the ideas being presented. Research reports should be typed on good-quality white bond, with plenty of white space, and mistakes should be neatly and unobtrusively corrected. Diagrams, figures, and tables should be easy to read and attractive. Even such a "minor" point as hyphenation can contribute to appearance. The right margin of a typed report will inevitably be uneven (unless the writer uses a word processor); therefore, hyphenate only lengthy words for which at least several letters appear on each line.

Documentation

Research reports require writers to document their facts and sources, whether primary or secondary. Any quotation, summary, or paraphrase of another person's words or ideas, or any reference to one's own experiments and observations, calls for careful citation so that readers may further investigate the source if they wish.

At times, writers, especially inexperienced writers, are troubled about whether or not to document certain information. A good question to ask in such cases is, "Would a mature, intelligent reader be likely to know the information?" The fact that John F. Kennedy was assassinated in Dallas, Texas, in November 1963 is common knowledge. His policy statements and specific decisions are not; they would need to be documented.

Although all writing about research requires documentation, different systems are used, depending on the conventions of the field in which the reports are written. No one form is standard for all reports. Two forms frequently encountered in college are the one prescribed by the Modern Language Association (set forth in the *MLA Handbook for Writers of Research Papers*, 2nd ed., 1984) and another by the American Psychological Association (*Publication Manual of the American Psychological Association*, 3rd ed., 1983). These two will be followed in this and the next chapter for illustrative purposes, the MLA form for the library paper, the APA form for the technical report. Your instructor may ask you to follow one of these models or the form of some other style manual, such as *The Chicago Manual of Style* or Kate L. Turabian's *A Manual for Writers of Term Papers, Theses, and Dissertations*. The important point is not so much what system you use but that you use only one system and use it consistently and precisely.

Steps in Writing a Research Report

Writing a research report entails many steps, beginning with the choice of a topic. Next we find material to develop the topic, evaluate the material, and plan specific strategies to appeal to the audience for the report. Finally we write and document the report.

Choosing and Limiting a Topic

The first step in writing a research report is choosing a topic—at least in the classroom. In the working world, however, the topic of a report is often assigned or simply in the course of events "chooses itself." Ideally, the topic should capture your interest and stimulate your curiosity. It should also reveal something of value to someone else, and it should be a topic you can live with for several weeks of intensive study and writing. It is well to remember that many topics that at first interest us not at all or only superficially become more rewarding as we delve into them. Virtually any topic can be *made* interesting and significant.

If a topic does not come to mind immediately, you can talk over possible topics with other students, your writing instructor, or instructors from other classes. The following list presents some topics that have been used successfully by students in the humanities and technical fields. Some may appeal to you or may nudge a possibility into consciousness.

Automobiles	Health
Woodworking	Inflation
Weather forecasting	Left-handedness
Microcomputers	Herpes
Antiques	Photography
Solar energy	Astrology
Drug abuse	Nutrition
Electricity	Women's liberation
Poetry	Aerobics

These topics, of course, are all far too broad for a research report written for a college class. They need to be narrowed. For example, you might narrow the topic "electricity" to emergency electric power generators. "Women's liberation" could be narrowed to job possibilities for women in nontraditional fields, "drug abuse" to the most overprescribed drugs.

Before investing much time in researching the narrowed topic, it is wise to measure it against certain criteria. Ask yourself these questions:

1. Do I have the necessary background to deal with the subject? Will I need to acquire extensive specialized information — of economics, electricity, literary theories, etc. — before I can begin my project? Can I perform the necessary investigations, experiments, on-site inspections?
2. Do I have enough time to complete the project? A ten-week quarter or fifteen-week semester with only part of the time set aside for research allows only short research projects. Committing yourself to a nationwide questionnaire or a semester-long test of some sort will doom your report to failure before you start.
3. Are there enough sources of information available on my subject? Run a preliminary check of books, journals, newspapers, and government documents in the library. If you can locate three to five good sources of background and specific information within an

hour, the chances are good that further efforts will turn up enough additional sources to make the topic feasible.

4. Will the subject allow me to write the kind of paper required? A topic that can only be handled by restating the information collected, say, a straight recounting of a person's life, is invalid. For technical topics, instructors are most likely to require a report of your investigative techniques or of the results of your investigations. For other topics, instructors are most likely to require a critical paper, one in which you analyze your findings and synthesize and evaluate them with critical commentary.

Stating the Problem

Before full-scale gathering of information begins, you need to isolate the problem that will guide your search and form the basis of your core statement. Knowing the purpose, what you want to accomplish, will keep you from wandering around in a forest of facts. To formulate a problem is to carve out a certain piece of the universe for inquiry. Here are some problems that lie within some narrowed topics based on the general ones listed in the preceding section:

What difficulties do left-handers face coping with educational institutions?

How do heel heights affect people's posture, therefore their health?

Who should choose one of the three proposed routes for a new freeway as the least expensive and most efficient? A group of civic leaders and directly affected citizens, or an independent consulting firm?

What can a microcomputer do?

In what ways does the dramatic structure of "The Love Song of J. Alfred Prufrock," in its interior monologue, help develop the theme of the poem?

Sometimes when investigations sift through all available information pertaining to the problem, the nature of the inquiry changes, as may be true for you. For example, you might start with the problem "What can microcomputers do?" but in the process of searching the literature, find many reports that apply microcomputers to a variety of functions in the home. If such a variation of the original problem appears to be fruitful, rephrase your problem accordingly and order your collection of facts to develop only home applications.

By keeping your problem as a constant focal point, it is easy to see which bits of information belong in your report and in which section and how to fit the parts together. By focusing on the problem, you can pull together all the information you need and ignore information you do not need to produce a complete, unified, and coherent report.

Obtaining Information

Once the topic is settled and narrowed and the problem is defined, the next step is to obtain information. Regardless of which type of research report you are writing, the first thing you do will probably be to call upon your memory for some facts and ideas about your subject, some personal experience with the problem. Jot down any information of this kind, and use these notes as leads to further exploration of your subject.

Memory, however, can only take you so far. There are other, more organized and productive methods for gathering information. They basically fall into two categories: obtaining information from secondary sources, that is, information that has already been gathered by someone else and that is usually held in libraries, and obtaining information from primary sources through observing, experimenting, or conducting surveys.

Obtaining Information from Secondary Sources. The early stages of research on the topic are when you should search the literature and compile a working bibliography. A working bibliography is a series of sources that offer potential information on your subject, usually noted on 3-by-5-inch file cards. (We use the term *bibliography* because it is a familiar one, even though literally *bibliography* refers to books, and your sources may include films, recordings, television programs, or other nonprint sources.) Often a working bibliography begins with a cursory search of general reference materials to reveal whether or not sufficient material is likely to be available for the chosen topic. The working bibliography will expand greatly as you search through the card catalog or consult a computerized data base.

Searching the Literature. A search of the literature begins with general reference works such as encyclopedias and bibliographical dictionaries. These reference works offer brief bibliographies at the end of each essay, and indexes and guides of various kinds. Almost every major discipline has an index that will help you find information on your topic. You may also want to consult some standard dictionaries. The following is a list of sources that will be helpful to you whether your topic is in the humanities, the social sciences, or the physical sciences. You can ask your librarian about other sources.

Encyclopedias and Dictionaries:
Encyclopaedia Britannica
Encyclopedia of Educational Research
Bartlett's Familiar Quotations
Oxford English Dictionary
Oxford Classical Dictionary
Book Review Digest

International Encyclopedia of the Social Sciences
Encyclopedia of World Art
Encyclopedia of Banking and Finance
Indexes:
 Reader's Guide to Periodical Literature
 Humanities Index
 Social Sciences and Humanities Index
 The Art Index
 The Philosopher's Index
 Music Index
 New York Times Index
 Wall Street Journal Index
 General Science Index
Bibliographies:
 MLA Bibliography
 The New Cambridge Bibliography of English Literature
 Bibliographic Index: A Cumulative Bibliography of Bibliographies
 International Bibliography of Historical Sciences
Abstracts:
 Abstracts of English Studies
 Psychological Abstracts
 Sociological Abstracts
 Women's Studies Abstracts
 Abstracts in Anthropology
 Astronomy and Astrophysical Abstracts
 Biological Abstracts
 Chemical Abstracts
 Bibliography and Index of Geology
 Physics Abstracts
Annual reviews:
 Annual Review of Anthropology
 Annual Review of Psychology
 Annual Review of Sociology
 Annual Review of Biochemistry
 Annual Review of Pharmacology and Toxicology
Handbooks and yearbooks:
 Second Handbook of Research on Teaching
 The Teacher's Handbook
 The Annual Register of World Events
 Demographic Yearbook
 Yearbook of the United Nations
 Monthly Catalog of United States Government Publications
 Biology Data Book
 Handbook of Chemistry and Physics

Handbook of Business Administration
Comprehensive Statistical Abstract of the United States

From general reference works, move to the card catalog, or computer catalog if holdings in your local library are computerized, to check further on possible sources of information.

Consulting Computerized Information Retrieval. A source of information that is becoming popular is computerized information retrieval. Many libraries provide access to a variety of data bases. The U.S. Government's National Technical Information Service (NTIS) offers computer searches of documents published or sponsored by the federal government. Some other data bases are DIALOG (Lockheed Information Retrieval Service, Palo Alto, California), BRS (Bibliographical Retrieval Services, Scotia, New York), and ORBIT II (Systems Development Corporation, Santa Monica, California). Bibliographic files are available in many areas, for example, agriculture, business, education, environmental studies, and physics.

A computer search has two distinct advantages: (1) although designing a search takes hours, once it is designed, a computer search saves time; (2) it will be more thorough than the ordinary library search because computer searches usually include several different indexing services. Computer searches, however, also have drawbacks: (1) the cost may be high (an average search costs a minimum of $50.00); (2) key references may be ignored if the search is too limited; (3) a wide search will pull in a considerable number of irrelevant references.

Compiling a Working Bibliography. As you find items of potential interest, first from general reference works, later from the card catalog or computer search, you will need to compile a working bibliography of all likely sources, typically recorded on 3 × 5 cards. Another system of keeping track of sources may work for you, but individual 3 × 5 cards have two distinct advantages: they can be shuffled and rearranged, and they can also be handily kept in a shoe box. Early on in your research — for example, when you are listing items from general reference works — write down the key information that you will need to identify a source and to match the source with notes taken from it later; leave room for other vital information that you will add when you move to the card catalog or computer catalog to check specific sources or when and if you consult a data base.

When you find likely specific sources, insert other vital information on the card, such as the library call number and publication information, and an informational note for the source as in the examples for the MLA and APA systems shown on pages 306 and 308. If you use a computer search, keep track of potential sources on 3 × 5 cards, as you would when searching the card catalog, but for materials found through

Corcoran, Paul E.

Political Language and Rhetoric,
1979

a computer search, be sure to insert the service's name and identifying document number also.

Continue the practice of recording vital information for each new reference, making sure that the publication information on each card is written strictly according to the documentation system you are using. Following a system carefully at this point will ease the later task of transferring the information to your typed list of references, an acknowledgment of sources.

Generally, if you follow the MLA system, you will have a section titled "Works Cited," although you may have "Works Consulted," a section for listing the works read but not specifically referred to in the paper. The APA system calls for a "References" section in which only the references cited in the text appear. "Works Cited" and "References" sections are alphabetized according to the author's last name or by the first word of the title (other than *a, an, the*) when the author's name is unknown.

Details on the MLA and APA systems of documenting sources within the body and at the end of a paper are set forth in the following lists. For model entries, see the complete library paper and technical report in Chapter 19.

MLA

According to the MLA system, items in each entry are treated as sentences, that is, followed by a period and two spaces. The normal arrangement of items is as follows:

1. Author's name as it appears on the title page. Last name first, then a comma, then first name, then initial if any, then a period. For joint authors, invert only the first author's name; use normal order for the other authors and insert commas or *and* as you would in a normal series. Anonymous works begin with the title.

2. Title of work, including any subtitles. Enclose within quotation marks the titles of articles, chapters, unpublished dissertations, episodes in radio or television programs, poems except those separately published as books, short stories, songs, and lectures. Underline (to indicate italics) the titles of books, journals, magazines, newspapers, plays, films, radio and television programs, separately published poems, operas, published dissertations, government publications, and works of art, including whatever punctuation is included in the title but not the period that follows the title. Capitalize the initial letters of all major words. If descriptive labels are needed, for example "editorial" or "computer software," add the information as a separate item immediately after the title. If two titles are required, say, for an article in a book, the title of the part of the book precedes the title of the book.

3. Name of editor or translator, if there is one. Editor and translator are abbreviated (Ed./Trans.) and placed before the name of the person.

4. Edition and volume specification. For any edition used beyond the first, indicate by number (4th ed.) the one used. State the total number of volumes in a multivolume work (6 vols.) regardless of the number of volumes used.

5. Publication information. For a book, note the place of publication (only the first city if more than one is listed on the title page), including state or country if the city may be ambiguous (Cambridge — MA? England?) or unfamiliar (Englewood Cliffs), followed by a colon; then the name of the publisher followed by a comma; and last, the date, followed by a period. For an article, note the name of the periodical, followed by a space; the volume number in Arabic numbers if there is one; the date in parentheses, followed by a colon; then the page or inclusive pages of the article, followed by a period.

Call number label

Publication information

Informational note

APA

In the APA documentation style, as with MLA style, items in each reference entry are considered to be sentences; they are followed by a period and two spaces. The order of items and treatment, however, are different.

1. Author's name. Last name first, then a comma, then initial or initials (not name) followed by periods, with no extra period for the end of the element. For multiple authors, give surnames and initials of all, no matter how many. (In the text, however, where there are six or more authors, use "et al." after the first author's name.) Invert names of all authors; place a comma between author's names, even if there are only two. Use the ampersand (&) with the comma for the last author's name. When a work is anonymous, its title moves to the author position. For edited works add "Ed." or "Eds." in parentheses after the editor's name, followed by a period.

2. Publication date. In parentheses state the year the work was copyrighted, or for unpublished works, the year the work was produced. A period follows the parentheses. For magazines, journals, and newspapers, place a comma after the year and add the month and day, if any.

3. Title of work. Titles of articles, chapters, and the like appear without quotation marks and end with a period. Titles of books are underlined to indicate italics and end with a period. Capitalize the initial letter of the first word of titles and subtitles, if any, and proper names. Enclose additional nonroutine, identifying information in brackets immediately after the title (e.g., [Letter to the Editor], [Cassette recording], [Film]) with no period separating the information from the title.

4. Editor's name when not in author position. When an article or chapter is cited from an edited work, use noninverted initials and surname of the editor or editors followed by "Ed." or "Eds." in parentheses before the period. [In E. B. Bernard (Ed.).]

5. Publication information. For a book, note the place of publication, with state or country when the place is unfamiliar (Bethesda, MD) or may be ambiguous (Cambridge — MA? England?) followed by a colon (if more than one publisher location is given, use the first location stated or home office if specified); then the shortened (but intelligible) name of the publisher, followed by a period. Enclose additional information such as an edition number beyond the first (3rd ed.), volume number (Vol. 2), or report number (Report No. 628) in parentheses immediately after the title with no separating period. A translation of a foreign title is placed in square brackets after the title. For an article, note the name of the periodical it is

published in. Titles of periodicals are typed with upper- and lower-case letters, followed by a comma. Give the volume number (not preceded by "Vol." or enclosed in parentheses) underlined, then the issue number in parentheses (only if each issue begins with page 1) and inclusive page numbers of the article (preceded by "pp." only in the case of newspaper and magazine articles and not enclosed in parentheses), with commas between elements.

Painstaking attention to bibliographical detail on note cards, even for sources that may not be used, may seem a nuisance, but accurately recorded entries save time later, and accurately presented entries help to establish an author's credibility.

Because the model library paper and technical report in Chapter 19 do not include all possible types of bibliographical entries, samples of frequently used ones are listed here in both MLA and APA formats for comparison.

A book by one author:

```
MLA:  Fraser, Antonia.  Mary Queen of Scots.  New York:
      Delacorte, 1969.
APA:  Fraser, A.  (1969).  Mary Queen of Scots.  New York:
      Delacorte.
```

More than one book by the same author:

```
MLA:  D'Angelo, Frank J.  A Conceptual Theory of Rhetoric.
      Cambridge, MA: Winthrop, 1975.
      ---.  Process and Thought in Composition.  3rd ed.
      Boston: Little, Brown, 1985.
APA:  D'Angelo, F. J.  (1975).  A conceptual theory of
      rhetoric.  Cambridge, MA: Winthrop.
      D'Angelo, F. J.  (1985).  Process and thought in
      composition (3rd ed.).  Boston: Little, Brown.
```

APA: Kirk, J. A., & White, S. D. (1983a). <u>Experimental</u>
        <u>procedures for the physical sciences</u>. New York:
        Harcourt.

        Kirk, J. A., & White, S. D. (1983b). <u>Experimental</u>
        <u>designs</u>. New York: Viking Press.

A book by two or three authors:

MLA: Young, Richard E., Alton L. Becker, and Kenneth L.
        Pike. <u>Rhetoric: Discovery and Change</u>. New
        York: Harcourt, 1970.

APA: Young, R. E., Becker, A. L., & Pike, K. L. (1970).
        <u>Rhetoric: Discovery and change</u>. New York:
        Harcourt.

A book by more than three authors:

MLA: Lauer, Janice M., et al. <u>Four Worlds of Writing</u>.
        New York: Harper & Row, 1981.

APA: Lauer, J. M., Montague, G., Lunsford, A., & Emig, J.
        (1981). <u>Four worlds of writing</u>. New York: Harper
        & Row.

A book by a corporate author:

MLA: Committee on Graduate Training in Scientific Writing.
        <u>Scientific Writing for Graduate Students</u>.
        Bethesda, MD: Council of Biology Editors, 1968.

APA: Committee on Graduate Training in Scientific Writing.
        (1968). <u>Scientific writing for graduate students</u>.
        Bethesda, MD: Council of Biology Editors.

A book by an author with an editor:

MLA: Whately, Richard. <u>Elements of Rhetoric</u>. 1828. Ed.
        Douglas Ehninger. Carbondale: Southern Illinois
        UP, 1963.

APA: Whately, R. (1963). <u>Elements of rhetoric</u>. (D.
        Ehninger, Ed.). Carbondale: Southern Illinois
        University Press. (Original work published 1828)

A book with an editor:

MLA: Berg, Stephen, and Robert Mezey, eds. <u>Naked Poetry</u>.
        Indianapolis: Bobbs-Merrill, 1969.

APA: Berg, S., & Mezey, S. (Eds.). (1969). <u>Naked poetry</u>.
        Indianapolis: Bobbs-Merrill.

A book with neither an author nor editor:

MLA: <u>College Bound Seniors</u>. Princeton, NJ: College Board,
        1979.

APA: <u>College bound seniors</u>. (1979). Princeton, NJ:
        College Board Publications.

A translation:

> MLA: Vygotsky, Lev Semenovich. Thought and Language.
>   Trans. Eugenia Hanfmann and Gertrude Vakar.
>   Cambridge, MA: MIT Press, 1967.
>
> APA: Vygotsky L. S. (1967). Thought and language (E.
>   Hanfmann & G. Vakar, Trans.). Cambridge, MA: MIT
>   Press. (Original work published 1934)

A selection from a book:

> MLA: Lowell, Amy. "Patterns." Literature. Ed. James
>   Burl Hogins. 3rd ed. Chicago: Science Research
>   Associates, 1984. 367–70.
>
> APA: Lowell, A. (1984). Patterns. In J. B. Hogins
>   (Ed.), Literature (3rd ed., pp. 367–370).
>   Chicago: Science Research Associates.

A work in multiple volumes:

> MLA: Horgan, Paul. Great River: The Rio Grande in North
>   American History. 2 vols. New York: Rinehart
>   1954.
>
> APA: Horgan, P. (1954). Great river: The Rio Grande in
>   North American history (Vols. 1–2). New York:
>   Rinehart & Company.

A republished book:

> MLA: Bain, Alexander. John Stewart Mill: A Criticism with
>   Personal Recollections. 1882. New York:
>   Augustus M. Kelley, 1969.
>
> APA: Bain, A. (1969). John Stewart Mill: A criticism
>   with personal recollections. New York: Augustus
>   M. Kelley. (Original work published 1882)

An article from a reference book:

> MLA: "Spartanburg." Encyclopedia Americana. 1973 ed.
>
> APA: "Spartanburg." (1973). Encyclopedia Americana
>   (Vol. 25, p. 459).

An article from a journal with continuous pagination:

> MLA: Haddock, Fred T. "Radio Astronomy Observations from
>   Space." American Rocket Society Journal 27
>   (1960): 600–02.
>
> APA: Haddock, F. T. (1960). Radio astronomy observations
>   from space. American Rocket Society Journal, 27,
>   600–602.

Note: The "27" refers to the volume number.

An article from a periodical with discontinuous paging.

MLA: Horn, Thomas D. "The Role of Bilingualism in
      Reading Difficulties." Journal of Research and
      Development in Education 14.4 (1981): 58–66.

APA: Horn, T. D. (1981). The role of bilingualism in
      reading difficulties. Journal of Research and
      Development in Education, 14(4), 58–66.

An article from a daily periodical:

MLA: Stowell, Linda. "Profile of the Executive
      Alcoholic." Arizona Republic [Phoenix] 20 Feb.
      1983: C1.

APA: Stowell, L. (1983, February 20). Profile of the
      executive alcoholic. The [Phoenix] Arizona
      Republic, sec. C, p. 1.

Note: In MLA format introductory articles such as *the* are omitted. If the name of the city does not appear in the newspaper's name, add it in brackets after the name. If pages are continuous, a section letter or number is not needed. In APA format, the city name appears within the newspaper's name.

An article from a weekly or biweekly periodical:

MLA: Morrow, Lance. "The Burnout of Almost Everyone."
      Time 21 Sept. 1981: 84.

APA: Morrow, L. (1981, September 21). The burnout of
      almost everyone. Time, p. 84.

An article from a monthly or bimonthly periodical:

MLA: Kupchan, Charles. "Solidarity's Future." Atlantic
      May 1985: 37–40.

APA: Kupchan, C. (1985, May). Solidarity's future. The
      Atlantic, pp. 37–40.

An editorial:

MLA: "Indefensible Defense Budget." Editorial. Los
      Angeles Times 16 Dec. 1983, sec. 5: 4.

APA: Indefensible defense budget [Editorial]. (1983,
      December 16). Los Angeles Times, part 5, p. 4.

A letter to the editor:

MLA: Cram, C. Paul. Letter. Los Angeles Times 16 Dec.
      1983, sec. 5: 5.

APA: Cram, C. P. (1983, December 16). Religion and
      politics [Letter to the editor]. Los Angeles
      Times, part 5, p. 5.

A review:

MLA: Rev. of Richelieu and Olivares, by J. H. Elliott.
      Saturday Review of Books 27 Sept. 1984: 3–6.

APA: Elliott, J. H. (1984, September 27). [Review of
        Richelieu and Olivares]. The Saturday Review of
        Books, pp. 3—6.

A public document:

MLA: United States. Senate. Special Committee to
        Investigate Organized Crime in Interstate
        Commerce. Report on Crime Investigation. 82nd
        Cong., 1st sess. S. Rep. 141. Washington, GPO,
        1951.

APA: U.S. Senate. Special Committee to Investigate
        Organized Crime in Interstate Commerce. 82nd
        Cong., 1st sess. (1951). Report on crime
        investigation (S. Report No. 141). Washington,
        DC: U.S. Government Printing Office.

A film:

MLA: Newman, Paul, actor. The Verdict. Dir. Sidney
        Lumet. Twentieth Century—Fox, 1983.

APA: Newman, P. (Actor), & Lumet, S. (Director). (1983).
        The verdict [Film]. Los Angeles: Twentieth
        Century—Fox, 1983.

Note: For a film, the author's name usually appears first, but if emphasis is being placed on the director or someone else connected with the
film or on the title of the television program, that name should appear
first.

A radio or television program:

MLA: Götterdämmerung. By Richard Wagner. Dir. Patrice
        Chereau. With Gwyneth Jones and Manfred Jung.
        Cond. Pierre Boulez. Bayreuth Festival Orch.
        PBS. WPBT, Miami. 6 and 13 June 1983.

APA: Wagner, R. (Composer), Chereau, P. (Director),
        Beyreuth Festival (Orchestra), Boulez, P.
        (Conductor), Jones, G.,` & Jung, M. (Singers).
        (1983, June 6 & 13). Götterdämmerung [Televised
        opera]. WPBT, Miami.

An interview:

MLA: Duncan, Gordon. Personal interview. 14 January
        1984.

APA: Guinn, D. M. (1984, January). [Interview with
        Gordon Duncan, Upjohn Research Manager]. Upjohn
        Newsletter, p. 1.

A computer program:

MLA: Shrayer, Michael. Electric Pencil II. Computer
        software. Michael Shrayer Software, 1978.
        North Star Horizon—CP/M, 16K, disk.

APA: Shrayer, M. (1978). Electric pencil II [Computer
      program]. Glendale, CA: Michael Shrayer Software.
      (Disk for North Star Horizon—CP/M, 16K)

Material from a computer service:

MLA: Nuveen, Mary, and Grace Smith. The CPSD 1978
      American National Election Study. Ann Arbor: UP
      of Michigan, 1979. DIALOG file 216, item
      1267409.

APA: Nuveen, M., & Smith, G. (1979). The CPS 1978
      American national election study [Machine—readable
      data file]. (DIALOG File 126, Item 126). Ann
      Arbor: University of Michigan Press.

Reading and Evaluating the Literature. After your literature search results in a list of potential sources, you are ready to begin to read and evaluate those references that seem most interesting and relevant, to take notes, and to verify information needed for the "Works Cited" or "References" sections of your report.

Before reading each source, supply yourself with something to keep notes on, preferably 5 × 8 note cards for space and ease of handling, although some researchers find that looseleaf sheets work well, beginning each new entry on a fresh sheet. Plan to limit the notes on each card to a single narrowed topic, labeling the card in the upper left-hand corner with a word or phrase that identifies the topic on the card. In the upper right-hand corner transfer the short label, often the title of a work in whole or part, that you have devised for the corresponding bibliography card. Both these labels will save time and effort in the long run. The topic label makes it possible to sort through an entire collection of note cards when note taking is finished and to order them into subgroups on the basis of the same topic identifier. Subsequent rearranging of the cards into ever finer subgroupings should end with the notes being in the appropriate order for the actual writing of the report. The short bibliographical label allows cross identification from notes to sources when it comes time to document the report.

With extensive reading, it is important to read economically. The most efficient way is always to read with the underlying problem of your report in mind. Notice divergent points of view, disagreements with authorities, general statements of theory and accepted facts, lines of reasoning. Whenever possible, read thoroughly and carefully only the material that pertains to your topic. Scan introductory material in books (preface, introduction, table of contents, etc.) and abstracts of articles as a way of pinpointing relevant material. In books and articles check headings, subheadings, and topic sentences of paragraphs for key points. As you read, you may discover references to other sources not on your original list in footnotes or in a bibliography. If you do, make bibliographic cards and add them to your list of references to read.

Components of the Communication   Kinneavy/"Basic Aims"
Process

Kinneavy represents the components of the composing
process as a triangle.

Encoder   Decoder
(Writer, Speaker)   (Reader, listener)
              Signal
              (Linguistic
              Product)

              Reality
(Something in universe)

Focusing on one of these components produces a
specific kind of discourse w/specific overriding aim.
                                                p. 303

It is important not only to read economically, but also to take
notes in the same way. Quote as little as possible. Quote primarily only
authors who are important authoriities on the subject and only when
their ideas are extremely important or stated extremely well. Remember
that words you have copied exactly should be enclosed within quotation marks, and recheck to make sure you have made no mistakes.
Instead of quoting, paraphrase an author's word whenever possible.
Summarize main ideas. From time to time jot down comments on what
you are reading. As you take notes, be sure to put the page number of
the original source at an appropriate place on the note card.

Obtaining Information from Primary Sources. Information obtained
from original investigation rather than from someone else's research is
primary data. Technical reports often depend heavily on firsthand information—information gained from experimenting, observing, or administering surveys.

Experimenting. After the hypothesis is formed or the problem fully
stated, the investigator attacks it by experimentation, testing it under
controlled conditions. For example, a researcher who hypothesizes that
iron exposed to damp air will rust would design a procedure to test that
hypothesis, collect data, classify, and then interpret the results. If she
measured the accumulation of rust over a period of days and found that
it increased at a fixed rate according to the length of exposure and
amount of moisture in the air, she could conclude from her experiment
that rust accumulation varies concomitantly with the duration of exposure to moisture.

Observing. Observation occurs, of course, in conjunction with experimentation. Experimentation includes observation under controlled conditions. Observation can also occur alone as a means of gathering data. For example, scientists, by observing the paths of stars and planets, established facts about the influences that define their orbits. A researcher attempting to improve the sound equipment in an auditorium would undoubtedly perform an on-site observation of the efficiency of the equipment currently in use. He might plan to observe at designated moments. These are examples of planned observations, but casual observation can also provide firsthand information. If a researcher were studying whether uniforms should be required for all bank employees, he might casually observe the present dress of the employees because a formal study would probably result in employees dressing nontypically.

Administering Surveys. Although both experiments and observations are important methods of obtaining firsthand data, undergraduate research reports that require firsthand information are more likely to depend on surveys. Questionnaires are a useful means of obtaining information from other people when more accessible sources, such as published books, articles, reports, and brochures, fail to supply what is needed. We must point out, though, that since questionnaires take time, effort, and money, it is best to be sure that a questionnaire is the only way to obtain the desired information before constructing and administering one.

There is no science of questionnaire design, but by following some basic guidelines, you can successfully handle a simple questionnaire of the limited scope your research report is likely to demand:

1. Include necessary information justifying the questionnaire, how the answers will be used, and why they will be beneficial. Place this information either at the head of the questionnaire or in a cover letter.
2. Give clear, exact instructions for completing the questionnaire.
3. Make the questionnaire as short as possible; ask for needed information only.
4. Arrange the questions in logical order. Avoid asking how much a company charges its employees for used typewriters before asking whether the company sells its used typewriters to employees.
5. Design the questionnaire so it is easy to answer. Provide boxes or blanks to be checked. These save time for the respondent and for the researcher when tabulating the answers.
6. Allow for all likely answers. Sometimes a simple yes or no is impossible. Include categories such as "no opinion" and "don't know," and shadings such as "agree strongly," "agree," "neutral," "disagree," and "disagree strongly."
7. When appropriate, provide for additional comments by leaving a blank space marked for that purpose or by using some open-ended

questions. Although comments are difficult to tabulate, unlike check marks, they may be more informative than the other answers.

8. Make the questions easy to understand and unambiguous. "Why did you buy your last home?" could elicit responses about price, location, style, and so on.
9. Phrase the questions so they focus on one topic only.
10. Ask for information that can be remembered easily.
11. Avoid questions that touch on personal bias. A question about whether the city council has been sufficiently concerned about providing for enough parks could call forth emotional, ephemeral answers based on anything from a respondent's dislike of one council member to fear of a tax increase, thus making the answer unreliable.
12. Avoid questions that appear to pry. Often age, educational level, income, and the like are important to a survey, but ranges rather than exact answers usually suffice. For example, you can bracket income: $0–$10,000; $11,000–$20,000; . . . $200,000 or above.
13. Word questions so that they do not suggest an answer.
14. If the questionnaire is mailed, include a stamped, addressed envelope for its return.

Questionnaires may be administered over the phone or in face-to-face interviews; in either case the questionnaire should be carefully planned as a guide, and the questions should be asked in a uniform way of all respondents.

Preparing a Preliminary Outline

Before progressing very far in gathering information, it is wise to formulate a preliminary outline to guide your further reading and note taking or gathering of primary data. This outline will be only a tentative plan, but should include the principal ideas of your topic as revealed in the topic labels on the note cards. Listing and arranging the ideas into major and minor categories is sufficient at this time to establish the framework of the report and suggest relationships among the ideas. If your topic is permanent part-time employment, your topic identifiers after reading a half dozen sources might look something like this:

Definition of permanent part-time employment
Retirees as part-time employees
Extent of part-time employment
Teenagers as part-time employees
Advantages of part-time employment
Disadvantages of part-time employment
Predominant sex of part-time employees

These could be arranged into major and minor categories, and, as relationships become clear, suggest other related topics that demand attention or the need for a questionnaire and the questions to be asked.

Definition of permanent part-time employment
    Similarities to temporary part-time employment
    Differentiation from temporary part-time employment
Typical part-time employees
    Predominant ages
    Predominant sex
    Predominant educational level
    Typical years of work experience
Advantages of permanent part-time employment
    Advantages to employer
    Advantages to employee
Disadvantages of permanent part-time employment
    Disadvantages to employer
    Disadvantages to employee
Sociological consequences of part-time employment

Constructing a Formal Outline and Table of Contents

When all information for the research report has been obtained, sorted, and ordered, it is time to write a formal outline. If the problem has been kept firmly in mind as the information was collected, the formal outline will be close to the rough outline formed early in the research process. On the other hand, if the collected information suggests a redefinition of the problem and another arrangement of points, another outline is needed. However it is achieved, a complete outline at this point can serve three important purposes. The first is to check on whether sufficient information is gathered for all subtopics. For example, if far more notes are found on the advantages of permanent part-time employment to the employee than to the employer, the researcher would be alerted to supply the needed information in order to expand the smaller part. In other cases, an imbalance might signal the need to reduce the size of some parts. The second purpose is to check the logic of the overall arrangement of the report. The third is to guide the actual writing of the report.

Typically, a library paper written for a college course is preceded by an outline. The sections of the paper are represented in the outline even though they are not distinguished by formal separation in the paper; that is, the library paper is written to be read in one continuous flow with transitions from one section to another indicated subtly rather than by headings and subheadings.

A technical report, on the other hand, is preceded by a table of contents, which is simply an outline transformed into a conventional contents format. The table of contents, like an outline, reveals the topics and divisions of the report. Entries in the table of contents must be identical to the headings and subheadings that appear in the report. (*Note:* no entry may appear in the contents unless it appears in the report; however, some subheadings may appear in the report that do not appear in the contents.)

As the model library paper and technical report in Chapter 19 illustrate, in both an outline and a table of contents the headings at each level are parallel in grammatical structure.

Planning Specific Writing Strategies

Before actually writing the draft of the report, the writer needs to plan specific strategies that will appeal to a specific audience for a specific purpose.

The ordering of the information itself is one strategy. Every research report needs a plan of presentation stating what will be treated in the report and in what order, although a formally stated plan typically appears only in a technical report, not a library paper. Even when the plan is not presented explicitly, it is needed to guide the writing. When it is explicitly stated, it guides the reader too. The ordering of information must logically develop the material so that readers can proceed from the known to the unknown, from the simple to the complex, from the more believable to the less believable, and from generalizations to specific support—through the report as a whole and within sections.

Technical terms that will be unfamiliar to the audience need to be defined, and so does any term used in an atypical way. The writer needs to decide what rhetorical operations will be appropriate, what examples and details to use, how many details to include so that generalizations receive adequate support, when to summarize along the way, when a clarifying analogy is needed, whether certain information is better footnoted or put in an appendix or included within the report proper, when graphics are needed and what kind, and so on. Although these elements of strategy are planned before the writer starts, the planning continues throughout the writing and revising processes.

Writing the Draft

For some writers, the easiest place to begin the draft is with the longest part, the middle sections. Successful introductions as well as successful conclusions require an overview of the entire development; therefore, they may be better left until last. Many writers, however, prefer to begin with the introduction as a way to set the purpose and plan firmly before them for reference. If this procedure is best for you, by all means follow it, but be prepared to revise your introduction if new ideas occur to you or if your organization changes as you discuss your topics. Writing for many people is a discovery process, even after much preliminary planning; simply accommodate yourself to new discoveries by restating your commitment to your readers.

Writing a draft is an individual process; nonetheless, we can all benefit from examining the practices of most experienced writers. These are summarized in the following paragraphs. Use those that make the writing task easier for you, and revise or discard those that do not.

Probably the most critical step is to start writing as soon as possible after gathering your information, planning the best organization, and settling on some specific ways of appealing to your audience. Eleventh-hour reports are rarely good, partly because of the pressure but partly because the information gathered much earlier is no longer immediate to the mind.

Another hint is to bring to bear everything you have learned previously about writing papers, about bringing an audience into agreement with you. (In one sense, *all* writing is writing from research. Research reports are simply an extended, formalized exercise of the regular writing process.)

Keep your note cards and other data gathered from firsthand observations nearby as you write. Glance through the note cards and data. Choose a pack or subpack or a section of the data that you think will be the easiest to write. With one section out of the way, the whole task will seem less overwhelming. Move from the easier sections to the harder ones. By proceeding section by section, you will, in effect, be writing a series of shorter, more easily handled discussions. Transitions between sections can be inserted during the revision process.

Try to write as rapidly as you can. The rough draft is not the place to worry about exact phraseology or words, certainly not spelling and mechanics. During this stage the best thing to do is get your ideas down on paper.

Write for at least an hour at a stretch. A student's time is often constrained, but if you work for any time shorter than an hour, you will fail to get into your material. Much longer than three hours and your writing may show the effects of exhaustion. Move away from your material only when you have some idea of where the next paragraph will be going. If you are "blocked," jot down a phrase or two that suggest an avenue of escape. When you return to your draft, reread the latest material to focus your thoughts and begin writing immediately.

Include more material than you need, not less. It is easier to delete material later than add it. This advice does not mean that your discussion should be "padded." It should, however, be complete. Readers typically want more substantiating detail rather than less. Any inappropriate or repetitive material can be cut during revision for the final copy.

As you write, mark spaces where visual aids need to be inserted, and try to incorporate them and direct quotations gracefully into the text with transitions before and after. Short quotations should flow with the text and be enclosed with quotation marks. Longer quotations (five lines or more usually) should be set off from the text and should not be enclosed by quotation marks. Visual aids and quotations always need some authorial comment. All quotations need to be documented according to the reference system you are following. The model library paper and technical report in Chapter 19 illustrate the use of visual aids and quotations and the placement of references.

Finally, write your introduction (or rewrite it) and your conclusion. Make sure that any conclusions are warranted by the information that has preceded them. Library papers often end with comments on the significance of the ideas that have been presented. Technical reports end with summaries, conclusions, recommendations, or predictions — or combinations of these elements. Look at the model papers in Chapter 19 and also the material on endings in Chapter 9.

Revising the Draft

Let the finished draft "cool" before revising it. Try to wait at least one day, several if possible, to gain some distance from the work so that you can more easily shift from the role of writer to the role of reader. Then come to the draft with an open mind, a pen, pencil, or word processor, scissors, and scotch tape.

Read the draft through, concentrating first on content and organization. Be particularly alert for sentences and paragraphs that do not logically follow one another, for questions that have been left unanswered, for clear expression of ideas, and for sufficient examples, facts, and details to support your generalizations. Make certain that your information is correct and your logic valid. Revisit the library or redo an experiment if there is even the slightest doubt about accuracy. Refigure any math or equations.

Test your ideas in different orders by cutting the draft, rearranging pieces of it, and taping them together in a new order. Or tape in additions and lengthy corrections. For example, if a transition paragraph is needed, cut the draft at the point where the transition is needed and tape the new paragraph in place. (It is a good idea to photocopy your draft each time before you rearrange so that you can compare the different arrangements and connections.) If you use a computer with word processing, rearranging pieces of a draft can be done simply by pressing a key. Be sure to save successive arrangements and revisions so that hard copies of each version can be compared for relative effectiveness. Whether you cut and paste or revise electronically, make sure that headings are informative and that they reflect the sections they head.

Reread the draft again, this time concentrating on style. Try reading it aloud. Look for pretentious words and phrases, garbled sentences, too many passives and nominalizations, and unnecessary jargon. Check sentence lengths. Are they varied? Are some too long, too complex? Break them into smaller units. If too many sentences in a row are short and choppy, combine the sentences into longer, more graceful units.

Once you have revised the discussion portion of your research report, you are ready to write or rewrite the introduction and write the conclusion. If you are writing a technical report, you are also ready to write the other necessary accompanying parts, such as the abstract, title page, and letter of transmittal, and to finish and insert visual aids.

It is time also to make sure references are correct. Although bibliographical form seems inconsequential compared to the rest of the report, incorrect form gives the impression of a careless reseacher at work and can lead readers to doubt the research itself.

Documenting the Sources

As mentioned earlier, there is no one universally accepted documentation system for the sources in a research report. Any system, however, includes two types of documentation, within and following the text, and has the same two aims: the first is to include sufficient detail to allow readers to verify the sources of the quotations, ideas, and facts included in the report; the second is to use as few parenthetical references as possible and to keep those used as brief as possible, while maintaining clarity and accuracy and giving credit to the source for original ideas and words.

The first type of documentation, that within the text, makes specific reference to sources in the text of the report, indicating what was derived, where it was derived from, and where in the work the words or ideas can be found or when the material was published. Both MLA and APA formats basically depend on parentheses for this information at the appropriate place in the text of a report. Both formats cite the author. Showing different emphases, however, the MLA format adds page numbers, and the APA format emphasizes publication date. APA format adds page numbers to the date only for direct quotations or when the material will be difficult to locate. Often, however, all information necessary to point to a source can be, and should be, gracefully integrated into the text. For example, if only one work of Lev Vygotsky's is used for a report and the entire work is cited, the first two of the following sentences would be preferred to the second two:

```
MLA:   Vygotsky has devoted an entire book to the origins
       and growth of intelligence in children.

APA:   Vygotsky (1956) has devoted an entire book to the
       origins and growth of intelligence in children.

MLA:   An entire book has been devoted to the origins and
       growth of intelligence in children (Vygotsky).

APA:   An entire book has been devoted to the origins and
       growth of intelligence in children (Vygotsky, 1956).
```

The second type of documentation lists the sources used, collected and alphabetized at the end of the report. The sources are unnumbered. As was mentioned earlier, a list of works quoted following the MLA format is headed "Works Cited"; another section, "Works Consulted," may be added for sources used but not quoted. A list following APA format is headed "References" and includes only sources cited. Both lists of works cited and references are started on a new page with "Works Cited" or "References" centered one inch down from the top of the page; all entries are double-spaced with hanging indentation. The first line of an entry is flush with the left margin in both cases. Successive lines are indented five spaces in MLA style, three spaces in APA style.

Within-Text Citation. Observe the application of MLA and APA style in the following representative examples of textual documentation.

When neither author nor date (in APA style) is part of the discussion:

```
MLA:   A recent attempt to bridge the relationship of
       writing and meditation focuses on the concept of
       inner speech, the verbalized segment of the stream of
       consciousness (Moffett 231-46).

APA:   A recent attempt to bridge the relationship of
       writing and meditation focuses on the concept of
       inner speech, the verbalized segment of the stream of
       consciousness (Moffett, 1982).
```

When the name of the author occurs naturally in the discussion:

```
MLA:   Moffett argues that for people who have highly
       developed inner speech capacity plus the ability to
       suspend it, "thought straightens out and deepens
       during the hiatus" (240).

APA:   Moffett (1982) argues that for people who have highly
       developed inner speech capacity plus the ability to
       suspend it, "thought straightens out and deepens
       during the hiatus" (p. 240).
```

When both the name of the author and the date appear naturally in the discussion:

```
MLA:   In a 1963 study Haddock, Schulte, and Walsh measured
       cosmic radio intensities (222-24).
```

APA: In a 1963 study Haddock, Schulte, and Walsh measured
              cosmic radio intensities.

Note: When following APA format, subsequent citations of three or more authors include only the surname of the first author, followed by "et al." and the year: "Haddock et al. (1963) found . . . "

When more than one publication by an author appears in the same year:

MLA: D'Angelo elaborates his own particular view of
              rhetorical principles and his understanding of
              rhetorical processes (<u>Conceptual</u> <u>Theory</u>) and applies
              his knowledge to identify five implications of
              emphasizing the structure of the discipline of
              rhetoric ("Search" 87).

APA: D'Angelo elaborates his own particular view of
              rhetorical principles and his understanding of
              rhetorical processes (1975a) and applies his
              knowledge to identify five implications of
              emphasizing the structure of the discipline of
              rhetoric (1975b, p. 87).

When one of two or more works by an author with different publication dates is cited:

MLA: The following discussion is based on the premise that
              "three movements in the thirties strongly affected
              the teaching of discourse: semantics, communication,
              and a second 'new criticism' " (Kinneavy, <u>Theory</u>
              14).

APA: The following discussion is based on the premise that
              "three movements in the thirties strongly affected
              the teaching of discourse: semantics, communication,
              and a second 'new criticism' " (Kinneavy, 1980, p.
              14).

When a work has a corporate author:

MLA: In <u>Freedom</u> <u>and</u> <u>Discipline</u> <u>in</u> <u>English</u> the Commission
              on English adopted the linguistics–composition-
              literature trilogy as a framework for the study of
              language arts.

APA: In <u>Freedom</u> <u>and</u> <u>Discipline</u> <u>in</u> <u>English</u> (1965) the
              Commission on English adopted the linguistics-
              composition–literature trilogy as a a framework for
              the study of language arts.

Note: The corporate author's name can also be used in parentheses, but if it is long, the parenthetical reference becomes an awkward interruption.

When a work has no author:

MLA: As the earliest treatment of prose style in Latin, <u>Ad</u>
              <u>Herennium</u> offers the oldest extant division of style

> into three kinds and the oldest extant formal study
> of figures.

APA: As the earliest extant treatment of prose style in
Latin, Ad Herennium (1954), probably written between
86 and 82 B.C., offers the oldest division of style
into three kinds and the oldest formal study of
rhetorical figures.

When citing literary works available in multiple editions:

MLA: Iago eggs Roderigo on by declaring that "it cannot
be that Desdemona should long continue her love to
the Moor," that "she must change for youth," and
that "when she is sated with his body, she will find
the error of her choice" (Othello 1.3).

APA: Iago eggs Roderigo on by declaring that "it cannot
be that Desdemona should long continue her love for
the Moor," that "she must change for youth," and
that "when she is sated with his body, she will find
the error of her choice" (Othello, 1952, Act I,
Scene 3).

Note: The page number is less helpful for literary classics; with other
information, such as act, scene, line, or chapter, readers can locate
quotes in any edition.

When citing an indirect source:

MLA: Aristotle's belief that an aim of discourse is to
refer to reality, that there is "a language
concerned with things," coincides with the beliefs
of other rhetoricians, but Aristotle also said that
there is "a language directed to the hearer" (qtd.
in Kinneavy 58).

APA: Aristotle's belief that an aim of discourse is to
refer to reality, that there is "a language that is
concerned with things," coincides with the beliefs
of other rhetoricians, but Aristotle also said that
there is "a language directed to the hearer"
(quoted in Kinneavy, p. 58).

Note: Whenever possible, quote or paraphrase from original sources.
When quoting from indirect sources, you may want to document the
original source in a note and explain why a secondary source was used.

Notes. There are two kinds of notes, content and bibliographic.
Content notes amplify material presented in the text with relevant comments. Such supplementary information should be as brief as possible,
not take the place of the text itself. Bibliographic notes acknowledge the
source of quotations — for example, full publication details for an original source cited as an indirect source. Superscript Arabic numerals mark
notes at appropriate points in the text, usually at the end of a sentence.
The numbers run consecutively through the text.

```
Aristotle's belief that an aim of discourse is to refer to
reality, that there is "a language concerned with
things," coincides with the beliefs of other rhetor-
icians, but Aristotle also said that there is "a language
directed to the hearer" (qtd. in Kinneavy 58).¹
```

The notes themselves are typed on a separate sheet and appear at the end of a report.

Note

```
¹Aristotle, Rhetoric, trans. W. Rhys Roberts (Oxford,
1924), qtd. in Kinneavy 58.
```

Although it is not apparent in this note because Aristotle is a single name, in note entries the name appears in normal order, unlike the entries in a works cited or references list, where names are alphabetized. Other differences between the two types of entries are few but important. One is numbering: superscript note numbers run consecutively through the text and correspond to notes at the end of the report, whereas bibliographical entries are not numbered. Another is indenting: in note entries the first line is indented five spaces, with subsequent lines placed flush with the left margin, whereas bibliographical entries have hanging indentation. A third is punctuating: a note entry is treated as one sentence with commas between elements instead of the elements being treated as separate entities.

The model library paper and technical report in Chapter 19 illustrate textual citations written according to the MLA and APA systems.

Editing and Typing the Final Copy

When all this work is done, you will be ready to edit and type the final copy. Make sure the documentary reference numbers in the text are correctly inserted and match up with the note or reference entries. As you type your paper, check for errors in mechanics, spelling, subject-verb agreement, pronoun reference, and so on. Use the chapters in Section Four, "Rhetorical Conventions," as a guide for common problems and how to correct them. And remember that even if someone else types your report, you are responsible for the final product. As a last step, proofread your typed report carefully (typographical errors are easier to catch if you read the pages from end to beginning and bottom to top).

EXERCISES

1. In the following excerpt from *Custer Died for Your Sins*, Vine Deloria, Jr., uses humor effectively to arouse his readers' indignation over the cavalier exploitation of Indians.

Read the excerpt; then revise its style and tone to conform to those of a typical report.

Into each life, it is said, some rain must fall. Some people have bad horoscopes, others take tips on the stock market. McNamara created the TFX and the Edsel. Churches possess the real world. But Indians have been cursed above all other people in history. Indians have anthropologists.

Every summer when school is out, a veritable stream of immigrants heads into Indian country. Indeed the Oregon Trail was never so heavily populated as are Route 66 and Highway 18 in the summer time. From every rock and cranny in the East *they* emerge, as if responding to some primeval fertility rite, and flock to the reservations.

"They" are the anthropologists. Social anthropologists, historical anthropologists, political anthropologists, economic anthropologists, all brands of the species, embark on the great summer adventure. For purposes of this discussion we shall refer only to the generic name, anthropologists. They are the most prominent members of the scholarly community that infest the land of the free, and in summer time, the homes of the braves.

The origin of the anthropologist is a mystery hidden in historical mists. Indians are certain that all societies in the Near East had anthropologists at one time because all those societies are now defunct.

Indians are equally certain that Columbus brought anthropologists on his ships when he came to the New World. How else could he have made so many wrong deductions about where he was?

While their historical precedent is uncertain, anthropologists can readily be identified on the reservations. Go into any crowd of people. Pick out a tall, gaunt white man wearing Bermuda shorts, a World War II Army Air Force flying jacket, an Australian bush hat, tennis shoes, and packing a large knapsack incorrectly strapped to his back. He will invariably have a thin, sexy wife with stringy hair, an IQ of 191, and a vocabulary in which even the prepositions have eleven syllables.

2. Assume that the following material will be useful to you in your report. Make up two bibliography cards for it, one according to MLA format, one according to APA format. Paraphrase the material on note cards with no direct quotations. The passage comes from *A Short Introduction to English Usage* by J. J. Lamberts.

There are several specific problems that have to do with prefixes. They have received far more attention than they perhaps merit, but they are regarded as crucial usage items:

Inflammable. This word is derived from the verb *inflame,* which means, as the name clearly suggests, "to burst into flames, or cause something (or someone) to do so." It came into English from Latin and is comprised of the morphemes {in_1} "into" and {flamma} "flame" and consequently anything *inflammable* may be regarded as likely to burst into flames. Many English words have the initial {in_2} morpheme, among them: *include, incline, incendiary, incandescent, incident, invade, infer, invent, intoxicate.* But it occurred to someone that *in* also means "not," as in *insane, indecent, incapable.* It could be argued that some very dull person might suppose therefore that *inflammable* meant "fireproof" and would deal with inflammable materials accordingly. To obviate that peril, the word *flammable* "likely to burn" was jacked into its place and a new meaning was pumped into it. There are those who feel that a useful distinction has been thrown away and that nothing has been provided to compensate for it.

Irregardless. The word has a prefix *ir-* which is an allomorph of {in₁} "not" before initial /r/. This is essentially a telescoping of two words, sometimes called a "blend," in this instance of *irrespective* and *regardless.* The principle objection raised against the word is that it is tautological: *in-* and *-less* say the same thing. *Irregardless* has four syllables, rolls off the tongue easily, and sounds literary; for that reason it has attracted many people who employ the language for show rather than for exact sense. There are, as we realize, those who are grieved that such a word should exist at all, standard or otherwise. It is ordinarily recognized as nonliterary and stands little chance of general adoption. Those who recognize the word for what it is are less irritated by its tautology than amused by its phony pretentiousness.

Disinterested. The meaning "not having a selfish interest or concern" is the principal one, and it has been in use for about three centuries. Earlier than that there was the meaning "not interested; unconcerned," but this meaning fell from general use several hundred years ago. Much has been said and written about *disinterested,* mainly taking the view that this word is beginning to be employed in place of *uninterested,* and that since the modifier *disinterested* is for some unspecified reason one of the bastions of Western civilization, the barbarian hordes will swoop down on us when the identification has taken place. The peril is vastly overrated. The development is proceeding in another direction. English has several doublets in which *un-* is contrasted with *dis-*: *un-* meaning "is not and never was," and *dis-* meaning "was once but is no longer." Thus: *unarmed, disarmed; unengaged, disengaged; unproved, disproved; unable, disable; unaffected, disaffected; unconnected, disconnected.* From here it is only a short jump to *uninterested, disinterested.* Even though many of us do not use it, this is a good word and the new meaning is a useful one: "no longer interested." It has more than an even chance of being adopted before long.

3. Now paraphrase the same passage, quoting one or two brief excerpts that seem to you to be the "most quotable."

4. Write a logical outline for the above passage, making sure that entries at the same level are in parallel structure.

5. Convert the following items into appropriate form for an MLA works cited list, then an APA references list. Then embed the same information in a sentence, using the various types of within-text citations of both MLA and APA forms.

a. The play *Betrayal* by Harold Pinter was performed at the Trafalgar Theater in New York in 1960 on April 2. Blythe Danner, Raul Julia, and Roy Scheider starred. Peter Hall directed it.

b. The third edition of Alexander Bain's *Education as a Science* was published in London by C. Kegan Paul & Co. in 1879.

c. Elaine P. Maimon of the Department of English, Gerald T. Belcher of the Department of History, Gail W. Hearn of the Department of Biology, Barbara F. Nodine of the Department of Psychology, and Finbarr W. O'Connor of the Department of Philosophy — all at Beaver College in Pennsylvania — wrote *Writing in the Arts and Sciences*, a composition text published by Winthrop Publisher, Inc., in Cambridge, Massachusetts. It was published in 1981.

d. A personal letter written to the author by Josephine Siltow on July 21, 1979.

e. *The Great Gatsby*, first published in 1925 by Charles Scribner's Sons and reprinted in New York by Scribners–Scribner Library in 1960. F. Scott Fitzgerald wrote the book.

f. B. D. Hale wrote an article, "The effects of internal and external imagery on muscular ocular concomitants," that was published in 1982 in the *Journal of Sport Psychology*, volume four, on pages 379 to 386.

g. G. E. Schwartz wrote "Psychological Foundations of Psychotherapy and Behavior Change." It appears in *Handbook of Psychotherapy and Behavior Change*. The book is subtitled *An Empirical Analysis*. It is edited by S. L. Garfield and A. E. Bergin and was published in 1978 by Wiley in New York. The article is on pages 219 to 228. It appears as a full chapter in the book.

h. Alexander Bain wrote *James Mill*, subtitled *A Biography*, that was published in London in 1882 by Longmans, Green, and Co. It was later republished in England by Gregg International Publishers Limited of Westmead, Farnborough, Hants, in 1970.

i. An editorial entitled "Babbitt's Loose Ship?" appeared in *The Sun-Times* of Wedfield, Illinois, in the Sunday edition of May 15, 1983. It appeared in Section A on page 16 and covers the first two columns about halfway down the page.

Chapter 19

Model Research Reports

This chapter presents a model library paper in MLA style and a model technical report in APA style.

A Model Library Paper

Michael Burke's library paper on the following pages is a successful student research effort with an aesthetically pleasing appearance. The *MLA Handbook* says that title pages for research papers are unnecessary. However, most other formats recommend a title page, and instructors in composition classes typically require them. Michael's paper, therefore, includes a title page, nicely arranged with all necessary information included. The titles of each part (outline, first page, works cited, and works consulted) are centered and spaced down from the top of the page. The type is double-spaced, and the pages have adequate margins. A lowercase Roman numeral marks the outline page; consecutive Arabic numerals mark each successive page, including works cited, in the upper right-hand corner, except page 1, which remains unnumbered.

The title states the subject of the paper in general terms but clearly. Although in the humanities catchy titles are used as often as informative ones, the practice is not very helpful. Informative titles with key words are becoming more the norm in the humanities as well as the sciences because of the requirements of computerized information retrieval.

The outline, a phrase outline (although sentence outlines are used too), maintains parallel structure at equivalent levels and is informative. With the core statement heading it and the plan for the development of the subject presented, the outline serves as a clear guide for the reader.

The Left-handed Student in a Right-handed World

by

Michael Burke

for

Dr. Dorothy M. Guinn

English 105

May 6, 1985

Outline

The Left-handed Student in a Right-handed World

Core Statement: In much of their daily life, left-handers
seem to work against the grain of the
rest of society as they try to cope in a
right-handed world, especially as
students learning to write in a
right-handed educational world.

I.   Introduction

   A.   General biases against left-handers in present
society

   B.   General biases against left-handers represented
in language

II.   The bias of a right-handed writing system

   A.   Alternative writing systems

   B.   Problems of left-handers with a right-handed
writing system

      1.   Manual dexterity

      2.   Anxiety

III.   Experts' views of the writing problems of
left-handers

   A.   The coercive approach

      1.   Past barbarous techniques

      2.   Arthur Linksz's techniques

   B.   Stephanie Harrison's supportive approach

      1.   Positive versus neutral influence

      2.   Constructive teaching techniques

   C.   Several experts' descriptive approach

      1.   Ralph Haefner's 1929 study

      2.   Recent studies

IV.   Conclusions

   A.   Some advantages for left-handers

   B.   Need for accommodation

The opening is catchy and arouses the reader's curiosity. Library paper openings may vary from a straightforward, serious approach to light humor. The opening details lead naturally at the end of paragraph 2 into the core statement, which lets the reader know the focus of the paper early. Michael's original opening was longer, more diffuse, included some questionable supporting details, and lacked a clear core statement:

> They live among us but their presence is ignored. One might live next door, another might be a close friend, another might be a member of your own family. While they do not appear to be handicapped or deformed, they face some of the same social and physical barriers as the disabled. However, their "handicap" is only noticeable under close scrutiny. They might request a seat at the end of a table or appear awkward as they struggle to dial a telephone or open a door or use a pencil sharpener. They often contort their bodies as they endeavor to write. They appear to stumble through their daily lives as if they had two left feet when in fact they are just left-handed individuals trying to cope in a right-handed world. The entire existence of these twenty-two million Americans (approximately 10 percent of the population) works against the grain of the rest of society. These persons write at desks intended for right-handed people, they drive on the right side of the road in cars with ignitions, stickshifts, and virtually all controls on the right side. They struggle with television dials located on the right side of the screen, they listen to records that play on turntables that have their arms on the right side, and, perhaps most noticeable to the public, they continually have smudges on their hand from trying to write from left to right—an action completely unnatural to them. In short, they are subject to a form of discrimination so subtle that it is virtually unnoticed by anyone who is not left-handed.

In the revised version, paragraphs take shape, repetition disappears, and a clear core statement appears.

In paragraph 3, one of the rhetorical operations, definition, is used effectively to set the problems of left-handers in historical and cultural contexts, with a divided comparison pattern as a framework.

1

The Left-handed Student in a Right-handed World

They live among us. One might live next door,   1
another might be a close friend, another a family
member. While they do not appear to be handicapped or
deformed, they face some of the same social and physical
barriers as disabled individuals do. Although their
"handicap" is only noticeable in certain situations, it
is none the less real. And despite the fact that
twenty-two million Americans--nearly ten percent of the
population--suffer from this "handicap," they are
ignored.

These forgotten people are left-handers living in a   2
world designed for right-handers. Left-handed people
contort their bodies at desks intended for the right-
handed. They struggle with scissor handles, telephone
dials, door handles, and pencil sharpeners, all shaped for
right-handers. They eat at tables with utensils
set for right-handers and dread a seat other than at the
end of the table. In sum, left-handers seem to work
against the grain of the rest of society in much of their
daily life as they try to cope in a right-handed world,
especially as students coping with a writing system
designed for right-handed people.

The bias under which "lefties" or "southpaws"   3
suffer is not common to our modern society alone. Its
long history is documented by the very language we use, by
etymology. For example, the word left has long carried
with it connotations of being wrong at best, bad or evil

Notice that *homophonous* is neatly defined by the context rather than explicit statement and that the parenthetical citation at the end of paragraph 3 is only a page number because Linksz's name is introduced in the text.

at worst. The Latin word for left is sinister, which to us today means "evil." Lyft, the Anglo-Saxon word for left, meant "weak." The French word for left is gauche, which in English is attached to people who are socially inept. In China, yin is the word for left and is associated with darkness, emotion, and femininity. Right, on the other hand, connotes goodness and correctness. In China, yang, the word for right, is likened to light, reason, and masculinity. Droit for the French means "straight" or "righteous"; the English borrowing adroit means "dexterous." For Germans, Recht means "law," and in English right means "correct." Furthermore, although write comes from a different etymological source than right, it is a homophone of right. Dr. Arthur Linksz, a leading American ophthalmologist who has researched left-handedness extensively, believes that the homophonous correlation between right and write may lead to much of the anxiety experts believe left-handed people experience because they must " 'rit' with a hand that is not 'rit' " (183).

And this brings us to a major problem that left-handers face in a right-handed society, a writing system that favors the right hand.[1] Before we look at that problem though, it is interesting to note that not all cultures have adopted writing systems that discriminate against left-handers. The Egyptians, for instance, wrote their hieroglyphics in vertical and horizontal lines from left to right and right to left. The ancient Greeks, perhaps recognizing the presence

4

Paragraph 5 starts with a nicely balanced sentence that leads into the basic problem left-handers face that the following pages will discuss.

Paragraphs 6 and 7 shift from the writing system to an analysis of the problems left-handers have with the system.

of sinistrals (left-handed individuals) in their society,
began their handwriting on the left, directed it toward
the right, and then returned on the next line beginning on
the right side--much like a farmer plowing a field. These
two examples of alternative writing styles are not meant
to suggest that a restructuring of our entire writing
system is a viable solution to left-handers' writing
problems, but they do illustrate the point that
left-handers' needs have been met at other times and in
other cultures.

   Most problems that left-handers face in our society   5
are more inconvenient than painful, more superficial than
profound.   But because writing is so basic and is done so
often, it looms importantly, particularly in the early
years in school. (Typing can relieve the problem in later
years because a typewriter does not discriminate on the
basis of handedness.) Left-handed children must learn to
form their letters and direct them across the page
according to a system specifically attuned to the right-
hander.

   Left-handers realize immediately their disadvantage   6
when they begin to write because unlike right-handers, who
naturally follow the easier path of pushing their pencils
and uncovering what they write as they write, left-handed
students must learn to push their pencils and pens rather
than pull them.   Moreover, unless they contort their hand
and arm, they cover what they write as they write--and
smudge it in the bargain.   They also quickly discover that
they lose time when they write at the right-handed desks
typically provided, and this disadvantage never disappears

Paragraph 7 includes a long quotation that is a good choice; it dramatizes the plight of left-handers. Notice the format of the quote. Because it is more than four lines, it is set off from the running text without quotation marks. Also, because the quotation is only one paragraph, it is not indented. If two or more paragraphs were quoted, each would be indented an additional three spaces. Notice too that the offset quotation is indented ten spaces from the left margin and that its parenthetical documentation comes after the period ending the quote.

Paragraph 8 is a transition paragraph that connects the anxiety spotlighted in paragraph 7 with the problems and solutions to be developed in the ensuing paragraphs. The paragraph sets up the comparison that will reveal the problems and solutions: the divergent viewpoints of experts.

Paragraphs 9 and 10 present advocacy of coercing left-handers to use their right hands. Dr. Linksz is the primary expert used in support of this view. Notice the reference to earlier mention of him that aids coherence, the proper use of double and single quotation marks, and the use of the ellipsis mark to indicate an omission from a quotation. Since the quotations are short, they flow with the running text of the paper. Notice too that Michael's commentary leads into and out of the quotations; the quotations are not simply "dropped in cold."

M. Burke 4

for the taking of tests where typewriters cannot be used.
A "solution" left-handers often resort to is to use
their laps as desks.

Because left-handed children appear awkward and   7
uncoordinated when they write, they are sometimes labeled
"slow learners" when they really are only slow writers.
Many left-handers face criticism for their struggle and
experience a sense of inadequacy. One student describes
this anxiety graphically:

> With clenched teeth and perspiring palms we
> hunched over our desks, holding our pencils with
> a death grip, and generally looking—and
> feeling—totally miserable whenever we had to
> write anything. Resigning ourselves to poor
> grades and extra homework in handwriting, we
> truly believed within ourselves that it was
> entirely our fault that our penmanship was so
> atrocious. (Harrison 385)

Experts stand on both sides of the fence on the   8
seriousness of the anxiety left-handers experience, the
learning problems they face, and how to deal with them.

Some experts believe that sinistrals should   9
experience little anxiety now because they are emancipated
from the dark days of "hand slapping" and "tying the
hands behind the back," techniques employed in the past
to discourage the use of the left hand. It should be
noted, however, that the word past is relative in this
context. Although these barbarous techniques died out
primarily in the 1930s, reports of adults coercing
students to use their right hands have appeared within the

Paragraphs 11 and 12 turn to a contrasting viewpoint: the case for a positive influence on left-handers and practical advice to teach left-handed students to cope with a right-handed writing system. Again, paralleling the previous method, one expert, Ms. Harrison, provides the primary testimony in support of the view discussed.

Notice the continuing coherence of the writing. Careful connections are made between sentences in a pattern of first old, then new information that guides readers through the material (e.g., in paragraph 11, "experts" in the first sentence, "one of these experts" in the second sentence, "an elementary schoolteacher" in the third sentence picking

past decade (Roper 2:1). Any coercion, as might be
expected, creates anxiety.

Arthur Linksz, whose theory about homophonous write
and right was mentioned earlier, is one of the experts who
believe that the problems created for left-handers by
their remaining confirmed in their left-handedness are
worse than any anxiety created by coercing them to adopt
right-handed ways. Linksz strongly advocates a totally
right-handed world. "If the right hand is the 'right'
hand, the 'better' hand, the 'dexterous' hand, why not use
it for writing? If coercion is necessary, why not all the
way?" (185). He does not believe that special techniques
should be employed to ease the burden of left-handed
children as they learn to write. Indeed, he believes that
"as far as the training of left-handed children is
concerned, . . . every reasonable effort is justified in
trying to redirect them to write with the right hand"
(180). Linksz advocates this redirection because he
believes that allowing left-handers to function as
left-handers in a right-handed society creates a form of
"artificial schizophrenia" that can only be detrimental
to children, leaving them confused and frustrated.

Other experts believe that not enough has been done
to relieve the anxieties of left-handed students and to
remove barriers to their learning that can only occur with
these anxieties. Stephanie Harrison is one of these
experts. An elementary schoolteacher who has written
perceptively on the problems of left-handers, Harrison
maintains that simply doing away with the coercive hand
manipulation that occurred in the past is insufficient.

10

11

up on "Stephanie Harrison" in the second, "its harmful effects" in the fourth sentence referring back to "coercive hand manipulation" in the third, and so on). Connections are equally good between paragraphs. The notion of teaching left-handed students at the end of paragraph 11 connects with the first sentence of paragraph 12. "Another of Harrison's suggestions" at the start of paragraph 13 connects with the start of the last sentence of paragraph 12: "She suggests some techniques."

Notice too the care taken to achieve effective emphasis; for example, the last words in the sentences and the paragraphs end them on strong notes. The numbered list of techniques in paragraph 12 is particularly effective in its clarity and care in using parallel structure, achieving both coherence and emphasis.

Paraphrase is used effectively and expertly in these paragraphs. Michael avoids stringing extensive quotations together.

M. Burke 6

Its harmful effects may be gone, but benign neglect of
left-handers is at best a neutral influence. She states
that seldom these days "is a left-handed child forced by
parents or teachers to write with his or her right hand.
But just as seldom is he or she taught to write with his
or her left hand" (116). Positive steps are needed to
teach left-handed students to use their left hands
effectively.

Harrison points out that while it may seem   **12**
insignificant to have only three inadequately trained
left-handed children in a class of thirty, the problem
looms much larger when we consider that the twenty-two
million Americans who are left-handed have nearly all been
deprived of adequate handwriting instruction. She
suggests some techniques to eliminate some problems
left-handed children face: (1) Place left-handed children
so they do not feel isolated, (2) provide left-handed
children with a parent or an older student as a model so
they will learn to write without feeling inferior, (3)
give left-handed children more and different writing
exercises than their right-handed classmates (for example,
blackboard writing encourages the use of the entire left
arm, a practice sinistrals tend to shun), (4) teach
left-handed students to hold their pencils and papers
comfortably, and (5) discourage left-handed students from
indulging in loops and flourishes when they write (117).

Another of Harrison's suggestions contradicts the way   **13**
left-handed students have traditionally been taught, that
is, to slant their letters to the right as right-handers
naturally do. She encourages left-handers to slant their

"Finally" at the end of paragraph 13 signals the close of this section of the paper. "Some experts" at the start of paragraph 14 continues the pattern established earlier and alerts the reader that another perspective will be given. Readers were not forewarned of a neutral perspective in the earlier cover sentences about experts on both sides of the fence, but since the biased approaches to left-handers' problems and solutions to those problems have been presented, it is logical to move to a neutral perspective, one that describes characteristics of left-handers rather than takes sides.

Paragraph 14 presents two important points from a 1929 study. The last sentence in the paragraph prepares the reader for further development of these points.

Paragraph 15 mentions recent studies in general that support one of Haefner's points, rephrasing it so the reader will be clear on which point is addressed. Again, following the pattern set up, authoritative evidence is presented. In this way the paper continues to achieve coherence on a larger level. Good attempts to connect sentences continue too: "One of these studies" in the second sentence of paragraph 15 is followed by "Other studies" at the start of the third sentence.

M. Burke 7

letters to the left since a left-handed slant does not
hinder the intelligibility of the handwriting but does
eliminate much of the constraint left-handers feel.
Finally, she believes that a model cursive alphabet should
be given to left-handed children so that they would have a
guide demonstrating this backslanted handwriting.

Some experts simply concentrate on describing the   **14**
characteristics of left-handed students as a group and the
disabilities or abilities they reveal, leaving to others
the "oughts" and "shoulds" that depend on their descriptions. For example, in his study published in
1929, The Educational Significance of Left-Handedness,
Ralph Haefner finds differences in physical stature
between left- and right-handers: "Right-handed children
are somewhat heavier and somewhat stronger than the
left-handed children" (79). But more to our point, he
speculates that "paragraph reading and arithmetical
computation might be of higher quality among right-handed
children as compared with left-handed individuals" (78).
However, despite his evidence to the contrary, Haefner
concludes that "in dealing with questions of mental
status . . . handedness is no better criterion to use
than would be color of hair or shape of face" (78).
Haefner may be right on both counts.

A 1982 Newsweek article reported on recent studies   **15**
that support Haefner's notion that poor reading skills are
more characteristic of left-handers than right-handers.
One of these studies, done by the Harvard Medical School
neurologist Dr. Norman Geschwind, points to left-handers
having twelve times as many learning disabilities as their

Paragraph 15 adds concrete details about dyslexia, a disability that may be unfamiliar to the reader, and uses as an example Nelson Rockefeller, with whom most readers will be familiar. Even though three different sources are used, the information is smoothly presented.

"On the other hand" at the start of paragraph 16 provides a transition to the support that will be provided for Haefner's other point, which is restated as a reminder for readers. Concrete details provide the support for this paragraph too. Their positive nature leads naturally into paragraph 17, which focuses on some advantages left-handers enjoy. Again we see one of the rhetorical operations, comparison, used effectively.

right-handed counterparts (55). Other studies point to
one of these, dyslexia, a complex disability in the use of
language, as affecting more left-handers than right-
handers (56). Dyslexics, among other problems they have,
may not be able to read or write without reversing
letters--b becomes d and dog becomes god. Researchers
often attribute the high rate of dyslexia among left-
handers to their being forced to use their right hands
(Brody AA8). A famous person who stands out as a clear
example of exposure to left-handed manipulative coercion
at least partially causing dyslexia is Nelson Rockefeller,
philanthropist, long-time governor of New York, and
forty-first vice-president of the United States. As a
child, among other restraining methods, Rockefeller's left
hand was pinned to his shirt to prevent him from using
it. Throughout his life he suffered and had to overcome
severe reading difficulties (Mastrangelo C3).

On the other hand, also supporting Haefner's
conclusions, recent studies point to left-handers'
intelligence being equal to right-handers' intelligence
and the possibility of their being more intelligent. The
Georgia Governor's Honor Program for Adolescents has at
least twelve percent more left-handers than right-handers,
and the Creative Problem-Solving Institute sponsored by
the Creative Education Foundation has over fifty percent
more left-handers than right-handers (Aliotti 36). Also,
Mensa, the famed organization of "geniuses," has a
greater percentage of left-handers than does the normal
population (Aliotti 36). And we all are familiar with the
achievements of some famous southpaws--Alexander the

Michael's original ending was as follows:

While the educational disadvantages of being left-handed are of great importance, the difficulties involved in the daily life of the left-handed student cannot be forgotten. The list of tasks that the right-handed individual finds no problem in performing can pose endless frustration for the left-handed person. Writing at a classroom desk is an easy accomplishment—if you are right-handed. If you are not, you probably find it easier to write on your lap rather than reach across your body to use the desk top. This is a time-consuming movement that poses serious problems during a test. Pencil sharpeners are also a challenge to the leftie. They are designed so that the right hand will turn the handle, but for the left-handed person, the right hand is usually weaker and less coordinated, making it next to impossible to sharpen the pencil. As a result, most lefties would rather have a shabby pencil than a confrontation with the pencil sharpener.

These problems do not disappear when the left-handed student goes home. He drives a car with all the controls positioned for the convenience of the right-hander—not a leftie. He struggles with kitchen utensils, scissors, telephones, and other modern "conveniences."

Left-handedness is not going to go away. It is not a bad habit; it is a trait. Therefore, every reasonable effort should be made to accommodate the left-handed individual. Left-handed children should be taught how to adapt to a right-handed world, and the right-handed world should accept left-handedness not as a deficiency but as a difference.

Michael revised his ending several times, each time reorganizing his ideas and attempting to unify them within the report as a whole. He also removed repetition and wordiness, excessive nominalizations, and the indefinite *you* to conform to the style and tone of the report. Many problems mentioned at the end were also discussed in the beginning, and nothing new was offered except for an analysis of the difficulty of sharpening pencils (which seems unwarranted in the context). Because these points remained undeveloped and are not the focus of the paper, their omission strengthens the ending.

The two clichés that appear, "out in left field" and "two left feet," were moved from early in the original draft; they appropriately bring some of the tone of the beginning to the end. No long summary of the material is needed; the brief phrases are sufficient. The last sentence is reasonable and a logical outcome of the information presented.

M. Burke 9

Great, Charlemagne, Napoleon, Michelangelo, Harry Truman,
and Albert Einstein—men who have formed empires, produced
masterpieces of art, led nations, and drastically advanced
scientific knowledge.

Left-handers, then, not only have disadvantages and
problems. Some advantages accrue to them from their
hemisphere dominance, advantages some right-handers would
like to enjoy, especially in the field of athletics.
Being a southpaw is a distinct advantage in baseball.
Witness Babe Ruth, Sandy Koufax, Lou Gehrig, Mickey
Mantle, Carl Hubbell (the first screwball pitcher), and
Ted Williams (last to hit over .400). It may be an
advantage in tennis; both Jimmy Connors and John McEnroe
are left-handers. And in a more serious vein, recent
studies reveal that left-handed individuals have a greater
recovery of speech function after brain injury (Brody
AA8).

17

With history as evidence, we can see that left-
handedness is not a bad habit that will disappear if
ignored. Even though many people, left-handers as well as
right-handers, are led to believe that left-handers,
especially young children, are "out in left field" or
typically act as if at the ends of their arms they have
"two left feet," every effort should be made to
accommodate them. Left-handed children should be taught
how to adapt to a right-handed world, and the right-handed
world should accept left-handedness not as a deficiency
but as a difference.

18

This content note follows MLA format. The content note is needed because this type of comment or explanation is too large to be accommodated within the text as parenthetical documentation.

M. Burke 10

Note

[1]This is not to say that there are not other and
serious problems. For example, as reported by William H.
Calvin and George A. Ojemann in Inside the Brain (71–72,
193), it has long been known that stuttering and left-
handedness show a close correlation, a tendency that
occurs with bilateral language representation. But this
complex matter would be the subject of another and more
technical paper.

The list of works cited and another of works consulted follow MLA form. Notice the Haefner entry under "Works Cited." No example for this type of entry was included in Chapter 18. *The Educational Significance of Left Handedness* is a book in a series. Therefore, the series name is included after the book title but neither underlined nor enclosed in quotation marks; the number 360 is the number in the series.

"Works Consulted" indicates that Michael read the material in the entries but, rather than quoting it, synthesized it for his general comments.

M. Burke 11

Works Cited

Aliotti, Nicholas C. "Intelligence, Handedness, and
     Cerebral Hemispheric Preference in Gifted
     Adolescents." Gifted Child Quarterly 25.1 (1981):
     36–40.

Brody, Jane E. " 'Diversity' of Woes." Arizona
     Republic [Phoenix] 24 Apr. 1983: AA8.

Calvin, William H., and George A. Ojemann. Inside the
     Brain. New York: New American Library, 1980.

"Dealing with Dyslexia." Newsweek 22 Mar. 1982: 55–56.

Haefner, Ralph. The Educational Significance of Left
     Handedness. Contributions to Education 360. New
     York: Teachers College, Columbia University, 1929.

Harrison, Stephanie. "Open Letter from a Left–handed
     Teacher: Some Sinistral Ideas on the Teaching of
     Handwriting." Teaching Exceptional Children 13.3
     (1981): 116–120.

Linksz, Arthur. On Writing, Reading, and Dyslexia. New
     York: Grune & Stratton, 1973.

Mastrangelo, Joseph P. "Sticking Up for Lefty's
     Rights." Washington Post 13 Aug. 1977: C3.

Roper, Carole. "Lefties Cope in a 'Right' World."
     Richmond Times–Dispatch 30 Oct. 1977, sec. 2: 1.

Works Consulted

Christian, Susan. "A Southpaw Who's Pushing for a 'Bill
     of Lefts.' " Los Angeles Herald Examiner 13 Aug.
     1981: B2.

Chrones, Angela. "Lefties, Speak Up for Your Rights!"
     Providence Journal 29 Jan. 1978: C2.

M. Burke 12

DeKay, James T. Letter. New York Times 1 Feb. 1981,

    Sunday magazine supplement: 78.

Edwards, Betty. Drawing on the Right Side of the Brain.

    Los Angeles: J. P. Tarcher, 1979.

Hunlein, Julia Heil. Preferential Manipulation in

    Children. Baltimore: Psychological Laboratory of

    Johns Hopkins University, 1930.

Held, Julie. "Lefties Left Out in a World Ruled by Right

    Hands." Birmingham News 8 Aug. 1977: C4.

Jones, W. Franklin. A Study of Handedness. Vermillion:

    UP of South Dakota, 1918.

McGowan, Dru. "Research Yields Few Facts, Much Dispute

    Over 'Lefties.' " Montgomery Advertiser 5 Aug. 1977,

    sec. 2: 4.

Needham, Rodney, ed. Right and Left: Essays on Dual

    Symbolic Classification. Chicago: UP of Chicago,

    1973.

Sanford, Robert. "Now the Lefts Want Their Rights."

    St. Louis Post-Dispatch 27 Nov. 1977: D6.

Schwartz, Harvey A. "Cerebral Organization, Handedness,

    and Education." Academic Therapy 16.1 (1980): 95-

    100.

Shenk, Mary Nic. "Finally Some Rights for Lefties."

    St. Petersburg Times 25 Aug. 1977: B2.

Warner, Edwin. "The Champ Who Never Made It." Time 5

    Feb. 1979: 20.

A Model Technical Report

Marie Bender's technical report on the following pages is a successful student investigative effort based on case-study materials. Like Michael Burke's library paper, it has an aesthetically pleasing appearance. It is neatly typed, double-spaced, with headings clearly set off from the running text and with adequate margins. All necessary parts are included: letter of transmittal; title page; table of contents; list of figures; abstract; a fully developed introduction with background, statement of problem, and plan of development; middle development sections; conclusions and recommendations; and references. Lowercase Roman numerals mark the introductory pages at the bottom; notice that the title page remains unmarked and that the letter of transmittal does not count as a page of the report because it lies outside the report itself. Consecutive Arabic numerals in the upper right-hand corner mark successive pages in the report proper, except page 1, which remains unnumbered.

A letter of transmittal covering a technical report briefly introduces the reader to the report. Contemporary business practice favors the full-block style used in Marie's letter, with elements aligned at the left margin, no paragraph indentation, and vertical spacing as shown. The first paragraph states submittal of the report and the authorization for the report. The second paragraph mentions the subject and purpose of the report and some special features of the report. The third paragraph includes acknowledgment of help, the fourth paragraph an offer for help and a pitch for a future assignment.

These features are typical in a letter of transmittal. Statements of transmittal or submittal, authorization or occasion for the report, and subject and purpose are necessary. The other elements may or may not be included and others may be added or substituted, such as background material, a summary of the report, recognition of an objective not met, and conclusions and recommendations. This letter of transmittal is appropriate for the report.

BENDER RESEARCH COMPANY
1282 South Marshall
Phoenix, Arizona 85200

July 21, 1985

Mr. A. J. Sayres, Executive Vice President
Future Motors Corporation
700 Fifth Avenue
New York, New York 10022

Dear Mr. Sayres:

Enclosed is the report of the three-month investigation
that you requested Bender Research to conduct at the
Future Motors carburetor plant in Hopeless, Utah.

The investigative team and I gathered information from
files, interviewed workers, observed groups, and conducted
several experiments in order to determine the causes of
poor workmanship. The data collected were recorded and
are reported objectively. Only the team's conclusions are
subjective.

I hope you will find the report useful for improving the
quality of workmanship at the Hopeless plant. I truly
appreciated the opportunity to conduct the investigation
and want to acknowledge the cooperation of Hopeless plant
employees in its timely completion.

Please call me if you have further questions or if I can
help you in any way in the future.

Sincerely,

G. Marie Bender

G. Marie Bender
President

GMB:dg

Encl

The Problem of Poor Workmanship

at the Hopeless Plant

Prepared by

G. Marie Bender, President

Bender Research Company

1282 South Marshall, Phoenix, Arizona 85200

July 21, 1985

The table of contents in the technical report functions much as the outline for the library paper. It shows the extent and nature of the topics covered and the organization and relationship of the sections within the report. It also, of course, indicates page numbers of the parts of the report. The titles of the preliminary and ancillary parts and the main headings appear in a combination of capitals and lowercase letters. Divisions are shown to be subordinate by indentation. All the headings and subheadings appear in the report, as they should. Often subheadings appear in the report that do not appear in the table of contents, but every entry in the table of contents must appear in the report.

Contents

Because the report includes only figures, the heading in the table of contents reads simply "List of Figures." If both figures and tables had been included, the heading "List of Illustrations" would have been used with subheadings "List of Tables" and "List of Figures."

List of Figures

iii

As we said in Chapter 17, there are two kinds of abstracts, informative and descriptive, although most abstracts combine elements of each to some degree. This abstract is primarily informative. It briefly restates the key information in the complete report. It gives a little background, the findings of the study, and recommendations. It can stand, as should be true of any abstract, as a substitute for the entire report for some readers.

Abstract

Future Motors conducted a study to determine why an exceptional number of faulty carburetors were being produced at its Hopeless plant. FM concluded that the difficulty lay with personnel and sent an investigative team to determine what the personnel problems were and what could be done to remedy the problems.

After observations and interviews, the team isolated three factors for further study: monotony of assembly-line jobs, extra breaks in Stan Softtouch's group, and an exceptionally high rate of production in Ignatz Hasen-fratz's group. Several experiments to curb monotony were performed: lighting was increased, the work area was repainted, jobs were rotated, and extra breaks were allowed. Increased lighting had no long-term effect on workmanship. Repainting the work area aqua, however, increased both quality of work and production rate. Job rotation and extra breaks increased quality of work but not quantity. From observations of the Hasenfratz group, the team decided that Hasenfratz was pushing his men too hard in hopes of a promotion.

The experiments and observations performed led the team to recommend painting the work area aqua, rotating men between tasks, giving the men two extra breaks per day, and replacing Hasenfratz as a group supervisor.

The introduction to a technical report should answer three basic questions: What am I doing? Why am I doing it? How am I doing it? The answer to the first question leads to a statement of the problem or the purpose; the answer to the second introduces the background leading to the particular problem and clarifies its importance or the particular purpose. The combination of these two answers locates the subject within an area of investigation or study and sets its limits or scope. The answer to the third question is the plan of the report.

These elements are all present in Marie's introduction to her investigative report; they add up to the meaning of the report. The reader's first question is always, Why should I read this? Marie's introduction answers that question clearly.

The "Background" section depends on the rhetorical operations narration and induction, the "Problem" section on definition, and the "Plan of Development" section on narration.

Marie's draft of the introduction was not nearly as well-organized and well-written as her final copy:

> In 1981 the comptroller for Future Motors reported the fact that the cost to Future Motors for repairing faulty carburetors in vehicles still under warranty had risen 48 percent from the preceding year. Knowing there had been no change in accounting procedures, he began to delve into company records to make a determination what the problem was. Company files showed that an exceptional number of these carburetors, returned for repairs, had been produced by one of FM's subsidiary plants in Hopeless, Arizona. These faulty carburetors accounted for 94 percent of the increased warranty expenditures.
>
> Various theories were developed to explain the cause of the situation. One suggested that the plant could be receiving defective parts. After consulting the engineers, it was found that the parts had been checked and had met required specifications. Another possibility could be poor machinery. Machinery experts were sent to the plant and found the equipment to be in excellent condition. This theory, then, was also discarded.
>
> It seemed the problem of poor workmanship could center on only one point. The difficulty had to lie with personnel: Whether the answer would be inadequate supervision, poor morale, objectionable working conditions, or something else was yet to be determined.
>
> Future Motors wanted someone to investigate this "people problem" objectively and offer suggestions for improvement. The author of this report, a behavioral scientist not associated in any way with the company, was selected for the undertaking.

Notice particularly the difference the subheadings make in enhancing the readability of her final version. Notice also that she reduces wordiness and improves her style in subtle other ways. For example, "Future Motors reported the fact that the cost" becomes "Future Motors reported that the cost," and "he began to delve" becomes "he

Introduction

This report presents the results of a study that analyzed the personnel problems involved in excess production of faulty carburetors at the Future Motors plant at Hopeless, Arizona.

Background

In 1981 the comptroller for Future Motors reported that the cost to Future Motors for repairing faulty carburetors in vehicles still under warranty had risen 48% from the preceding year. Knowing that there had been no change in accounting procedures, he delved into company records to determine what the problem was. Company files showed that an exceptional number of carburetors returned for repairs had been produced in one of FM's subsidiary plants in Hopeless, Arizona. These faulty carburetors accounted for 94% of the company's increased warranty expense.

Various theories were developed to explain the cause of the situation. One theory suggested that the plant could be receiving defective parts. However, when company investigators consulted the engineers, they found that the parts had been checked and had met required specifications. Another theory centered on the possibility of poor machinery. Machinery experts were sent to the plant and found the equipment to be in excellent working order. Both theories were discarded.

At this point a third theory was advanced, that the problem of poor workmanship could lie only with the personnel. Future Motors decided to call in an outside investigator to study this "people problem" objectively delved." "After consulting the engineers, they found" becomes "However, when company investigators consulted the engineers, they found." Although this last change adds words, the revised structure is clearer because it puts the agent of the action into the subject.

The discussion of a technical report is the longest section and varies in form more than introductions and conclusions. The aim, the kind of report, and the content largely determine the form. In this investigative report the discussion is divided into three sections, "Isolating Factors," "Experiments for Improvement," and "Observation of Hasenfratz Group," that serve as segments of the bridge that reaches from the questions raised by the problem to the answers given in the conclusion.

"Isolating Factors," the first section of the discussion, has its own introduction, or overview, that reveals the procedures used (gathering data from company files, interviews, etc.) and what facts the procedures were intended to uncover (the men's attitude toward the job and working conditions). The overview also spells out the classification system that controls the subsections to follow. Employees are grouped according to their status into three categories: top management, group supervisors, and assembly-line workers.

2

and offer suggestions for improvement. G. Marie Bender,
the author of this report, a behavioral scientist not
associated in any way with the company, was selected,
along with a team of five assistants from Bender Research,
to conduct the investigation.

Problem

The investigative team focused on the problem of poor
workmanship in terms of the personnel producing the
carburetors.   The question was whether poor workmanship
was the result of inadequate supervision, poor morale,
objectionable working conditions, or something else yet to
be determined.

Plan of Development

The report that follows will first discuss the
isolating factors the team observed as possibly contributing to poor workmanship: the three different
employee levels at Hopeless, the production output of the
five shop groups, attendance, and performance records.
Next it discusses the experiments with lighting, colors,
job rotation, and work breaks that were performed as
possible indicators of a solution to the problem. The
report continues with a summary of the Hasenfratz group,
followed by conclusions and recommendations.

Isolating Factors

The investigative team first examined the people or
group of people with whom the difficulty might rest. For
study purposes the people were divided into three
different levels of employee status. At the Hopeless
plant, the first level was top management, which consisted

In a pattern that coherently follows the overview of the whole section, each employee level is treated in turn by describing the specific procedures used for that employee level and the results obtained.

Notice that throughout "Isolating Factors," word choice is neutral, maintaining an appropriately objective tone. Cohesion is created within each subsection by sentences moving from old to new information. Transition words and phrases such as "The team, however," "with these facts," and "for example" are used as needed. There is no need for transitions between subsections because the headings provide demarcation and information about the group to be treated next.

3

of a marketing executive, the chief accountant, and the
manager. It also included the immediate staffs supervised
by these managers. The second level consisted of five
group supervisors. The third or bottom line of employee
status consisted of the assembly-line workers.

The team checked the company's personnel files and
gathered as much information on top management as possible
for data that would indicate skill and job satisfaction.
The supervisors were studied next. The team then checked
the production records of various groups and noted any
obvious variations among them. Next they interviewed each
supervisor and asked his opinion about the job. The
supervisors also answered a job satisfaction questionnaire. From the assembly-line workers a random selection
of men were interviewed. The team hoped to learn the
men's attitudes toward the job and working conditions.
Any plant records that pertained directly to this group
were studied.

Top Management

Since the team was studying the manufacture of faulty
carburetors, it seemed improbable that the difficulty lay
with the top managers, who were not directly involved in
the actual assembly process. The team, however, judged it
wise to make relatively sure nothing was troubling the
group because if these managers were incompetent or
dissatisfied with their jobs, their problems could filter
down to those more directly involved with production.

The team first investigated the top managers' job
satisfaction and absentee rate. Personnel records showed
that the three department heads all had college degrees

4

fitting them for their positions. This match of training
to job led the team to assume that the managers were
genuinely interested in their respective fields. Past
data on the executives showed they had participated in a
job satisfaction study conducted by Bartlett and Bradley
(a motivational research team) in 1979. They were 89%,
91%, and 94% satisfied with their jobs according to this
study. Personnel records also showed that the two men and
one woman each had received a merit raise during the past
year. Apparently FM felt the managers were skilled and
doing an excellent job. Absenteeism was less than 1% of
total work time for these top managers. With these facts,
the team felt fairly certain the difficulty lay elsewhere
and so moved on to study the next level of employees.

Group Supervisors

The five group supervisors were the next group to be
investigated. Each headed a group of twenty men and his
own assembly line. One line could completely assemble a
carburetor.

The team first attempted to determine job satisfaction. Each man was interviewed by a member of the
investigation team. He was then given the same questionnaire that Bartlett and Bradley had used in their
previously mentioned study. Each man scored at least 85%
satisfaction with his job. All the supervisors believed
they had been treated fairly by the company. For
example, they all felt they were receiving good salaries
and excellent vacation benefits (every supervisor was
entitled to four weeks paid vacation) and that the company
supported them when problems arose with subordinates.

5

They also felt there was room for advancement in FM
Corporation. Though they could not be promoted further at
Hopeless plant, they believed that there was always the
possibility that a good supervisor could be transferred to
a higher position in another FM factory.

On the negative side, four of the supervisors felt
that the fifth, Stanley Softtouch, was far too lenient
with his men concerning breaks. He often gave his men two
extra short breaks during the day. This leniency created
difficulties for the other two supervisors, whose men felt
they should not have to obey the rules when Stan's group
ignored them. Also, one supervisor, Ignatz Hasenfratz,
said that although he liked his job, he did not like
living in the small town of Hopeless.

Having learned as much as they could from the
supervisors themselves, the team checked the production
records of the five groups for any pertinent information
they might hold. Two facts about the five groups stood
out. The production of four of the groups was nearly
equal, but the group under Ignatz Hasenfratz produced
nearly 7% more per day than did the other four. Yet
although there was more output from this group, the
workmanship was as poor as or poorer than that found in
the other groups, according to the quality control
engineers. The output of the group under Stanley
Softtouch had been rated of slightly higher quality than
that of the four other groups, although production was no
higher. These being the only outstanding facts the files
revealed, the team moved on to investigate the next
group.

6

Assembly—Line Workers

To investigate the assembly—line workers, the team
checked time cards and found absenteeism extremely high.
It was equal to nearly 5% of the total work days in a
year.

The only other records that gave any information
about the assembly—line workers were those kept by the
small supplies office, located one quarter mile from the
assembly line. When an employee's tool broke, he came to
the small supplies office to obtain a new one. In order
to receive a new tool he had to sign a slip showing it had
been given to him. Nearly 10% of the assembly—line
workers signed for new tools every day, compared to an
average of 5% in other FM subsidiary plants. Since the
tools had been checked by the supplies office and had met
specifications, there seemed to be no reason for these
tools, which FM purchased from one supplier, not to hold
up at Hopeless as well as those in other factories.

Since performance records could not possibly be kept
on each of the 100 assembly—line workers, these two
sources proved to reveal the only written information of
any value to the investigative team.

The team decided to draw 20 names at random from the
list of assembly—line workers to be interviewed. The only
question asked the workers was, "What is your opinion of
your job?" Every worker said that, above all, the job was
monotonous. Some felt that the work was unchallenging
and the surrounding area depressing. All workers except
those in Stanley Softtouch's group commented on the
unfairness of his workers taking extra breaks.

7

Experiments for Improvement

The investigative team believed that the problem of greatest importance was to find a way to improve the monotonous and unchallenging jobs of the assembly—line workers since these factors affected the largest number of people. In order to attack this problem knowledgeably, the team decided to observe the assembly—line workers for three days.

During these three days, the team made some important observations. One was that the men in Stanley Softtouch's group did, in fact, take extra breaks. Their production, however, never fell below that of the other groups. A second observation was that at least one person walked to the supply office every hour to get a new tool because his old one had broken. The time elapsed from the start of the journey to the supply office, which was one quarter mile away, until the return was approximately 50 minutes. When one of the investigators made the same trip, she walked at a steady, though not fast, pace, and returned to the plant with the new tool in 25 minutes. The team's conclusion was that the walk to the supply office likely provided a nice "break" for the workers and that, although they could not document any occurrence, it seemed likely that employees were damaging their tools to take advantage of this break.

The team decided to see if a change in the working atmosphere would improve the quality and perhaps rate of production. Two changes suggested were lighting and color of paint since both could possibly affect employee morale, hence the quantity and quality of production.

"Experiments for Improvement," the second discussion section, like "Isolating Factors" has its own introduction, or overview, for the subsections that discuss experiments with lighting, colors, job rotation, and breaks. This overview, too, reveals procedures (observation of the assembly-line workers and experimenting with changes in the working atmosphere) and the facts that the procedures were intended to uncover (effect of breaks and changes in the working atmosphere on quality and rate of production). Although the subsections to be covered are not as explicit as those for "Isolating Factors," and such explicitness is not always possible, they are suggested.

Certain parallel handling of the facts presented creates overall coherence among the subsections. Each subsection ("Lighting," "Colors," "Job Rotation," "Breaks"), following the by-now-familiar pattern, outlines the procedures for the particular experiment, the facts that the procedures were intended to uncover, and the results of each experiment. Each subsection also mentions the length of time devoted to each experiment, and each includes figures to illustrate the results mentioned in prose. As with "Isolating Factors," cohesion is maintained by sentences moving from old to new information so that each sentence logically fits its context.

8

Such effects were cited in a 1975 study by the psychol-
ogist H. E. Mann, who experimented with light and
color changes on 500 Sinclair factory employees as they
manufactured staplers. His study showed that where two
fluorescent bulbs were installed above each workbench,
production increased 3% over that with only one bulb, and
quality of workmanship increased 2%. When three bulbs
were installed, production and quality dropped close to
that with one bulb. The study also showed that workers
surrounded by dull colors such as grey and beige produced
the least staplers. Workers surrounded by bright colors
such as red and orange produced the most staplers, but had
the sloppiest workmanship. Those surrounded by cool
colors such as blue and green showed the second highest
rate of output and produced staplers of the best
quality.

Lighting

    The first experiment created a change in lighting.
The project ran two weeks. Employees were told at the
start of each week that their lighting was to be changed
but not in what way. During the first week, lighting was
increased 10%. During the second week, lighting was
returned to normal. Production was recorded during both
weeks. Quality was measured by the team disassembling a
carburetor (chosen at random) and recording the number of
faulty parts as a percentage of the total number of
assembled parts. Change in quality was checked by
comparing the percentage of faulty parts produced to
previous records of the quality control engineers.

Notice the generous white space surrounding the figures, their closeness to the point being made, and their easy readability. Notice too that the figures are not simply dropped in "cold" but explained in the running text. The comments tell readers what they should see in the illustrations.

Although description, supported by illustration, is the major rhetorical operation for presenting the data produced by the procedures, classification and analysis are used to arrange the data for graphic illustration. Line graphs, such as those used in this section, are drawn from summaries of raw or processed data.

9

As Figure 1 shows, when lighting was increased,
quality increased by 5% for the first two days of week
one. The last three days showed a steady decline so that
at the end of the week quality had dropped down to the
original level. Figure 2 shows the effect of the return
to normal lighting. During the second week when lighting
was dropped to its original level, quality increased 5%
for the first two days. During the next three days,
quality again made a steady descent until it reached its
original level by the end of the week. Output remained
virtually level throughout the two weeks.

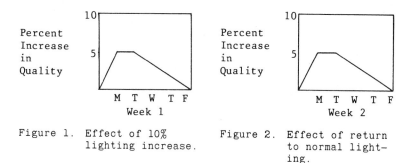

Figure 1. Effect of 10%   Figure 2. Effect of return
           lighting increase.   to normal light-
                                             ing.

At first it seemed strange that when lighting levels
were returned to their original levels, quality increased
for a time. However, the employees knew only that the
lighting had been changed and that they were being
watched. Apparently the attention they received by being
subjects of an experiment gave them (in a Hawthorne
effect[1]) the incentive to produce better quality goods for
a short time even under regular conditions. The results
of this experiment contradicted the results of the Mann

study because increased lighting did not prolong the production of better quality goods for more than a few days.

Colors

The standard color for the walls surrounding all of the five groups was gray. The floor in the assembly area was a mixture of brown and beige. All these colors had been shown in the Mann study to lower productivity, but the team decided that experimenting with wall paint in a limited number of groups would be the most feasible approach. The team chose groups 2 and 3. Their work areas were painted in cool shades, but not concurrently. Group 3's work area was painted second to serve as a check on the results found in group 2. The color experiment ran four weeks.

Group 2's walls were painted aqua. After the room was painted, quality and production were checked for two weeks. As Figures 3 and 4 (page 11) show, during the first two days quality improved 6% and the rate of production increased 2%. On the third day the increase in quality dropped to 4% and the production increase dropped to 1%. This increase remained constant throughout the rest of the experiment.

Group 3 was tested next using the same procedures, with almost identical results. The team concluded that color certainly had a constructive effect on the workers.

Job Rotation

The team next experimented with job rotation to curb monotony. This experiment lasted six weeks. Twenty men from each group were chosen, with 16 men in each group

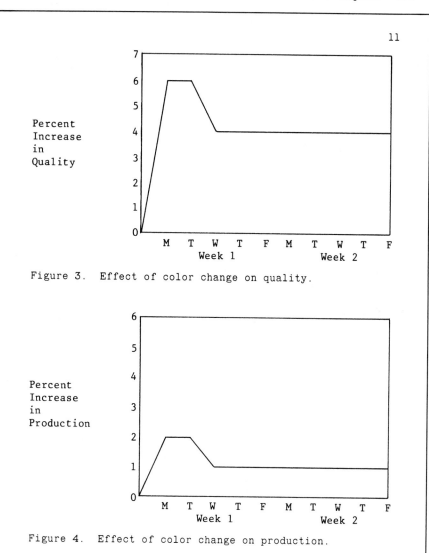

Figure 3.   Effect of color change on quality.

Figure 4.   Effect of color change on production.

12

performing a specific task and four men trained on many
jobs used as "floaters," wherever needed. During the
three-week training period each man was to learn three
more tasks. In other words, he was supposed to perform
four out of the 16 tasks. During the next three weeks the
men were rotated among the various jobs they had learned.

When the second three-week period began, the team
began recording the quality of workmanship and production
rates. As shown in Figures 5 and 6, during the first
week, there was a 3% increase in quality and a 1% increase
in production. At the end of the second week quality
increased 5% (as the men perfected new tasks), but
production dropped to its original level. This production
rate remained constant for the rest of the test period,
and the increase in quality leveled off at 4.5%.

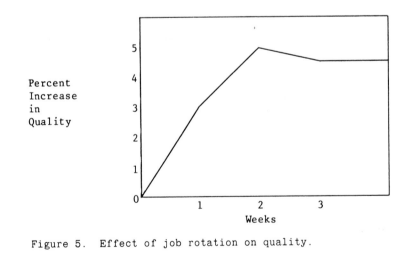

Figure 5. Effect of job rotation on quality.

13

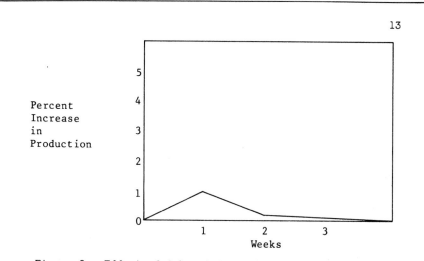

Figure 6.   Effect of job rotation on production.

        Thus job rotation, though not increasing pro-
ductivity, did increase quality. When workers were asked
why they thought quality had increased during rotation of
jobs, many said that having to be ready to perform any of
several tasks kept them more alert and forced them to pay
close attention to what they were doing.

        The supply office during this period showed fewer
requisitions for new tools. The average rate for men
coming to get new tools dropped to 5%, on par with the
rate at the other subsidiaries. (The reader will recall
that the average rate in all FM carburetor plants of men
who obtained new tools during a work day was also 5%.)

Breaks

        Breaks were the next target of experimentation. Each
plant set its own rules for breaks. Four of the five
groups under investigation followed the plant rules and

took only one midmorning break of 15 minutes and one afternoon break of the same length. Another plant rule was that only two men in one line could be gone at the same time. The "floaters" performed their tasks until the men on break returned.

Group 5, however, did not follow the plant rules. Group 5's supervisor, Stanley Softtouch, allowed his men as many as two extra short breaks. Though group 5's production was no higher than the other four groups, the team observed that its quality checks indicated better workmanship. Approximately 3% fewer faulty parts came from this group.

The team decided to run a test to see if extra breaks could improve quality in other groups as well. Fred Friendly's group was selected for this experiment. The men were given the regular 15-minute break morning and afternoon, plus a ten-minute break in the morning and afternoon.

Quality check and production rate records were kept during the two-week test period. As shown in Figure 7, quality levels increased by 1% by the end of the second day, 2% by the third day, and 3% by the fourth day. This quality level held firm for the remainder of the test time.

As shown in Figure 8, although production increased slightly the first two days, by the third day it returned to previous levels, and it remained there for the rest of the experiment.

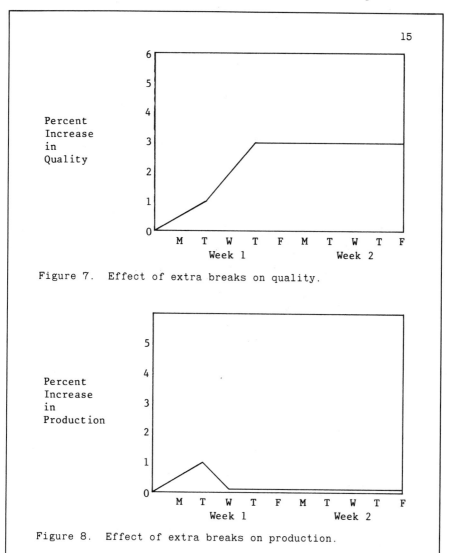

Figure 7. Effect of extra breaks on quality.

Figure 8. Effect of extra breaks on production.

"Observation of Hasenfratz Group," the final discussion section, differs in length and format from the preceding discussion sections. Because it is brief, no need exists for separate subsections. Its first paragraph, again following the pattern established, briefly states its procedures (observations and timing of the assembly belt) and what the facts of the procedures are intended to reveal (why the low quality of output from Hasenfratz's group was combined with higher production).

The section goes on to report the results of the team's observations, its interviews, and its notice of the speeded up assembly-line belt. It ends with an evaluation of group supervisor Hasenfratz.

16

Observation of Hasenfratz Group

With the facts from the experiments recorded, there remained one more area to be investigated. That was the group supervised by Ignatz Hasenfratz. The team wanted to determine why the quality of output from this group was rated lower than that from the other four, although production was rated higher. The investigation began with a one-week candid observation of this group and its supervisor. The team's initial superficial overview revealed nothing significant. Later the assembly belt was timed and found to be running slightly faster than that of the other groups. The team also noticed that Hasenfratz constantly stood over his men criticizing their work.

On the third day of the one-week observation, a significant incident was observed. Hasenfratz had been standing over one worker for some time, and when he finally turned to leave, the worker let a carburetor pass without performing his task on it. Later, when questioned about his behavior, he said that he felt Hazenfratz was always pushing the men to produce faster, yet criticized them when their increased speed resulted in flawed work. The worker felt he and the others could produce quality goods only so fast and became obstinate under Hasenfratz's constant needling. This obstinacy could contribute to faulty workmanship, such as that observed in the incident earlier in the day when the worker let the carburetor roll by untouched.

When the team interviewed other men in the group, they added that they thought Hasenfratz pushed his men in hopes of quality and production records that would get him

The ending of the report is the goal, the fulfillment of what was promised at the beginning. In an investigative report such as this one, the ending presents the answers; it solves the problem. Although some organizations recommend placing conclusions and recommendations at the beginning of the report, most follow the inductive system used in this report. Conclusions placed at the beginning suspend the readers' full understanding until they have read through the discussion sections. When the rhetorical operation induction is used and conclusions placed at the end, the readers accumulate full understanding as they read.

An ending may include a summary section, conclusions, recommendations, or predictions, or a combination of any or all of these. Sometimes, as in this report, conclusions and recommendations are combined to form the ending section. Although the word *summary* does not appear in the heading, a good share of this section is summary combined with brief concluding statements along the way. Often, recommendations are listed, as they are in this report. Since they are the ultimate purpose of the report, it is well to draw attention to them by this graphic means. If there is an order of importance to the recommendations, the most important is listed first. In this report, the recommendations are virtually of equal weight; they are ordered to correspond to the presentation of material in the report.

17

promoted to another plant in a larger city and away from
Hopeless. Their views coincided with Hasenfratz's
opinions expressed earlier.

   The team reported these facts to the plant operations
manager and discussed the speed of the assembly-line
belt. They suggested that slowing it down might help,
although the investigators believed that the main problem
lay in Hasenfratz's desire to leave Hopeless. Even if the
belt slowed down, Hasenfratz would probably still pressure
his men with constant criticism. Therefore, the company
had to decide whether he was valuable enough to be transferred to another plant, whether he should be counseled,
or whether he should be terminated.

                Conclusions and Recommendations
   At the end of the three months allotted for the
investigation, the team was asked to summarize its
findings and suggestions for improvement for both the
operations manager at the Hopeless plant and the
vice-president in charge of operations at the Detroit
office.

   The team had, at the beginning of their investigation, isolated several noticeable factors. They were as
follows:

1. One supervisor, Stanley Softtouch, gave extra breaks;
    quality of workmanship in Softtouch's group was rated
    higher than in the other four groups.
2. Another supervisor, Ignatz Hasenfratz, was highly
    dissatisfied with living in the town of Hopeless;
    production in the Hasenfratz group was 17% higher than

in the other four groups, but quality of workmanship
was poorer.

3. An exceptionally high number of men went to the small
    supplies office to replace broken tools.

4. Assembly-line workers felt their jobs were boring and
    monotonous.

Since monotony and boredom were the problems that
seemed to affect the greatest number of people, several
experiments changing the work atmosphere were performed to
seek ways of curbing them. The first experiment increased
lighting; this increased lighting improved quality for a
few days before it returned to normal. When lighting was
returned to normal, quality increases were again recorded
for a few days. The team concluded that the attention the
employees had received from being the subjects of an
experiment encouraged them to produce better quality
carburetors even under regular conditions.

The second experiment changed the color of the work
area. Two groups had their areas painted aqua, though not
concurrently. The first group's production increased 1%,
while quality increased 4%. The second group's increases
were almost identical. This color appeared to increase
quality and production rate significantly.

The third experiment rotated jobs. The men were
taught three new tasks during a three-week training period
until they could perform four of the sixteen tasks in
their group. When the men were allowed to rotate among
these tasks, the production rate remained the same, but
quality increased 4.5%. (During this experiment the
number of requisitions for new tools dropped in half.)

19

The fourth experiment added extra breaks. When the men were given an extra ten-minute break both morning and afternoon, the production level remained normal, but the quality level rose 3%.

The team finally looked at Ignatz Hasenfratz's group specifically to find the reason for his men's high production of poor-quality carburetors. The investigators saw Hasenfratz push his men too hard, which led to obstinacy and poor workmanship. Interviews with the men supported the team's conclusions. Apparently Hasenfratz hoped through high production records to be promoted out of Hopeless.

With the experiments and observations completed, the team recommends the following:

1. Paint assembly-line areas aqua or some similar color in the blue range.
2. Rotate workers between four tasks.
3. Give the men an extra ten-minute break morning and afternoon.
4. Bring in a new supervisor for the Hasenfratz group.

The team believes that these recommendations if carried out would do much to improve the quality of the carburetors manufactured at the Hopeless plant.

Because Marie's report is an investigative report, research into pub-lished materials played only a small role. The two references cited, however, do conform to APA style.

20

References

Bartlett, J. E., & Bradley, S. M. (1979, February). Job satisfaction study: Future Motor's Hopeless plant (Report No. 65–79). Los Angeles: Bartlett and Bradley Research Associates.

Mann, H. E. (1975). Effects of light and color changes on quality and quantity of production (Report No. A–5). Aberdeen, OH: Sinclair Manufacturing.

Footnote

[1]The "Hawthorne effect" comes from a famous
industrial relations study conducted by Elton Mayo for
approximately five years during the 1930s at Western
Electric's Hawthorne plant in Chicago. The study is
mentioned in numerous books on management and productivity. The official account of the whole range of
experiments appears in Management and the Worker by F. J.
Roethlisberger and William J. Dickson (Cambridge, MA:
Harvard University Press, 1939). The mysterious result of
the experiments was that women in a relay assembly test
room continually increased their production no matter
whether conditions were improved or worsened. The
explanation for this result was that the close supervision
and counseling provided caused the women to become a team
and outdo themselves in cooperating with the experiments;
increased production, then, had to do in large measure
with the attention paid the women as members of an
experimental group.

Chapter 20

Kinds of Business Letters

All good business letters persuade to the extent that they maintain goodwill in addition to the message they impart. In most instances, goodwill is inherent in the very process of receiving a letter. People who do not fear bill collectors or anticipate threats or legal papers are pleased to open an envelope addressed specifically to them. They feel the pleasure of encountering something new, a touch of wonder or mystery. Even junk mail retains some of this sense for those who seldom receive letters. And even though the greeting they encounter is formal, "Dear Ms. Alworthy," it is endearment nevertheless. From the moment of greeting to the moment of closing, the writer's tone will either enhance, maintain, or destroy the minimum goodwill inherent in the letter-writing situation.

Writers of business letters want the reader's goodwill not only because of the immediate benefit — to help persuade the reader into a favorable decision or attitude — but also because goodwill is a basic desire of all healthy human beings and their organizations. An ambience of goodwill is also useful for future negotiations. It represents respect, trust, and confidence.

Goodwill is enhanced without effort when the writer imparts information the reader desires. If the information is disagreeable, however, the reader will have at least a tendency to react as ancient kings did with bearers of bad news; the meaning of the message may destroy the minimum of goodwill the greeting inspires. In this situation, extra efforts are necessary to enhance and maintain goodwill. Whether the message is agreeable or disagreeable, however, goodwill is threatened by incorrect spelling and grammar, trite and fuzzy language, incoherence, illogical reasoning, and frosty or silly tone.

Often, the writer's persuasive effort extends beyond the need to impart agreeable or disagreeable information. The goal of the writer may be to influence or change the reader's thought, attitude, or action. Such persuasive letters are written to propose, request, apply, sell, complain, or claim. The following scheme classifies most business letters into these three information situations, according to effect on the reader:

Agreeable	Disagreeable	Persuasive
Orders and acknowledgments	Negative acknowledgments	Sales or proposals
Favorable adjustments	Denial or unfavorable adjustments	Complaints or claims
Appointments	Refusals	Applications
Provisions, grants, payments	Denial or inadequate provisions	Requests for information, favors donations, collections

We will examine the general principles to follow in selecting the appropriate content, language, and arrangement in these letter-writing situations.

Agreeable Situations

We usually "break" bad news. We "handle" the situation with some delicacy in order to alleviate the pain of it. Good news, however, is agreeable, and so we give it to the reader at once because it instantly generates goodwill: "Your application for credit has been approved"; "We are pleased to provide the information you requested."

After the announcement of the agreeable news, the details follow. In the euphoria of pleasing another, however, the writer may wax magnanimous; the tone may puff a bit:

> We are pleased to satisfy your claim and render full restitution. Gabriel's stresses the integrity of its products and the comfort of those who use them. The customer's happiness is paramount at Gabriel's.

While the reader is ready for the details of the adjustment, the writer is bent on self-gratification. The tone reveals an attitude focused on the writer, not the customer, in spite of the letter's claim. The writer should follow the direct opening with details that specify the conditions of the adjustment, anticipating the reader's questions as they arise.

Orders

In ordering and acknowledging orders, the writer states exactly what is wanted: the size, color, model, listed price if available, and even the inventory number. A proper close for the order is an instruction for delivery and date. The acknowledgment expresses appreciation for the order and affirms or adjusts the conditions of shipment.

Adjustments

Letters offering favorable adjustments should do so wholeheartedly, omitting such negative feelings as we find in this example:

> We will replace the transformer you claim is malfunctioning when we receive your equipment, but we feel our product is not at fault. We suggest that you follow more closely the printed installation procedures and operational instructions.

The natural goodwill of a favorable adjustment is destroyed in the writer's begrudging tone. An agreeable adjustment letter might read:

> We will be glad to replace your transformer with a new one if you will ship your equipment according to the enclosed instructions. Our technician will then analyze the performance of the returned transformer to learn whether the malfunction is caused by the design or by our installation and operating instructions. Please do not install or operate your new transformer until we are able to determine the cause of its improper performance.

A suitable conclusion for this adjustment situation would attempt to reestablish the customer's goodwill:

> By calling this problem to our attention, you help us follow our tradition of customer service.

Appointments

Letters that appoint or grant are always happy occasions, and it is appropriate to mention that feeling from the start:

> I am happy to inform you that Atlas Standard has appointed you to our review board.

> We are glad to grant your proposal to investigate the effects of ethnic differences among our employees in Singapore.

> The Core Company takes pleasure in offering you the position of Chief Engineer.

Again the specific details follow: the duties to be performed or the results expected, the money to be involved, the date for beginning, and, in the case of grants, the date for ending the project.

Requests and Responses

Letters requesting information about products for sale are always agreeable, but requests also seek other information that the reader may not always be able or willing to provide; extra persuasion may be required. When writers ask for information about products or services, they can proceed directly, as in all other agreeable letters. The reader's interest in promoting his or her own product can be assumed. However, if the request is dissociated from the possibility of sales, it is the asking of a favor. To respond, the reader has to take the time to reflect, collect the information, and write. Therefore, you will want to tell the reader you are grateful for the effort. If possible, appeal to some benefit for the reader — usually the natural desire to share knowledge with others. Students seeking information for reports or investigators asking the reader to fill out a questionnaire can offer to acknowledge the reader's contribution and to send a copy of the final report.

Inquiries that request information should begin a bit more cordially than the brusque "Please send me information about . . ." Remember, you are asking a favor. You also need to know just what you want. "Please send all the data on . . ." is likely to be ignored. A good opening describes the writer's identity along with the need for the information: a student in a sociology class seeking facts about alcoholism among teen-agers who have sought refuge at the YMCA for the last two years, a committee member seeking citizen aid for a community transportation project, a government engineer needing advice on the solution to a particular problem. If possible, try to spark your reader's interest with some familiar detail, especially if it compliments the reader:

> Gathering data for a report on interurban transportation, I encountered your article in *Urban Affairs* (December 1982), and I would be grateful if you would let me benefit from your knowledge.

> At the Annual Meeting of Associated Design Engineers, John Silver mentioned your work in color research. Several of us at the Institution Testing Center have been attempting a composite chart of color and operational relationships. Specifically, we would like to know . . .

The information requested should be specifically and clearly stated. If there is more than one question, make a list. Indent the questions and number them. If you ask more than five or six questions, a questionnaire is appropriate. Make it a separate attachment to the letter and leave enough space for the answers. Above all, make the questions clear and as easy as possible to answer. The more one-word answers the reader can supply, the more he will appreciate the writer's efforts. (See Chapter 18, p. 295.)

Conclude by telling the reader how you plan to use the information. Here is the place to indicate how the reader may benefit, at least by receiving a copy of the finished report or word about the outcome of your project. And of course, close with a final word of appreciation. A sample inquiry requesting information appears on page 397.

Although the request for information requires extra persuasive effort, a positive response is an agreeable situation. As in all letters of agreement, the persuasiveness derives from the maintenance of goodwill

AZ Engineering
1200 Lime Street
Oklahoma City, Oklahoma 73001
July 10, 1983

Ms. Diane Atwood, Director
Products Division
U.S. Chemical Company
16 Westfield Road
Springs, Maryland 20031

Dear Ms. Atwood:

You may remember our brief exchange at the last
annual meeting of the Chemical Society of America in
Houston. At the time you mentioned your work in the
silicone field, particularly with water-resistant
additives having a silicone base. We are now engaged in
the development of a paperlike material from synthetic
fibers which will be water resistant, and we need your
assistance. Perhaps we can mutually benefit from the
development. Specifically, we need to know the following:

1. Any new silicone products that may be used as
   additives to attain water repellency.
2. The properties of these silicone products.
3. The procedures for applying them.

We are in a particularly critical stage in our
development and would like to share with you our progress
reports as well as our final report. Of course your
contributions will be fully acknowledged. We appreciate
your time and effort in responding to this request.

Sincerely yours,

Gene Starr

Gene Starr, Chemist

as well as the credibility and accuracy of the information, logical reasoning, completeness, and clear language. The questions should be answered in the order asked. Frequently the information requested is procedural, as in the request for information about silicone products. The response appears on page 399.

Disagreeable Situations

Denying credit, refusing claims or information, and turning down applications or proposals are obviously disagreeable situations. No matter how justified the writer's decision, the reader will be disappointed. Knowing this, the writer may adopt a defensive tone — "I can't help it," or, "It's not my fault" — which only aggravates the situation. Instead, the writer should extend amenity, not only through politeness but by means of explanation as well. A reader who understands the reason for the refusal may accept it more easily. At least the reader will not think ill of the person who is refusing. The writer's strategy should be to prepare the reader for acceptance of the bad news. If it is presented at the outset, the reader may not go on to learn the reasons for the refusal. The writer should begin with a buffer statement, neutral and relevant yet not misleading. The first of the following sentences is a good beginning; the second example would be misleading:

> We studied your application, among many others, with a great deal of care.
>
> We are pleased to have your application and find it most intriguing.

The explanation that follows is specific and complete. The very length of it will tend to convince the reader that the writer has taken the request, claim, or application seriously and has considered it fully. The usual reasons for refusal can be found in the logical facts of the case, company or organizational policy, or comparisons for a best choice:

> The position requires at least five years of actual experience in display design in addition to formal education at an accredited art school with an outstanding reputation.

To avoid an implication of acceptance, the buffer and explanation should not be too thankful or gratified with the request or application, and it should not use such words as *however, although, but, will not, cannot,* and *unable.* On the other hand, do not be overly apologetic: "We regret to tell you," is sufficient. If you fall back on company policy, be sure to explain why it is the policy. Above all, do not talk down to the reader, as if giving lessons to a child:

> Our experience over the past twelve years has taught us . . .

U.S. Chemical Company
16 Westfield Road
Springs, Maryland   20031
January 2, 1985

Mr. Gene Starr
AZ Engineering
1200 Lime Street
Oklahoma City, Oklahoma   73001

Dear Mr. Starr:

I am sending you a sample of our silicon compound 50
(SC–50) for evaluation. It is an additive that imparts
water resistance to paperlike materials. This product is
new and still in the experimental stage. The enclosed
data sheet describes all the properties we have determined
so far. We have not yet settled the question of
application, but I shall describe the procedures we are
most favoring at this time, and ask that you follow them
with care and caution.

Because of its high alkalinity (pH 13), the SC–50 cannot
be added as received. It must first be acidified and
allowed to stand until completely gelled. Procedures for
this gelling have been worked out with alum or acetic
acid. One may work better with your synthetic fibers.

With Alum

1. Dilute the SC–50 to 15 percent silicone solids.

2. Allow the mixture to stand until gelation is
    complete (usually overnight).

3. Adjust the alkalinity, if necessary, between pH 5
    and 6.

With Acetic Acid

1. Dilute the SC–50 to silicone solids and slowly
    add acetic acid, stirring constantly until the
    solution turns cloudy.

2. Allow the mixture to set for several hours until
    gelation is complete.

3. Add more acetic acid until the alkalinity is
    between pH 5 and 6.

Of course, I appreciate any interest in our work.

Sincerely,

Diane Atwood

Diane Atwood, Director
Products Division

At the end of the explanation, as a conclusion to the reasoning, the writer states the refusal. Of course, if the reasons are clear enough, the reader can infer a refusal, and an actual statement may not be necessary. Instead of a cruel statement, such as, "Therefore, the selection committee found it necessary to turn down your application," the writer might imply the refusal by announcing the person appointed or the recipient. The clearer the reasons for refusal, the less necessary an explicit statement of refusal.

Whenever possible, try to suggest some alternative that may benefit the reader. In the refusal to a job or grant application, for instance, the writer might indicate other positions or grants that more closely fit the applicant's qualifications. In refusing information requested, the writer might offer what information he or she can and then suggest other sources. Alternative products or services, other companies and organizations, and other courses of action may all benefit the reader who has been disappointed.

Before the end, writers who must refuse should offer some gesture to restore good feelings. Although they have refused, they are sensitive to the disappointment:

> I appreciate your interest in our company and wish you well.

Persuasive Situations

We have seen that all writing situations are more or less persuasive, depending on the degree of agreement already existing between writers and readers. Among the more persuasive situations are the occasions for writing requests and claims, sales letters and proposals, and applications for jobs. In all these situations the writer aims to influence the reader's thought or action.

Favors, Donations

Letters requesting favors, votes, or donations always require more persuasion than mere inquiries. They are essentially sales letters or proposals. Readers more readily vote for a candidate or give a donation when they can perceive a reward or some benefit they desire, either personal or communal or both. The benefit to a donor is usually the enhancement of the citizen's sense of communal well-being, credit for helping others, or quite simply human sympathy for the less fortunate. People give most often for the same reasons they go to church or synagogue, attend communal functions, or despair at the plight of a jobless worker with six children. Donations offer no specific returns, but favors do. Although it is brash to call upon a favor due, it is not unwise to suggest that a favor granted now may be repaid with dividends someday. Here is a politician implying an appeal for the vote and going much further. He requests campaign help and suggests the possibility of a governmental appointment in return.

> With work from all of us, Spartan City can move forward again. We are going to restore competence as well as leadership in the Mayor's office. As you contemplate the crucial issues facing the city, I hope you will decide to commit some of your valuable time to our campaign. The Mayor's office has more than 600 appointments to fill, and the Mayor is the chief budget officer.
>
> All we are asking you to do is to volunteer some time so that we can elect a leader and not a politician to the Mayor's office. Please fill out the enclosed card, specifying what area of work you prefer and how much time you can contribute.
>
> We are counting on you for better city government.

Claims, Complaints

Letters that claim and complain are both disagreeable and persuasive situations. A reader in the position to grant or reject initially tends to the negative, assuming an attitude of one who is waiting to be convinced. A claims adjuster, for instance, must decide between the monetary cost of adjusting and the goodwill cost of not adjusting. The claimant assumes that companies and organizations, like individuals, fear loss of reputation. The appeal to goodwill should be suggestive, through a description of the faulty product, or service, or mistreatment. After a clear and complete description, the writer should state directly what adjustment is sought.

The major pitfall in writing letters that claim and complain is the tendency to emotional excess. From the writer's point of view, a claim is a cry of injustice and a demand that justice be restored. To some degree the writer feels victimized. The tendency, therefore, is to react with some anger, manifesting itself in discourtesies and even insults, which are self-defeating.

To counteract this tendency, the writer assumes that the reader, whether company or individual, seeks to maintain goodwill, that the fault or error was unintentional, and that once the readers know the problem, they will desire to make the proper adjustment. Obviously, however, they cannot begin to adjust unless they know all the details. Rather than go on about the devastation caused by the error or fault, the writer should give specific details of the situation, completely and reasonably. At the end the writer spells out the adjustment desired, and perhaps expresses some confidence that the reader will be able to make the adjustment. Throughout the letter the writer assumes that no one intends to take unjust advantage of anyone else. No one likes to bear guilt unnecessarily. An example of a fair letter of complaint and claim appears on page 402.

Ace Industries
411 South Houston Avenue
Aberdeen, Maryland 21001
October 1, 1983

President
The Atlas Computer Corporation
1410 South Garden
State College, Pennsylvania 16801

Dear President:

The new Atlas computer 611 we purchased last fall
performed without significant flaws until the guarantee
expired last month (September 10). During that time we
have appreciated your company's faithful adherence to the
terms of the guarantee. For the past month, however, we
have been denied the use of the computer, with the
exception of a day or two immediately following repair,
but we can no longer make legal claims for malfunctions.

In addition to the expense of extensive repairs this
month, we have incurred significant loss of revenue
because of the computer's downtime. Over the past year,
when the guarantee was in effect, this loss was not
significant and we made no claim for restitution. But now
we have lost nearly a month's business.

Since we are programmers ignorant of electronics, we will
not attempt any diagnosis of the malfunction, but the
results never check out the same when we run a program
more than once. At this point, we think the equipment has
basic weaknesses that will continue to cause downtime no
matter how often it is repaired. Therefore, we request
either a replacement or a refund. We also feel justified
in asking for remuneration for some of the financial
losses, but we have no agreement to that effect.

Although our Atlas 611 is past the period of the
guarantee, we believe that you will want to uphold the
reputation of the Atlas Computer Corporation. May we hear
from you as soon as possible?

Sincerely yours,

Alton Jones

Alton Jones
Vice-President

The writer of this letter must persuade the reader to make an adjustment beyond the company's legal responsibilities. Notice that the letter is polite yet firm and direct. It uses the strategy of restraint, indicating that it could claim more. This strategy is intended to work on the reader's sense of justice. In view of the customer's greater loss, the least the reader can do is grant the lesser request.

Collection

Letters requesting payment can often undo the goodwill an organization establishes through advertising, public relations, and employee training. To maintain goodwill in an essentially disagreeable situation, collectors have resorted to series of letters mailed in a predetermined sequence. The tone of the first is friendly, a mere reminder; it is followed by a stronger reminder, then an outright inquiry, and finally an urgent message that veils or states a threat of legal action.

At first, the writer assumes the reader has merely overlooked the bill: Perhaps you have forgotten? Misplaced? We missed your payment. May we remind you? In the second reminder the writer retains the same assumption. It is basically a repetition of the first, with the added prod that this is the second notice. In both these stages, retail organizations usually follow the custom, wise or not, of pushing their products for further sales. However insensitive this addition may be, it does tell the reader that credit is still good.

In the third stage, the writer asks why the bill has not been paid. Some trouble perhaps? Please come in and discuss it with us. Or may we hear from you? Arrangements can be made. The writer's motive is to get some reader response. Appeals are directed to the reader's pride or credit rating or sense of fairness. If there is still no response, the situation becomes urgent. A letter is now sent out threatening the reader in either direct or veiled statement:

> Since we have not heard from you, it has become necessary to take measures. Please send the $200 owed on your account within the next five days to avoid impairing your credit and possible legal action.

The tone should avoid stridency but leave no doubt about the resolve to collect.

Sales, Proposals

Collection letters have the benefit of a final appeal to law in order to persuade the reader, but sales letters and proposals do not. The sales letter must rely almost exclusively on arousing the reader's desires. They are largely made up of sugar and spice, while the proposal is made up of facts and argument. People are seldom interested in reading unsolicited sales letters or proposals. (Those that are solicited are actually responses to inquiries; therefore, the reader's interest has already been stimulated.)

The first requirement of an unsolicited sales letter is to rouse the reader's interest, usually with a startling fact or appeal to a particular desire to obtain a bargain, comfort, luxury, status, and so on:

> By the year 2000 you won't need money.
>
> Would you like a free subscription to the *Morning Post?*
>
> In four years you could be driving this Ferrari on the French Riviera if you invest now.

Triteness is the danger in all attention-getting devices; timeworn gimmicks usually turn the reader away:

> We're number one. And so are you!
>
> You don't need a million to enjoy the best things in life.

Foolish questions also repel readers — "Why not buy from us?" — as does emphasis on the writer — "It pays to watch the growth of Hammond Incorporated." The dignified sales letter allows the product or service to sell itself. It emphasizes from the start a particular feature that will most appeal to the reader:

> The ACME home generator produces electricity for half what it costs from the electric company. And keeps you in light when all other power fails.

The information has to be adapted to the reader, of course. What readers will likely use the products or services being offered? What is their age group? Economic level? Where do they live? What do they do? Why aren't they getting these products and services now? What do these people want? What do they dream? Market research usually seeks the answers, but any writer can conduct a brief analysis if the results of market research are unavailable.

Once attention is stimulated, the writer describes the product, emphasizing its advantages over competing products. The major appeal may be to quality, safety, convenience, economy, sophistication, luxury, exclusiveness, elegance. The description of the product builds upon the reader's desire and shows how the product fulfills it. Finally the writer asks the reader to act — to buy — for his or her own benefit. Examples of unsolicited sales letters are so abundant they clog the daily mails.

Proposals appeal by means of fact and reason rather than emotion. They define problems and offer solutions or investigations to discover solutions. In letter form, proposals are much briefer than in reports, but they follow the same pattern:

1. They establish a situation or background of a problem.
2. They define the problem.

3. They propose a solution or investigation to discover a solution.
4. They describe the means — procedure or method — to be used.
5. They estimate the feasibility or limitations of the solution or anticipated solution.
6. They present qualifications, if not already known, of personnel and the organization.
7. They estimate the cost and time involved.

Letter proposals seldom fulfill all these requirements. They usually refer to other information about qualifications and may briefly mention cost, but they seldom give a full cost estimate. The tone is neutral. No selling is apparent. Reader interest is assumed, but background information appeals to it without obvious efforts to sell. The writer might say that the proposal aims to find ways of increasing productivity or improving labor conditions, but he or she does not sell these solutions. The conclusion, however, restates the proposed benefits, which are the purposes for undertaking the project proposed. A proposal letter appears on page 406.

Job Applications

Among the most significant letters you will ever write are those applying for a job. Job application letters are emissaries. They are all about you and represent you. Clarity, vagueness, correctness, an excessively confident or timid tone, all tell the reader the sort of person you are. Careless spelling and grammer represent a careless person. "I was told you had a job I might be interested in" represents a vague one, and "If you want an energetic and competent man, I'm it!" suggests a silly, artificial, overconfident one.

The major difficulty in writing a job application letter is maintaining the reader's perspective when the subject is you yourself. This difficulty increases when the application is unsolicited because you do not know of any particular need you might satisfy for the reader. The way to solve the problem is to know something about the organization and something about yourself. With such information, you have a better chance of offering contributions to the organization, of writing your letter from the reader's perspective. You must ask yourself, "What can I do for them?"

You can begin to answer the question by learning what the organization does, where installations are located in the United States and abroad, what its major undertakings are, and what problems it has encountered. To get information, read the company's advertisements and talk to friends and acquaintances who might know something about the organization. If a company has a magazine, find it and read it. Request copies of brochures and annual reports. Look up the orga-

Energy Research Institute
2400 Coalton Road
Kansas City, Kansas   63021
July 2, 1983

Mr. Frank Logan
Research and Development
Huff Energy Incorporated
1502 Carl Place
Oklahoma City, Oklahoma 74111

Dear Mr. Logan:

   I was pleased to hear from our sales manager, Cynthia
Leeds, about the double-glazed solar collector your
organization has recently developed. But Ms. Leeds
indicated that you have not acquired significant
efficiency data.

   The Energy Research Institute has facilities capable
of recording maximum efficiency of both active and passive
solar energy systems. These facilities include several
thousand feet of superstructures mounted at various tilts
and directions.

   I propose to test your solar collector prototypes to
determine their efficiency under as many conditions as
possible. We would test them under all conditions of
available sunlight. Data on the energy output would then
be compared with similar data from your single-glazed
collectors and with data from other manufacturers tested
under the same conditions. The results should give a
rather reliable estimate of efficiency for the
double-glazed solar collector.

   Because we are receiving maximum sunlight hours at
this time, I would like to begin the series of tests as
soon as possible.

   Qualifications of our personnel to be assigned are
attached along with a breakdown of costs. You will notice
that both engineers have advanced degrees and more than
five years of solar experience in radiation studies.
Please notice also that costs are below $50,000.

                    Sincerely yours,

                    Anne Adams

                    Anne Adams
                    Chief Engineer

nization in such sources as *College Placement Annual, Standard Statistics, Standard Corporation Reports,* and *Middle Market Directory* and *Million Dollar Directory* (both Dun and Bradstreet publications). Also consult newspapers and magazines that emphasize business news such as the *Wall Street Journal* and *Business Week.* These sources may tell you about the organization's achievements, current condition, and future goals. As a result, you may be able to indicate more specifically how you can contribute with the qualifications you have.

You should also know something about yourself, your strengths and weaknesses. Just what are your qualifications for the job you seek? Try to narrow the range of jobs to real possibilities so that you will not waste time and energy seeking positions your qualifications do not fit. Your most obvious qualifications are shown by your achievements. What applicable courses have you taken? Grades? What grade average did you maintain? What grade average in your major field? Use only the information that will impress the reader. What did you learn on jobs you have held? How is that experience applicable to the job you are applying for? Less obvious qualifications are matters of personality development. Have your educational and working experiences shown that you have initiative? That you can handle heavy responsibilities? That you are a team player? That you are creative? What evidence can you offer?

In planning the letter, think about your tone. It ought to be somewhat confident but not overly so, and not overly humble either. It should be somewhat eager, but not fawning. Even in the most desperate situations, it is unwise to say you must have the job. And use active verbs as much as possible. Rather than saying, "I was in the sales department," say what you did — sold merchandise, trained other clerks, kept books, planned displays and newspaper ads. Your letter should be the best representation of yourself — your education, work experience, interests, and abilities — put forward with maturity, care, and an appealing tone.

Solicited applications. The advantages of a solicited application are those of accepting an invitation or having someone introduce you. In both cases, you can respond more specifically to the job requirements because you know something about them:

In the 1982 issue of *Spectrum,* I noticed Fairchild's advertisement for digital design engineers. I have been doing research in digital design at the University of Tulsa for the past year and will receive my B.S. in electrical engineering this spring. During the year I have designed three different interfaces for my Apple computer. I would like to apply my training, experience, and enthusiasm to future developments in digital design engineering at Fairchild.

Dr. Allan Richards of Amoco informed me of an available research position in the application of mathematical equations to the solutions of problems tested recently by petroleum engineers. In May I will graduate from the University of Tulsa with a B.S. in applied mathematics and an engineering option. I would like to contribute my learning and creativity to Amoco as a research assistant, and, if possible, work with Dr. Richards.

Both examples contain the three basic ingredients of a strong introduction: they identify the applicant, set forth the most appealing qualification, and ask for a position. Notice also the tone; each introduction offers a contribution to the organization.

Unsolicited applications. To avoid the drab "I am interested in working for your company," writing the introduction of an unsolicited application requires some ingenuity, but no stunting or bragging:

Surely an organization as huge as Sunlight Inns could profit by hiring a junior manager with a B.S. in hospitality management from the University of Houston, a leading school in the arts of hotel management. My internship has proven my commitment to quality service; my customer relations experience has gone far beyond textbook learning. Please consider this application for a beginning position with Sunlight Inns.

Perhaps it is only the tone of the first sentence that would jar the reader. A great improvement could be accomplished with the substitution of one word, "perhaps" for "surely." Still, such an opening is risky. The writer has either been pumped up to a show of overconfidence or is a "fast talker" in the making. In any event, the opening sounds artificial. A more humble and appealing approach might show the reader some intelligent awareness of the world outside the self, especially an awareness of the profession:

On Friday, April 3, the Channel 2 news mentioned an increase in production at Wells' Tulsa Refinery. I am in the upper eighth of my class in petroleum refining and will earn my chemical engineering B.S. in June from the University of Tulsa. Before then, however, I am confident that I can ably assist a refining engineer at Wells Refining.

While reading the latest *American Chemical Society Journal,* I found your article on the opening of a new McCoy Refinery. It mentions a need for chemical engineers experienced in estimating costs of processing equipment. Since receiving my M.S. from the Massachussets Institute of Technology, I have acquired more than ten years experience with processing equipment, including cost estimations. I would like to explore the possibility of joining McCoy Refinery.

The last example, we notice, subordinates college education to working experience, which is most important to the employer. When you have only a smattering of experience, however, the appropriate education is the strongest qualification. The middle paragraphs of the letter concentrate on these qualifications. They elaborate and specify with evidence. In addition to an overall grade average in the field of concentration — if high — you can mention courses specifically applicable to the job, and further, some particular knowledge you gained. Make the jobs you have held and your extracurricular activities significant by showing the qualities of character they have helped develop — initiative, a sense of responsibility, leadership, ability to solve actual problems outside of classroom setups. Always be aware that prospective employers are interested in you for their own benefit.

At the end restate your interest in the position and request an interview, or if the employer is at a distance, request a phone call. Such response, we must remember, is the whole aim of the letter. Be sure to extend the courtesy of flexible time; that is, the interview should be at the reader's convenience. Of course, if you cannot be available at certain times, say so.

Writers may follow all these instructions and still fail to attract an interview by unwittingly annoying the reader. They run the risk when they discuss salary, which is premature, or when they tell the prospective employer at length what he already knows about the profession or about the qualifications for the position within it:

> Your ad suggests a person who is versatile, accurate, reliable, and responsible. I believe I have the necessary qualifications.

Just say instead that your previous job experience had demonstrated such qualities. The virtues we have described can be found in the developing and ending parts of the letter about employment as a digital design engineer at Fairchild.

> In addition to my electrical engineering courses, I will have completed 24 hours in computer science courses at the time of graduation. I am in the top 20 percent of my class. My senior project, under the supervision of Dr. H. B. Smith, is the design and construction of an analog-digital interface for an Apple II computer.
>
> I assisted a digital design engineer at Texas Instruments last summer, helping to design hardware for its home computer. I also designed interfaces for the TI–440. Last summer was an extra education for me. In addition to the practical work in design, I learned to be versatile and to use my ingenuity. I also learned to be responsible to others and to the job. On the enclosed résumé, please notice my three years of training in maintenance. This training helped me enormously in overcoming mechanical difficulties I encountered in design problems.
>
> The résumé should answer other questions about my past work and educational experiences. I have had little time for extracurricular activities, as you can see, but I did prove myself as something of a leader in my role as chairman of the Student Engineering Board. If you would like copies of the final reports I wrote on my digital designs, I will be glad to send them.

I would appreciate an opportunity to discuss possibilities of my joining Fairchild as a digital design engineer. Please call or write to arrange an interview at your convenience.

Applicants can increase the chances for an interview if they are on the scene. They can suggest traveling to the employer either deliberately for that purpose or because they are going to the locale anyway:

In June I will be visiting relatives in New York. Would it be possible for me to come by and talk with a Fairchild representative then?

Résumés

The résumé or vita accompanying the letter of application is the applicant's report on the self. It is wise to compose it before writing the letter and then draw upon this report on the self for the most appropriate details. The résumé usually contains six blocks of information:

Heading
Career objectives
Educational experience
Work experience
Activities — interests, awards, special skills
References

The *heading* begins with the word *Résumé* or *Vita* and lists the name, address, and phone number where you can always be reached, as well as a temporary address and phone number if applicable. The résumé is not dated. A photo may be included, but usually it is not because it reveals information that employers are not supposed to evaluate, particularly sex, race, and age. Here are the most common forms:

RÉSUMÉ OF SUSAN FINCH

1601 Dayton Avenue
Daytona, Florida 32001
(904) 555-6770

June and August:

1800 Michigan Boulevard
Chicago, Illinois 60610

RÉSUMÉ

Susan Finch
1601 Dayton Avenue
Daytona, Florida 32001
(904) 555-6770

Some résumés add a date of availability, but it can more easily be included in the letter, especially at the end.

The *career objectives* show the prospective employer how clearly the applicant can define goals. Applicants with clear-cut goals are usually seen as more mature and ready for a professional career than those without:

> Objective: I seek a career position in design engineering with the opportunity of increasing responsibility.

This sort of statement lets the employer know the applicant's long-range ambition as well as immediate goal. Often the immediate goal is omitted, since it does not fit a variety of job situations. The writer might add a willingness to relocate and travel at this point in the résumé. Such information is relative to goals, or at least shows a realistic sense of achieving them. Applicants writing after they have accumulated significant experience often drop the statement of career objectives. The objectives should be apparent in the description of the work experiences.

Applicants without significant work experiences emphasize *educational experience* by setting forth these details before those of working experience. The most advanced degree comes first. High school details are omitted unless they imply something extra or special. List dates of attendance, institutions, degrees and dates, fields of concentration, grade-point averages if high, and a few courses that specifically prepared you for the chosen career. If you financed your own education wholly or in part, say so.

Applicants with substantial *work experience* place these details before those of education. They include dates of employment, job titles, name and location of employers, responsibilities, and accomplishments. Work from the present backward.

The *activities* section of the résumé is the place to put in extracurricular participation, community work, interests, honors and awards, and skills.

The *references* should be confined to three or four people who can evaluate your professional potential or performance, usually professors, supervisors, and colleagues. Never list a person for reference until you have gained permission. Then list names, titles, addresses, and phone numbers. References are often withheld until the interview stage, and then used as the basis for a follow-up letter. Even when they are withheld, however, a statement at the end of the résumé should indicate that you are aware of the prospective employer's need for references: "References will be supplied upon request," or "References are on file at the Student Employment Services, University of Southern California."

The résumé reproduced on page 412 appears to fulfill most of the requirements.

RÉSUMÉ OF DAVID R. GRANGE

1330 New Brunswick Avenue
Tulsa, Oklahoma 74112
(918) 555-5321

Job Objective: I wish to pursue a career in chemical
engineering, preferably in the field of
industrial design.

Education: University of Tulsa, Chemical Engineering.
B.S. expected in spring 1982. In upper 10
percent of class with 3.8 overall average
and 3.9 in major field. Emphasis on field
equipment design. Specially applicable
courses include pump design and truck
design.

Business Experience:

1978–1982   Assistant Engineer, Dowell, Inc., Tulsa,
Oklahoma. Worked fifteen hours per week
during academic year, full time during
summers. The first two years worked in the
Analytical Laboratory, primarily in organic
section. Last two years promoted to
Process Design and Engineering where I
designed a pump to be used for enhanced oil
recovery. Also designed acid sled for use
in acidizing projects.

Summer 1978   Delivery, Yale Cleaner, Tulsa,
Oklahoma. Delivered draperies and ran
truck route to satellite stores.

1976–1978   Janitor, Crown Lutheran Church, Tulsa,
Oklahoma. In charge of total complex,
heating and cooling systems, and building
security.

Activities: Valedictorian at Will Rogers High School in
Tulsa. Played in the marching band at the
University. Am interested in sports,
music, and church activities.

References: I will be glad to provide references from
former employers and professors upon
request.

Although you may find it convenient to reproduce your résumé by means of a printer or photocopying machine, avoid using a service that advertises expertise in résumé preparation. The product may be impressive, but too much so. Employers may recognize the source and conclude that you are incapable of effective communication on your own.

If your letter of application and résumé do not bring any response, you may send a *follow-up letter,* in which you suggest that your application may not have been received. If you have received an interview, you will want to follow up with a letter of appreciation, and at the same time take the opportunity to raise or answer any questions that may have occurred during the face-to-face discussion. The follow-up letter is also the place to formally present your recommenders if you have omitted them on the résumé. Of course, you will want to show enthusiasm for the job and organization. You may mention something you were shown that had special appeal, such as a new process or the way a company is organized, or the *esprit de corps* of the employees.

If you are offered a job, the follow-up letter is one of acceptance or refusal. Acceptance is an agreeable situation, so begin with the immediate answer, "Yes, I accept." Remember, though, that this acceptance letter may serve as part of a contract, and so be sure to spell out the terms of what you are accepting, the salary, and the conditions of employment. If you are in a position to refuse a job offer, cordially explain your reasons, as in all disagreeable situations, but in this one, leave the door open for future possibilities.

EXERCISES

1. Criticize and rewrite the following passages. Errors are in tone, formalized expressions, wordiness, and vagueness.

   a. A feasibility study of the conversion from water flooding to steam flooding in order to enhance the oil recovery from this field is proposed.

   b. Once again you have sent us faulty equipment; just what is it with your people?

   c. It has come to my attention that you are now accepting proposals for projects that improve productivity.

   d. In the current job market, I could not turn down any reasonable offer and would certainly love to apply my talents to your splendid company.

   e. As for your request, I enclose the following.

   f. Ajax humbly requests the proper acknowledgments of our offer.

   g. Pursuant to our regulations, we feel it inappropriate at this time to grant exclusive rights to nonprivileged customers.

   h. This decision theory is nonoperative in pure-theoretical competition.

i. Faultless as we feel in this instance, we are sending you a full refund to satisfy your claim, but the guilt should ride more heavily on your shoulders than ours.

j. We are cognizant of your situation and although we assert various preferences in methodology, we basically adhere to the initial principle of full-scale manipulation.

k. It is with regret that I am forced to tell you that we shall not be able to attend the ballet on the night for which you have invited us.

l. I remain in hopes that you will respond with alacrity.

m. Realization has grown that improvement of the curriculum is a function of the degree of cognizance, adaptability, and manipulatability of those involved in analyzation of our educational goals and of their capacity for increasing their skills in performance of tasks and responsibilities necessitated by our newly defined objectives.

2. Are the situations for the following letters agreeable, disagreeable, or persuasive? Rearrange the parts to suit your answer and rewrite to improve tone, adding or deleting material as necessary.

a. Dear Mr. and Mrs. Jones:

Congratulations to the Newlyweds!

As time passes and you and your wife become potential home-owners, you will find our free counseling service a great advantage in planning your finances so that home ownership will be possible. We also extend home loans at the lowest possible interest rates.

Meanwhile, you may pick up your check for $1000, the exact amount you requested in the loan application. Your late model automobile proved to be more than enough collateral.

Again, let me urge you to take advantage of our financial counseling service at no cost to you.

b. Dear Ms. Lawrence:

Would you please fill out the enclosed questionnaire? I need the information for my class project at the University of Arizona.

In addition to these questions, I would like to know just why your company cannot extend to students the opportunity of interviews with your key employees? I have asked several by phone and always got the same answer, that it was against company policy. You are such a magnificent company that I just don't understand.

c. Dear Ms. Everett:

I'm sorry to inform you that we cannot honor the claim of your company for release of contractual obligations. We are all in the same boat. Our contracts with others are just as binding as this one with you, and if we were to renege on them, they in turn would have to renege on others, and so on. You see, then, why we must hold you to your legal obligations?

Again let me say how regrettable we feel this situation to be and if we can be of any further help, do not hesitate to get in touch.

3. Criticize the following letter for tone and content, and rewrite:

Mr. I. A. Richards
Vice-President, Marketing
Ace Dog Foods
Belevidere, Illinois 61008

My Dear Mr. Richards:

As you may know I am the founder and vice-president of Convenent Food Stores, in charge of our market projections. We have just been taken over by Allswell and as a result I now seek a new position.

The enclosed résumé will show you how my career has advanced through innovative marketing of new products. Most of my experience lies in this field, consumer products and services, although I have achieved some outstanding successes as field representative in my younger years.

I would prefer a position as general manager or better, overseeing marketing opportunities, but I would consider a lesser role. My salary expectations are in the $40,000 to $50,000 range, with an incentive or equity opportunity in addition.

Perhaps you are not the most appropriate individual for me to address in your company; if not, I would appreciate your passing this letter on. Be assured that I am interested in the intriguing merchandising Ace Dog Foods has been pursuing and would welcome an opportunity to join in.

Your response will be greatly appreciated.

Sincerely,

4. Does the résumé on page 416 report most effectively on the writer? Study the résumé to determine what could be said better and what might be added, deleted, and rearranged for the most effective presentation.

5. Write a letter requesting information about a topic you are investigating or will investigate for a research report. Remember to specify what you want to know, to let the reader know why you want the information, and to appeal to the reader's willingness.

6. Write a letter proposing a project for study. Remember to describe the reasons and possible significance of the study in a background, to define precisely what you are proposing to find out, and to offer a means of precedure.

7. Write a letter telling a trainee how to run some machinery, or a colleague how to get to a difficult place or how to run a committee meeting, an election, a sales campaign.

8. Write a letter applying for a job and a résumé that reports on you.

Résumé of Grace Bittleman
1011 South Woodlawn Avenue
Chicago, Illinois 60610
April 1, 1982

PERSONAL INFORMATION

Age: 28

Height: 5'5"
          120 lbs.

Health: Excellent

Married
Status: Single

EDUCATION

1971   Graduated from Charles High School, Chicago,
       Ill.

1975   University of Tulsa, Tulsa, Okla.
       Bachelor of Science Degree, Chemical Engineering
       Tau Beta Pi fraternity

1977   Massachusetts Institute of Technology,
       Cambridge, Mass.
       Master's Degree in Chemical Engineering

WORK EXPERIENCE

1980—present   Hunter Oil Company, Tulsa, Okla.
               Engineering Plant Manager

1977—1980   Plant Design and Engineering

1973—1976   Metal Designers, Tulsa, Oklahoma
               Drafting
               Standard Oil of Indiana, Tulsa, Okla.

JOB—RELATED ACTIVITY

Active member in American Chemical Society and
American Institute for Chemical Engineers.

Rhetorical Conventions

Rhetorical conventions help writers establish their ethos — their credibility — and enhance the readability of their writing. Following the conventions is a negative virtue; that is, writers get little recognition for following them but blame if they fail to follow them. Readers become annoyed with mistakes that interfere with their train of thought about the ideas being presented, and they lose faith in the validity of the ideas if many mistakes occur. Whether reasonable or not, people lose faith in a writer who misspells or punctuates randomly.

Because this text is not meant to cover basic writing skills, what follows attempts to review only the more common errors of grammar, punctuation, and mechanics. With control over the conventions practiced by good contemporary writers, you can gain confidence in your writing, a confidence that will enable you to concentrate more on what you say than the rules that control how you say it.

Chapter 21

Grammar

One of the most common grammatical mistakes for inexperienced writers is taking something less or more than a sentence for a sentence. In the one case a fragment occurs, in the other a run-on sentence. Often these errors stem from lack of attention rather than lack of knowledge. Other frequent mistakes are disagreement between subject and verb, faulty pronoun reference, dangling modifiers, and misused parts of speech. Many of these are caused by the complexity of the grammatical situation; for example, a plural verb might seem appropriate because the subject appears plural but is actually singular.

Sentence Fragments

A sentence fragment occurs when a writer sets off with a capital letter and a period a group of words that lacks either a subject or finite verb or both. Not all fragments are faults, however. Some are used deliberately by experienced writers to create particular rhetorical effects. For example, dialogue, representing actual speech, depends on them:

"But what shall we lecture about?"
"The English Novel."
"I don't read novels."
"Great Women in Fiction."
"I don't like fiction or women."

> Dylan Thomas, "A Visit to America," *Quite Early One Morning*

Fragments, most often used to create emphasis, abound in advertisements, as in these examples, both of which are endings of the advertisements in which they appear:

So when I need work on my car I look for a Mr. Goodwrench sign. It's at more than 5,000 GM dealers. Across America.

All this at your fingertips with a Nikon EM. At a very small price. Especially for a Nikon.

Fiction writers, too, employ fragments:

> *Ten o'clock.* The sun came out from behind the rain. . . .
>> Ray Bradbury, "August 2026:
>> There Will Come Soft Rains"

> Not a move. Even her expression hadn't changed.
>> William Carlos Williams, "The Use
>> of Force"

> But to return to my story. The crocodile began by turning the unhappy Ivan Matveitch in his terrible jaws so that he could swallow his legs first. . . .
>> Fyodor Dostoevsky, "The
>> Crocodile"

Fragments are used conventionally to answer questions, exclaim, and command. These fragments are considered elliptical sentences in which the missing words are understood:

> Do you understand what a fragment is? Yes [I understand].

> Of course! That is the route we always take.

> [You] Please mail the film for developing.

Nevertheless, sentence fragments should be used rarely, particularly in the kind of writing most of you will be doing in college and after ward. And they should always be used deliberately, not accidentally. Effective sentence fragments are produced by writers who know the rules well enough to break them by choice. Accidental fragments damage a writer's credibility and may confuse the reader.

The italicized segments in the following examples are ineffective fragments:

> Joan Stein, my college roommate, is now a fading photo in a box. *Last heard from Christmas '65 with a married name and a Maryland postmark.*

> Television can be extraordinarily worthwhile. *When it finds the proper formula of time, talent, and inspiration.*

> He stood looking out to sea. *With eyelids slitted against the setting sun.*

The two ways to correct sentence fragments are to attach the fragment to the preceding or following independent clause or add needed grammatical elements to transform the fragment into an independent clause. The choice you make between these alternatives depends upon the rhetorical effect desired. The three fragments just given can be corrected in the following ways:

Joan Stein, my college roommate, is now a fading photo in a box. I last heard from her Christmas '65 with a married name and a Maryland postmark.

Joan Stein, my college roommate, last heard from Christmas '65 with a married name and a Maryland postmark, is now a fading photo in a box.

(It will not do to attach the fragment to the end of the previous sentence because the fragment modifies *Joan Stein, my college roommate,* not *a box.* Modifiers are usually best kept as close as possible to the word they modify.)

Television can be extraordinarily worthwhile when it finds the proper formula of time, talent, and imagination.

He stood looking out to sea, with eyelids slitted against the setting sun.

"He stood looking out to sea. His eyelids were slitted against the setting sun" is grammatically correct but rhetorically ineffective because of awkward separation of ideas and clumsy prose rhythm.)

EXERCISE

Examine the sentences below. Decide whether the fragments are effective or ineffective. Correct ineffective fragments by making them independent clauses or attaching them to independent clauses. Be prepared to justify those fragments you choose to leave as they are.

1. Andrea Saylor spent twenty-four hours in O'Hare Airport. The unfortunate situation resulting from a severe snowstorm which blanketed the Great Lakes area.

2. In spite of our pleas and threats. Mark persists in playing loud rock music in his dorm until midnight. Preventing the rest of us from studying.

3. Dusk. A dark cloud like a black fist descended on the silvery, silent street. Everyone knew the stranger lingered in the saloon. Drinking several drinks too many.

4. The crippled plane circled for a half hour before it could land. Waiting for its fuel to be consumed.

5. A balanced budget. The promise of every politician. All of whom have different ideas about how to achieve the balance.

6. It is a rare graduate who can resist comparing unfavorably the winning teams of his or her four years in college. With the winning teams of today.

7. Before a bill becomes law, so much study, debate, and compromise occur. That one wonders how the legislators manage to pass as many laws as they do.

8. Darkness. Inky black darkness. The path marked by only an occa-

sional Christmas candle, settled in a paper bag weighted with sand. Forming a sporadic but welcome beacon.

9. At a gasoline refinery serious accidents may happen. Unless, of course, proper safety precautions are taken.

10. Prescriptive grammar addresses how language should be used. Descriptive grammar how language is actually used.

Run-on Sentences

A run-on is a sentence error that occurs when a writer uses a comma or no punctuation at all to join two or more complete sentences (independent clauses, each with their own subject and finite verb). The result is a comma-spliced or a fused sentence, both confusing to readers. Two independent clauses need something stronger than a space or a comma to join them. A semicolon (;) does the job. So does a comma and a coordinating conjunction used together. Of course, you can also choose to separate the independent clauses with a period, starting the successive one(s) with a capital letter, thus making separate sentences out of the run-on sentence. At times, you can also make an independent clause into a dependent clause. The correction you choose depends upon the rhetorical effect you want, because all the choices are grammatically correct.

Here are some examples of how run-ons can be corrected:

FUSED SENTENCES:	It is snowing the expressway will be a mess.
COMMA SPLICED:	It is snowing, the expressway will be a mess.
REVISION 1:	It is snowing; the expressway will be a mess.
REVISION 2:	It is snowing, so the expressway will be a mess.
REVISION 3:	It is snowing. The expressway will be a mess.
REVISION 4:	Because it is snowing, the expressway will be a mess.

Any of the options work with the two independent clauses in question, but not just any alternative will do to correct this next run-on. The question here is not only of grammatical correctness but also of rhetorical effectiveness:

Float trips down the rivers of eastern Oklahoma and western Arkansas are becoming popular the Illinois River is always crowded on weekends the White River is less crowded because it is farther from population centers.

The first two clauses are not close enough in thought to warrant a semicolon, although the second and third are. Making a three-clause compound with coordinating conjunctions would not result in logical coherence. The best revisions are these:

Float trips down the rivers of eastern Oklahoma and western Arkansas are becoming popular. The Illinois River is always crowded on weekends; the White River is less crowded because it is farther from population centers.

Float trips down the rivers of eastern Oklahoma and western Arkansas are becoming popular. The Illinois River is always crowded on weekends, but the White River is less crowded because it is farther from population centers.

EXERCISE

Apply any of the four means of correcting run-on sentences to correct the sentences below. Remember, the means are as follows:

Use a period and capital at the start of a new sentence.
Use a semicolon.
Use a coordinating conjunction — *and, but, for, or, nor, so,* and *yet* — with a comma preceding it.
Keep one independent clause as a main clause and turn any others into dependent clauses.

Make sure that your revisions are not only grammatically correct but also rhetorically effective.

1. Gobbledygook flourishes in government agencies it also grows rank in the legal profession and it sometimes blooms in business and academia.

2. We attach labels to people such as "Chinese" or "cripple," the living, complex individual is lost to sight.

3. When a woman marries, she exchanges one man's surname for another man's surname in almost all facets of life she is required to use her husband's surname.

4. Susan Drake has metastatic carcinoma, she has been in the hospital for three weeks, she has considerable pain.

5. It is not always possible for us to escape, sometimes it is not even possible to dream of escaping so we soothe ourselves by thinking that staying is the noble choice we even invent a fancy name for our self-sacrifice.

6. A wasp's actions are to the point, they are not automatic and can be modified to fit a situation.

7. In Mediterranean cultures houses are surrounded by walls the rooms face not out, but in, toward a patio, activities of the family are sheltered from the public eye.

8. Our view of the world is conditioned by our own experiences since other people have different experiences, they see things differently and express themselves differently.

Agreement of Subject and Verb

It is a principle of sentences that subjects and verbs agree in number. In uncomplicated sentences, subject and verb agreement usually causes little problem. Other sentences, however, require monitoring to avoid common usage errors, those that occur when material intervenes between the subject and verb, or when sentence elements are inverted from normal word order, or when the writer is not sure whether the subject is singular or plural.

Here are some guidelines for avoiding subject-verb agreement errors:

1. Do not be misled by words coming between the subject and verb. Determine the simple subject of the verb, the word that controls agreement, by finding the verb and then asking, "Who or what _____?" filling in the blank with the verb in the sentence. Be particularly alert for prepositional phrases modifying the subject. The noun of the prepositional phrase is not the subject of the sentence.

> One of the books is overdue. (*One* is the subject of *is*, not *books*, which is the object of the preposition *of*.)
>
> Each of the football players weighs over two hundred pounds. (*Each* is the subject of *weighs*, not *players*, which is the object of the preposition *of*.)

2. Be especially careful to find the subjects in sentences that have been inverted, particularly in expletive *there* sentences:

> He sold the first edition on whose flyleaf were scribbled several names and dates. (*Names and dates were scribbled.*)
>
> There are only one or two companies bidding on the deal. (*Companies are bidding.*)
>
> There are, in the final analysis, two viable alternatives to completing the requirements. (*Alternatives are.*)

3. Sometimes it is difficult to decide whether the subject is singular or plural. Meaning determines choice in some cases, rule in others.

a. Collective nouns or words such as *audience, part,* and *half* may be either singular or plural, since the reference may be to a unit or to separate entities.

> Part of the football team are in their uniforms.
>
> Part of the cake is eaten already.
>
> Half of the audience are walking to their seats. (notice *their*)
>
> Half of the audience is applauding vigorously.
>
> The team is winning most of its games this year.
>
> The team are granting interviews on their individual performances.

424   Rhetorical Conventions

(*Note:* If you feel uncomfortable with the variation in agreement, try recasting the sentences — "Team members are granting interviews.")

b. The word *number* preceded by *a* takes the plural verb form, when preceded by *the,* the singular verb form.

A number of examples are used to clarify a complex point.

The number of examples used to prove the point is small.

c. Compound subjects treated as a unit take a singular verb:

The sum and substance of their argument is persuasive.

d. A noun retaining the plural form of the original language, such as *data,* takes the plural verb form in English even though the noun does not conform to English pluralization and so sounds "singular":

The data from the study are significant.

The phenomena are rare.

(This usage, however, is no longer universal.)

e. Nouns ending in -*s* generate questions about agreement. Plural nouns of measurement when used as a unit take singular verb forms:

Six dollars is too much to pay.

Six inches appears to be maximum growth.

Some nouns such as *news, mumps, linguistics,* and *physics* regularly take the singular verb form:

Mumps is a childhood disease.

Linguistics is the study of phonology, syntax, and semantics.

Other nouns such as *scissors, trousers, clothes,* and *glasses* (spectacles) usually take the plural verb form:

Trousers for portly men are on sale today.

His glasses slip down his nose in hot weather.

Still other nouns ending in -*s* such as *athletics, economics,* and *politics* take either the singular or plural form depending on meaning:

The economics of buying a house are easy to understand.

Economics is known as the dismal science.

f. Singular subjects joined by *or* or *nor* take the singular verb form. If the subjects joined by *or* or *nor* differ in number, the subject closest to the verb determines agreement:

Either the President or our congressional representatives are responsible for the problem.

Neither the swimmers nor the coach is able to predict the winning time.

g. When the subject and predicate nominative do not agree in number, the subject determines agreement:

Her chief flaw is her frequent absences.

Her frequent absences are her chief flaw.

Many people, however, feel uncomfortable with these oddly coupled subjects and predicates. Recasting avoids the subject-verb agreement problem:

Her chief flaw is that she is frequently absent.

She has one chief flaw: frequent absence.

h. Words spoken of as words, even when plural in form, call for the singular verb form:

Clothes is an interesting word to study etymologically.

(Notice that words used in a special way are italicized.)

EXERCISES

1. Check subject-verb agreement in the following sentences. Correct only those sentences that reveal errors. Mark "correct" those that have no errors.

   a. Each of the students who work on the school paper major in journalism.

   b. The example of other swimmers who practices for months before winning one race spur me on.

   c. The progress of most brain-damaged people is measured in small leaps followed by long plateaus.

   d. It is obvious that the possibility for many far-reaching changes in personality and physical growth have to be faced.

   e. The vice-president and presiding officer of the Senate has the responsibility for casting the deciding vote in case of a tie.

   f. Neither the players nor the coach tell us why the team lost the game.

   g. Every man and woman in the group are potentially able to lose twenty pounds.

   h. Semantics is the study of meaning.

   i. A tennis court, as well as a swimming pool, are adjacent to the hotel.

   j. The number of us attending the baroque music concert are sufficient to fill the hall.

2. Recast the following sentences to eliminate conflict in number between the subject and the predicate nominative.

   a. Sixty laps of the pool are the reason I am tired.

b. The first prize was three boxes of tennis balls.

c. Six pages of reading are the assignment.

Pronoun Reference

Pronouns are words that substitute for nouns. Categories of pronouns are as follows:

Personal: he, she, . . .
Reflexive or intensive: myself, yourself, . . .
Relative: who, which, . . .
Demonstrative: this, these, . . .
Interrogative: who, what, . . .
Indefinite: one, all, few, . . .

The only pronoun that does not substitute for other words is the impersonal *it*. This *it*, distinct from the personal *it*, is an empty word serving as subject of usually short sentences talking about the weather, time, or space:

It is snowing.

It is two o'clock.

It is four and a half hours by plane from Los Angeles to New York.

Writers must choose pronouns carefully and place them carefully so that readers know exactly to what word reference is being made. Pronouns should not have more than one possible referent. In "Tom told Dick he passed astronomy," *he* ambiguously refers to either Tom or Dick. Direct discourse can solve the problem:

"I passed chemistry," Tom told Dick.

Or else clarifying information could be added:

Tom, who had worried all semester about his chemistry grade, told Dick that he finally passed.

Even when ambiguity is not a problem, keep pronouns as near as possible to their antecedents (the word for which a pronoun substitutes) for easier reading.

The antecedent should exist within the body of written material. The reader should not have to guess at one or manufacture one. In the following sentence the referent for *he* must be generated by the reader:

In Stephen Crane's *The Red Badge of Courage*, he tells the story of a naive young soldier's first battle.

References to the title of a discourse or to items entirely outside the discourse also force readers to create antecedents, sometimes erroneously. Mystery openings such as "I'll never forget it" (referring to a title: "The Night My Car Plunged Off a Cliff in Yellowstone Park") or "This reminds me of a star" (referring to an object being described) discourage rather than attract readers. Some pronoun forms and reference are especially troublesome:

1. Indefinite *you* and *they*. These pronouns should be avoided in formal writing, but avoiding them is not an easy matter for two reasons. Both these pronouns are used frequently in conversation, and we find it difficult to think of a single person when talking about a concept that applies to no one in particular. This situation often leads unwary writers into use of indefinites:

> When a person engages in physical activities like jogging or swimming, you don't need to worry about having someone else participate with you.

> When a person engages in physical activities like jogging or swimming, they don't need to worry about having someone else participate with them.

The traditional solution to the problem has been to use the masculine reference for an indefinite singular antecedent:

> When a person engages in physical activities like jogging or swimming, he doesn't need to worry about having someone else participate with him.

But because masculine reference seems sexist to many people, they choose other options. The following were discussed in Chapter 10:

Use *he or she* or *he/she*.
Repeat the noun.
Substitute an article.
Reconstruct the sentence to avoid pronoun reference.
Shift to the plural.
(For longer pieces) Use *he* in one paragraph, *she* in another.

Here are some possible revisions of the sentence cited previously:

> When a person engages in physical activities like jogging or swimming, he or she doesn't need to worry about having someone else participate.

> When a person engages in physical activities like jogging or swimming, that person doesn't need to worry about having someone else participate.

> A person who engages in physical activities like jogging or swimming doesn't need to worry about having someone else participate.

Other indefinite pronouns which cause reference problems are *anyone, anybody, everyone, everybody, no one, nobody, someone, somebody, each,* and *one.* Since all are regular, they require a singular pronoun reference.

> Anyone who wants to win at tennis will have to give up some of his leisure activities to practice every day.

Plural *their* would be the automatic choice of nearly everyone in conversation or in very informal writing. For formal writing, the best options are to revise the sentence to avoid the need for pronoun reference or to require plural pronoun references:

> Anyone who wants to win at tennis will have to give up some leisure activities to practice every day.

> Tennis players who want to win will have to give up some of their leisure activities to practice every day.

The choice you make to avoid exclusive masculine reference will depend upon the rhetorical effect you want, but be sure to choose a grammatically correct option.

2. *As* and *that* in elliptical comparison. When the verb in the second half of a comparison is omitted, you must distinguish whether the remaining pronoun is a subject or an object of the omitted verb. Failure to distinguish between *I, he, she,* etc. for the subject and *me, him, her,* etc. for the object can distort meaning.

> Mary likes tennis as much as I. (to the same extent as I like tennis)

> Mary likes tennis as much as me. (as much as she likes me)

3. Reflexive pronouns, the ones that end with *-self* or *-selves.* These pronouns function as objects and revert the action of the verb back to the actor. Thus, subject and object have the same referent:

> Joe hit himself.

Errors in using reflexive pronouns occur most frequently when writers try too hard to be complimentary and become obsequious:

> I feel that having leading businessmen like yourself come to speak to our students is a great learning tool for them.

> We hope some of our most successful graduates, like yourself, will respond to our fund raising effort.

In neither case is *yourself* appropriate; *you* should be substituted.

4. Pronouns, especially personal and relative pronouns, that change form for the nominative, possessive, and objective cases.

   a. Major trouble lies in the use of *who* (nominative case) and *whom* (objective case). A parenthetical insertion between a pronoun and verb can cause confusion; ignore this insertion when determining proper case form.

> The head basketball coach is the one who I believe will recruit the heaviest this year.

> Who do you suppose will be the most sought-after high school forward this year?

Test the subject of the verb by mentally subtracting parenthetical material. (In the first sentence *who* is the subject of *will recruit;* in the second *who* is the subject of *will be.*

b. Trouble also occurs when the pronoun is both object and subject. The subject function determines the form of the pronoun.

> Dr. Johnson nominates *whoever* gets an A in three writing courses for the intern program.

(*Whoever* as subject of *gets* overrules its function as object of *nominates.*)

> The prize of a trip to Bermuda goes to *whoever* has garnered the highest dollar pledges to the fund drive.

(*Whoever* as subject of *has garnered* overrules its function as object of the preposition *to.*)

In formal writing you will want to use *whom* for all objects, even though in conversation *who* is often used.

> The scientists *whom* we all recognize as the first to describe the molecular structure of DNA are James Watson and Francis Crick.

> The scientist *whom* we owe chief credit to for eradicating the scourge of polio is Jonas Salk.

> *Whom* did you ask for the assignment?

If you are unsure which form to use in your own writing, mentally rearrange the sentence so the pronoun in question follows the verb or preposition ("You did ask whom for..."). If you are still in doubt, substitute a personal pronoun for the relative pronoun in question ("We all recognize him"); and if that personal pronoun is in the objective case, then *whom* is the correct form.

c. Errors may also occur when pronouns form part of compound objects. All parts of the object must be in the objective case.

> Jim wrote the letter to Liz and *her.*

> The IRS refunded John and *me* a hundred dollars on our income tax.

Mental subtraction of the first object (which rarely presents a problem) will help you decide the correct case form for the remaining objects(s). (You would not say "Jim wrote the letter to she.")

EXERCISE

Find all misused pronouns in the following sentences and correct them.

1. Few men have encountered more adversities than him.

2. The more experienced divers — Jan and me — will bring up the lost chest.

3. The award should be reserved for whomever received the highest grades in his or her class.

4. Samantha plays as much tennis as me.

5. Several of we swimmers are swimming extra practice laps Saturday morning.

6. Whom did you say knows the contents of the treasure chest?

7. I wrote to the admissions office and asked them to send transcripts to my sister and I.

8. No one except they had seen the cave at the end of the canyon.

9. No one will complete their task unless someone such as yourself encourages them every day.

10. The dean of admissions told Mark and I that us boys would have to make an appointment for another day.

Dangling Modifiers

Modifiers dangle when there is no word in the vicinity to attach themselves to, causing confusion, or if the word in the vicinity is inappropriate, causing hilarity. The three most common constructions resulting in dangling modifiers are the participial phrase, the prepositional phrase containing a gerund, and the elliptical clause. Infinitive phrases cause problems less often.

1. A particular trouble spot for participial phrases is at the beginning of a sentence:

Walking down the street, the sun blinded my eyes.

(The sun was not walking down the street.)

Having enjoyed the holiday, the flight home was a letdown to John.

(The flight did not enjoy the holiday.)

2. Prepositional phrases with gerunds may also misfire:

After driving only five hundred miles, the new tire blew out.

(The tire did not drive.)

Before attending college, my experience with dorm life was nonexistent.

(Experience cannot attend college.)

These errors may be corrected by supplying the missing word or moving the word modified closer to the modifier:

Walking down the street, I was blinded by the sun in my eyes.

Having enjoyed the holiday, John felt the flight home was a letdown.

Before attending college, I had no experience with dorm life.

Or the phrase may be changed to a clause:

> As I was walking down the street, the sun blinded my eyes.
>
> Because John had enjoyed the holiday so much, the flight home was a letdown.
>
> After we drove only five hundred miles, the tire blew out.
>
> Before I attended college, my experience with dorm life was nonexistent.

3. Dependent clauses become elliptical when they are missing words that are understood nonetheless. Such clauses dangle when the subject of the independent clause is taken as the missing subject of the elliptical clause.

> As a May graduate with a B.A. in education, my application is being submitted now for teaching positions in several schools.

(The application did not graduate in May.) To correct the confused sentence we supply the missing words or give the clause a word to modify:

> Since I am a May graduate with a B.A. in education, my application is being submitted now for teaching positions in several schools.
>
> As a May graduate with a B.A. in education, I am submitting my application for teaching positions in several schools.

4. Infinitive phrases at the beginning of a sentence can also dangle:

> To qualify for the match, six games out of seven must be won.

To revise, the writer inserts a noun or pronoun for the phrase to modify.

> To qualify for the match, you must win six games out of seven.

EXERCISE

Examine the following sentences. If you detect any dangling modifiers, revise the sentences in which they occur. (Mark "correct" sentences that have no errors.)

1. Intrigued by the challenge of waterskiing, I decided to take some lessons.

2. Having taken all thirty-six pictures, my film was ready for unloading.

3. When invited to a dance, some excuse was generated by Kathleen every time.

4. The cruise ship came into view, looking out over the ocean.

5. Our mistake was recognized when fifty miles out of our way.

6. Marie asked a friend to help her with the costumes, thinking she could finish quicker that way.

7. To watch salmon spawn, rivers in Alaska are a good place to go.

8. When only three years old, my father moved the family to America.

9. After graduating from high school, college was next in line for Jeffrey.

10. To achieve good grades in college, one must attend classes regularly and study hard.

Adjectives and Adverbs

Adjectives modify a noun or pronoun. *Adverbs* modify a verb, an adjective, or another adverb. Many adverbs can be identified by their *-ly* ending: *easily, quickly, devastatingly, weekly.* However, some adjectives end in *-ly* too: *ghastly, kingly, friendly, weekly.* Some adverbs have both an *-ly* form and an unmarked form: *close, closely; late, lately; near, nearly.* (And the unmarked forms can be adjectives too.)

Determining whether a word, then, is an adjective or an adverb is a complex matter if adjectives and adverbs are considered in isolation. In a sentence, however, adjectives and adverbs can be distinguished easily. Adjectives modify nouns or pronouns. Adverbs modify verbs, adjectives, or other adverbs. Adverbs can be identified as words that answer the questions, How? When? Where? How much? With what degree of certainty? Most of the time the correct form moves easily into place, but some troublesome choices occur with particular words and in particular spots.

1. The adjectives commonly misused as adverbs are *fine, bad, good, smooth, sure,* and *most.* All these are substandard usage:

She played *fine.*

She wants to win *real bad.*

The car ran *good.*

The engine ran *smooth.*

He is *sure* tall.

Most everyone liked the film.

Standard English demands these forms.

She played *finely.*

She wants to win *really badly.*

(*Note:* Although both of these sentences are grammatically correct, neither is rhetorically sound. Both exhibit ineffective word choice. A good writer would revise with more specific verbs: "She played expertly"; "She fervently wants to win.")

The car ran *well.*

The engine ran *smoothly.*

He is *surely* tall.

Almost everyone liked the film.

2. Adverbs are often misused for adjectives after certain linking verbs: *feel* (the most common), *look, smell,* and *taste.* All these are substandard usage:

The team feels *badly* about the score.

She looks *well* in that new dress.

The room smells *mustily.*

The coffee tastes more *bitterly* than it should this morning.

Standard English demands the following:

The team feels *bad* about the score.

She looks *good* in that new dress.

The room smells *musty.*

The coffee tastes more *bitter* than it should this morning.

3. Comparisons sometimes cause problems in choosing the correct adjective form. Use the comparative form when comparing two items, the superlative form when comparing three or more items. Both these sentences reveal substandard usage:

Of the twins, Andy is the friendliest.

If you compare transportation costs by rail, air, truck, or ship, you will find sending goods by ship is less expensive.

Standard English usage requires these forms.

Of the twins, Andy is the friendlier (or the more friendly).

If you compare transportation costs by rail, air, truck, or ship, you will find sending goods by ship is least expensive.

Your reader will understand your meaning even if you use incorrect forms, but your ethos, or credibility, will suffer. What you say may be discounted because of the substandard way you express it.

EXERCISE

Examine the following sentences for misused adjectives or adverbs. Correct any errors. (Mark "correct" sentences that have no errors.)

1. This herb butter blends especially well with cheese to produce a more delicious sauce.

2. I feel real well about my promotion.

3. Nancy Lopez plays golf quite expertly.

4. The diver arched above the board and sailed graceful into the pool.

5. Sandy feels badly about Bruce's leaving for college.

6. Most of the tennis players on the court looked awful amateurish.

7. Most everyone tried to walk as quick as possible toward the exit.

8. The coach looked sternly to him.

9. The coach looked sternly at him.

10. Of the five courses I am enrolled in this semester, chemistry is the more difficult.

Verb Forms

The chief causes of misused verb forms are ignorance of the historical present and subjunctive, and uncertainty about troublesome verbs.

Historical Present

Misuses frequently occur when inexperienced writers discuss completed works that are narrated in the past tense, as are most literary, historical, and scientific investigative works. Since these works still exist in the present, a writer referring to them uses the historical present. Notice that we used *are narrated,* not *were narrated.*

For example, Stephen Crane wrote *The Red Badge of Courage* in 1894, but if we discuss the novel we would say that it *is* about a naive young man's response to his first battle experience, or that Stephen Crane vividly *describes* the battle scenes in the book. In contrast, if we talk about the work of James Watson and Francis Crick on DNA, we would say they *did* their investigations from 1951 to 1953 (because these took place once and for all); we might go on to say that their model *shows* us the structure of the DNA molecule (because it still does).

The Subjunctive

Although the subjunctive or conditional mood is not used as often today as it once was, discriminating writers still employ it to express a condition, an uncertainty, or a wish. The subjunctive of *to be* is *be* for present tense and *were* for past tense. Other verbs have a subjunctive form only in the present tense with third-person singular subjects (*he win* not *he wins:* "We insist that he win one match before quitting.")

We use the subjunctive in *that* clauses expressing a suggestion, request, demand, or motion.

Ann suggests that the contract *be* accepted.

Charles asks that final approval *come* in ten days.

The captain demands that each pilot *fly* in very close formation.

I move that the new rules *be* adopted immediately.

It is also used in certain idiomatic expressions:

Be that as it may.

Come rain or shine, classes start at 8:00 A.M. Monday.

The subjunctive form is appropriate in contrary-to-fact or hypothetical statements:

If I were to enroll for an advanced degree, it would be in physics.

She wishes she were in Washington, D.C., to see the cherry blossoms in bloom.

Many people in recent years, however, have begun to omit the subjunctive in contrary-to-fact or hypothetical statements:

If I was to enroll for an advanced degree, it would be in physics.

She wishes she was in Washington, D.C., to see the cherry blossoms in bloom.

However, if you wish to mark yourself a careful writer, you will opt for the traditional form. It will grate on no one's ears, while the newer form will annoy those who appreciate convention.

Troublesome Verbs

1. A major problem occurs with certain verbs whose forms are often confused: *sit* and *set*, *lay* and *lie*. Acceptable usage for these verbs is as follows:

Present Infinitive	Past	Past Participle	Present Participle
(to) sit	sat	sat	sitting
(to) set	set	set	setting
(to) lie	lay	lain	lying
(to) lay	laid	laid	laying

To avoid incorrect usage, remember that *set* and *lay* are transitive verbs that take objects; *sit* and *lie* are intransitive verbs that do not take objects:

She sits in the chair.

She sat in the chair.

She set the book on the table.

She is setting the new china plates on the table.

I lie down in the shade after a grueling tennis match.

I have lain down in the shade after almost every grueling tennis match.

They lay new carpet very quickly.

They laid the new carpet throughout the house.

2. Confusion of past tense and past participle forms of certain verbs also causes trouble for some writers. The most common of these verbs and their principle parts are as follows:

Present Infinitive	Past	Past Participle
(to) break	broke	broken
(to) choose	chose	chosen
(to) drive	drove	driven
(to) freeze	froze	frozen
(to) ride	rode	ridden
(to) run	ran	run
(to) sink	sank	sunk
(to) speak	spoke	spoken
(to) tear	tore	torn
(to) wear	wore	worn

We thought he *had broken* (not *broke*) the contract.

The judge who *had been chosen* (not *chose*) was a Republican.

They *had driven* (not *drove*) the camper across the ice.

When the ice cream *had frozen* (not *froze*), we dipped our spoons in it.

She *had ridden* (not *rode*) horses since she was twelve.

The meeting *had run* (not *ran*) its course by the time we arrived.

The ship must *have sunk* (not *sank*) its hull deep in the mud.

You should *have spoken* (not *spoke*) to the professor first.

The wind *had torn* (not *tore*) the curtains during the storm.

If you were Irish, you would *have worn* (not *wore*) green.

3. A third problem is inconsistency of tense within a sentence or longer passage. Inappropriate shifts in tense should be avoided:

We *drove down* the street slowly in the fog when a car *comes out* from a driveway with no headlights on.

In the excitement of telling someone about a stressful moment, people often shift from past to present tense. It creates a sense of immediacy. In standard usage, however, shifts in tense have to be handled more subtly or avoided. The simplest revision of the sentence would be this:

As we drove down the street slowly in the fog, a car came out from a driveway with no headlights on.

More often shifts in tense occur over a longer stretch of discourse:

Solitude. Walking back to the college dormitory on a cold, damp, gray afternoon, while mulling over the main points of the history lecture I just heard, I realize that I feel very much alone — not only physically, but spiritually too. My friends seem preoccupied of late, and Mom hasn't called once this week. "What an uneventful, dreary day," I comment out loud to no one but the stiff, young, bare trees, standing rigid in their unbending straitjackets of ice. Allowing the gloomy weather to dampen my spirits, I trudge into the stuffy dorm foyer with an unattractive scowl crisscrossing my face and glance out of habit in the direction of my usually empty mailbox.

Once present tense has been established for the sequence of actions, it needs to be maintained: *realize, comment, trudge, glance.* The shift to past perfect in referring to the lack of phone calls from home, however, *is* appropriate; the mother's failure to call is the past, not part of the writer's current revelation.

EXERCISE

Examine the following sentences for incorrect verb forms. Where you find inappropriate forms, substitute correct forms. If there are alternate forms, make a note of those too. If you find no errors in verb forms in a sentence, mark it "correct."

1. After he begun to realize the consequence, he halted his actions.
2. Henry James's heroine in *The Portrait of a Lady*, Isabel Archer, married a man who abused her.
3. Her hope was that she be awarded the promotion.
4. The books set on the library shelf in neat rows.
5. He had lain the confidential papers out on the desk as if he was expecting to be back immediately.
6. If the new client were to mistake our intentions and suppose us to be dishonest, we would be in trouble.
7. Until the next to the last award was made, he had expected to win the competition.
8. Last night I laid awake for a long time and watched the moonlight laying across the bedspread.
9. If you are setting out on a road trip this summer, you should set down and plan your route carefully.
10. Not a word was spoke until they chose the new leader.

Chapter 22

Punctuation

When we speak, we use intonation and stress to indicate whether we are stating something or asking a question and whether we are continuing with a thought or have reached the end. We "punctuate" our speech. Punctuation marks in writing substitute for those we use orally. The choice of punctuation marks is not completely automatic, but since the symbols that are used do have fixed meaning, the process is governed by rules. The standard conventions for the use of punctuation are designed to facilitate the comprehension of written material. Following these rules is a negative but essential virtue. No one praises a piece of writing because it is punctuated correctly, but not following conventions can damage the effect of a piece of writing. Except in fictions, which readers anticipate may depart from conventional usage, nonstandard use of punctuation will annoy readers or, worse, cause them to misunderstand the meaning and judge the writer incompetent. Properly used, punctuation becomes a valuable technique for achieving clarity and occasionally emphasis.

The Comma

Basically, there are two uses of the comma: to separate elements and to enclose elements. Five sentence structures require commas to separate elements. Seven sentence structures require commas to enclose elements.

Commas to Separate

1. Independent clauses joined by a coordinating conjunction are separated by a comma:

An independent clause has a subject and a main verb, and we often combine two or more independent clauses into one sentence.

2. Items in a series, including the last item, are separated by commas. Newspapers and magazines consider the comma before the last

438

item in a series to be optional and often omit it, but omitting it *may* cause confusion:

> The high temperatures were caused by faulty operations, poor design and improper installation of the air-circulation system.

Does the design, as well as the installation, modify the circulating system? To avoid possible misinterpretation and inconsistency (and having constantly to decide whether or not misinterpretation may result), always use the comma before a conjunction in a series:

> The high temperatures were caused by faulty operation, poor design, and improper installation of the air-circulation system.

3. Coordinate adjectives are separated with commas. The problem with applying the rule is deciding whether the adjectives are coordinate or not. There are two ways to test for coordinate adjectives. One is to mentally insert *and* between them. If the result is idiomatic English, that is, if it sounds natural to you, then the adjectives are coordinate. You could say, "able and experienced scientists"; you could not say, "the big and black dog." Another test is to reverse the order of the adjectives to see if the result is idiomatic English. You could say "experienced and able scientists," but you could not say "the black and big dog." Correct punctuation is demonstrated in these examples:

> The committee is composed of able, experienced scientists.
>
> The big black dog crashed against the fence as it caught the ball.

4. Certain introductory modifiers are separated with commas. Following this rule depends almost as much on rhetorical effect as on usage standards. Commas are generally not used after introductory prepositional phrases unless they are exceptionally long or need to be emphasized:

> During the afternoon siesta time we strolled through the park.
>
> In this dream world of sky and sea melding into one gray eminence, we sat silently and damply for hours.

Commas are usually found after introductory adverbial clauses, and the most conservative writers consistently use them in such situations:

> When you start a sentence with an introductory adverbial clause, you should separate the clause from the rest of the sentence with a comma.

But they may be omitted when the clauses are short or when there is no need for special emphasis:

> When in Rome do as the Romans do.

Commas also separate interjective elements: exclamations, a *yes* or *no*, adverbs that modify whole sentences, and discourse facilitators:

Oh my, what a funny purple cake.

Yes, Danya picked out the cake.

Fortunately, the damage to the brain was mostly in the right hemisphere, so he can still talk.

Well, that is true, of course, but we need to look at the other side of the picture.

Commas are also used consistently after absolutes and introductory phrases containing a participle, gerund, or infinitive:

His foot tapping with the beat, the violinist introduced the tarantella in the fourth movement.

Sitting down at the table, the tax attorney opened his brief case and drew out several forms.

After playing the Schubert String Quartet No. 15 in G Major, the two violinists, the violist, and the cellist were pleased with the enthusiastic applause.

Because of his desire to leave quickly, he became impatient.

5. Words that might be misread together are separated by commas:

While we were walking, the dog was found. (*not:* Walking the dog)

After eating, Sue brought out a new game. (*not:* After eating Sue)

After eight, twenty musicians took their seats on the stage. (*not:* After eight twenty)

Sometimes commas are inserted to separate sentence elements that should not be separated. This practice disturbs the reader's comprehension, forcing her to reread material. Some places where commas are mistakenly inserted are the following:

a. Between the subject and verb:

A writer, should not separate subjects from verbs in well-written sentences. (*should be:* A writer should not . . .)

b. Between a verb and its object:

You can use, a handbook of English grammar to check on usage problems. (*should be:* You can use a handbook . . .)

c. Between a restrictive clause and the word or word group it modifies:

The article, that advocates abolishing pass-fail grading for all but a few electives, was praised. (*should be:* The article that . . . electives was praised.)

Commas to Enclose

1. Commas are used to enclose nonrestrictive clauses and phrases. The problem here comes in determining which clauses and phrases are

restrictive, which nonrestrictive. Restrictive modifiers are essential to the meaning; they identify the word modified while implying that the opposite also exists. They are not enclosed by commas:

> Pilots whose minds are dull do not live long.

"Whose minds are dull," a restrictive relative clause, identifies the pilots in focus and implies that there is another group of pilots whose minds are not dull. On the other hand, nonrestrictive modifiers comment on an already sufficiently identified word:

> Pilots, whose minds are dull, do not live long.

Now we have only one group of pilots. None live long and all have dull minds. Compare the difference in meaning between these two sentences:

> Azaleas which are acid loving thrive in the shade.

> Azaleas, which are acid loving, thrive in the shade.

In the first, particular azaleas that are acid loving thrive in the shade, but in the second, all azaleas thrive in the shade.

Relative clauses beginning with *who, whom, which,* and *whose* may be either nonrestrictive (requiring commas) or restrictive (no commas), but all relative clauses beginning with *that* are restrictive:

> The people that I am principally interested in are my family members.

> A desk that has a marproof finish is practical.

Participial phrases can also be restrictive and nonrestrictive:

> Any pilot knowing the heavy traffic patterns near major airports will keep close visual watch for other planes.

> The pilot, knowing the heavy traffic patterns near major airports, kept a close visual watch for other planes.

2. Commas are used to enclose loosely attached appositives. Appositives are parenthetical words or phrases that rename the noun or pronoun they immediately follow:

> Two professors, Dr. Johnson and Dr. Watson, teach the American literature survey in alternate semesters.

One- or two-word appositives very close in meaning to the word they modify are not set off by commas:

> The subordinating conjunction *although* is among the last children learn to apply in their writing.

3. Commas are used to enclose an adjective series or adjective phrase following the noun or pronoun modified:

> Her hair, short, blonde, and wavy, was convenient for her because she swam or played tennis every day.

The Jaguar, shiny yellow in the bright afternoon sun, was parked at the front of the Frank Lloyd Wright house on the hill.

4. Commas are used to enclose absolutes. Absolutes consist of a participle with its own subject and any attached modifiers or complements. They usually modify the sentence as a whole rather than some part of it and may be placed at the beginning, in the middle, or at the end of a sentence:

My exams finally being finished, I drove off to the beach for the day.

The theater, a heavy rain furiously drumming on its copper roof, became an echo chamber that drowned out the actor's voices.

She crossed the street swiftly, her hair blowing off her shoulders in the wind.

5. Commas also enclose parenthetical expressions, "asides" that explain, qualify, emphasize the main thought, or provide transition:

James Watson's *The Double Helix* was written, as Mary Elizabeth Bowen and Joseph A. Mazzeo point out in their book *Writing About Science,* to be a best seller, and it succeeded.

The answer she gave, I recognized immediately when I heard it, was based on outdated information.

A holiday at an isolated beach is a peaceful respite, indeed a much-needed respite, from urban noise and bustle.

The project, furthermore, was one I believed would help many people.

6. Commas are used to enclose negative insertions:

Her body became frail and weak with age, but not her memories.

7. Commas are used to enclose addresses, degrees, titles, direct address, geographical names, and, with direct quotations, the speaker as subject with accompanying verb:

Gregory Solt, who rescued the boy from the flooded Rubio Wash, lived at 1400 Rubio Drive, San Marino, California 91108. (no comma between the state and zip code)

Don A. Anderson, D.D.S., has been our family dentist for years.

Frederick T. Haddock, Professor of Astronomy, designed the radio telescope at the University of Michigan.

There is no reason, Stephen, to fight with your younger brother.

Balboa Park in San Diego, California, is the site of the world famous San Diego Zoo.

"USC will make it to the Rose Bowl again this year," I shouted, "and the opposing team will be Michigan."

Dates may or may not use commas:

> The flight schedule will change in March, 1987, for three airlines, and remain in effect until September 30, 1987.

> The flight schedule will change in March 1987 for three airlines, and remain in effect until 30 September 1987.

EXERCISE

In the following sentences insert commas where needed or cross out commas that are unneeded or misused. Mark "correct" the sentences that have no errors.

1. He left the heavy backpack for the guide had warned him of the steep hill ahead.

2. The route is difficult to follow but the alternative routes are all longer.

3. It was a difficult year, filled with unexpected trips home, new instructors, and shifting schedules, but I managed to graduate with my B average intact.

4. If I were elected president of the Symphony Council I would bring in musicians to demonstrate their instruments.

5. Throughout the first day and night, and well into the night of the second day, ash from the forest fire kept falling.

6. He walked up the path across the patio and into the garden.

7. An old dilapidated house with vines growing from its windows leaned to the earth.

8. One bright sunny morning in early June my sister's big black cat climbed in my window and tracked dirt all over the bedspread.

9. A boat that has only sails no auxiliary engine presents a challenge on a calm day.

10. Our new boat, which is painted red and white, has sprung a leak.

11. Carl Sandburg the biographer of Lincoln was awarded the Pulitzer Prize.

12. The poet Sandburg has written a biography of Lincoln.

13. Her writing is on the whole the best in the class both in style and originality of ideas.

14. Please send the package to 1116 North Main Street Chicago Illinois so that it will arrive by June 10 1987 for her birthday.

15. Inside the room was elegantly decorated.

16. He learned at an early age, the necessity of saving money.

17. James grew gigantic, deep-red, roses, in his garden.

18. A woman who hopes to succeed in business must work hard.

19. The players worked together, and gained a victory.

20. I enjoy the study of, history, art, and literature.

The Semicolon

With one exception, the semicolon functions like a weak period. It is occasionally used instead of a comma between independent clauses connected by a coordinating conjunction to emphasize balance or contrast. Its most frequent use, however, is between independent clauses not joined by coordinating conjunctions, that is, where a period could be used. Its rhetorical effect is to draw independent clauses closer together than a period would. Therefore, even though using a semicolon between independent clauses may be correct grammatically, the clauses drawn together have to be judged for rhetorical effectiveness too.

The three examples that follow show sentences that are effectively drawn together by a semicolon:

> The dream home they say they have always wanted is an English Tudor brick; however, they seem perfectly happy in their California ranch-style house.

> England was conquered by the Normans in 1066; after that, many French words entered the English language.

> AIDS is a new disease; but it has reached epidemic proportions.

The next example shows the semicolon used with grammatical correctness but rhetorical ineffectiveness.

> Minnie Brown knew the victim; she was at the shopping mall when the shooting occurred.

The only other place a semicolon is used is to separate a series of items that contain internal commas. Using the semicolon for this purpose helps readers easily distinguish the main divisions of a series:

> Committee members include representatives from the College of Arts and Sciences, a history professor, a literature professor, and a physics researcher; the College of Law; and the College of Business, a management professor, an economics professor, and an accounting professor.

EXERCISES

1. In the following sentences insert semicolons where needed or cross out the semicolons that are misused grammatically or rhetorically. Mark "correct" the sentences that have no errors.

a. At the end of each week; however, she became more familiar with the work.

b. The lake is useful as a source of electrical energy, pouring its water through the huge turbines, as a reservoir, holding at bay flood waters from the overflowing rivers, and as a recreation spot, providing swimming, boating, and fishing.

c. The semicolon acts like a weak period; it draws together related independent clauses more closely than a period.

d. The committee consisted of Ms. Marie Bender, the high school principal, Mr. Samuel Brown, the retired engineer, Dr. Leslie Wall, the dentist, and Mr. Michael Ryan, a computer programmer.

e. The mountain snow melted swiftly under the summer sun; causing the rivers to flood the lowlands.

f. Our rented beach house, which had been described as being in excellent shape, had a broken window and no lights, the beach, instead of being sandy, was virtually paved with rocks, and the dock had been half washed away by the winter storms.

g. A semicolon can be used instead of a comma between independent clauses joined by a coordinating conjunction to emphasize balance or contrast; but such use happens only occasionally.

2. Write five sentences illustrating proper use of the semicolon.

The Colon

The colon is a sign of inclusivity; what follows the colon is entailed in what precedes it. An independent clause usually precedes the colon; an independent clause, a phrase, or a list may follow the colon. An independent clause following the colon can be signaled to the reader by starting the clause with a capital letter, in contrast to starting a phrase or list with a lowercase letter.

The colon calls attention to the explanation, summary, amplification, list, or illustrative quote that follows. It is a formal mark that corresponds to the informal dash.

The colon is also used in business letters following a salutation (Dear Ms. Brown:) or a subject line (Subject: Order Number 1248), between a chapter and verse from the Bible (John 4:10), and between hours and minutes (8:00 A.M.).

Be sure not to confuse the semicolon and colon. Remember that a semicolon must be both preceded and followed by an independent clause.

The following sentences illustrate the use of the colon:

The colon may direct attention to at least three things: an explanation, a series, or a quotation.

The problem can be formulated this way: Can you imagine a three-dimensional space that turns around and closes in on itself?

Some of the most beautiful lines in the Bible are spoken by Ruth to Naomi: "Whither thou goest, I will go. Wither thou lodgest, I will lodge."

Her plans were as follows: to visit relatives in England, to tour castles in France, and to live in Germany for six months to learn the language better.

EXERCISE

Supply colons or substitute colons for incorrect punctuation marks where needed in the following sentences. Capitalize any independent clauses that follow a colon. If a sentence is correct as it stands, circle the number of the sentence.

1. His plans were as follows first he would find a job, then he would save his money, and later he would attend college.

2. There is only one way out of this forest we must go back the way we came.

3. Among the guests were several of George's friends Mr. and Mrs. Al Bateman, neighbors of long standing, Mr. Joe McNichols, his business advisor, and Dr. Kay Sands, his colleague at the university.

4. The orchestra played easy-to-dance-to tunes such as "Greensleeves," "Yesterday," and "You Light Up My Life."

5. I do not remember the details; therefore, I shall not try to answer the question.

6. After graduating from high school, I faced one of the most difficult tasks of my life; I had to choose a college major.

The Dash, Parentheses, and Brackets

The dash, as we said in the section on the colon, can be used to direct attention informally to what follows:

When the circus came to Leigh, the whole town forgot everything else — politics, budgets, traffic congestion, and the heat.

It is also used, along with parentheses and brackets, to set off interruptions. Dashes and parentheses often set off illustrative or supplementary material or sudden shifts in thought or tone. Brackets enclose editorial changes.

Writers have some options in the use of dashes, parentheses, or commas to isolate parenthetical material, depending upon the effect they want to create. Commas tend to create the most neutral tone and connect the offset material more closely with the rest of the sentence than dashes or parentheses.

Scholars in higher education need to form public opinion, not simply follow it.

Parentheses lessen the importance of the offset material and disconnect the material more sharply from the rest of the sentence.

Middle schools in Zimbabwe (formerly Rhodesia) have been renamed for prominent Africians.

Parentheses enclose the full form of acronyms when first used in a piece of discourse or the acronyms for the full form:

The MLA (Modern Language Association) meets each year between Christmas and New Year in a major city in the United States.

The Modern Language Association (MLA) . . .

Dashes set parenthetical material off most decisively from the rest of the sentence and emphasize it. (In typewritten manuscripts, a dash is two hyphens with no space between, before, or after.) Dashes also convey a more informal tone:

I shouted to him — I've forgotten just what — when I saw the bull come charging toward him.

Brackets enclose editorial changes and explanations, such as *sic* to indicate an error in the original. They also serve as parentheses within parentheses:

The Red Badge is a veritable echo chamber of sound: the regiment "weeze[es] and bang[s] with mighty power. . . ."

At the other end [of the room], orange crates served as furniture.

The newspaper article was headlined, "Freinds [*sic*] of the Library Donate $50,000."

In a letter to Nellie Crouse (Dec. 31st [1895]), Stephen Crane castigates language as "an infernally bad vehicle for thoughts."

EXERCISE

Insert dashes, parentheses, or brackets as needed in the following sentences:

1. Queen Victoria's death 1901 more or less ended the period named for her, a period marked by a rapidly expanding British Empire.

2. The elements Turner painted sunlight, water, rich shadows, and sky are all infused with luminescent color.

3. For all her life ninety-five years my great-aunt never left Lancashire.

4. He renovated houses mansions, actually for a living.

5. According to the newspaper report, "The tornado cut a wide swath thru sic the center of the city."

Quotation Marks

Quotation marks are double or single inverted commas that enclose short direct quotations, words used in a special sense, and some titles. Single quotation marks are reserved for enclosing quotations within quotations. Quotation marks signal the beginning and end of a quotation; both of the set must be used. Quotation marks are not used with quoted material of five or more lines (except dialogue); instead, these long quotes are set off by indenting the left margin ten spaces. In such set-off quotations, marks are used only within the body of the quotation itself as they appear in the original. Occasionally, short quotations are set off in this fashion for emphasis.

Quotations include passages borrowed from someone else's work and dialogue:

> Professors Guinn and Marder contend that "in all ages, of course, people have deliberately or inadvertently experimented with the variables of rhetoric in response to their communication needs." (Exact quotation from "Experimenting with the Limits of Rhetoric," appearing in the *Rhetoric Society Quarterly,* Vol. 2, No. 2 [Spring 1980], p. 83.)

> Susan said loudly enough for us to hear: "I'm planning on setting up my dental practice in Chicago or some other big metropolitan area."

> Robert Persig in *Zen and the Art of Motorcycle Maintenance* argues that the attitudes finally to be reached are the traditional Zen values: naturalness, spontaneity, acceptance of the "suchness" of things, and the absence of rigid categories. As he writes in his discussion of coming to terms with a key word for him, "quality,":

>> You want to know how to paint a perfect painting? It's easy. Make yourself perfect and then just paint naturally. That's the way all the experts do it. The making of a painting or the fixing of a motorcycle isn't separate from the rest of your existence. . . .
>> The real cycle you're working on is a cycle called yourself. The machine that appears to be "out there" and the person that appears to be "in here" are not two separate things. They grow toward Quality or fall away from Quality together.

> Barbara asked, "Do you know that *lagniappe* is a word of Spanish origin meaning something like the extra roll in a 'baker's dozen,' a trifle given

'free' in the Mideast when you have not bargained as hard as you might for an object you wanted?"

The standard rules for using other punctuation with quotation marks are these:

1. Always place periods and commas inside quotation marks.
2. Place semicolons, colons, question marks, and exclamation points outside quotation marks unless the punctuation belongs to the quotation; then place them inside the quotation marks.

Quotation marks enclose words referred to in a special sense:

When asked to pay, his statement "no sweat" puzzled the foreigner.

Some words in English, such as "cleave" and "hew," have two meanings that are virtual antonyms.

(*Note:* Often you will find words referred to as words *italicized* rather than enclosed in quotation marks.)

Quotation marks enclose titles of short stories, essays, poems (unless separately published as single works), songs, articles from periodicals, subdivisions of books, television programs, and unpublished dissertations or theses:

In Henry James's "The Pupil" the young boy's tragedy is his excessive comprehension and awareness.

T. S. Eliot wrote both "The Love Song of J. Alfred Prufrock" and *The Wasteland.*

"The Impossible Dream" was a hit song from *Man of La Mancha.*

An exception to this practice occurs with references to parts of the Bible and legal documents.

The New Testament of the Bible begins with the Gospels, Matthew, Mark, Luke, and John.

The U.S. Constitution was hammered out after the Revolutionary War.

EXERCISE

Insert quotation marks where needed in the following sentences. Mark "correct" the sentences that have no errors.

1. The song Yesterday was made famous by the Beatles.
2. The words guarantee and warranty in English both come from the French.
3. The man, the police officer reported, cried Fire! and caused a wild rush for the nearest exit.
4. Who said Give me liberty or give me death?

5. Martin Luther King is remembered for his stirring I Have a Dream speech.

6. Shakespeare used the phrase salad days to refer to youth.

7. Mark Twain joked once that reports of his death were greatly exaggerated.

8. Talleyrand said once of Mme Patterson-Bonaparte With what grace she would have reigned, had she been Queen.

The Apostrophe

The apostrophe shows possession, contraction, and pluralization of certain letters, abbreviations ending in periods, and numerals.

Use the apostrophe to form the possessive of nouns and indefinite pronouns. For singular and plural nouns not ending in -s, add the apostrophe as well as -s:

The boy's bike   The children's storybook

Anyone's guess   The men's locker room

For singular nouns ending in -s, add either the apostrophe and -s or only the apostrophe:

Dolores's dress   or   Dolores' dress

Yeats's poetry   or   Yeats' poetry

For plural nouns ending in -s, add only the apostrophe:

The scissors' mark

The students' goals

If you are forming the possessive of a compound or word group, add the apostrophe and -s to only the last word:

My mother-in-law's birthday

The queen of England's crown

To indicate separate possession with compound nouns, use an apostrophe after each noun; to show joint possession, use an apostrophe after the last noun:

Ann's and Cleve's houses

Don and Helen's daughter

Do not use the apostrophe with the personal possessive pronouns: *his, hers, its, ours, yours, theirs, whose. Its* is most often misused. Remember that *it's* is a contraction for *it is.*

Very often you will find the possessive with apostrophe used for people, but avoided for inanimate objects or abstractions:

Mr. Jackson's economic problems

The economic problems of the United States

Using the possessive apostrophe where possible and appropriate will tighten your writing by reducing the number of function words:

The claimant's case   *rather than*   The case of the claimant.

The apostrophe is also used to mark omission in contractions: *didn't, can't, won't, wouldn't,* etc. Be sure not to confuse *you're* with *your, they're* with *their* or *there, we're* with *were* or *where, there's* with *theirs.*

Use of the apostrophe with *-s* to form plurals of isolated letters, numbers, abbreviations, acronyms, and words referred to as words is optional (italicize [underline] only the letter referred to, not the *-s*):

the 1980s	or	the 1980's
6s and 7s	or	6's and 7's
ps and *qs*	or	*p*'s and *q*'s
two *Bs*	or	two *B*'s
six *ands*	or	six *and*'s
two MCs	or	two MC's

Use of the apostrophe with *-s* to form plurals of the letter *s,* words ending in *s,* and abbreviations or acronyms followed by periods is mandatory:

s's and *t*'s
many *perhaps*'s
two Ph.D.'s
six C.O.D.'s

EXERCISES

1. Insert necessary apostrophes and cross out the unneeded ones in the sentences below. Mark "correct" the sentences that have no errors.

   a. The values of the 1920s are eloquently protrayed in F. Scott Fitzgeralds *The Great Gatsby.*

   b. There are six misused *and*'s in the passage.

   c. It's easy to learn to drive a car with automatic shift.

   d. He didn't watch his *ps* and *qs* carefully enough at the presidents monthly board meeting.

   e. Some critics think that Keats's poems are romantic poetrys finest examples.

   f. Workers incomes have risen over the past decade but not enough to keep up with inflation.

Rhetorical Conventions

g. "Who's books are these?" asked the instructor.

h. The promotion to marketing manager was her's for the asking because she had two M.A.'s, not your's with only a B.A.

i. I didnt get to sleep until after twelve oclock.

j. The yellow maple sheds its leaves around Thanksgiving in Oklahoma.

2. Write a sentence showing separate possession using two people's names and a sentence showing joint possession using the name of a law firm with several partners.

3. Write a sentence using the possessive case of a compound word.

End Marks: The Period, Question Mark, and Exclamation Point

End marks signal intonation; using them helps to reveal sentence meaning. The period means you are stating something, the question mark means you are interrogating, and the exclamation point means that you are stressing something. Remember to use the question mark only with direct questions, not indirect questions. Also remember to rely as much as possible on sentence structure and word choice rather than exclamation points to emphasize, command, and express amazement or sarcasm.

Professor Markham met with Dr. Norris, Mr. Sandborn, and Ms. Lee to discuss the layout of the offices in the new building.

I did not know whether to use a semicolon or a period between the two independent clauses. (The question in the statement is indirect so needs no question mark.)

Did you know that an abstract for a report, no matter how long the report, usually runs only 100–125 words?

John said, "I cannot condense my fifty-page report to 125 words!"

The man whose parked car had been hit was most emphatic. "I'll see you in court," he roared. (*Emphatic* and *roared* do the work of the exclamation point.)

The period is also used with abbreviations and acronyms. The following are some common abbreviations that take periods:

A.D.	D.C.	M.A.	Mr.
A.M.	Dr.	M.D.	p.
B.A.	e.g.	Ms.	Ph.D.
C.O.D.	i.e.	Mrs.	P.M.

R.S.V.P. on an invitation means that a reply is requested.

Ms. Samantha Marder received her B.A. degree in 1983.

If an abbreviation comes at the end of a sentence, its period suffices for the sentence period.

Historians question whether he was born in 1 B.C. or 1 A.D.

The periods are typically omitted from abbreviations for organizations when more than two words are being abbreviated: EPA, HUD, USC, UCLA, ASU, IBM, UPS, NFL. The postal abbreviations for the states omit the periods: AZ, CA, MD, NJ, PA.

Acronyms are abbreviations that form pronounceable words from the initial letters of the words in a name. They never require periods:

MC	NOW	SNAFU (or snafu)
NASA	RADAR (or radar)	UNESCO
NATO	SONAR (or sonar)	VISTA

Besides being used with direct questions, the question mark is also used within parentheses to indicate that the accuracy of a number or date is in question:

In a letter to John Northern Hilliard written in January 1986(?), Stephen Crane writes about his desire to write "plainly and unmistakably."

EXERCISE

Correct the end marks as necessary in the sentences below. Mark "correct" the sentences that have no errors.

1. Did he plan the riot? agitate the prisoners? give the signal to begin?
2. Alaric was born in 376(?) and died in 410.
3. "Halt!" cried the guard at the gate.
4. He asked whether the shipment had arrived?
5. I first attended Moravian College, then U.C.L.A., and finally graduated from U.S.C..
6. He replied that his family had come from Poland
7. "Close your books and take out a clean sheet of paper!"
8. The newspaper headline reported a snafu in the local E.P.A. office.
9. Our road system is in a mess! Two bridges were destroyed in the flood! The main highway leading to Benton is full of potholes! Can't our state government take care of something besides the pay increase they recently voted themselves!
10. Did you see the sign, "John Jones, MD," hanging over the door?

Chapter 23

Mechanics

Many conventions of standard written English are mechanical; that is, they are arbitrary. We follow them because readers expect writers to observe them, not because of any particular logic behind them. One convention has to do with spacing. We leave one space between words or between internal sentence punctuation and a word, but we leave two spaces between a final period and the next sentence. We indent paragraphs five spaces, not eight or ten and not randomly. Other conventions have to do with the use of abbreviations, italics, numbers, capital letters, and so on. The conventions that you are not likely to be completely familiar with are covered in this chapter.

Capitals

Capital letters mark the beginnings of sentences and proper nouns. Usually titles awarded to people are not capitalized unless part of a proper noun, except for titles of particular distinction.

> Governor Anderson held office for sixteen years, but his good friend Stephen Stanfield, the lieutenant governor, held office for only eight years.

> Where does the President live? In the White House. (The leader of the United States is referred to, not the president of any organization. And the White House is a particular house in Washington, D.C., not one down the block.)

Kinship terms are ordinarily not capitalized unless substituted for a proper name:

> I'll ask my father and mother if they would like to attend.

> Tell Mother I'll be home later.

Words derived from proper nouns tend to drop the initial capital when used as common nouns. In the first sentence "Kleenex" is a specific brand; in the second the word is used generically:

I bought a box of Kleenex in the stylish new container.

Most people use kleenex when they have colds rather than cloth hand-
kerchiefs.

Titles of the papers you write and of books, chapters in books,
articles, and works of art begin with a capital, as does any word after a
colon. All other words in titles are capitalized except short function
words — articles, conjunctions, and prepositions of less than five letters. In hyphenated words capitalize the second word only if it is a noun
or an adjective, or if it is as important as the first word.

"Corrosive Without Corrective" and "The Rhetoric of Hitler's 'Battle' "
are chapters in Kenneth Burke's *The Philosophy of Literary Form:
Studies in Symbolic Action.*

Through the Looking-Glass

"The Tribulations of a Left-Hander in a Right-Handed World"

"The Breakup of Poe Engineering"

If technical reports are divided into sections with headings, major headings may consist of all capitals to distinguish them from lower level
headings, although both the *MLA Handbook for Writers of Research
Papers* and the *Publication Manual of the American Psychological Association* discourage the practice.

PARTS OF SPEECH
   Nouns and Verbs

(Most organizations have their own rules for distinguishing titles, headings, and subheadings. They will be consistent within the organization
although not necessarily between organizations.)

Italics

Italics are indicated in typewritten and handwritten material by
underlining.

Typewritten: <u>The Sound and the Fury</u> by William Faulkner

Handwritten: <u>The Sound and the Fury</u> by William Faulkner

Titles of books (exception: the Bible), periodicals, newspapers, plays,
separately published long poems, films, musical pieces, and works of art
are italicized.

Ernest Hemingway wrote *For Whom the Bell Tolls.*

The film *Gone with the Wind* is based on Margaret Mitchell's book of the same name.

The musical *Man of La Mancha,* based on *Don Quixote,* opened first in Los Angeles, and then moved to Broadway.

Among the highly rated newspapers and magazines are the *New York Times,* the *Washington Post,* the *Wall Street Journal, Time,* the *Atlantic Monthly,* and the *New Yorker.*

Foreign words and phrases that have not yet become Anglicized and names of ships, aircraft, and spacecraft are italicized:

The Swiss linguist Ferdinand de Saussure referred to a message to be communicated as the *signifié* and the set of signs that communicate the message as the *signifiant.*

In April 1981 the spaceship *Columbia* took off on man's first commuter run into space.

Words, letters, or figures referred to in a special sense are italicized:

In and *during* are alternate choices only in a limited context, where the meaning is "at a point in the course of something."

His *3*s look like *5*s sometimes.

Avoid italicizing for emphasis. Restrict it primarily to situations where the exact meaning or reference might be overlooked otherwise:

Stephen Crane uses verb clusters to express simultaneous activities, adding a dynamic quality to his description of battle scenes:

The men *bending and surging in their haste* were in every impossible attitude.

The Ellipsis Mark

The ellipsis mark consists of three spaced periods to indicate omission of one or more words in a quoted passage. If the ellipsis runs to the end of the sentence, a period is added at the end.

The river, a central symbol in *The Adventures of Huckleberry Finn,* is described idyllically by Huck as he floats downstream with Jim: "You see the mist curl up off the water, and the east reddens . . . then the nice breeze springs up . . . so cool and fresh, and sweet to smell."

The Senator said: "If the President's program works, the country will remain immensely strong. . . . The President has merely set the stage, and the drama will be more than a one-act play."

Notice that even though the text of *Huckleberry Finn* begins before the quoted passage and continues afterward, the ellipsis mark is not used at the beginning or the end of the quotation.

If one or more lines of poetry are omitted from a quotation, a separate line of ellipsis marks running across the full width of the quotation indicates such an extended break. This practice has also been followed when paragraphs of prose are omitted, but this practice is no longer universal.

The Hyphen

The hyphen is used to divide words between syllables at the end of a line, to join prefixes to words, to connect parts of a compound, and to avoid misreading.

Before hyphenating words at the end of a line, be sure to look up the syllable division in your dictionary, but do not depend upon these divisions totally. Some divisions are inappropriate at the end of a line even between syllables. Here are some guidelines:

1. Do not hyphenate if it means leaving one or two letters of a word at the end or beginning of a line: *cream-y, frequent-ly, re-play, a-gainst.*
2. Hyphenate already hyphenated words only at the hyphen: *court-martial, self-analysis, commander-in-chief.*
3. Avoid hyphenating proper names: *Jeffrey, Gregory, Louisiana, San Marino.*

In general hyphenate at line end as little as possible. Restrict yourself to hyphenating only lengthy words, and when possible, only at the more natural breaking points, such as frequently used suffixes (*establish-ment*). Always avoid hyphenating already hyphenated words at any point other than the standard hyphenation, and do not hyphenate at places in words that may momentarily confuse the reader because the first part by itself forms a pronounceable or unpronounceable unit that does not coincide with the whole:

ANNOYING: Teachers who are alert to the problems of left-hand-ers will find left-handed desks for them.

REVISED: Teachers who are alert to the problems of left-handers will find left-handed desks for them.

CONFUSING: Because they were written incorrectly, we will read-dress the envelopes.

REVISED: Because they were written incorrectly, we will re-address the envelopes.

EVEN BETTER: Because they were written incorrectly, we will readdress the envelopes.

It is impossible to achieve a uniform right margin in any case, and incorrect hyphenation or a series of word divisions at the ends of lines are annoying to readers.

There is no general rule to follow for hyphenating compounds.

Many present-day compounds have progressed from being separate words to hyphenated words and then one word. But this is not a uniform progression. Some compounds, such as *ice cream,* remain two words. Consult your dictionary when in doubt. When current dictionaries do not agree on the form a compound can take, any of the forms recorded are in general use, and you may choose among the options.

If you coin your own compound, you will need to hyphenate between words:

The my-way-is-better-than-your-way person is hard to get along with.

In fact, any two or more words functioning as a single adjective before a noun must be joined with hyphens:

The snow-covered mountain

His twenty-second birthday

Her do-it-yourself attitude

Suspension hyphens are used in a series:

The first-, second-, and third-graders lined up in the gymnasium.

Hyphens are used to avoid misreading:

Revision of your paper means a re-vision of your content, arrangement, and style.

And hyphens are used with many prefixes, such as *self-, well-,* and *great-,* and with prefixes connected to proper names.

self-made man

well-proportioned body

great-grandmother

pro-Irish

Abbreviations, Numbers, and Symbols

Ordinary writing presents few problems with abbreviations, numbers, and symbols. Only certain abbreviations are permissible and desirable, such as Mr. and Ms. before names, Jr. and Ph.D. after names; standard forms such as A.D., B.C., A.M., and P.M.; and certain common Latin expressions, such as i.e. (that is), e.g. (for example), cf. (compare), and etc. (and so forth). Names of many organizations, agencies, and entities, particularly governmental, often appear in abbreviated form as acronyms, nearly always without periods: IRS, HEW, CIA, NASA, DOD, CETA, U.S. (used adjectivally), C.O.D.

Numbers ten or under or that can be expressed in one or two words are written out: *ten, twenty-six, one hundred,* unless the amounts are mixed; then all numerals are used: "95 to 120 students." Numbers are used for pages and divisions of a book (page 10, chapter 6), for decimals and percentages (a 3.2 average, 10 percent), statistics (a score of 7–4, 12 feet wide), and large round numbers ($2.3 billion). Numbers beginning a sentence are always written out, so if the number is three or more words, revise the sentence to shift the number:

> Nine hundred fifty to one thousand two hundred students will graduate this year.

> This year 950 to 1,200 students will graduate.

Symbols are few and standard: $, ¢, &, %, °F, or °C. Unless copying official titles — A&P — write *and* out.

In business and technical writing, however, abbreviations, numbers, and symbols are used more frequently and according to somewhat different rules. In fact, many organizations have their own systems of abbreviations, numbers, and symbols. Whatever system is adopted, it should be used consistently.

Abbreviations are worthless unless readers understand them. If you plan to repeat a term often in a report and its abbreviation is unfamiliar, spell it out, and then put one version in parentheses. The reader will expect the abbreviation thereafter.

> 1,800 feet per second (fps)
> 1,800 fps (feet per second)

Effective writers observe these guidelines for abbreviations:

1. Abbreviate only those units of measurement following an exact number: several feet, 16 ft.
2. Do not abbreviate a term when it is the subject of discussion: "The alternating current (not AC) was changed to direct current (not DC)."
3. Spell out rather than abbreviate short words: *mile, ton, cord, sine.*
4. Do not punctuate an abbreviation unless it is identical with a word: diam, doz, in., emf
5. Do not add *-s* to form the plural of an abbreviation: 500°C, 3,000 cal, 50,000 kw.

In professional writing the trend is to use as many figures as possible rather than write numbers out. The most commonly accepted rules are these:

1. Numbers above ten are written as figures. If numbers above and below ten appear in the same passage, only figures are used: "ten units"; "18 tubes"; "a 5 to 25% variation." (Compare with the rule on the use of numbers in nonprofessional writing given previously.)
2. Units of measurement, below or above ten, are written as figures: 6 volts, 2,000 fps, 3%.
3. One of two numbers that appear together in different context is

expressed as a figure; the other is written out: "six 12-volt batteries."

4. A zero does not precede the decimal point in decimal numbers less than one: .007, .987, 9.02.

5. Fractions are spelled out when they stand alone; with units of measurement they are expressed as figures. Mixed numbers are always figures: "with three-fourths the power"; "1/16 sec"; "6½ times as fast."

6. Numbers are never written in both figures and words, except in legal documents. Readers are likely to feel their intelligence insulted if they read, "Five (5) shots were fired."

Business and technical writing tends to use many symbols: " for inches, ' for feet, × for by, # for number, / for per, % for percent, ° for degree. However, if an organization has no ironclad rule for the use of symbols, it is best to observe the general rule that the only symbols used in textual material are mathematical and chemical expressions; all other symbols are used only in tables and drawings.

The symbols in mathematical expression should be defined the first time they are used, even when the report contains a list defining the symbols (necessary when a report uses a large number of symbols). A list of symbols is arranged alphabetically in this order: lowercase English letters, uppercase English letters, lowercase Greek letters, uppercase Greek letters, subscripts, superscripts, and special notes.

EXERCISES

1. In the following passages all punctuation and capitals have been omitted. Punctuate and capitalize. Also find incorrect use of abbreviations, numbers, or symbols, and correct them:

although word processing equipment was first introduced in the 1960s the need for utilizing its cost saving features did not become urgent until the economic recession and inflation of the early 1970s today international data corporation estimates that over one hundred and fifty thousand companies in the u s use at least one word processing system and that the market will increase annually at a production rate in excess of fifty thousand units.

word processing systems range from automatic editing typewriters to the sophisticated hybrid systems used for merging word processing and data processing due to low cost and high reliability stand alone systems essentially electronic typewriters with removable storage media lead in units installed ninety eight % at year end 1977 the word processing systems analyzed in this report will refer to such stand alone models with the following features text editing dual media station automatic tab memory automatic margin adjust automatic input underlining backspace correction control by word line or sentence revision modes permitting the operator to selectively retrieve characters words lines sentences paragraphs or pages automatic output centering and hyphenation logic

2. Examine the following sentences for punctuation or mechanical errors, correcting any you find. Mark "correct" the sentences that have no error.

   a. Father said that we should take the old highways to avoid the construction on the new bypass.

   b. Professor Smith who teaches history 101 told two superior students notice I said superior that they could skip the final examination.

   c. The chapter Watching The Brain At Work in Inside The Brain was especially interesting researchers were surprised that the cortex could be mapped for different functions.

   d. We have missed the start of the first showing of the film Elsie said but we can see it later this evening.

   e. The bill of rights was not part of the original U.S. Constitution.

   f. The rust laden railing bent from years of neglect barely held it's grip on the concrete steps.

   g. The linguistics text deals with three major areas: phonology, syntax, and semantics.

   h. He did not know whether the Young Mens Christian Association sponsored a masters swimming program?

   i. Basketball now a world famous sport was invented in 1891 by Dr. James Naismith it's popularity has grown immensely since then.

   j. Psittacosis which can be transmitted to humans occurs in parrots, pigeons, ducks, turkeys and chickens however it's danger to man has lessened since the discovery of antibiotics.

Index